Samuel L. Graham

The Navigation of the Caribbean Sea and Gulf of Mexico

Samuel L. Graham

The Navigation of the Caribbean Sea and Gulf of Mexico

ISBN/EAN: 9783744795760

Printed in Europe, USA, Canada, Australia, Japan

Cover: Foto ©Andreas Hilbeck / pixelio.de

More available books at **www.hansebooks.com**

U. S. HYDROGRAPHIC OFFICE.
No. 86.

THE NAVIGATION

OF THE

CARIBBEAN SEA AND GULF OF MEXICO.

VOL. I.

THE WEST INDIA ISLANDS, INCLUDING THE BAHAMA BANKS AND ISLANDS AND THE BERMUDA ISLANDS.

REVISED AND COMPILED BY

LIEUTENANT S. L. GRAHAM, U. S. NAVY,

AND

LIEUTENANT F. E. SAWYER, U. S. NAVY.

WASHINGTON:
GOVERNMENT PRINTING OFFICE.
1888.

Compliments of
   Lieutenant George L. Dyer, U. S. N.,
                              Hydrographer.

PREFACE.

In this edition of Sailing Directions the effort is made to avoid mention of such matters as are necessarily of an ephemeral character. The chart is the principal guide, showing in a graphic form that which is usually duplicated in the pages of the Sailing Directions. As the former can be readily corrected, it is considered advisable to restrict the contents of the latter to such matters as cannot be easily delineated on the charts and which will not require the continual defacement of the Sailing Directions by corrections.

The coasts of Cuba, Santo Domingo, and Puerto Rico are imperfectly laid down on the charts, and doubtless many dangers exist there of which there is no record.

In this compilation notes were taken from—

Hydrographic Office Publication, No. 63.   Lieutenant Commander F. M. Green, U. S. N.

Hydrographic Office Archives.
Office of Naval Intelligence, Bureau of Navigation.
Consular Reports and Commercial Relations, State Department.
Hydrographic Office, Coast Survey, and British Admiralty charts.
Notices to Mariners.
Port Charges of the World, Hunter and Patten, 1884.
North Atlantic Memoirs. A. G. Findlay.
West India Pilot, Part II, Admiralty, 1887.
Puerto Rico and the Virgin Islands. J. Imray & Son.
West India Directory, Part I, Cuba, &c. J. Imray & Son.
Reseña de los Principales Puertos, &c., de la Republica Dominicana.

Bearings and courses are true. The direction of the wind is the point from which it blows; that of ocean currents, the point towards which they set. Distances are expressed in nautical miles.

G. L. DYER, *Lieutenant, U. S. Navy,*
Hydrographer.

U. S. HYDROGRAPHIC OFFICE,
Navy Department.

CONTENTS.

	Page.
Preface	III
Note	V
Table of contents	VII
Index chart	VIII
Index	329

CHAPTER I.
General remarks on winds, currents, and tides.................................... 1

CHAPTER II.
The straits of Florida, with the coast from Cape Canaveral to the Tortugas. 8

CHAPTER III.
The Bermuda islands 14

CHAPTER IV.
The Bahama islands and banks... 21

CHAPTER V.
The island of Cuba 68

CHAPTER VI.
The Windward channel and Jamaica, and the neighboring banks and cays.. 127

CHAPTER VII.
The island of Santo Domingo or Haiti 158

CHAPTER VIII.
The Mona passage and the island of Puerto Rico 209

CHAPTER IX.
The Virgin islands 231

CHAPTER X.
The Windward islands, Sombrero to Barbadoes, inclusive......................... 259

Harbor and special charts arranged according to sections occur within the limits of general charts.

Within limits of—	Title.	Number.
27	Bermuda islands, with plans of	
	Grassy bay and Ireland island	
	Narrows or Ship channel and St. George harbor..............	
	The Banks southwest of the Bermudas	
	BAHAMAS.	
	The Great Bahama bank, Great Isaac to 23° 40′ north	26a
	———— ———— Great Exuma to New Providence...........	26b
	———— ———— Old Bahama channel to Exuma	26c
	———— ———— 23° 40′ north to Old Bahama channel.......	26d
	Harbors of Great Exuma, Nurse channel............................	340
	Raccoon cut, Ragged Islands anchorage	341
	New Providence island	335
31	Nassau harbor	949
32	Salt Cay anchorage and Hanover sound	337
943	Whale Cay channel and Green Turtle Cay anchorage	998
944	Crooked Island anchorage	957
946	Cockburn harbor	1050
947	Turk's islands	1000
	Alfred sound, Mathew Town road	422
	Egg island to Eleuthera, Great Stirrup cay, Ship and Fleeming channels, Wide opening, Royal Island harbor................	338
	Clarence harbor, Douglass road, Ragged Island harbor, Highborne cut, Wax Cay cut..	339
	CUBA.	
	Bahia Honda, Port Mariel	520b
	Havana harbor	307
	Port Matanzas, Cays Francés and Confites anchorages...........	270
	Cárdenas and Santa Clara bays, Piedras, Mono and Monito anchorages, Port Cabañas..	520a
26d	Ports Nuevitas, Nuevas Grandes, and Manati	520c
31	Ports Gibara, Banes, Padre, Bariay...................................	519b
32	Port Jururu	158
35	Porto de Vita...	159
36	Ports Sama, Yaguaneque, Cananova, Naranjo.....................	519a
373	Port Nipe	16

Harbor and special charts arranged according to sections occur within the limits of general charts—Continued.

Within limits of—	Title.	Number.
	CUBA—Continued.	
944	Carbonico and Livisa	161
946	Ports Tanamo and Cebollas	518b
947	Port Cayo Moa, Jaragua, Yamaniguey, and Cañete anchorages	518a
948	Ports Niguero, Escondido, Cueva, Aguacate, Navas, Sigua, Boma, Mata, Baracoa, Maravi, Baitiqueri, Cayaguaneque, Taco, Yumuri, Naguarage, Port Miel and Guanito bays	377a
	Guantanamo	377b
	Santiago de Cuba	1003
	Approaches to ports Casilda and Masio	916
	Cienfuegos	521
	Sagua la Grande harbor	45
	JAMAICA.	
	Port Royal to Pedro Bluff	815
	Port Royal and Kingston harbor approaches, Morant cays	718
	—— —— —— —— harbors, Port Royal Ship channel	348
35	Morant bay, Fisherman bay to Belvidere point	719
347	Port Morant	708
373	Dry, Manchioneal, Green Island, St. Lucea, Mosquito Cove harbors, Port Maria, Carlisle, and Montego bays, Blewfields anchorage	349
	Falmouth harbor, Port Antonio, Aunatto and St. Ann bays, Savannah la Mar and Black River anchorages	350
	Navassa island, Bajo Nuevo, Seranilla bank	379
	Grand and Lesser caymans, Georgetown anchorage	43
	HAITI AND SAN DOMINGO.	
	Jacmel harbor	951
	Cayes, Flamand, St. Louis and Meste bays	168
	Cayemites, Baradaires and Aquin bays	954
	Port au Prince	1012
	Port au Prince approaches	1015
	Gonaives bay	922
36 40 373	Acul, Tierra Baja, Tiburon, Chouchou, Salt River, Moustique bays, Juan Rabel anchorage, Port à l'Ecu	953
948	Port Paix, St. Mark, Petit Goave and Fond La Grange bays	952
	St. Nicolas Mole	950
	Cape Haiti harbor	818
	Monte Christi to Fort Dauphin bay	625

Harbor and special charts arranged according to sections occur within the limits of general charts—Continued.

Within limits of—	Title.	Number.
	HAITI AND SAN DOMINGO—Continued.	
	Manzanillo bay	393
	Puerto Plata	959
	Samaná bay, Barracota and Yuna rivers	917
	Santo Domingo harbor	914
	Caldera bay	1014
	PORTO RICO AND VIRGIN ISLANDS.	
36	Mayaguez and Aguadilla bays, Mona island, Puerto de Guanica	372
40	Port San Juan	372a
948	Port Ponce	720
1001 1002	Virgin passage, St. Thomas and adjacent islands	965
	Anegada passage with adjacent islands	1002
	Santa Cruz, Christiansted harbor	1058
	St. Thomas harbor	977
	Road harbor	137
	Gorda sound	569
	WINDWARD ISLANDS.	
	Sombrero island	371b
	Crocus, Grande, and Marigot bays, Oyster pond, Gustaf harbor	371a
	Barbuda	367
	St. Eustatius, St. Christopher, Nevis, and Montserrat islands, Orangetown and Plymouth anchorages	1011
36	Falmouth and English harbors, Antigua	366
40	Guadeloupe and adjacent islands	363
	Port Louis, Guadeloupe	1065
	Port du Moule, Guadeloupe	1059
	Approaches to Point à Pitre, Petit Hâvre	364
	Guadeloupe, Salée river, Petit Hâvre anchorage	531
	Basse-Terre roads, Guadeloupe	1063
	Marie Galante, Grand Bourg	532
	The Saintes	362
	Dominica	810
	Roseau roads, Prince Rupert and Woodbridge bays, Dominica	513
	Martinique	1009
	La Trinité bay, Martinique	1064
	St. Pierre roadstead	1020
	Cul-de-Sac Marin	1021
	Fort de France	1022

Harbor and special charts arranged according to sections occur within the limits of general charts—Continued.

Within limits of—	Title.	Number.
	WINDWARD ISLANDS—Continued.	
	St. Lucia island, Marigot harbor to Gros island, Grand Cul-de-Sac bay, Marigot harbor	707
	Port Castries, Gros Islet bay, Kingstown, Greathead and Calliaqua bays, St. Vincent	359
	St. Vincent	157
	Barbadoes, Carlisle bay	1010
	Carriacan to Battowia, Tobago Cays anchorage	357
	Admiralty bay, Grenadines	358
	Grenada, St. George harbor, South and Northeast coasts	356
	Tobago island	354
	Tobago, East coast, Scarborough and Courland bays	355
	St. François anchorage, Guadeloupe	1073
	St. Anne anchorage, Guadeloupe	1086
	Galet anchorage, Desirade	1082
	Port St. Marie, Guadeloupe	1083

CHAPTER I.

GENERAL REMARKS ON WINDS, CURRENTS, AND TIDES.

The West India islands and the neighboring banks lie within the limits of the NE. trade-winds, which blow from the eastward so constantly throughout the year as to have given rise to the terms "windward" and "leeward," universally employed to signify that a point is relatively to the eastward or westward.

These trade-winds are subject to diurnal and annual modifications, and are at times temporarily interrupted by other winds of varying force and direction.

The diurnal variations to which the trade-winds are subject are called land and sea breezes, which have especial characteristics for each locality. The sea-breeze generally sets in about 9 a. m., and blowing either directly on shore, or according to the trend of the coast-line, at an angle to it, continues till about sunset, when a calm interval is succeeded by a light air off-shore, attaining its greatest strength about day-dawn, and being succeeded by an oppressive calm, to be again followed by the sea-breeze. On the coasts of Cuba, Santo Domingo, Puerto Rico, and Jamaica the regular sequence of land and sea breezes is seldom interrupted. In the Virgin and Windward islands, as well as among the Bahamas, the land-breeze does not usually occur, but during the night the trade-winds are apt to die away, regaining their strength in the morning. Sailing-vessels therefore usually endeavor to go to sea at early daylight.

The changes of seasons in the West Indies, as elsewhere, are produced by changes of the sun's declination. There is a dry and a rainy season, the exact dividing line between them varying somewhat from local causes, but speaking generally, the rainy season lasts from June till November. During this season the wind inclines toward the SE., with torrents of rain. Calms and heavy squalls frequently occur, and hardly a year passes without a hurricane of more or less severity. This season is also known as the sickly season, from the great prevalence of dangerous fevers.

From November to June the wind draws more to the NE. and increases in strength, sometimes blowing a strong gale from this direction for two or three successive weeks in December, January, and February. Rain, though less frequent, is not of rare occurrence.

Occasionally strong winds from N. and NW. interrupt the trades, and blow very hard in the Gulf of Mexico and among the Bahama islands. These are called northers, and occur from November to April.

These gales of wind bear a strong resemblance to the *pamperos* of the Rio de la Plata. Always heralding their approach by a heavy bank of clouds in the NW., and preceded by a light air from the contrary direction, accompanied by a falling barometer, they commence with a violent squall, gradually settling down into a fresh gale, which hauls to the NE. and E., ending with fine weather.

As the sun gets toward its extreme northern declination the rainy or hurricane season begins, and toward the middle of June rain falls in abundance.

July, August, September, and October are the months in which hurricanes occur most frequently, as graphically illustrated by the following table:

Relative frequency of West India hurricanes, as illustrated by the number recorded during three hundred years.

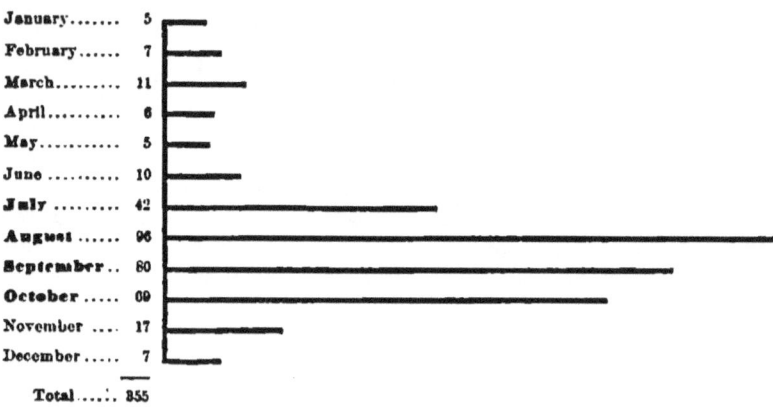

January	5
February	7
March	11
April	6
May	5
June	10
July	42
August	96
September	80
October	69
November	17
December	7
Total	355

These terrific cyclones are the most dangerous which the navigator of the Gulf of Mexico and Caribbean sea is likely to encounter. During the hurricane season—July, August, September, and October—he should be constantly on his guard. The following brief account has been compiled, chiefly from the Pilot Chart of the North Atlantic Ocean, issued the first of each month by the U. S. Hydrographic Office.

A West Indian hurricane is a great whirlwind which forms near the limits of the belt of equatorial rains and calms, to the eastward of the Windward islands, and then moves bodily to the westward. Sometimes it will continue on a course about WNW. across the Gulf of Mexico, but oftener curves to the northward before reaching the Gulf, and follows the Gulf stream up the coast. The wind whirls around the center in a direction opposite to the motion of the hands of a watch. The storm field is divided for convenience of reference into two parts, called, respectively, the dangerous and the navigable semicircles. When the storm is moving to the westward, that portion lying north of the track is the dangerous semicircle, and while moving in a northerly direction the portion to the eastward is the dangerous semicircle. In other words, the right-hand semicircle is by far the more dangerous portion of the storm, and for three reasons: First, because the progressive motion of the storm along its track (about 17 miles an hour) increases the velocity of the wind in this semicircle, while decreasing it by the same amount in the other semicircle; secondly, because both wind and current tend to carry the vessel directly in front of the storm, and if obliged to scud she will run into still greater danger; and, finally, because this is the side towards which the track is liable to recurve at any moment. Advantage should therefore be taken of the earliest opportunity to find the bearing of the center and the probable track of the storm, so that every possible precaution may be taken.

EARLIEST INDICATIONS OF THE APPROACH OF A HURRICANE.

The first indication is, generally, the passage of an *anti-cyclone*, which is revealed by—

(1) Extraordinary *rise* in the barometer.
(2) Cool, dry, fresh winds of considerable duration.
(3) Dry, bracing, and beautiful weather, clear sky, and exceedingly transparent atmosphere.

These anti-cyclonic winds change direction very slowly, and sometimes blow for a long time from the same point of the compass. As soon as the barometer commences to fall and the sky cloud over, the cirrus cloud veil appears most dense in a particular part of the horizon, where a whitish arc is formed, and this arc, which surrounds the hurricane, is the first indication which enables us to fix its bearing. This cloud veil thickens gradually and causes solar and lunar halos. At this period, when the sun rises and sets, the clouds are remarkable for their dark red and violet tints. Very soon peculiar *cirro-stratus* clouds appear. These look like white and delicate feathers or showy plumes crossing the sky, and usually remain fixed for hours without change of form. The weather then becomes heavy and the heat oppressive and sticky. In a short time the *cloud-bank* of the hurricane appears in the horizon, the wind freshens every moment, and passing squalls with light rains prevail.

The bearing of the center of the hurricane, while yet at a distance, can be determined approximately by noticing the focus of divergence of the *cirro-stratus* clouds before mentioned. This focus can be obtained

4 HURRICANES.

by supposing the *cirro-strati* to be prolonged until they meet, and its bearing corresponds nearly to that of the hurricane center.

The bearing of the center of the *cloud-bank* corresponds with the bearing of the *vortex*. This *cloud-bank* is easily distinguished from any other cloud by its *appearance*, its *relative fixity of position*, and the *direction which the scud takes in relation to it*. It differs from a squall cloud in *appearance*, as its base, consisting of a nimbus cloud, cannot be entirely seen, while the base of the squall usually forms a dark band above the horizon. It is *fixed* in relation to the other clouds, remaining in the same point of the horizon. The clouds of a squall, on the contrary, change position frequently. Finally, it will be noticed that the *scud flies in horizontal lines;* that is, an observer who is looking at the *cloud-bank* sees the scud fly from left to right in parallel lines. This does not happen when the observer looks at any other point of the horizon, where there may be a heavy cloud. He will soon see that the scud does not fly in horizontal lines, or does not move from left to right, relatively to himself.

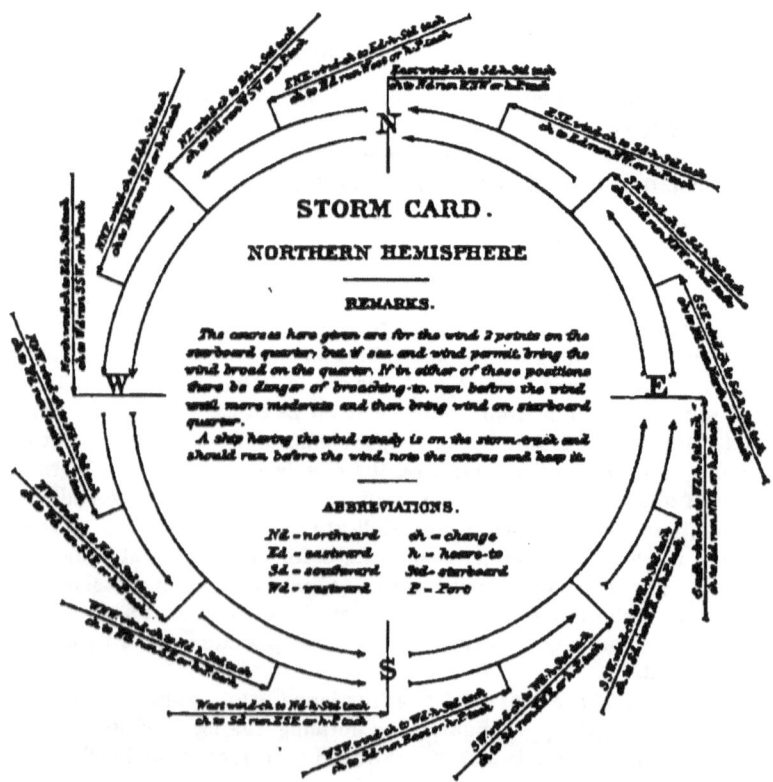

WEST INDIAN HURRICANES.

(From the Pilot Chart of the North Atlantic Ocean, September, 1887.)

DIAGRAM A.—Illustrating the circulation of the wind towards and around the center of low barometer in a tropical cyclone, northern hemisphere. The dangerous winds occur in the inner whirls.

DIAGRAM B.—For practical use in finding a ship's position relative to the center of a tropical hurricane, northern hemisphere, by means of the direction of the wind and fall of the barometer.

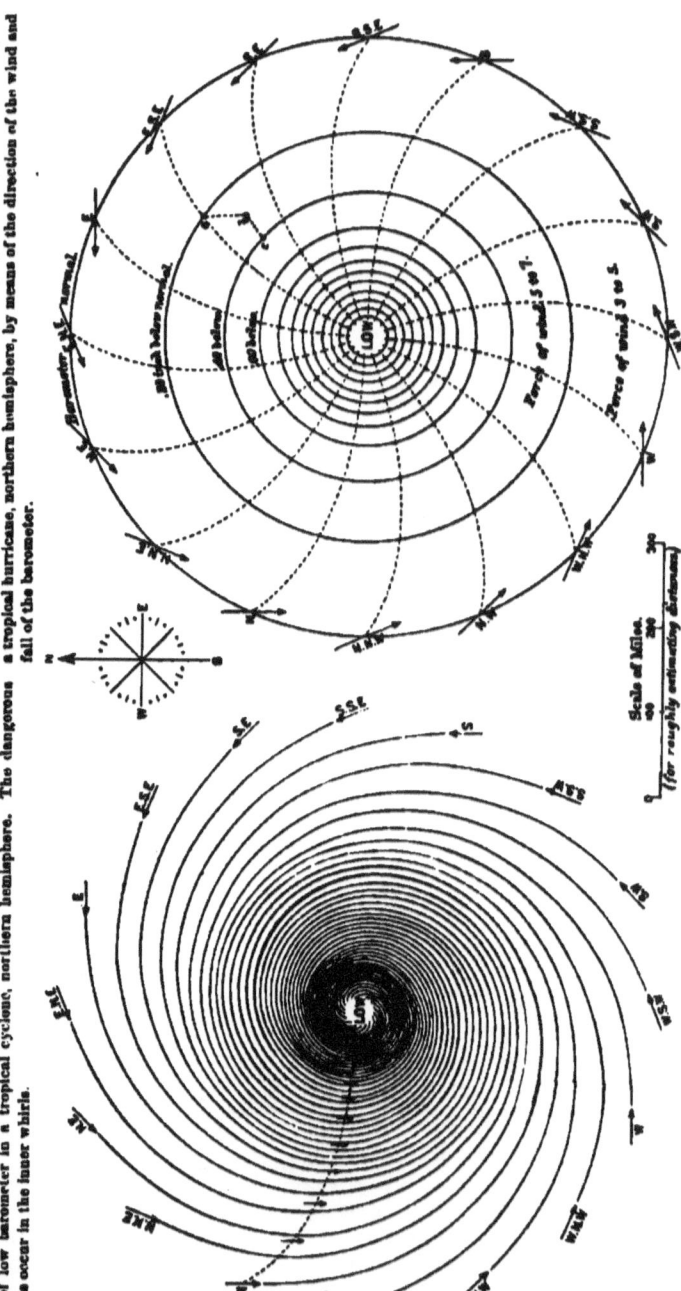

DIAGRAM A.—The spiral lines illustrate the circulation of the wind in a tropical cyclone, northern hemisphere. The diameter of the area represented may vary in different storms and in different latitudes from about 100 to about 800 miles, and is generally least in low latitudes. The air is drawn in towards the center of low barometer, gradually takes up a more and more nearly circular path as its velocity increases, and finally whirls around the center with hurricane force. At the center is a calm spot from 10 to 30 miles in diameter; this is marked LOW, and here the lowest barometer reading is obtained. It will be noticed how similar the motion is to that of water in a whirlpool or eddy, and very naturally, as this is nothing but a gigantic whirlpool in the atmosphere, with the suction or draught at the center upward instead of downward. The direction of the wind at any point on this diagram is the same as the direction of the curve at that point, and the arrows show this direction at the points where they are plotted. By plotting arrows at all points having the wind from the same direction, north, for example, and joining them by a dotted line, we find that this dotted line curves towards the center, as shown. The angle of bearing of the center therefore gradually decreases from about 10 points to about 8 points in the inner whirls, where the well-known "2-point rule" becomes true.

PRACTICAL USE OF DIAGRAM B.—Suppose that at 4 p. m., for instance, the wind is E. SE., and the barometer .20 inch below the normal: Find at the margin of the diagram the wind-arrow marked "E. SE.," and follow the dotted line in toward the center as far as the isobar marked ".20 inch below normal"; this intersection (marked a) is your position on the diagram; for, by the method of construction just explained, this is the place, and the only place, where the wind is E. SE., and, at the same time, the barometer .20 inch below the normal. Referring to the compass and scale which accompany the diagram, you will find that the center (LOW) bears SW. by S., distant 250 miles. Plot this 4 p. m. position of the center on your track chart, from the 4 p. m. position of your vessel.

Later in the day, say 8 p. m., suppose that the wind is SE. by E., and the barometer is .30 inch below the normal (having fallen .10 during the interval): With this wind your position must be half-way between the dotted lines leading in towards the center from the arrows marked "SE." and "E. SE.," and with this barometer reading it must be half-way between the isobars marked ".20 inch below normal" and ".40 below"; it is therefore at the point marked b, and the center bears SW.,

DIAGRAM B.—Here dotted lines are drawn from each wind-arrow at the margin to the center, in the way shown above, so that to find the direction of the wind at any point follow the dotted line out to the margin and read it there. The circles are ISOBARS, and the barometer falls .20 inch as you go from one of these circles to the next inner one. This illustrates very clearly the rate at which the barometer falls as you approach the center—at first slowly, as the broad outer ring is traversed, then more and more rapidly. Near the center, where the isobars are very close together, it has been known to fall an inch in 50 miles. Of course as you recede from the center the barometer rises, .20 inch as you pass from one isobar to the next outer one, just as it fell on entering the hurricane. This diagram involves as much of our latest knowledge of cyclones as can be safely used as a general guide, and extends out beyond the regions where the barometer is falling rapidly and the wind and sea have become violent. No attempt will be made to draw up a set of rules for action, but only to indicate how to plot your position on the diagram and obtain from it the probable bearing and distance of the center and the track and velocity of the storm, leaving it to yourself to decide what action to take, having proper regard to the strength and speed of your ship, the lay of the land, and the passage you are making.

distant 200 miles. Plot this 8 p. m. position of the cyclone center on your track chart, from the 8 p. m. position of your vessel.

You thus have the position of the cyclone center at 4 p. m. and at 8 p. m. plotted on your chart, and the line joining the two positions is the track of the center and distance it has moved in four hours.

Suppose, again, that at 10 p. m. the wind is still from SE. by E., but the barometer stands .40 inch below normal, having fallen .10 in two hours. Your position is now at the point marked c on the diagram, found by exactly the same course of reasoning as before, and the center now bears SW., distant about 175 miles. Plot this 10 p. m. position of the cyclone center on your track chart, from the 10 p. m. position of your vessel. If you have been lying-to, this will evidently indicate that the storm's track has recurved, and that you are directly in front of the center. But no matter whether you have been lying-to or not, your vessel's track and position at any time, and the track and position of the cyclone center, are both plotted on your chart, and you can closely watch every change of relative position in order to avoid the center and dangerous semicircle of the hurricane.

1018—No. 85

THE LAW OF STORMS CONSIDERED WITH SPECIAL REFERENCE TO WEST INDIAN HURRICANES.

Every one who has made any study of the law of storms has probably found much that seems contradictory and confusing. For this reason the following brief statement has been prepared for the use of practical men, as no set of rules can be used intelligently without a clear general idea of the facts on which they are based.

The above "Storm-Card," based on the circular theory of the rotary motion of the wind in a cyclone, has been of infinite service to mariners during the past half century, and it is still thought that no better set of brief, practical rules for instant action in a hurricane, when the barometer has fallen five or six tenths of an inch and the wind has risen to a force of 7 or 8, can be framed, with all our latest knowledge. Occasional disasters must occur, in spite of all human foresight, in these terrific whirlwinds, which carry havoc and destruction along a track which may be several thousands of miles in length and several miles wide. Indeed, it is astonishing to find how few cases there are where vessels actually involved in a hurricane have failed to profit by these rules. Such cases are so rare that no stronger proof is needed of the value of this card for use when the barometer is about five-tenths below the normal and the wind is as high as 7 of Beaufort's scale.

Certain additional and very important advances, however, have been made in our knowledge of this subject during the past fifty years. Here, as in every branch of science, our horizon has been enlarged. Guided by the work of the ablest meteorologists and the results of thousands of observations made by mariners and accurately plotted and thoroughly discussed, we can now detect the approach of a hurricane very much earlier than was formerly possible. The time thus gained is of the greatest value in enabling a vessel to shape her course so as to escape from the track of the storm before the wind and sea have become so violent as to make her almost unmanageable. We know, too, that at some distance from the center the wind does not blow in a strictly circular direction, but rather spirally, in towards the center, so that near the limits of the cyclone area, where the force of the wind is from 3 to 5 and the barometer has just begun to fall, the center may bear 10 points or more to the right of the wind.

GENERAL RULES FOR THE HURRICANE SEASON.

Watch carefully for the earliest indications of an approaching hurricane; constantly and carefully observe and record the barometer, thermometers, wind, and weather. When one is evidently approaching, heave-to, carefully make and record your observations every half hour, or even more frequently; make every effort to find the probable bearing of the center, direction in which the storm is moving, and the semicircle you are in. Unless you heave-to when thus observing the fall of the barometer and the shifts of wind, you may be led into serious error; a fast steamer, for instance, may run into the dangerous side of a hurricane, and yet get shifts of wind characteristic of the navigable semicircle. Any attempt to cross the storm-track is dangerous, but if you decide that it must be attempted, crowd sail and keep the wind well on the starboard quarter. If obliged to lie-to, always do so on the coming-up tack; in the dangerous semicircle this will be the starboard tack, the ship will head away from the center, and you should make all the headway you can; in the navigable semicircle it will be the port tack, the ship will head towards the center, and you should make as little headway as possible. In scudding always keep the wind well on the starboard quarter in order to run out of the storm. So long as the barometer continues to fall, the center is getting nearer; when it steadies and begins to rise, this marks the nearest point, and here the shifts of wind will be most sudden and violent and the sea highest and most confused. If, when lying-to, the wind begins to shift in the opposite direction to what it did at first, it is evidence that the storm-track is recurving, and your semicircle is changed; immediate action must be taken to suit the new conditions. But if your vessel is making any great headway it may give you a shift of wind contrary to what you would have if lying-to; this must be always borne in mind. Cool weather is characteristic of the navigable semicircle, owing to the indraft from the northwestward; warm weather, on the contrary, indicates the dangerous semicircle, where the air is drawn in from the southeastward.

There are two cyclone currents to be considered—a current moving in a circular direction around the center, caused by the wind, and a current which follows the storm along its track. These vary considerably with different storms, but should always be taken into account when near the coast.

Squalls of more or less severity are common throughout the West Indies, especially during the summer months. They are generally of the arched form well known to sailors, and are almost always accompanied by thunder and lightning. They are most frequent near the land. White squalls, so called, are said to occur, giving little or no warning except the ripple on the water made by the wind. They are fortunately of very rare occurrence. Flaws of wind are frequently met with when coasting under high land, sudden gusts rushing down through the valleys. They should be carefully guarded against.

Among the Windward and Virgin Islands, in the Mona, Windward, and Bahama passages, on the shores of Puerto Rico, Haiti, and Jamaica, and on the north coast of Cuba as far west as Matanzas, the current almost always sets to the westward with a force varying from one-fourth of a knot to 3 and even at times 4 knots. This westerly current is felt, but with less constancy, on the eastern side of the Bahama banks and islands, and is due partly to the constant trade-wind acting on the surface of the sea, and is partly a continuation of the great equatorial current which is deflected to the NW. by the coast of South America and rushes furiously through the passage between the islands of Trinidad and Grenada.

Though not invariably experienced, the navigator should vigilantly guard against the effects of this probable current by never losing an opportunity by night or day of verifying his position.

In very many places the currents are much affected by the tides and still more affected by any interruption of the trade-wind, as will be shown particularly when treating of such localities.

The leeward side of the Mona passage in the vicinity of Cape Engaño and the shores of the island of Anegada, before the establishment of the light on Sombrero island, have been strewn with numerous wrecks, owing to vessels being set to leeward by this current.

Along the south coast of Haiti, inshore, a current of at least a knot an hour has often been encountered setting to the eastward.

The most westerly point in the Florida strait where the influence of the Gulf stream may be felt is difficult to determine. Sometimes an easterly current of 2 miles an hour may be felt as far west as the meridian of the mouth of the Mississippi, but more frequently it commences between Havana and the Tortugas.

The navigator is referred to the general examination of the Atlantic ocean, published by the U. S. Hydrographic Office, for detailed statements concerning the winds and currents of the Atlantic ocean, which constantly influence with greater or less force the winds and currents of the Caribbean sea and Gulf of Mexico.

Slight shocks of earthquakes are very frequent among the islands of the West Indies, especially in the Virgin and Windward islands. They are sometimes strong enough to do serious damage on land, the most severe shocks having occurred at Guadeloupe and St. Thomas. The large majority of the shocks are, however, slight, their principal effect being the heavy sea waves, which frequently are seen to rise without any apparent cause, and which dash heavily against the shores of the islands. These rollers are most frequent in the eastern part of the West Indies, but occur at times on all the islands. They frequently make landing dangerous, and have been known to tear vessels from their anchorages and dash them ashore. They have been attributed to gales of wind prevailing at a distance, but more careful observation and research indicate that they have their origin in earthquake shocks.

It is very possible, however, that occasional gales in the Atlantic may make their effects felt in this manner, and navigators would, by noting all the attendant circumstances when these phenomena are perceived, assist greatly in finding out the laws that govern them.

CHAPTER II.

THE STRAITS OF FLORIDA WITH THE COAST FROM CAPE CANAVERAL TO THE TORTUGAS.

The straits of Florida form a most important thoroughfare for vessels bound from the United States and British America to Matanzas, Havana, and the ports of the Gulf of Mexico, and for vessels bound from the Gulf of Mexico to the United States and Europe.

Cape Canaveral is low and sandy. A shallow bank, on which the sea nearly always breaks, extends from it in a southeasterly direction.

There is good anchorage, sheltered from northerly and westerly winds, with the light-house bearing about N. 33° 45' E.

The anchorage is marked by an iron can-buoy with black and white perpendicular stripes. A vessel seeking anchorage should bring this buoy and the light-house in range, bearing N. 33° 45' E., and anchor when within half a mile of the buoy.

Ohio shoal lies N. 30° 56' E. from the light-house. Bull shoal bears N. 47° 49' E. from the same point. These two shoals are quite small. N. of the Ohio shoal there is also a small shoal patch. In rough weather the sea breaks on these shoals, but at other times they can not be seen, and as they are steep-to, and quite dangerous to approach, by keeping east of the whistling buoy off Hetzel shoal all danger will be avoided.

The coast in the neighborhood of cape Canaveral is like the cape itself, low, barren, and sandy. All along the shore as far S. as Jupiter inlet a narrow lagoon extends, separated by a strip of sand beach from the sea and having inshore of it extensive cypress swamps.

Life-saving stations have been established by the United States Government at intervals along the shore.

From Indian river to Jupiter inlet the coast-line has the same general direction, and continues low and sandy. Off this part of the coast there are several small shoal lumps, which will be avoided by keeping 10 miles off shore north of St. Lucie inlet.

From Jupiter inlet the coast takes a southerly direction to Virginia cay, where the sandy shore ends and the Florida reefs commence. The coast is generally formed of sandy hillocks covered scantly with brushwood, black rocks being interspersed here and there. The shore is generally clear of danger.

Florida keys.—From Virginia key a chain of small islets, covered with mangrove trees, and called the Florida keys, extend to the W.

and SW. for nearly 200 miles, ending at the Dry Tortugas. These keys are fringed on the seaward side with a net-work of coral reefs, perfectly steep-to, and extremly dangerous to the navigator in former times, but much less so now from the numerous beacons and lights which mark their positions. Between these reefs and the Gulf stream there is a narrow belt of navigable water uninfluenced, or nearly so under ordinary circumstances, by the current of the Gulf stream, and consequently frequented by steamers bound into the Gulf of Mexico.

As the passages inside the reefs and between the keys, although navigable for vessels drawing 6 feet or less, necessitate accurate local knowledge for their navigation, no account will be attempted of them, but to aid vessels bound along the reefs a description will be given of the artificial aids to navigation.

Reef beacons.—To warn vessels of their approach to these dangerous reefs, beacons have been planted at intervals along the seaward edge of the dangers, and so marked as to distinguish them from each other. These beacons, as shown in the accompanying plate, are of iron, each of the series marking the line of the reef being surmounted by a lattice-work cylinder, the top of which is 36 feet above high water. They are distinguished by vanes marked by a letter or number large enough to be distinctly seen from a safe distance, as they may be approached from seaward within a few hundred yards.

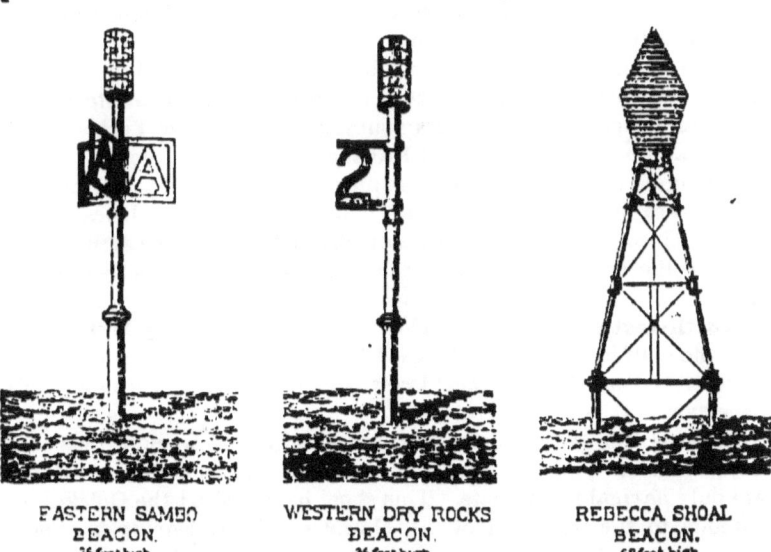

EASTERN SAMBO BEACON. 36 feet high.

WESTERN DRY ROCKS BEACON. 36 feet high.

REBECCA SHOAL BEACON. 68 feet high.

In passing along the edge of the reefs it must be remembered that the current frequently sweeps very strongly on to the reefs; the navigator should, therefore, constantly verify his position by bearings of the beacons and light-houses.

Virginia key is separated by a narrow cut from key Biscayne, the southern point of which is called cape Florida.

Soldier key, a small islet west of the Fowey rocks, has a number of buildings on it and is used as a buoy depot.

Legaré anchorage is to the southward of Fowey rocks, and just inside of Triumph reef.

Turtle harbor.—There is good anchorage which may be reached by passing around to the northward of beacon "K," giving it a berth of half a mile, and anchoring midway between this beacon and the one surmounted by a cross.

From a point abreast of Pickle beacon and 1 mile distant a vessel under steam may safely steer along the edge of the reefs to Tennessee reef. In the night-time the ship's position should be constantly checked by bearings of Alligator reef light, to avoid being set on to the reef by the current.

Key West harbor is sheltered by the reefs and keys, and affords commodious and secure anchorage to vessels of any size. The island, on the western end of which the town is situated, is low and sandy, and covered with brush. The town is an important commercial place, with 5,016 inhabitants. Supplies of all sorts, coal, ice, and fresh provisions, can be obtained here at all times. Tow-boats, steam-pumps, lighters, anchors, etc., to assist vessels ashore or in distress, are always ready. There is no dock here, and vessels whose bottoms need repair must be docked at Havana or hove down to a wharf.

There is telegraph communication between Key West and the Northern States and with Havana. There is a United States naval store-house and coal depot here. Steamers running between New York and Galveston and between Tampa and Havana touch here en route.

Entrance channels.—There are numerous channels leading between the reefs to the harbor of Key West, but most of them need local knowledge. The entrance by the main ship-channel or by the western channel is, with the assistance of the Coast Survey chart, perfectly easy and safe.

Northwest passage.—The channel leading from Key West harbor into the Gulf of Mexico can be used by vessels not drawing more than 17 feet. To use it safely, local knowledge or the assistance of a pilot is necessary. It is only 60 feet wide.

Between Key West and the Marquesas keys there are numerous small keys and islets lying on a shoal bank. The passages between these keys are only navigable for boats. This shoal bank, called the Quicksands, extends to the westward of the Marquesas keys, leaving a passage between these keys and the Dry Tortugas, a cluster of low islets lying to the westward of Key West.

Rebecca shoal obstructs this passage. It lies to the westward of the west end of the Quicksands, and S. 78° 45' E. from Fort Jefferson, and is marked by an iron pile light-house. S. 68° 16′ E. is a small patch called the Isaac shoal.

Vessels should take the passage between the Rebecca shoal and the Tortugas rather than that east of the Rebecca shoal, and should keep at a distance of 2 miles from the light-house.

The Tortugas keys, frequently called the Dry Tortugas, form a cluster of low, sandy islets, rising from a bank of coral and sand. On Garden key, one of the easternmost of the islets is Fort Jefferson, a large brick fortification, not garrisoned at present. The keys are generally bare of vegetation. Bush key has, however, a scanty growth of brush upon it.

There are numerous excellent anchorages among the keys, and, as this neighborhood is constantly frequented by fishermen who supply the Havana market, pilots may be readily obtained. If temporary shelter only is required it may be reached by bringing Loggerhead key light to bear N., distant 4 miles, and steering for it till Garden key light bears N. 56° 15′ E., when good holding ground will be found in 10 fathoms of water, and sheltered from northerly and easterly winds.

Loggerhead key is bordered by low bushes. From both its northern and southern ends shallow sand pits extend, having one or two spots nearly or quite bare at low water.

The navigation of the straits of Florida has always been considered difficult and dangerous, and justly so, till the establishment, within the last few years, of beacons and lights along the Florida reefs. At the present time, with the exercise of ordinary care and prudence, there is no danger to be feared except the encountering of a hurricane without sufficient sea-room to drift.

Reefs.—The annual number of wrecks on the reefs has very greatly diminished since the present excellent system of lights and beacons has been established, so that the numerous wreckers who formerly constituted a large proportion of the inhabitants of Key West have been driven to seek other means of livelihood. It may be truly said that nearly all of the cases of vessels grounding on the Florida reefs are due to ignorance, carelessness, or, as the records of the admiralty court at Key West indicate, to willful running of vessels on shore to defraud underwriters.

These reefs are lighted throughout so that a vessel can not approach nearer than 5 miles at night without sighting a light, and in the daytime the vicinity of danger is indicated in ample time by the change in the color of the water.

It must be borne in mind while in the vicinity of these reefs that the Gulf stream, influenced by the wind, frequently sets strongly onto the reefs, especially in the space between the Alligator and Carysfort reef light-houses. For this reason vessels when beating up the straits should not stand close in shore in the night-time, especially in thick weather.

Under the usual circumstances of wind and weather—that is, with a NE. wind and the Gulf stream running two or three knots—the navigation of the straits by steamers and sailing-vessels is entirely different. They will therefore be considered separately.

Steamers bound South, running between the northern ports of the United States and the Gulf of Mexico on their outward passage generally steer a course to pass cape Canaveral at a distance of from 12 to 15 miles; in thick weather or in the night sounding frequently and taking care not to shoal the water to less than 11 fathoms. From abreast of this light a course S. 12° 28′ E. may be steered, keeping in not less than 12 nor more than 16 fathoms, till Jupiter inlet light is seen from the deck, when the ship may be hauled in toward it till a depth of 5 or 6 fathoms of water is reached, three-fourths of a mile or 1 mile off shore. This distance off shore may be preserved safely in the day-time from Jupiter inlet to Hillsboro' inlet, but as the shore curves outward here, care must be taken in the night-time not to come too close, and a depth of 10 fathoms had better be kept, which will carry the vessel about 2 miles off shore. From Hillsboro' inlet to the northern end of the reef a S. course may be steered.

Fowey Rock light is a very valuable aid to navigation. All dangers between it and the N. end of Virginia key will be avoided by taking care not to bring the light to bear to E. of S.

In coasting along the reef in the day-time the beacons may be passed at a distance of 500 to 800 yards, but in the night a vessel should haul off shore as soon as Fowey Rocks light is made, and until abreast of it, whence she can run on courses parallel to the reefs at a distance of 1 or 1½ miles, constantly checking her positions by bearings of the lights as they are made and passed.

Vessels bound to Havana generally shape a course for that place when abreast of Alligator Reef light, but those bound to Key West or the Gulf of Mexico continue their course between the Gulf stream and the reef.

Captain Timmerman, commanding the steamer *City of New York*, a very skillful and experienced navigator, says: "My experience has been that from Fowey rocks to Carysfort reef the Gulf stream runs parallel to and seldom more than three-fourths of a mile from the general line of the reefs; but with fresh easterly breezes, which are the prevalent winds, the current runs close to the reef, the color of the water almost invariably marking its edge. To the westward and southward of Carysfort reef, the line of no current gradually widens until abreast of Alligator reef, where it is about 2 miles wide, or even wider, with northerly winds. From abreast of beacon 'E' on Couch reef, there is frequently with northerly winds a strong westerly current between the Gulf stream and the reef." The courses and general directions here given must, of course, be somewhat modified according to circumstances of wind and weather.

FLORIDA STRAIT.

Steamers bound to the northward will find it advantageous to pass the lights on the Florida reefs and coast at such a distance that they can be just seen from the deck. This course will give them the full strength of the favoring currents and will enable them to frequently verify their position, a point which can not be too urgently insisted upon.

Sailing-vessels bound from ports in Europe, or from the Atlantic ports of the United States or British America, to the Gulf of Mexico, and intending to pass to the westward of the Great Bahama bank, shape a course for the southern end of Abaco island, generally known as the "Hole in the Wall." Hauling to the westward between the S. end of Abaco and the N. side of the Great Bahama bank, those vessels drawing not more than 12 feet may safely cross the bank, leaving its westward edge at a point about 15 miles S. of Orange cay. Vessels drawing more than 12 feet keep on to the westward through the NW. Providence channel between the Great and Little Bahama banks, haul round the Great Isaacs light-house at a distance of 3 or 4 miles, and follow down the western edge of the bank to a point about 15 miles S. of Orange cay. The wind is generally from the eastward, so that the water is smooth, but vessels becalmed are sometimes carried helplessly by the Gulf stream to the northward of the Little Bahama bank and have to make the best of their way to the Hole in the Wall again.

From the edge of the bank 15 miles S. of Orange cay a course should be steered to pass close along the northern edge of the Salt Cay bank, and having passed Elbow Cay light haul over for the Pan of Matanzas and coast along the Cuba shore at a distance of 3 or 4 miles till westward of the Tortugas, when a course may be shaped for the port of destination.

Vessels bound to Key West would, of course, haul to the northward sooner, being governed by the strength and direction of the wind in choosing a point to cross the Gulf stream.

Sailing-vessels bound North with a fair wind would, of course, follow the track used by steamers, skirting the circles of illumination of the lights along the reefs. As, however, the wind generally blows from between NE. and E., it is almost always necessary to beat for a portion of the way at least, and it is while by the wind on the starboard tack that most of the wrecks take place. While beating up through the stream, if a vessel can not get hold of some landmark along the reefs during the afternoon, she should not approach the Florida shore after dark in thick weather, but remembering that current frequently sets strongly over the reefs, the vessel should be kept under short sail on the off-shore tack during the night. By complying with this simple precaution the much-dreaded navigation of the Florida strait will be deprived of all its dangers, which were formerly considered so great that vessels were instructed to keep entirely away from the Florida side of the channel.

CHAPTER III.

THE BERMUDA ISLANDS.

This group was formerly called the Somers islands, from Sir George Somers, who was shipwrecked here in 1609.

They were first settled by the English 1612, and have remained ever since in their possession. The group consists of over 360 islands, most of which are small and surrounded by dangerous reefs nearly even with the surface of the water. Access is extremely difficult. The principal ones which are inhabited are St. George, St. David, Hamilton, Somerset, and Ireland. The population is about 14,500, of whom 6,000 are white.

The government is administered by a military governor appointed by the British Government. This group forms a most important military and naval station, all commanding points being strongly fortified.

The United States is represented by a consul and vice-consul.

There is a complete dock-yard establishment at Ireland island, with every requisite for refitting and docking the largest ships. The enormous iron floating-dock has had a basin excavated for it, and can take up vessels of the largest size. Although intended for Her Majesty's vessels, other vessels in distress can be repaired there, or have their steam machinery repaired at the dock-yard.

The principal trade is with the United States, large quantities of fresh vegetables being exported there. Steamers from New York arrive and depart every two weeks, and the steamers running between Halifax and St. Thomas touch twice a month at St. George.

Being situated between the parallels of 32° and 33° N., about an equal distance from the West India islands and British North America, the climate is a mean between the two, partaking neither of the extreme heat of the one nor of the excessive cold of the other. Owing to the Gulf stream, which passes between the Bermudas and the American continent, the climate is greatly ameliorated, the winter months resembling the early part of October in England, but without its frost. Gardening is pursued during this part of the year, while the tropical productions of the West Indies are cultivated during the heat of the summer.

The winter, or cold season, is the most agreeable, and lasts from November to March. In the latter part of February spring commences, and the weather usually continues mild, with refreshing showers and gentle breezes from S. and W., until the end of May. In June the summer sets in, and the weather becomes hot. Calms now succeed to the gentle breezes of May, the air is sultry and oppressive, and long droughts are common, which are often broken up by heavy thunderstorms. In September the weather changes its character, and becomes again mild and agreeable. Hurricanes and tempests are frequent, and few autumns pass without them, of more or less violence; the squalls are heavy and sudden, occurring particularly in the winter season.

The whole of these islands lie on the SE. side of an oval-shaped coral reef. On the northern and northeastern edge the reef is under water, with a ledge here and there showing above it at low water, with a single rock called the "North Rock," rising to the height of 8 feet. Approaching from the southward the land is low, rising nowhere to a greater height than 260 feet, but by far the greater part forming gentle undulations of from 20 to 60 feet above the sea-level. The area of the islands is about 12,000 acres, but only 1,200 are under cultivation. The principal islands are well wooded, chiefly with the Bermudian cedar, which with its close and rigid foliage of the darkest green gives a gloomy character to the woods at a distance. They are irregularly hilly, and the valleys contain a rich vegetable soil, capable of producing abundant crops of arrowroot, potatoes, and other vegetables, which are largely exported, as is also a small quantity of straw plat and tropical fruits. There is a total want of springs and wells of fresh water, and it has become an almost universal custom to collect the rain-water from the roofs, which is carefully led into tanks and forms the only supply of pure water. The roofs as well as the walls are whitewashed, and the white roofs gleaming among the dark trees is characteristic of Bermuda.

Signal stations.—There are four signal stations on the islands—one at St. George, the headquarters on the east; another at Mount Langton, near Hamilton; another on the SW. coast 3 miles from the SW. end of the islands; and another at Gibb's Hill on the W. coast.

Pilots can be obtained off St. David's head upon a signal being given for one. Information is telegraphed from one part of the island to another by the chain of signals. The pilots are competent, but for the St. George channel do not go out very far. They use small boats, either whale-boats or gigs, which are very sharp. They are divided into two classes—government or first-class pilots and second-class pilots. There are 26 in all, 16 at the W. end and 10 at the E. end of the group. The pilot charges are reasonable, being so much per foot, more being charged for going in than coming out and more for sailing vessels than for steamers. When a vessel shifts her berth half pilotage is charged. Ten shillings per day is charged for detention. The rates are regulated by government, and the captain-superintendent of the royal dock-yard on Ireland island is the commissioner-in-chief to see that the pilotage rules are complied with. Complaints against pilots can be made to him.

Coal can be obtained either at Grassy bay, Murray bay, or at St. George. Anthracite, Cardiff, Welsh, or Cape Breton is kept on hand, but the former in a limited quantity. Price varies from $7 to $9 per ton. In the port of St. George coaling is done with wheel-barrows and is rapid; at Murray anchorage, from hulks with baskets, and very rarely interrupted by storms; at Grassy bay, from hulks and at the rate of 10 tons per hour, and interrupted by winter gales. Water costs one-half cent per gallon delivered in casks from Hamilton. It is rain-water. It can also be procured from the dock-yard in steam tank-vessels. Provisions cost 30 per cent. more than in New York. Butcher's meat is imported from New York. Fruit is scarce, except bananas.

Channels.—The channels through the outer reef, commencing at North Rock, the most northern, are as follows:

North Rock channel.—There are two channels on either side of this rock, and they can be navigated by vessels of large draught, but as they are narrow and intricate and only known to a few pilots they are seldom used.

Mills Breaker channel is the next to the southward, and the entrance is half a mile to the northward of the Mills breaker, which is marked by an iron buoy, bearing N. 25° 18′ E. from St. David's head. It is only used by Bermudian vessels. The narrows, or ship channel, is regularly buoyed, and is the principal entrance to the interior of the reef.

St. George's channel.—S. of the seaward extreme of the narrows is the channel over the bar to St. George harbor.

Boiler channel is southeastward from St. George's channel and along the shore of St. David's island. It is only used in moderate weather and by vessels of not over 15 feet draught.

Hog Fish cut is at the SW. end of Hamilton island, about 2 miles westward of the light-house, through which small island vessels thread their way by the eye into Elies harbor. This snug little basin is formed between the ends of Hamilton and Somerset islands. On the NW. part of the former there is a small conical hill about 150 feet high, called Wreck Hill, which is very conspicuous and a useful object in approaching from the North or South.

On the NW. side of the reef are three more openings, through which small traders find their way into Grassy bay and Hamilton harbor, passing close along the NW. side of Ireland island, but no directions can be given for them.

Tides.—Northerly winds cause the highest and southwesterly the lowest tides. The force of the stream is also variable and probably affected by the current prevailing outside.

The flood from the eastward round St. David head sets into St. George harbor and through the Narrows nearly in the direction of the channel to off St. Catherine point, where it sweeps around to about WSW. and sets one-quarter of a knot to 2 knots an hour according to the force of the wind. The ebb runs with the same force from the SW. toward St. Catherine point, where it diverges to ESE., trending more southerly eastward. Off St. George it is strengthened by the stream through the ferry and harbor to seaward. About the Sea Venture shoals, on the N. side of the narrows, it sets in all directions and stronger about the buoys near these shoals, which is the narrowest part of the channel. The floods in the offing set to the NE. and the ebbs to the SW., but, as has already been seen, nearer the shore they set in various directions.

Anchorages.—Murray anchorage, lying inside the reef and entered through the narrows or ship channel, is safe for well found vessels, there being from 6 to 10 fathoms of water and good holding ground. With a NW. gale there is a heavy sea, which cuts off communication from shore.

The boat landing at old naval tank is very poor, the sandy beach just beyond, sheltered by the rocks, being better.

At Murray anchorage foreign vessels-of-war anchor till permission is received from the governor to go nearer the dock yard.

Grassy Bay anchorage is not much better than Murray anchorage, unless a vessel can go to a naval buoy. A breeze from any direction raises a disagreeable sea, its advantage being its proximity to the drydock.

St. George anchorage is an excellent one, well land locked, and with good holding ground. Having to cross the bar at the entrance is the only drawback. There is an anchorage in the Five-fathom hole outside the Narrows, but it is not desirable.

St. George is the northeastern island of the group. On the S. side of the northern part the land forms an elbow, and here there is a considerable town, formerly the seat of government, and in front of it a secure harbor, protected by St. David and other islands, for vessels of 14 or 16 feet draught, which can cross the bar at high water.

There is a marine railway at St. George, where vessels of 800 tons can be taken up, and repairs of all kinds, except to machinery, can be well and quickly made.

On the bluff of St. Catherine point, the NE. extreme of St. George and of the whole group, Fort St. Catherine stands conspicuous from its isolated appearance, a narrow strip connecting it to the higher land at the back, which is steep, and moderately wooded on its northern side, Fort Victoria crowning the summit, about 150 feet above the sea. To the SW. of the latter is Fort St. George, 164 feet above the sea, distinguished by its flag-staff and yard, and here every vessel approaching the island is signaled.

St. David island.—Its shores are very irregular, and its E. end terminates in a bold rocky promontory, between 70 and 80 feet high, thickly covered with cedar, called St. David head, which forms the eastern extremity of the group.

1018—No. 85——2

Hamilton, Long, or **Bermuda island** is the largest of the group. Its shores, however, are very irregular, and so is its surface. The highest part, called Gibbs hill, near the SW. end of the island, is 256 feet high.

Hamilton stands near the center of the island, on the N. side of Hamilton or Crow Lane harbor, and is the seat of government. The harbor is convenient, well sheltered, and capable of receiving vessels of 10 or 12 feet draught alongside the wharf in front of the town.

Large numbers of visitors, attracted by the mild climate, come here from the United States to spend the winter.

Somerset island is generally not so elevated as the others.

Ireland, the northern island, is entirely occupied by the government establishments.

Grassy bay, just to the eastward of Ireland island, is the principal anchorage for men-of-war.

A buoy has been placed near Mills breaker, but it frequently goes adrift and can not, therefore, be depended upon.

Five-Fathoms Hole anchorage, sometimes called Jervis roadstead, is open to all winds from WNW. round by N. to SSW., with no protection from the sea except what the reefs afford, and that only from the former bearing to NNE. It may, therefore, be considered nothing more than a stopping place for a pilot. In favorable weather, with the wind from NW., a vessel may anchor in from 7 to 9 fathoms of water, with St. Catherine point bearing N. 67° 30′ W., but care should be taken to select a clear sandy spot; for the darker ones, which may be generally detected from aloft, especially on a bright sunny day, are rocky coral heads, and by anchoring on them the loss of the anchor is risked. Be prepared to leave the anchorage the moment the winds begin to veer.

Currents.—The surface currents during the sounding operations of the *Argus* were found to be weak and irregular. On Argus bank on one occasion the current set to the SE. at the rate of three-fourths of a knot per hour.

General directions.—In steering for Bermuda at night or in thick weather it is advisable not to go to the northward of the parallel of 32°. In coming from the SE., the light should not be brought to the southward of S. 73° 7′ W., or during the night approached nearer than 6 or 7 miles. Coming from the westward, it should be kept at the distance of 10 or 12 miles until it bears northward of N. 56° 15′ E. A vessel from the northward sighting the light should haul off immediately, as the reefs extend off in that direction 16 miles.

The Bermuda islands are about 240 miles to the southward and 400 to the eastward of the outer limits of the Gulf stream. Hence the current in the neighborhood is exceedingly variable, both in force and direction. Generally, however, it appears to be greatly influenced by the wind, particularly if it has blown from the same point for several days, when its velocity may be found to be 1 knot an hour, or more, in the opposite direction. The utmost attention to the reckoning is therefore requisite, and should the vessel's position be at all doubtful, and the weather unfavorable for seeing the light, the parallel should not be crossed in the night time, for the edge of the bank is too close to the reef for soundings to give safe warning.

The Bermuda islands appear to lie near the northern limit of the variable winds, and also on the track of hurricanes and revolving storms passing off and along the shore of America, which is distant about 600 miles. The revolving winds which pass over the islands vary in strength from breezes to storms. In the summer season the winds are light and usually steady for a considerable time, blowing in straight lines or on one point, with but little fluctuation in the barometer. But after the commencement of November veering winds, of various degrees of force, set in and gradually become frequent, yet they seldom follow in such rapid succession as that one gale becomes confounded with another. Light winds and very fine weather usually intervene between the passing of revolving winds, while, at other times, hard-blowing straight-line winds with a high barometer are experienced.

The arrival of such succeeding progressive rotary winds is indicated by the barometer falling, as well as by the increase of the wind's force, which will often occur suddenly. Except in the case of great storms perfect regularity in the fall and rise of the barometer, and in the changes of the wind, will not be found; for the direction of the wind, as well as the atmospheric pressure, is no doubt modified by other revolving gales or strong winds blowing at the same time, but when whirlwinds, tempests, or hurricanes blow they overpower such irregularities.

In the winter season northerly winds sometimes blow hard without veering for two and three days together. The air is then dry and cold, and while the thermometer falls the barometer remains stationary, or rises a little. Misty weather is very uncommon, but it constantly happens that a change of weather is first announced by increase of both temperature and moisture in the air. The December gales generally commence from the S., veer round by the W., and terminate at about NW. or NNW.

During the winter months most of the gales which pass along the coast of North America are revolving gales. Vessels from Bermuda, bound to that shore, should therefore put to sea when the NW. wind, which is the conclusion of a passing gale, is becoming moderate, and the barometer is rising to its usual level. The probability is, more particularly in the winter season, that after a short calm the next succeeding wind will be easterly, the first part of a fresh revolving wind coming up from the SW. quarter.

A ship bound to New York or the Chesapeake might sail while the wind is still W. and blowing hard, provided the barometer indicates that this W. wind is owing to a revolving gale which will veer to the northward. But as the usual track which gales follow in this hemisphere is northerly or northeasterly, such a ship should be steered to the southward. As the wind at W. veers toward NW. and N., the vessel would come up, and at last make a westerly course, ready to take advantage of the E. wind at the setting in of the next revolving gale.

A vessel at New York and bound to Bermuda, at the time when a revolving gale is passing along the American coast, should not wait in port for the westerly wind, but sail as soon as the first portion of the gale has passed by and the NE. wind is veering toward the N., provided it should not blow too hard; for the N. wind will veer to the westward, and become every hour fairer for the voyage to Bermuda. A great number of gales pass along the coast of America, following nearly similar tracks, and in the winter make the voyage between Bermuda and Halifax very boisterous. These gales, by revolving as extended whirlwinds, give a northerly wind along the American continent, and a southerly wind on the whirlwind's opposite side far out in the Atlantic. In sailing from Halifax to Bermuda, it is desirable for this reason to keep to the westward, as affording a better chance of having a wind blowing at N. instead of one at S. as well as because the Gulf stream sets vessels to the eastward.

When vessels from Barbadoes or its neighboring West Indian islands sail to Bermuda on a direct course, they sometimes fall to the eastward of it, and find it very difficult to make when westerly winds prevail. They should, therefore, take advantage of the trade-wind to make the meridian 68° or 70° of longitude before they leave the parallel of 25° N.

CHAPTER IV.

THE BAHAMA ISLANDS AND BANKS.

The Bahamas.—Until 1783 the Bahamas frequently changed masters, but since that time they have remained British possessions. Until 1848 they were under one government, but Turk's island and the Caicos are now attached to Jamaica. The larger islands are inhabited, the population being 44,000.

This remarkable group is composed of numerous irregularly-shaped white sandstone islets and rocks, thinly wooded, the loftiest about 400 feet high, most of them under 100 feet, and many only a few feet above the surface of the sea. They are generally situated on the edges of coral and sand banks, some of which are of the most dangerous character. They are remarkable for being steep-to, as the lead from 10 fathoms or less will frequently drop into 100 fathoms.

One or two of the largest islets are clothed with wood of moderate dimensions, of sufficient size for the scantling of vessels of from 150 to 200 tons burthen. Brazilletto, yellow-wood, lignum-vitæ, and fustic are exported in small quantities. The soil in general is of so light and stony a character that the vegetation is scanty, and it is only capable of producing fruit, Indian corn, and vegetables. Cotton was at one time a valuable article of commerce, but it is not now cultivated to any large extent. Lately cocoanut trees have been planted extensively. Sugar-cane grows luxuriantly on many of the islands and is being more largely cultivated.

The most important product is salt, which is raked in great abundance at many of the islands. Fruit and a coarse description of sponge are also largely exported. Good water is rather scarce, and on some of the islands the inhabitants depend chiefly on rain-water. Poultry is readily obtained at most of the inhabited islets, but cattle are scarce, although generally obtainable at Nassau; the breed of sheep is excellent.

Custom-houses are located at Nassau, Abaco, Eleuthera, Harbor Island, Exuma, Rum Cay, Long Island, Long Cay, Inagua, Ragged Island, and Bemini.

A most remarkable feature is the exceeding clearness of the sea-water, which enables the bottom to be seen from aloft at considerable depths and at some distance; the navigation of the banks is consequently conducted almost entirely by the eye, but care must be taken not to run with the sun ahead of the vessel.

Winds.—The Bahama islands are all within the influence of the trade-winds; their lowness, of course, exempts them from the regular land-wind, but in the summer season a light breeze frequently comes from the Florida shore in the night, and reaches the western side of the Little Bahama bank, but no farther. At this period the wind generally prevails to the southward of E., and the more so as their northwest extreme is approached; the weather is then very variable, and squalls rush down with great violence, accompanied with heavy rains and an oppressive atmosphere. They are within the zone of hurricanes, and a year seldom passes without their being visited by a heavy gale at least, from the SE., which inflicts serious damage both on shore and at sea.

Northers.—In the winter months, from about November to the middle of March, the trade-wind is frequently interrupted by NW. and N. winds. In December and January this may be expected almost weekly. previously to this change the wind will draw round to the S. and SW. About twenty-four hours after or less, dark masses of clouds will be seen raising from the westward, and in a short time the wind will rush suddenly from that quarter with the force of a double or treble-reefed topsail breeze. It will soon veer round to NW. and N. with clear weather, and remain between these points for two or three days. It will then haul gradually to NE. perhaps with increased force, accompanied by heavy squalls, and wear itself out at E. in the course of a few days.

The barometer is scarcely any guide; a small fall may be detected as the wind draws to the S., and it will rise rapidly with the N. wind. The mariner may be sure of the action of the wind, and that it will not back at this period, and this will enable him to seek shelter, if necessary, with every confidence in the change that will follow. On the southern edge of the group this change may be more sudden on account of the partial interference of the winds from the highlands of Santo Domingo and Cuba on the regular trade, but it seldom takes place without a previous indication of dark masses of clouds to the westward.

Current.—A feeble stream, seldom exceeding half a knot, generally sets to the westward on the S. side of the Bahama islands and to the NW. on the NE. side; but it is liable to change, and often suddenly, especially in the Northwest Providence channel and on the NE. side of the Little Bahama bank. Here it will sometimes be found running strong to windward. Some observations tend to show that this is more frequently the case after northers, or on the increase of the moon. The opinions of the wreckers and Cayman fishermen appear to agree on these points, but there is no certainty in the matter and, consequently, more than ordinary attention is required when navigating among the islands. Near the northern and eastern bank of the Little Bahama the current sets strongly towards the bank.

Tides.—The tidal stream runs directly on and off all the banks at the rate of from 1 to 2 knots, except in the narrow channels between the cays on the Great and Little banks; here its velocity is greatly increased and in some places it is scarcely possible to contend against it.

Bank Blink is a phenomenon described as a bright reflected light hanging over the clear white sand-banks and serving to point them out for a long distance. From lengthened experience, however, we warn the navigator most strongly not to trust to so fallacious a guide. It will be far better for him to depend upon the eye from aloft, the lead, the reckoning, and especially the latitude, which should be unremittingly checked.

The Little Bahama bank is of irregular shape and lies to the northward of the Great Bahama bank, from which it is separated by the NW. Providence channel.

Great Abaco island is the largest of the numerous islands which skirt the Little Bahama bank on all sides but the NW. and W.; it rises on the eastern side of the bank and is inhabited. The southeast extreme is 2 miles in breadth and 90 feet high; at the eastern end of this headland there is a small, narrow tongue of low, flat rock, which projects about 300 yards to the southward, and close off it a very small rock. This remarkable point is called the Hole in the Wall, from the sea having worn a large arch through the rock, which is visible about 3 miles off, from SSW. to WSW., and the opposite bearings.

Anchorage in 10 fathoms will be found on the W. side off the SW. point of Abaco, three-quarters of a mile from the shore, with the light-house bearing N. 73° 7' E.

Cheerie sound.—From the Hole in the Wall the eastern shore of the island rises gradually to a height of 120 feet, and the sandy beach which borders it is steep-to. Thence the coast bends in, forming a deep bight, called Cheerie sound, which is everywhere foul, except at the NE. corner, where, with local knowledge there is shelter for small coasters. The coast-line becomes exceedingly irregular, and is skirted by numerous small cays, between which are several narrow openings navigable for wreckers and vessels of light draught. The first opening lies about 400 yards NE. of NE. point, and 13 feet may be carried through it into Little harbor.

Little Harbor cay, the first of the islets, lies NW. of the sandy bluff; the reef extends half a mile off shore, and there are 10 or 12 fathoms of water the same distance farther out. About 400 yards from the N. end, between it and Channel rock, there is another small cut, which carries a depth of 15 feet, and leads into Pelican harbor; but all these places are too difficult for a stranger to enter without a pilot.

Pelican and Abaco cays, next to the northward, are skirted by the reef the same distance off shore as at Little Harbor cay.

Little Guano or **Elbow cay** is separated from Abaco cay by a narrow channel; at its N. end is a high sandy bluff, and about a mile to the southward of the bluff there is a small settlement. This islet is at the NE. extreme of the Little Bahama bank, and a reef stretches off nearly 3 miles to the northeastward; it is one of the most dangerous and fatal elbows in the Bahamas.

The Elbow Reef cay lies N. 19° 41' E. from Abaco light, and in thick weather is likely to pick up all vessels bound to the SW. should they happen to fall to the westward of their reckoning. It is therefore advisable for a vessel to strike the parallel of 26° 30' N. well to the eastward of the cay. Should the wind be to the southward when in this neighborhood and the light not in sight, or the reckoning doubtful, it will be prudent to keep the vessel's head to the eastward in the night, as the lead will not give sufficient warning of the danger. The current generally sets to the NW., and the tides run through the openings at the rate of 2 to 3 knots.

From Elbow cay the range of small islets takes a NW. by W. direction for more than 100 miles, and skirts the shore of Abaco at a distance of from 3 to 6 miles.

The Elbow reef sweeps round these islets at the distance of about 3 miles, and joins the NW. end of Man-of-war cay, leaving an opening from a half to a quarter of a mile wide with a depth of 14 feet between it and the reef, which commences again to leeward. The channel lies close to the eastward of some small rocks nearly half a mile N. 22° 30' W. from the cay, as there is a small rocky head to be avoided lying about 400 yards NW. from the end of the cay; and a snug harbor for coasters drawing under 12 feet, off the mainland about 6 miles S. 45° W. of the opening. In a case of absolute danger a vessel of the above draught may save herself by running in here, but, without local knowledge, it would be attended with very great risk.

Whale cay.—About 8 miles farther to the NW. there is another opening between Whale and Green Turtle cays. There are two channels through, one between Whale cay and Channel rock, which lies 1 mile to the NW., with 13 feet water in it, and named Southeast channel; and another to the westward of the rock, named Northwest channel, about 400 yards wide and 3 fathoms deep, but the eye must be the guide. This channel should, however, not be used, as the reefs have extended. The sea breaks heavily on the edges of the reef in strong NE. gales, and the breakers on either side serve to point out the opening.

There is a settlement on the SW. end of Green Turtle cay, where wood and water may be obtained.

Walker cay, about 65 miles from Green Turtle cay, is the westernmost of the Grand cays, and is woody and 55 feet high. The islets between are skirted, to the distance of from 3 to 4 miles, by a solid reef, which presents no safe opening whatever. Between the cays and Abaco there is a passage, through which may be carried 12 feet water to the western part of the Little Bahama bank, entering by Whale cay channel.

Matanilla shoal, a dangerous coral patch, lies 4 miles westward of Middle Shoal, 2 miles within the northern edge of the bank and 3½ miles from the NW. extreme, and at 5 miles N. 67° 30′ W. of it the bank will be struck in 13 fathoms. The patch is not half a mile in extent, and on one small spot there are only 12 feet. All this part of the bank is extremely dangerous. The bottom being rocky and covered with dark weed, the water is not discolored, and the shoals do not break; the rock is so flat that no dependence can be placed on anchors.

Tides.—The tidal streams run on and off the Little Bahama bank, and near the edge are at times strong. The current in the offing is very uncertain for some distance to the northward.

The whole of this part is closely skirted by narrow, shallow sand-ridges and detached coral patches, and is extremely dangerous. The Florida stream strikes the edge of the bank sideways, with a strength of from 2 to 3 knots, and the lead gives scarcely any warning. There are small openings here and there with 3 and 4 fathoms water in them, and in a case of absolute danger a vessel might be guided by the eye into safety, on the bank, but she would run imminent danger of shipwreck.

Memory rock is a little, dark, barren, rugged islet, only 14 feet high, lying N. 22° 30′ W. from the W. end of Bahama island, about midway between it and the western limit of the bank, and three-fourths of a mile within its edge. At 3 miles NW. of it there is a most dangerous small coral patch, on which the sea generally breaks. Between the rock and patch there are from 3 to 4 fathoms water, about a mile within the edge of soundings, under the lee of a sand ridge, on which there are 2 fathoms. To the southward of the rock there is no safe opening for vessels drawing over 12 feet. The edge of the Florida stream comes generally close home to the rock. Between it and Bahama island vessels are only influenced by the tides, which set regularly on and off the bank at the rate of from a half to a knot an hour.

Sandy cay is very small, and covered with bushes to the height of 14 feet above the sea.

Indian cay lies close off the NW. point of Bahama island, leaving between a channel for small craft drawing 6 feet, round to the settlements on the N. side of the latter island.

Bahama island is inhabited, thickly wooded, but generally level, and about 40 or 50 feet high. At Settlement point, the W. end, it is a mile broad, N. and S., and anchorage will be found under it in 8 or 9 fathoms water, about half a mile off shore, with the NW. point, bearing N. 56° 15′ E., and the SW. point S. 25° 18′ E., but a vessel must quit the moment the wind threatens to change.

Soundings appear to extend off a short distance, and anchorage is marked on the chart under the latter point, but this part of the island is very little known. Thence the coast line takes an ENE. direction, and toward the E. end of the island sweeps round to the southward, forming a deep and dangerous bight, with southerly winds. This part appears to have a foul shore the whole way, without any anchorage; but it is also very imperfectly known. From the SE. extreme of the island the edge of the Little Bahama bank trends to the S. and round to the SE., and connects itself to the W. side of Abaco at Rock point. It is closely skirted by numerous small islets and dangerous ledges without any navigable openings between them, as far as Gorda cay, which lies N. 56° 15′ W. from Rocky point.

There is a well on Gorda cay and anchorage under the W. side. There is also water to be found abreast the anchorage under SW. point of Bahama island.

Great Isaac, at the NW. extreme of the Great Bahama bank, is a barren, narrow, honey combed rock, about three-quarters of a mile long and about 40 feet high, and being foul, yet very steep-to, landing is sometimes difficult even in moderate weather. There are 4½ fathoms water between it and the NE. rock, and the same depth between it and the Brothers; but, as before recommended, it will be better to pass outside of all. The ground to the SW. of the Great Isaac is foul to the distance of half a mile.

The Hen and Chickens form a group of barren, rocky islets. A vessel may round their N. end at a quarter of a mile distance, and anchor on the bank in 4 fathoms; but the ground to the SW. is foul to the distance of three quarters of a mile, where the depth is 2½ fathoms. In passing this neighborhood in the night, do not come within the depth of 10 fathoms.

From the Hen and Chickens to the Moselle shoal the edge of the bank is clear, and vessels can run just within its edge in from 6 to 16 fathoms.

Moselle shoal is dangerous in the night-time, having only 4 feet of water on its S. end, but in the day-time it is very conspicuously marked by a large black buoy with staff and basket-work ball upon it.

To avoid this shoal the Great Isaac light-house should not be brought to bear to the northward of N. 42° 11′ E. till the shoal is passed, or at night till the Gun cay light is opened W. of the Bemini islands bearing S. 5° E.

The North and South Bemini are two irregularly shaped, sandy islands, covered with small wood to the height of about 40 feet, and occupy a space of nearly 6 miles N. and S. They are separated by a very narrow cut, which opens out to the eastward, and forms a secure harbor for wreckers drawing 8 feet. There is a small settlement, custom-house, and a resident magistrate; and vessels in distress may obtain water and supplies sufficient for the moment.

Anchorage will be found in 8 or 9 fathoms water, fine sand, about midway between the extremes, and a mile off shore; be careful, however, not to shoot too far in, and look out for a clear spot. A little more than a mile northward of the N. end of the islands there is a remarkable small black rock, 8 feet high, called North rock.

Henry bank is stated to lie about NNW., half a mile from the S. point of South Bemini island, and a quarter of a mile from the shore. It is believed to have a depth of 3 feet upon it, with 3 fathoms on its in-shore side.

Spar beacon.—There is a spar beacon, surmounted by a barrel, on the N. extremity of Picket rock to serve as a guide to Barnett's harbor. Vessels drawing less than 14 feet may find shelter against southwesterly winds on the Great Bahama bank by entering the channel midway between the rock awash, N. of the beacon and triangle rocks. The course is E. until clear sandy bottom is struck in 3 fathoms; there anchor with Gun cay light-house bearing S. 8° 26′ E.

Gun cay is a mile long, but very narrow.

When 5 miles to the northward of the light, it should not be brought to the southward of S. 45° E., in order to avoid the low rocks between it and the Bemini islands, which sweep slightly outward, and, being so close to the edge of soundings, the lead will be of little use. There is temporary anchorage, with easterly winds, in 7 or 8 fathoms water, about three-quarters of a mile off shore, with the light-house bearing E. Wreckers find good shelter within the cay by passing round the S. end.

Cat cays are two narrow woody islets, 40 feet high, lying from 1 to 2 miles within the edge of the bank, and extending about 4 miles S. 33° 45′ E. off Gun cay, from which they are only separated by the small channel mentioned above. Round the S. point of the southern cay there is good anchorage for vessels drawing under 12 feet called Dollar harbor, where they will lie sheltered from all points but the S. The point is bold and steep-to, and the only danger to be avoided is the Rabbit rock, which is nearly awash, and lies N. 67° W., a mile from the point. There are some small barren rocks about 14 feet high at three-quarters of a mile to the SW. of the point, and they must be left to the southward in going in.

Some wells of good water will be found on the E. side of North Cat cay, about a quarter of a mile from its southern end.

The flood runs ENE.; the ebb, WNW.; springs rise 3½ feet.

Caution.—By bearing in mind that Orange cays are entirely barren and that the Riding rocks are covered with bushes, and, moreover, there is a beacon on the S. rock, they may be easily distinguished.

A vessel may anchor on the edge of the bank, which is here entirely clear, in from 6 to 9 fathoms, with the Riding rock bearing E. There is also an anchorage for small craft S. 67° E. of Castle rock, but in approaching it from the eastward a vessel must cross a shallow sand-bank extending N. and S. To cross this bank in its deepest part, which has 15 feet of water, keep the South Riding rock open just to the southward of Castle rock, and anchor in 3½ fathoms of water.

Gingerbread ground extends from Great Isaacs to a point 30 miles west of Little Stirrup cay. It is a very dangerous ledge of rocks and low cays. It is from 2 to 5 miles in width, and, as it lies close to the edge of soundings and is not easily seen from a distance, many ships have been lost upon it. There are several low rocks upon it and several cuts through it, but, except in case of emergency, strangers had better avoid them.

From the Gingerbread ground the northern edge of the Great Bahama bank takes an easterly direction to a point abreast of the Stirrup cays, a distance of 35 miles. In this space it is quite free of danger, and the lead will be a safe guide.

The majority of sailing-vessels bound from Europe and the Atlantic ports of North America to Cuba, Key West, and the northern ports of the Gulf of Mexico run through the NW. Providence channel. Those drawing 12 feet or less may cross the bank from the vicinity of Great Stirrup cay to a point about 14 miles S. of Orange cay, saving about 55 miles of distance.

The Berry islands are a group of small, narrow, wooded cays, from 50 to 60 feet high, which, from Great Stirrup cay, sweep round to the eastward, forming nearly a semicircle, and a good guide in the night.

Great Stirrup cay, the northernmost of the Berry islands, is a necessary landmark for vessels intending to cross the bank from the NW. Providence channel to the westward. At about half a mile from the W. end there is a small sandy cove and some wells of good water, and landing is generally easy, except with northerly winds. In moderate weather, with the prevailing easterly winds, a vessel may anchor in 7 fathoms, sandy bottom, with a flag-staff on the hill S. 8° 26′ E. about three-quarters of a mile off shore. A small supply of stock and vegetables may also be obtained.

Great harbor.—Great Stirrup cay is separated from Great Harbor cay by an opening 800 yards wide, and within it there is a limited anchorage, with a depth of $3\frac{1}{2}$ fathoms. It is completely exposed to the NE. and, except in a handy fore-and-after, a vessel might meet with considerable detention. Those under 10 feet draught can get close up under Great Harbor cay, or lie more snugly in Panton cove at the SE. end of Great Stirrup cay. Goat cay, which is about half a mile within the opening, forms a remarkable steep, rounded, woody hill 80 feet high.

Directions.—Should a vessel be forced to run for the anchorage in Great harbor, bring the S. end of Goat island to bear S. 47° 49′ W. and just clear of the N. end of Great Harbor cay, which is bold and steep-to at the distance of 200 yards. This mark will lead just clear of the E. end of the bar which extends out from Stirrup cay; give the N. end of the Great Harbor cay a berth of rather more than 200 yards and anchor with it bearing E. in 3 fathoms water; or shoot the vessel farther into the SE. of the point, according to her draught.

Slaughter harbor is a small basin between Great and Little Stirrup cays, scarcely 400 yards in diameter, but has a depth of 15 to 18 feet.

The channel, however, is barred, and only navigable at high water, with the assistance of a pilot, for vessels drawing 12 feet. It is quite open to the northward, but the bar, which generally breaks across in this wind, protects the anchorage.

On **Anderson** and **Cistern cays** there are remarkable clumps of dark trees 100 feet above the sea. Between the latter and Bamboo cay there is a small snug inlet, called Bullock harbor, for coasters drawing 8 feet. The channel is through Great harbor, between Goat and Lignum-Vitæ cays, or from the westward round Little Stirrup cay.

Great Harbor cay, about 60 feet high, is nearly connected to Haines cay, and is the largest of the Berry islands, and has a few settlers. Its eastern shore forms several sandy bays, separated by low white stone cliffs. Near the center, at about three-quarters of a mile off shore, there is a small islet called Patit cay, with a boat channel within it. Shallow rocky ground extends from the NW. end of this islet to within about 1½ miles of the N. end of Great Harbor cay, and a wide berth had better be given to it. The soundings are so regular that in the night-time they scarcely give warning of approach, and great care must be taken not to come within the depth of 10 fathoms.

Fish cays should not be approached from the NE. within 2 miles between Market Fish cay and Haines cay, which bears N. 67° 30′ W. from it. There is an opening 3 miles wide and an anchorage in it for small craft.

The **tides** are strong in all these passages between the cays, and sometimes run at the rate of 3 knots. The flood runs to the W., the ebb to the E.

In crossing the bank from the vicinity of Great Stirrup cay to Orange cay, follow the courses and distances as laid down on H. O. charts.

Mackie Bank buoy is intended to guide vessels in crossing the Bahama bank and to correct their positions in running from Stirrup cay to Orange cay; it is visible at 5 or 6 miles distance.

If it is desired to leave the bank between the Riding rocks and Orange cay, after steering 25 miles on a S. 39° 22′ W. course from the commencement of the flats or middle ground, steer S. 84° 22′ W. 25 miles and the western edge of the bank will be reached.

In crossing the flats the eye must guide the vessel between the numerous clear white sand-ridges and small black heads, which are easily seen, even in the night time, if the weather is clear. Some attention, however, should be paid to the tide on the first course. Should the vessel enter upon the bank with the first of the flood with a commanding breeze, she had better steer half a point farther to the westward, and the contrary on the ebb, judging at the same time according to the depth, which should generally decrease up to the sand-ridges.

Elbow bank.—Although the water is so shoal and clear, the lead should be well attended, and the line marked to feet (when wet), as the vessel may be set by the tide too far to the windward on the Long banks, or on the Elbow bank to leeward, which will be indicated by the gradual decrease of depth as she approaches either way, should the wind be scant. If she gets to the eastward of the track, toward what is called the long bank, the little heads of sponge and dark fans will become more numerous. In the winter months, should the wind haul to the southward, a sure indication of a northwester, instead of beating about among the shoals it will be better to anchor and await the change that will soon follow.

Tides.—The stream runs from one to half a knot an hour to within a short distance of the N. side of the Middle ground. On the flats there is very little set, and on the S. side of the Middle ground the stream goes regularly round the compass from E. to S. and W., from high to low water and the contrary. On the parallel of 25° N., about 16 miles eastward of Orange cay, a vessel will carry two hours more of high water across the shallowest part of the bank; therefore, by entering upon the S. 33° 45' W. course at three-quarters flood a steamer of 13 feet draught may cross the flats before the tide begins to fall.

Northwest channel.—At the NW. end of the Tongue of the Ocean is a narrow intricate channel between sand-ridges, through which may be carried a depth of 10 feet at low water on to the bank, and it is usually used by the wreckers. These small vessels leaving Nassau generally anchor under the Chub cays for the night, and contrive to be at the entrance of the channel by sunrise in order to be able to see the numerous heads which skirt the edge of the bank for about 1½ miles inward before they come to the sand-bores. The clearest route will be found by striking soundings with Blackwood bush (a small, low, bushy cay, the westernmost of the Berry islands), bearing N. 75° 56' E. 5 miles.

Andros island, about the largest of the Bahama islands, forms the W. side of the Tongue of the Ocean. It is low, swampy, thickly wooded, and intersected by numerous shallow creeks, which almost cut the island into three parts at high water. Along the eastern side, however, from High cay to the southward, there is a narrow ridge of hills from 70 to 90 feet high. This shore is skirted by numerous small cays and reefs to the distance of from 1 to 2 miles, and, being steep-to, is very dangerous, particularly in the neighborhood of High cay, where the tongue is only 15 miles across. The western shore of the island is composed of slimy mud, like pipe-clay, and is so low that, in NW. gales, it is overflowed to a considerable distance inland. The water is here so shallow that in some places a boat cannot come within many miles of the shore.

There is no harbor whatever, but boats and small craft drawing 4 or 5 feet find their way through the reefs on the eastern side of the island into some of the creeks, for the purpose of collecting sponge, which is found in large quantities, and shipping the wood, which is floated into them from the lagoons in the interior. There are but few inhabitants, and the only settlement of consequence is at Red bay, near the NW. end of the island. From this end an extensive flat of sand, dry in many places at low water, runs off 12 miles to the NW., and on it are several small islets, the northernmost of which are called Joulter's cays. About 2 miles to the northward of Morgan's bluff, a remarkable rocky headland forming the NE. point of the island, there is an opening in the reef, abreast of a small rock called Golding cay, and it will admit a vessel of 9 feet draught into shelter within in moderate weather.

Hurricane hole.—This entrance also leads into Hurricane hole, a snug anchorage for vessels of small draught to the NW. of Pigeon cays.

South side channels.—On the S. side of the Tongue of the Ocean there are several small channels leading across the bank to the SE. and southward, available for vessels of light draught.

They are called Queen's, Blossom, Thunder, and Lark channels. Through Thunder and Blossom channels vessels of 14 feet draught may pass.

The navigation depends entirely upon the eye, but is not difficult.

Coming to the southward, however, the channels are not so easily discovered. The tides run rapidly through and sometimes across these ridges, so that the navigation is unsafe in the night. A vessel may, however, anchor any where between them. From the entrance to Queen's channel the edge trends to the NW. and is clear for about 8 miles, but from this point it is full of rocky heads and reefs all along the western side of the Tongue of the Ocean.

Green cay is 60 feet high near its center. To the southward of it and just on the edge of the bank, which is here very steep-to, anchorage may be found. It requires very great care not to shoot too far in.

These dangers are on the edge of the bank, which is very steep-to, and from here sweeps round to the eastward and then to the southward. This part of the bank is impassable.

The edge of the bank takes a NW. by N. direction for 28 miles to SW. reef, and is very foul, there being several rocky heads nearly awash, and it is consequently dangerous to approach in the night.

Southwest reef.—This very dangerous rocky ledge lies on the edge of soundings SE. from Clifton Bluff, N. P. It is nearly awash, and the ground is foul for a mile to the northward of it.

New Providence island, being the seat of government, and possessing a safe harbor for a few vessels of 15 feet draught, is the most important island of the Bahamas. A narrow ridge of wooded hills from 80 to 120 feet high skirts the northern shore almost the whole way. The N. side of the island is skirted by several small cays covered with brushwood, and within less than half a mile of the edge of the soundings.

Hog island is the easternmost of these, and bounds the N. side of Nassau harbor; the western end gradually falls from low sand-hills to a flat rocky point on which is the light-house.

Silver cay lies 1,200 yards westward of Hog island, and half a mile from the shore of New Providence. At about 400 yards further westward is Long cay, and 1½ miles beyond this is North cay. There is a navigable opening for small vessels between the two latter cays; and also an opening through the foul ground about a mile to the westward of north cay leading into Delaport bay, a small anchorage for vessels of light draught, but seldom used. The shore to the westward of these cays should not be approached nearer than a mile.

Nassau stands on the northern slope of a ridge about 5½ miles from the E. end of the island, and is one of the most picturesque and well-built towns in the West Indies. It is much frequented by visitors from the United States and Canada, and has an excellent hotel, which is the property of the government.

Coal can not generally be obtained. Provisions can be obtained, but are high priced and not in great quantity. Water can be obtained (rain water), and some of poor quality can also be had from the wells in the city. Beef and mutton can be had, but the price is high. There is a marine railway on the S. side of Hog island, where vessels of 400 tons displacement can be hauled up.

The health of the place is good. Yellow fever has been epidemic, but not lately. The sickly season is from July 1 to October 15. There is a health officer and quarantine is maintained. There are three hospitals—the military, which is used only by the soldiers; the quarantine, which is situated on Athol island; also a public hospital, called the New Providence Hospital. Sick mariners are admitted to this hospital at $1.50 per day. The capacity is about 300 patients.

The place is fortified and has an English garrison.

The authorities to be called upon are the governor and chief justice. The United States is represented by a consul and vice-consul.

The exports are pineapples, oranges, grape fruit, shaddocks, bananas, cocoanuts, sponges, and dye-woods; also the following woods: Brazilletto, cedar, ebony, satin-wood, lignum-vitæ, logwood, and mahogany.

The imports are the usual commodities of life. There is a small ad-valorem duty on nearly all imports and exports to defray the expenses of the government.

Pilots are found in numbers, and if services are offered pilotage is compulsory, and it is necessary to take them if going over the bar inside. The pilotage fees are—

	£	s.	d.
8 feet and under	1	1	0
10 feet and under	1	9	0
12 feet and under	2	2	0
14 feet and under	2	15	0
16 feet and under	4	0	0
17 feet and under	5	0	0
18 feet and under	5	10	0

And 5 shillings for every half foot above 18 feet.

NASSAU.

The Nassau Mail Steamship Company sail from Jacksonville, Fla., three times a month with mails for the Bahamas, also a line from Tampa, Fla., and the Miller and Henderson line twice a month.

The southern portion of the island is low, and covered in great part with extensive pine barrens or woods. The shore is generally sandy, swampy, and shallow; flat sands run off from it for some distance. An excellent carriage road runs along the northern shore, and another crosses the island from the town to the Blue hills. The N. side is skirted by several small, low cays, covered with brushwood, and within less than half a mile of the edge of soundings.

Besides Nassau, the anchorages are Delaport bay, West bay, and Southwest bay.

Nassau harbor.—The entrance to this harbor lies between Hog island and Silver cay; but between them a rocky bar runs right across, which breaks heavily with strong NW. and N. winds, and is sometimes impassable for several days. The greatest depth at low water springs is 17 feet, but this is only in a space not 50 yards wide, and vessels drawing over 13 feet can not enter safely.

When bound to Nassau from the N. or NE., a wide berth should be given to the NE. elbow of the Little Bahama bank until the parallel of 26° 30′ N. is reached. Approaching from the eastward the latitude of 25° 45′ N. should be most carefully maintained until either the N. end of Eleuthera, which may be seen about 12 miles off, is sighted, or the Abaco light-house, which is visible in clear weather 16 miles away.

The current, as the Bahama islands are approached from these points and also from the E. and SE., generally runs to the NW., but not strong. To the northward of Eleuthera, however, a strong set in the opposite direction will sometimes be found after NW. and N. winds, and probably after fine weather on the increase of the moon, but it will be safer not to depend upon this. Should the land of Eleuthera be made, haul round Egg Island reef at the distance of 3 or 4 miles, and when Great Egg island bears E. the course will be about S. 33° 45′ W., and the distance nearly 32 miles to Nassau light-house.

The first objects seen when approaching Nassau harbor will be Forts Fincastle and Charlotte, and soon after the government house, a large square building on the top of the ridge, between them. When near the entrance a stone obelisk will be observed on the hill a short distance to the eastward of Fort Charlotte, which is the westernmost fort; and when the light-house bears S. distant about a half a mile, a small, low rock will be opened out close under the land, called Tony rock, on which is a pole beacon with a triangular frame on the top.

Tony beacon open a little to the E. of the obelisk; bearing S. 10° 20′ W. will lead over the deepest part of the bar, westward of a red buoy on the extremity of the spit off Hog island; when the light-house bears N. 80° 35′ E., turn sharply to port till heading SE., when run in by the chart.

1018—No. 85——3

Anchorage.—The best anchorage is abreast the ordnance wharf. Vessels drawing 13 or more feet should moor head and stern, with the heaviest anchor to the eastward. The anchors must be planted in mid-channel, with a sufficient scope of chain to swing clear of the upper flukes and hove well taut.

The depth of water in the harbor is said to be decreasing; it is not advisable for a vessel drawing more than 13 feet to attempt to enter. The holding-ground at the anchorage is not good. A red light is exhibited from the flag-staff near the light-house at night when the bar is impassable or dangerous. This light is obscured by the light-house when bearing S. 79° 40′ E.

Vessels merely wishing to communicate with Nassau, or with the wind to the southward, will find a temporary anchorage off the N. side of Hog island, in about 8 fathoms, on the very edge of soundings. This anchorage must, however, be approached under easy sail, and care must be taken not to shoot too far in; in the winter months be prepared to quit the moment the wind threatens a change.

The best berth is with the government house bearing S. 22° 30′ W., just open to the eastward of Christ church and Hog Island light-house S. 70° 19′ W.

The light-house must not be brought to the westward of this bearing on account of the shoals which run off the N. side of Hog island.

Eastern channel.—Vessels drawing under 11 feet may enter Nassau harbor from Douglas road or Cochrane anchorage, but this is only to be done by the eye. A depth of 9 feet may be carried at low water over the eastern flats of Fort Montague, and the channel lies close under the S. sides of Athol and Hog islands.

Boat landings.—There are two principal landings, the eastern or government landing near the center of the town, at the foot of the public grounds. The other is about one-fourth of a mile to the westward, at the foot of the street leading down to the governor's house. At high water boats can land anywhere along the sea-wall.

Bar signals.—If the harbor is approached with a northerly wind, and there is an uncertainty as to the state of the bar, should it be dangerous to cross, a red flag will be hoisted on the signal staff near the light-house, and at night a red light exhibited. In this case it will be more prudent to proceed to the Douglas channel, or to the anchorage at the SW. end of the island. Should it be passable, but too dangerous for a boat to get out, a white flag will be hoisted, and the pilot boat will be seen waiting just within the breakers, showing a flag red and white horizontally. In this case, cross the bar, steer for the boat, and receive the pilot. This, however, is a dangerous experiment for a vessel of heavy draught, and, except in a case of great emergency, it will be far more prudent to act as above stated. No attempt should be made to cross the bar when dangerous. Recently a boat capsized, and four men were drowned in attempting to cross.

Abaco anchorage.—Should a strong northwester overtake a vessel at the entrance of either of the Providence channels, it will perhaps be better to remain under the lee of the S. end of Abaco, or anchor under the W. side of the Hole in the Wall, and wait until the wind moderates and the sea goes down. It may still continue to blow hard as the wind draws round to the NE., but when it reaches this quarter the sea generally subsides on the bar in a short time. A good sheltered berth will be found under Abaco in 11 fathoms water, with the lighthouse N. 75° 56′ E., about three-quarters of a mile from shore.

West bay.—The W. end of New Providence forms a small bay which affords good shelter for small craft drawing 7 feet water from all points but the W.

Southwest bay.—The SW. end of New Providence is formed of remarkable bold white perpendicular cliffs about 30 feet high. The best anchorage will be found with Clifton bluff N. 36° 34′ W., and the S. extreme of the island S. 81° 34′ E., in $4\frac{1}{2}$ fathoms water, just on the edge of soundings, and about half a mile off shore. A vessel may go farther in, according to her draught, and be guided by the lead. Should she have to work up, be very careful to avoid a small rocky patch of 11 feet, lying close to the edge of the bank with the bluff bearing N. 25° 19′ W. nearly 2 miles, and the Conch rock S. 78° 45′ E. The latter, however, is only about 8 feet high, and so small that it will scarcely be visible from the deck of a small vessel. A vessel may also anchor southward of this patch in $5\frac{1}{2}$ fathoms, with the bluff N. 25° 19′ W. and the above rock E.

From New Providence island the bank runs to the northeastward about 35 miles to Eleuthera, and has on its edge a number of small islands and rocky reefs, separated by narrow channels, the principal of which are the Douglas and Fleming channels.

Among these small islands are several anchorages, which may be picked up from the chart.

Salt Cay anchorage.—Salt cay is a little more than 2 miles long, but very narrow. Under its western point is a snug anchorage for two or three vessels of 14 or 15 feet draught.

There is a rocky ledge with 13 feet of water on it, reaching off a quarter of a mile from the W. end of Salt cay, where the sea only breaks with strong NW. winds.

Athol Island anchorage lies between Salt cay and Athol island, and is a good berth for two or three vessels drawing under 18 feet. As the entrance is only 200 yards wide and open to the NE., it is difficult for a sailing vessel to get out, and in the winter season she may be detained for a long time.

In approaching this anchorage from the NE. care must be taken to avoid the range of low islets and coral patches which skirt the N. side of Rose island to the distance of $1\frac{1}{2}$ miles, and outside of which soundings extend for three-quarters of a mile.

The leading mark into the harbor is a remarkable conical bush on New Providence island, near the creek village, just open E. of the quarantine officer's house on Athol island.

Steer in on this line till the E. point of Salt cay bears N. 19° 41′ W., when haul up S. 19° 41′ E., and anchor in 3 fathoms of water with the west end of Rose island rocks bearing N. 45° E.

A pilot should be taken if one can be obtained.

A light is shown from the quarantine officer's house.

Green Cay anchorage.—To the SW. of Green cay there is a snug anchorage for small vessels, well sheltered, except to the westward. Anchor in 3 fathoms of water with the W. point of Green cay bearing N. 22° 30′ W., and the S. point of Sandy cay bearing W.

This anchorage is unsafe with NW. winds.

Douglas channel is distinguished by two pole-beacons on small black rocks in the center of the opening. It is navigable for vessels of 20 feet draught, but it is so narrow and crooked, and the tides so rapid, that a pilot is absolutely necessary. However, in the event of a vessel being forced to run in without assistance, the following directions may be useful:

Directions.—Wait for the flood tide, and strike the edge of soundings with the beacons in one S. 50° 37′ E., which line will lead close to the westward of Booby Island ledge, and when the small pile of stones on the W. end of that island bears N. 87° 11′ E., haul up about S. 67° 30′ E., so as to pass to the windward of the black buoy on the NE. edge of the shoal ground of the Douglas rocks. It is seldom, however, that the wind will allow a vessel to do this, but the tide is so strong under the lee, that by proper attention she may shoot through the narrows, which is only about 300 yards wide. Should she be forced to make a board, it had better be done under the W. side of the Douglas rocks, where they are steep-to. If under 14 feet draught, she may shoot into the southward of the beacons; but there is a very dangerous small rock, with 4 fathoms around it, right in the middle of the opening between the Douglas and South Channel rocks, which, on account of the strong ripplings over the dark bar that runs across, is not seen.

If it be determined to take the latter channel a boat had better be placed over this rock, for the tide runs here so strong that without a good commanding breeze the vessel would be scarcely under control. Having passed the buoy off Douglas passage, a S. 53° 26′ E. course will lead between the Turtle head and the black buoy off the N. end of the Hook sand, whence the course may be gradually shaped to S. 45° W., for Douglas road or Cochrane anchorage, guided by the eye and chart.

Cochrane anchorage.—A convenient berth will be found in about 4 fathoms water, sand and marl, with the block house on Potter cay nearly in one with Montague fort on New Providence N. 78° 45′ W., and the house on Rose island N. 5° 37′ W., about 8 miles from the town of Nassau. An anchorage may also be taken up a short distance within the Douglas channel in Shoe Hole road, in 4 or 4½ fathoms, but it is not good holding ground, and in a strong norther vessels are liable to drag. The sea in these winds seldom breaks across, and they may, therefore, run in here when the bar at Nassau is impassable.

Water.—There are wells of excellent water near the house on Rose island, but difficult and inconvenient to get at.

The opening between the Six Shilling cays and the Samphire cays is 6 miles wide, but the channel is only about 1½ miles in breadth, and lies about a mile southwestward of the former islets. It is capable of admitting vessels of 20 feet draught without much difficulty, provided they have some little knowledge of the locality.

Shannon beacon.—On the southwesternmost of the Six Shilling cays is the outer or Shannon beacon, triangular shaped, 50 feet high, and visible 7 or 8 miles. The Quintus rocks have two pole beacons, on the southern rock; they bear N. 22° 30′ E. and S. 22° 30′ W. from each other.

Directions.—When approaching the Fleming channel from the northward run down close to the edge of the bank, which is about a mile from the cays, and enter upon soundings with the Shannon beacon bearing S. 78° 45′ E., when the Quintus beacon will be just open S. of it, and then steer S. 47° 49′ E. This course should lead about a mile southwestward of the Shannon, and when it bears N. 5° 37′ W. bear up S. 25° 19′ W., which will lead into Douglas road or New anchorage.

As the tides run right across the inner part of the channel, the flood to the SE., the ebb to the NW., at the rate of 2 or 3 knots, steer accordingly, so as to pass 400 yards to the eastward of a black buoy with flag, moored S. 59° 04′ E., 2 miles from the upper or NE. Samphire cay, and S. 36° 34′ W., 6¼ miles from the Quintus poles; these latter, therefore, will be a good guide. The buoy lies in 2 fathoms water, at the inner and narrowest part of the channel, which is little more than a mile wide. A short distance to the NE. of the buoy there is a small ledge of 14 feet, called the Middle ground, with 21 feet on either side, but it had better be left to the eastward.

When the buoy eastward of the Samphire cay bears southward of S. 56° 15′ W. do not stand farther eastward than to bring the Quintus beacons in line, and to the westward keep the Pimlico islands open eastward of the Six Shilling cays. The edge of the shoal ground on either side of the channel, however, may be seen from aloft. A vessel may anchor in the channel, or take up a convenient berth for quitting about a mile to the SW. of the Quintus rocks, but she will be exposed to the westward. The shoal ground extending southward from the Shannon Beacon cay should be carefully avoided.

The Pimlico islands are a range of small, barren, low, rocky islets. At about 2 miles within the Pimlico islands is Current island, which is only separated from the W. end of Eleuthera by a narrow channel, called Current cut, through which the tide rushes with the force of a rapid.

Current or Egg islands, lying off the N. end of Eleuthera, are very low, but well wooded. They are separated from Eleuthera by a narrow channel sufficiently deep for small vessels.

There is anchorage in 8 fathoms of water on the edge of the bank, with Great Egg Island hill in one with Little Egg island, N. 22° 30′ E. about a mile from the latter; but the holding ground is not good, and a heavy swell generally rolls in round the elbow of Egg reef. Vessels drawing under 16 feet may go so far in as to bring Little Egg to bear N. 67° 30′ W. and the paps on Royal island N. 5° 37′ E., where they will have 3 fathoms at low water. In beating up they may stand towards the cays by the lead, observing that the S. end of Little Egg is foul to the distance of a long half mile. When standing to the southward be careful when approaching the SW. reef.

Great Egg island is a wooded islet about 67 feet high. The opening between it and Royal island is a little more than 200 yards across, and the elbow of Egg reef terminates near the middle of the islet.

Royal island, the largest of the group, lies parallel to and within Egg Island reef. Near the center of the island there is a conspicuous large stone house, and about three-quarters of a mile to the SW. of it are two remarkable woody paps or hummocks, close together, and about 74 feet high. On the S. side of the island there is a snug little harbor for small craft drawing less than 9 feet. In the middle of the entrance lie two small dry rocks, and on entering it will be better to pass close to either of the points E. or W. of them. The best berth is with the house bearing N. 11° 15′ E. or N. 22° 30′ E. in 10 feet at low water. At about 1¼ miles S. of the harbor there is a narrow rocky ledge, nearly dry, and in working up from the SW. it will be better to keep to the northward of it.

A well of good water will be found near the house on Royal island.

George island, the easternmost of the group of islands NW. of Eleuthera, is separated from it by a narrow channel leading round to Harbor island. On the sandy point at the E. end of the island there is a small village of fishing huts. Russell island is woody and about 80 feet high.

Egg Island reef.—Along the NW. side the depths are 9 and 10 fathoms at three-quarters of a mile from the reef, but at the elbow the edge of soundings is close to the shore. This neighborhood is very dangerous, and requires the greatest attention to the lead.

A short distance from this western elbow, and outside of the reef, lie two dangerous rocks, called Landrail and Lorton rocks. Landrail rock bears N. 11° 15′ W. from the hill on Great Egg island, and N. 59° 04′ W. from the western pap on Royal island. Lorton rock bears N. 14° 04′ E. from the hill on Egg island, and N. 28 07′ W. from the western hummock of Royal island. There are numerous other rocks along the edge of this reef, having a depth of 3½ to 4½ fathoms between them.

Eleuthera island is of a very irregular shape, and may be said to form the NE. elbow of the Great Bahama bank. It is thickly inhabited, and the soil is peculiarly adapted to the cultivation of pine-apples, which are largely exported. From Bridge point, the northern point of Eleuthera island, a range of small low islands sweep around for about 5 miles to the N. end of Harbor island, and are fringed by a reef to the distance of about half a mile. These islets, the largest of which is Harbor island, trend for 2½ miles to Glass window. They are bold and steep-to, forming deep coves and bays, within which there is good shelter for small coasters.

Northeast bank.—From Man island, which forms the elbow of the above cays, a spit or tongue of bank about 2½ miles broad, with 12 and 14 fathoms of water on it, runs off 5 miles N. 45° E., and, with careful attention to the lead, it serves as a valuable safeguard in approaching this very dangerous neighborhood in the night; but the latitude is the great point to be attended to here, and, if not certain of this, a wide berth should be given to this locality, which is generally the land-fall for vessels bound into the NE. Providence channel.

On Harbor island, W. side, there is a considerable town, which is considered the healthiest spot in the Bahamas; the S. end is about the same height, but rocky and woody, and is separated from the main by a narrow channel, through which vessels of 12 feet draught may enter into a small but well-sheltered anchorage named East harbor. The entrance for small vessels into the western harbor is through a small intricate cut, close off the N. point, but it requires the aid of a pilot.

East harbor has a bar at the entrance on which the sea breaks in heavy weather, but there is not less than 14 feet at low water. The opening is easily recognized by the sand-hills to the northward, and the ridge of bold rocky cliffs to the NW. of the Cow and Bull southward of it. Bring the opening to bear S. 45° W. and run boldly in, bordering towards Harbor island, and anchor just within the bar in 3½ fathoms water, with the S. end of that island bearing N. 22° 30′ W. The tide runs through with great rapidity, and it is therefore necessary to moor. Vessels are prevented from going farther in by an extensive shallow sand-flat, which separates this anchorage from that off the town, and, being exposed to the NE., this place is difficult to get out of, and consequently seldom visited. It would be found, however, a safe refuge for a vessel caught in the bight between it and James point.

Vessels entering this harbor by the S. bar should steer for the entrance on a course S. 35° W., and keep near the N. side of the channel, as the shoal extends from the S. shore nearly half way across. There is always a swell on the bar, even in light winds, and the tides run strong.

Anchorage can be found in 3¾ fathoms with Dunmore point bearing N. 10° W. and S. entrance point N. 74° 20' E.

At Savanna sound there is a settlement containing about 300 inhabitants. There is a small but good salt pond here, but the fresh water is not good, the well being used by cattle.

From **Bamboo point** the western shore takes a NNW. direction for 3½ miles; it then turns abruptly to the SE. and round to the eastward, forming Rock sound, where is situated one of the largest settlements, containing about 500 inhabitants. To the northwestward of Powell point there are many shallows and sand-ridges, on several of which low sand cays, called schooner cays, have formed, and between which are channels capable of admitting vessels drawing less than 12 feet; those, however, bound here for fruit or stock, above this draught, generally enter on the bank from the NW., through the Fleeming or Douglas channels.

Tarpum bay is the next settlement on the W. side of Eleuthera. Small vessels may anchor here close to the shore, protected from the westward by numerous sand-bores nearly awash at high water. There are 500 persons at this settlement, and there are good wells bored in the rock.

Governor harbor is a small cove, about 11 miles farther northward. In entering this cove keep close to the S. point, to avoid a small rock having only 12 feet of water over it, lying about 100 yards off, with 3 and 3¼ fathoms between it and the shore. The anchorage is exposed to westerly winds, but with good ground tackle and proper precaution there is no danger. The best berth is in 3½ fathoms, with the S. point bearing S. 47° 49' W. and W. end of Cupid cay N. 56° 15' W.

There are some wells near the opposite shore about 1½ miles from the village, but the water is not very good. About a mile to the northward of this, near the beach, is what is called James cistern, where after heavy rains abundance of good water may be obtained, but it is scarce in the dry season.

Pitman cove, generally called The cove, is the northernmost settlement on Eleuthera. This part of the shore is bold and steep to, and a vessel may anchor in 4½ or 5 fathoms within half a mile of it.

Directions.—Vessels bound to any of the above settlements from the westward will not have less than 21 feet water across northward of the Middle ground, on a clear sandy bottom. The depth is 15 feet on the northern edge of the Middle ground, at about 4 miles from Finley cay, which is very low and sandy, and in beating up the lead must be the guide. The channel between the Middle ground and the low rocks to the NW. is about 4 miles wide in the narrowest part, abreast the Samphire cays, from whence it gradually opens out to the NE.

Exuma sound.—From the S. end of Eleuthera island the edge of soundings sweeps around to the northwestward and westward as far as the Ship channel, then in a SE. direction for nearly 100 miles to Great Exuma island, forming Exuma sound.

Long island.—From the S. extreme, named South point, the western shore trends N. 22° 30′ W. for about 14 miles, and then bends round westward, forming an extensive bay. Soundings extend from 1½ to 4 miles off this part of the shore, and good anchorage will be found anywhere with the prevailing easterly winds. The most convenient position for communicating with Clarence settlement is with Stephenson rock, bearing N. 56° 15′ W., in 7 or 8 fathoms water, 2½ miles off shore, where there will be room to weigh should the wind veer to the westward. Stephenson rock is 25 feet high, and lies about 1½ miles from the shore and N. 45° W. from the S. end of the island. Population 5,209. Pineapples are extensively grown on this island.

Abreast Stephenson rock there is a well of excellent water near the beach.

At about 1½ miles to the NE. of South point there are some conspicuous white cliffs about 50 feet high, and from thence the eastern shore of Long island curves slightly round and takes a N. 22° 30′ W. direction to Clarence harbor. At about 4 miles northward of South point Mavors hill rises to a remarkable sharp peak 150 feet high, and between it and the harbor the interior is cut up by numerous salt ponds. There are about 140 persons residing along the shores of this harbor.

Clarence harbor is formed between the shore and some small low islets which extend off about 1½ miles to the E. It is capable of admitting a few vessels of 13 feet draught, but, being open to the northward, it is much exposed and frequently very difficult to get out of. The assistance of a pilot is necessary.

Wood and water may be obtained in Clarence harbor, also a small supply of beef and vegetables.

Directions.—Should a vessel be forced to run into Clarence harbor without a pilot, the following directions may be useful: The S. shore of the harbor is skirted at the back by a ridge of low hills, and on the western fall of the highest part there is the ruin of a large building, and about 1 mile to the NW. of it, at the end of the ridge, a house, and near it a flagstaff. Run in with the staff in line with Harbor point, bearing S. 14° 4′ W. until the ruin bears S. 22° 30′ E., when haul up directly for it, and anchor on this line in 18 feet water, just within the W. end of Strachan cay, the northernmost of the larger islets. A beacon 40 feet high, the base and upper part red and the middle part white, is erected on Lark point, the SW. extreme of this cay, to point out the position of the harbor.

The channel within is little more than 200 yards wide, and the outer part generally shows itself on either side by the breakers, which extend out nearly 400 yards from the Booby rocks off the N. end of Strachan cay. Being open to the NNW., it is by no means a desirable place in the winter months for large vessels that can not get under shelter of the cay. The salt ponds are close to the shore, very productive, and the salt is readily shipped.

A bank of moderate depth extends out at least 4 miles to the NE. of Clarence harbor, but its exact limits have not yet been determined.

Little Exuma island is very narrow and low. It contains about 160 inhabitants, and the chief settlement is about 3 miles from the E. end, in the vicinity of a valuable salt pond. There is anchorage off this part of the shore, but it is an extremely exposed position, and only visited by a few small vessels, who take a favorable opportunity to ship the salt. Those employed for this purpose generally come from Nassau, with a pilot on board, and no stranger should attempt to approach this island without one.

Great Exuma island is merely separated from Little Exuma by a small, shallow channel, almost fordable at low water.

The S. shore is generally low and swampy, and skirted by sand-banks and small cays, among which boats can only navigate at high water. The north shore is more firm and elevated, varying from 50 to 100 feet in height.

The island contains 2,300 inhabitants, but as there are no large salt ponds they are scattered about and employed in raising stock and provisions; it is, consequently, only visited by small coasters, who convey the produce to Nassau. The whole of the northern shore is skirted by a line of narrow, woody islets and small, barren rocks to the distance of from 1 to 1½ miles, and within them there are several secure harbors for vessels drawing as much as 14 or 15 feet. The channels, however, are so exceedingly narrow and intricate as to be quite impassable to strangers, and even with the assistance of a pilot there would be considerable risk in a vessel of this draught beating out. Those, however, drawing 12 feet will not have this difficulty, as they can run in at the E. end and out at the W.

Stocking island, the largest of the islets on the northern shore of Great Exuma, is 3 miles in length. Under its western side small vessels may careen alongside the rocks.

Beacon.—Near the center there is a remarkable round hill, 100 feet high, and on the summit a well-built solid stone pillar, 28 feet high, which is the first object seen from the offing, and an excellent guide.

Exuma harbor.—The eastern channel lies between the small, low rocks, about 4 miles to the eastward of the beacon, and N. 11° 15′ E. of the ruins of Rolletown, which are conspicuously situated on the E. end of the rising ground on Great Exuma. Man-of-war cay extends off about a mile from this part of the shore, and on its N. side are the ruins of a small battery. No safe directions can be given for this channel, the pilotage depending entirely upon the eye.

The western channel is 3 miles to the NW. of the beacon, and is much easier of access than the other. The opening between Conch and Channel cays is a mile wide, and serves to point it out, for the low, small rocks lying between Stocking island and the former cay are close together. The entrance, however, is barred right across, leaving a small cut, 400 yards wide, close up to the reef, which runs off about 400 yards from Conch cay; 21 feet may be carried through this cut into an anchorage, with 5 fathoms water, within 200 yards of the SW. side of the above reef. It is, however, scarcely safe in the winter season, as it is quite exposed to northwesters.

Directions.—The mark to cross the bar is Industry tree (a remarkable large tree, standing on the summit of the highest hill on this part of the shore), in line with the E. side of some small, low, black rocks, named Smith cays, lying under it, a short distance from the land, bearing S. 11° 15' W., but the vessel should be hauled up the moment she is within Conch reef, for the space is very confined. As before stated, vessels of 11 and even 12 feet may proceed as far as they like to the eastward, provided they take high water to cross the flats westward of the beacon. All these outer cays lie within about half a mile of the edge of soundings, and commence nearly abreast the middle of Little Exuma, about 3 miles from the shore.

There are several small intricate openings between the cays, leading onto the bank, the first of which, after passing Great Exuma island, is Galliot cut.

Adderly cay lies about 25 miles to the NW. of the beacon on Stocking island. A stone beacon, 30 feet high (10 feet of the middle part being red, the upper and lower parts white), stands on the cay. To the southward of this beacon there is a channel and harbor for small craft. There is a well of good water on the W. end of Lee Stocking island and a cultivated salt-pond on Norman Pond cay, westward of it.

Conch cut is difficult to recognize, from the similarity in appearance of the adjacent cays, which are from 30 to 50 feet high. It has, moreover, more water and is more easily navigated, but still only adapted to small, handy, fore-and-aft coasters.

Highborn cut, 10 miles northward of Wax cut, is a much better opening to run through, but extremely difficult to beat out of. It is easily recognized by Highborn cay, which bounds the S. side of the channel, being the highest of the whole range.

Allen cays are on the N. side of this channel. These cays are numerous, and on one of them, near the center of the group, are some cocoanut trees. There are several rocks in mid-channel, both above and below the surface. A pilot is necessary for this channel, for it is very narrow and crooked. The charts of it are trustworthy.

The **tides** run through this cut at the rate of 3 knots at the springs.

Ship channel is the northernmost and by far the best of these openings. The entrance lies between Bluff cay on the S. and Dog rocks on the N. side. From the latter a sand-bank strewn with rocky heads extends half a mile to the southward.

As the entrance is approached, an inner range of small cays about 30 feet high will be seen 1¼ miles inside of the outer islets. The northernmost of these is a bold, black rock called North rock, and having on it a beacon 50 feet high, with the upper half red, lower half white.

Bush cay is at the S. end of Ship Channel cay, which bounds the S. side of the channel, and has a small beacon on it. There are some conspicuous sand-cliffs 60 feet high, which, with Highborn cay, are a good guide for the opening.

Directions.—After recognizing these rocks and cays the channel may be approached, taking care to avoid a rock with 5 feet of water on it lying in a line between the South Dog rock and Bluff cay, and one-third of the apparent width of the channel from the latter.

To enter the channel steer in to the westward, keeping the South rock just open of the N. point of Bluff cay till the beacon on North rock bears N. 64° 41′ W., when haul up and run for it till in a line between the South Dog rock and Bluff cay. Then steer N. 47° 49′ W., which will carry the ship about half a mile to the northward of Mushroom rock, avoiding the shoal which runs off to the northward of it.

At the entrance to this channel the bottom is dark-colored and is, in consequence, deceptive, but the shallow part of the bar on the N. side generally shows itself by strong tide-ripplings.

The **tides** run regularly in and out of all the above openings with great velocity, according to their breadth. In the Ship channel its rate is from 2 to 3 knots, gradually decreasing as the vessel advances upon the bank.

Vessels bound to Nassau round the W. end of New Providence island, having entered Ship channel and being about half a mile N. of the Mushroom rock, should steer S. 84° 22′ W. 8 miles, or until they have brought the sand-cliffs of Ship Channel cay to bear S. 56° 15′ E., as the run may be influenced by the current. The course will then be S. 67° 30′ W. 18 miles, which should take the vessel southward of the Yellow and White banks, and to a depth of 3 fathoms at low water, as will be seen by reference to the chart. Thence by steering W. 8 miles it will bring her to the edge of soundings. Should the water not deepen as above, the tide will have set the vessel too far northward, and she must haul a little more to the southward until she has done so. Many small patches will be met with, and by no means attempt to run in the dark, or when the sun or weather prevents the shoals from being distinctly seen. A vessel may anchor anywhere, provided she has 2 feet to spare at low water.

Vessels drawing less than 10 feet may, after bringing the sand-cliffs to bear as above, steer N. 59° W., which will lead across the Middle ground in 10 feet at low water, avoiding the small coral heads, which are easily seen.

The small islets on the N. side of Ship channel terminate about 5 miles from the entrance; thence the edge of the Bahama bank sweeps round to the eastward about 20 miles, and presents no opening whatever as far as Powell point, on the west side of Eleuthera island. Here there is a channel of 10 feet at low water.

Cat island is very fertile and generally well cultivated; but, possessing no large salt ponds, the inhabitants are scattered over it from one end to the other.

The NE. side, from Columbus point to Bird point, is generally rocky, bold, and steep-to; but from thence it becomes foul, and is skirted by a reef which runs round the NW. end of the island at the distance of two-thirds of a mile. There is shelter for boats within, and deep soundings will be found 2 miles outside of it.

The features of the southern shore are not quite so regular. At 11 miles S. 78° 45' W. from Columbus point, the S. extremity of the island terminates at some remarkable white cliffs. About 2¾ miles west of the cliffs a dangerous reef leaves the shore, and sweeps eastward to a remarkable bluff. About midway between the bluff and the cliff there is a small cut, which admits vessels of 12 feet draught into good shelter at Port Howe. This end of the island should be avoided in the night, and very carefully approached in the day-time.

Port Howe.—To enter, bring Williams' house, situated on a hill close to the water and easily distinguished, to bear N. 33° 35' E., and steer for it until inside the reef, when haul up sharply to the eastward and anchor. There is an anchorage in 7½ fathoms of water outside the reef with Williams' house bearing N.

A pilot should always be taken for entering the harbor.

Vessels bound to Bight settlement and having passed Hawks-nest sand-spit, should not attempt to cross the bank until about 4 miles northward of that sand-spit. There is a conspicuous bare patch about 2 miles S. of the settlement.

Conception island is a dangerous uninhabited islet, irregular in shape. Close off the E. point there is a small islet one-third of a mile in diameter, called Booby cay. On the NW. side there is a clear, open bay, with good anchorage on a sandy bottom, sheltered from NNE. round easterly to SSE. The depth is 6 fathoms at about one-fourth of a mile from the edge of soundings, but farther in the bottom becomes foul.

The approach to its SW. side is extremely dangerous, even in daytime, as the dark, rocky heads are difficult to distinguish. The bank extends off 3½ miles from the N. side of the island and is equally dangerous; it is pretty clear in the center, with variable soundings; but along its western side there is a dry reef on which the sea always breaks, and extends N. 3½ miles from some small cays near the NW. end of the island.

San Salvador or Watling's island.—The interior is largely cut up by salt-water lagoons, separated from each other by small woody hills from 100 to 140 feet high; it is, however, considered to be the most fertile of the group, and raises the best breed of sheep in the Bahamas. The inhabitants, about 500 in number, are scattered about the island in consequence of there being no safe anchorage except at the N. end, where there is a reef harbor for coasters.

On the NE. side of the island the tower of the light-house makes an excellent landmark, being seen long before the island is made out.

There are several small cays on and within the reef off the N. side of the island. White cay, so called from its appearance, is the northernmost.

Green cay is about a mile N. of the NW. point of the island, and round the S. end of it is the channel, with 7 feet water leading into the anchorage for coasters.

Soundings do not reach more than a half mile from the W. side of San Salvador island, in many parts much less, and the edge is generally very foul. At about 2 miles eastward of the SW. point, in a small bay just under some houses on rising ground, there is a confined anchorage for small craft under the lee of the reef, which extends a short distance from the shore.

Rum cay.—The SE. end rounds a little and forms two remarkable white cliffs about 90 feet high, which may be seen during the day 9 to 12 miles off. A reef commences at the S. point of the cay and, sweeping off nearly a mile from the shore, terminates off some dry wells at the SE. point. It is nearly steep-to, and should be carefully avoided in the night. The eastern side of the cay, to the northward, is bold and free of danger. The population of this cay is 650.

The water on Rum cay is good, but the supply is small. Fresh meat and poultry may be obtained.

In **St. George bay** is the principal settlement, and near it is a valuable salt pond. The bank of soundings extends southward about 2 miles from the shore, with a general depth on it of from 4 to 6 fathoms, but from Sumner point, the S. extreme of the cay, the edge of the bank is fringed with a narrow, broken ledge of coral, which extends westward about 5 miles, with from 9 to 15 feet water on it, and the sea breaks in heavy weather.

St. George anchorage.—Within the reef there is excellent anchorage in St. George bay, and secure at all times, except in the hurricane season. Vessels leaving the anchorage at Rum cay for the northward had better pass round the W. end of the cay, but they should clear Conception island before dark, as the current frequently sets strong to the NW.

Port Nelson.—The entrance is through a break in the reef about one-fourth of a mile in breadth, and the least water is 4 fathoms. The channel, however, is intricate, and should not be attempted by a stranger, although the bottom is easily seen, but the least dark spot would probably mislead. Stand in with two small houses on Cotton Field point, at about 1¼ miles westward of the settlement, bearing N.

until the flag-staff bears E.; then steer for the flag-staff and anchor in 4 fathoms water, fair holding ground, and well protected from all winds.

Commander H. D. Grant, of H. M. S. *Steady*, says the entrance through the reef is known by a white house, which can hardly be mistaken, bearing N. 2° 48' W.; the depth of water is about 4½ fathoms, and a vessel can anchor anywhere E. or W. of the entrance in 5 fathoms, but not with it open, as a rather heavy swell sets in. Or a vessel may steer in between Sandy point and the W. end of the reef fronting St. George bay. This passage is clear of danger, except such as may be avoided by the eye.

Currents.—The currents are variable and irregular in their force. They may generally, but by no means as a rule, be expected to set strongest at full and change of the moon, and then to the NW. or SE.

Samana or **Atwood's cay** is uninhabited and lies out of the usual track of vessels. Its surface is hilly and broken, and about one-third from the W. end rises to the height of 10 feet.

On the N. side, at about 1½ miles from the W. end, are three dry rocks close to the edge of the reef. The W. point is low and sandy, and from it a narrow reef, nearly dry and steep-to, extends westward.

This very dangerous reef is said to extend from 4 to 5 miles from the W. end of the island, the extreme point lying 2 miles farther out than is represented on the charts.

At about half a mile from the E. point is a cay, and 2 miles eastward of it another, but much smaller and lower. The reef which skirts the southern cays continues in an unbroken line for more than a mile eastward of the latter islet, terminating in a detached breaker at the eastern extreme.

There is an anchorage in 8 fathoms of water on the SW. side of Samana cay, about 2 miles from the W. point, and 600 yards off shore, but the ground is not good.

Good water may be obtained by digging wells.

The Plana or **Flat cays** are two islets separated by a narrow channel. The W. end of the cay forms a narrow point, is steep-to, and at about a mile from its extremity there is a hill 70 feet high, but the rest of the cay is low and flat. A bank of soundings, 3 miles broad, extends from the E. end, but on the southern edge there are some dangerous shallow spots and, the whole bank being a dark rocky bottom not easily distinguised, this end of the cay should be approached very cautiously.

The western cay is oval-shaped. All the eastern side of the cay is fringed with a reef to the distance of about a quarter of a mile, terminating at the SW. sandy point.

Anchorage.—On the W. side of the western Plana cay, near the SW. point, there is a clear bank of soundings extending about a third of a mile from the shore, on the edge of which anchorage will be found in about 7 fathoms water, with room enough to weigh, should the wind come unexpectedly from the westward.

At the back of the SW. point of the western Plana there are some wells of excellent water a little beyond the sand-ridge; the casks can be rolled up and rafted off very conveniently; indeed, it is the best place for watering among these islands, with the exception of Nassau.

The Crooked Island group of islets rises from a triangular shaped bank. The NE. point of Acklin island, the SW. point of Castle island, and the Bird rock form the angular points.

Castle island.—The SE. end forms a remarkable bold sand-cliff; the SW. end runs off to a low, sandy point. A bank extends off to the distance of 3 miles from the E. side. The NE. rock is very remarkable, resembling an old castle—hence the name of the island; and between it and Acklin there is a passage for boats.

Acklin island.—Salina point is low and bushy. There is good temporary anchorage in Jamaica bay, with the prevailing winds, in 9 fathoms water, on the edge of the bank.

Abreast the Fish cays the edge of the bank is clear for about one-third of a mile inward, but elsewhere it is foul and dangerous until close up under Fortune island, where there is a small, clear space on which a vessel will find good shelter from northers, with the S. point of Fortune island bearing N. 33° 45′ W. distant three-quarters of a mile, and a small sand-bore which breaks E. 5° 37′ S. Be careful not to shoot in too far, as the ground becomes foul a very short distance within the line of the soundings.

Fortune island, or Long cay.—About 2 miles from the S. end a hill rises, and is a good landmark coming either from the northward or southward. One and one-fourth miles from the S. extreme of the island, on the W. side, there is a small settlement containing about 350 inhabitants, and at the back of it a very productive salt-pond. A post-office is located here. The whole shore is steep-to; nevertheless, with the usual easterly winds, the few vessels that come here for the salt find a temporary anchorage off the pond, but so close in that there is not room to swing, and they must be prepared to quit the moment a change threatens. There is frequent communication by steamers to and from the West Indies and America.

Crooked island is separated from Fortune island by a small channel, through which wreckers drawing under 7 feet water find their way into shelter from NW. winds. There is an anchorage on the edge of the bank full three-quarters of a mile off shore, but not to be recommended. The shore is low; woody, generally foul, and soundings do not extend off more than 400 yards. A dangerous reef extends off in a NW. direction from the NW. point of the island.

Bird rock, about 10 feet high, lies N. 22° 30′ W. about a mile from the NW. point. Close to the southward of it there is a narrow intricate opening in the reef, leading into a small well-sheltered basin, named Portland harbor, in which there are 3½ and 4 fathoms water; but it requires the assistance of a pilot. Vessels approaching the light must pay careful attention to its bearings, as the point of the reef extends about 1¼ miles N. 22° 30′ W. of the tower, and the current to the northward of Crooked island is variable.

Crooked Island anchorage is 2½ miles southward of the NW. point, nearly abreast a remarkable large house standing close to the shore.

Landrail point, a short distance to the northward of it, is low and rocky, and has a small flagstaff near the extremity. The shore to the northward of this forms a low, sandy beach.

The **anchorage** must be approached with great care, under easy sail, and be prepared to come to the moment the soundings are obtained, or to back off if necessary. The edge of the bank will be seen from aloft; the bottom is sand and grass, good holding ground. In the winter season it must be left the moment the wind veers to the southward of E., but in the summer months a vessel may remain, as the wind is generally light from this quarter; it will, however, be more prudent to keep off under sail.

A supply of stock and vegetables may generally be obtained here, but it will probably detain a vessel some hours. Population, 627.

During strong westerly winds the best landing place is close northward of Landrail point, inside a reef running a little to the northward, and which affords shelter. There are some wells of good water on the S. end of Crooked island, called the French wells; but as the anchorage here is full three-quarters of a mile from the shore, it is inconvenient for watering. There is also a convenient well of excellent water near Landrail point, and a good landing place on the beach to the northward of it.

Acklin island, the largest of the group, and containing about 370 inhabitants, is separated from Crooked island by an opening about 2¼ miles wide, but so shallow that it may be waded across at low water.

Northeast breaker is a dangerous rocky patch, nearly awash, about a quarter of a mile in extent, which generally breaks.

About 2 miles from Creek point there is a small harbor for wreckers.

Abraham's bay is the opening in the reef leading into an exposed anchorage; but this side of the island is very dangerous, and had better be avoided altogether. The western side of the island is irregularly shaped, and only accessible to boats, or very small coasters, from the shallow water on the bank.

The **Mira-Por-Vos** is a cluster of small, low, barren, rocky islets.

South cay is the largest of the cluster. Close off its eastern side there is a remarkable square black rock. In the center of the cay there is an uncultivated salt-pond; and on the S. shore are two remarkable sand hills, about 30 feet high, which may be seen from the SE. point of the bank. In moderate weather, with the usual easterly winds, a vessel may anchor about half a mile from the W. end of this cay, in 8 or 9 fathoms, clear, sandy bottom.

To the SE. of the above cays there are several detached coral ledges, on which there are only 3 fathoms water, and a heavy swell generally rolls over them, which renders them dangerous. The lead will be of great use in approaching from the southeastward, and a bearing of the cay will indicate when southwestward of the coral ledges.

Current.—It generally sets to the SW. over the bank a mile an hour.

Diana bank is composed of sand and coral. It has from 9 to 15 fathoms water on it, and 20 fathoms on its edge, and may be made a useful guide to vessels beating through Crooked Island passage in the night.

Crooked Island passage is the best one for vessels bound to the northward or northeastward from the passage between Cuba and Santo Domingo. It is also constantly used by vessels bound from the United States to ports on the S. side of Cuba, to Jamaica, and the Isthmus of Panama.

Since the establishment of the excellent lights on Bird rock, Castle island, and the Great Inagua, there is not the least difficulty.

Currents.—Before Bird rock light was established several vessels were lost on Watling's island, being swept there by the current, which almost everywhere through these islands sets to the westward at the rate of from half a mile to a mile an hour.

This set is occasionally stronger or weaker, according to the varying force of the trade-wind. In the neighborhood of Conception isle it is said generally to run strong to the NW. Some observations tend to show that after northers, or on the increase of the moon, the current sets to the NE., and on the decrease of the moon, as it approaches to change, there is a similar set to the SW.

Caution.—There is, however, no certainty in the case, and consequently more than ordinary attention is required when navigating among the West India islands; the navigator, therefore, should not fail to take advantage of every opportunity of determining the ship's position at night by observation.

Should a sailing vessel be caught in Crooked Island passage by a northwester, instead of beating about, which would be attended with considerable risk, it will be better to seek shelter under the S. end of Fortune island, or run out and keep under the lee of Acklin island, under easy sail, until the wind draws round to the NE., which it will do in two or three days at the farthest.

Mariguana island is generally low, about 30 feet above the sea, and thickly wooded. Near the center of the island there is a hill 110 feet high, and toward the E. end there are several small hummocks from 40 to 60 feet high. Abraham hill, at the back of Start point, is about 80 feet, and a long flat ridge behind the SE. point 90 feet high. There is no good water to be found on the island, but wood in abundance.

To the eastward of Start point the shore forms a deep bight, called Abraham bay. A dangerous reef sweeps round to the eastward, at a distance of about 2 miles from the head of the bight and is steep-to. About a mile eastward of the Start there is a small opening through which coasters may carry 2 fathoms into a good harbor within the reef.

The Caicos group consists of a number of small islands and cays, rising from a large, shallow sand-bank, having a very irregular outline.

It is extremely dangerous on every side, particularly so on the southern part. Nowhere in this portion of it can a sheltered anchorage for a large vessel be found. The northern, and a large part of the eastern, edge is formed by a chain of narrow wooded islands very thinly inhabited. They produce a very small quantity of fruit and vegetables for the markets of Nassau and Turk's island. Most of the inhabitants are fishermen and wreckers. Population, 2,845.

The six principal islands of this group are West or Little Caicos, Providenciales, North Caicos, Grand Caicos, East Caicos, and South Caicos.

Philips reef is a dangerous patch of coral, about 1 mile long, and on which the sea always breaks heavily. The soundings do not extend more than one-half a mile to the northward of the reef; to the eastward they run off 2 miles, varying from 10 to 20 fathoms, and to the southward from 7 to 10 fathoms. A ship, therefore, approaching from either direction should pay great attention to the soundings.

In a case of emergency a vessel might take the channel between Cape Comete and the reef, where a depth of from 6 to 7 fathoms may be carried.

Grand Caicos island.—Near Haulover point is a large square house and a small settlement on the side of the hill. All along this shore the reefs extend at a distance of from 1 to 2 miles from the beach, having shelter inside for boats.

To the northward of Haulover point the reef extends about 2 miles in an easterly direction, and between it and the shore a temporary anchorage may be found for small vessels. This anchorage is open to the eastward, and a heavy swell is generally felt there, but a strong current always sets to the eastward, which will enable a handy vessel to beat out in moderate weather.

From Haulover point the shore trends to the westward to Juniper hole, the opening between the islands of Grand and North Caicos. There is here, between two bluff points, a shelter for boats.

North Caicos island.—The N. side is skirted by a reef at about half a mile from the shore. The NE. point of the island is prolonged for about 2 miles by a dangerous rocky ledge. This part may be easily recognized, as it rises into a chain of small hills about 100 feet high and having on the three easternmost the ruins of some large houses.

The coast takes from here a SW. direction, forming a dangerous bight, skirted by a reef which extends more than half a mile from the shore.

Between North Caicos and Providenciales there is a continuous chain of small islets.

Fort cay is a low sandy islet, covered with bushes and situated about 7 miles SW. from the Mary cays. There are some wells of poor water on it. There are also the ruins of a fort and a magazine.

Anchorage.—The reefs which skirt this cay to the westward form a small but well sheltered harbor, having a depth of from 15 to 18 feet.

Providenciales beacon, on the NW. point of Providenciales, is formed of a pile of stones. From this peak the ground falls to the NNW. and terminates in a low sharp point, from which a dangerous reef extends for a mile to the eastward, having outside of it a bank of soundings.

Malcolm road is to the westward of this point, and is about half a mile wide, in which a vessel may anchor in from 6 to 7 fathoms. This anchorage is dangerous and should only be made use of in a case of emergency and with the greatest caution.

Vessels from the northward are apt to mistake the Providenciales for the West reef, and, by hauling too soon to the southward, run upon the West reef. With proper attention to the latitude, which should be checked upon every possible occasion, this mistake need not occur.

West Caicos island.—The western shore is bold, the soundings only reaching 200 yards from the shore, and in many places a less distance. The island is uninhabited and has no fresh water.

There is good anchorage under the southern shore in 5 or 6 fathoms of water, with a sandy bottom, sheltered from all but westerly winds, and large enough for a vessel to get under weigh with any wind. The best berth is in 5 fathoms, with the hill on the SE. point bearing N. 11° 15' W.

The anchorage in Cockburn harbor is about half a mile wide, having a depth of 20 feet, shoaling to 12 feet at its upper end. It is entirely exposed to winds from SE.

Cove cay is a rocky islet in the entrance. The channel is to the westward of it.

A pilot (procurable at Grand Turk island) is necessary to enter the harbor.

Buoys.—Fine large iron can-buoys have been placed in Cockburn harbor. Vessels usually drop an anchor to leeward of one of these buoys, and make fast to it with a hawser to assist the anchor, as the bottom is hard rock and very smooth. The best berth is with the W. point of Cove cay bearing S. 73° 07' E. about 300 yards distant. If desirable a ship may anchor outside the harbor, with the flagstaff on Government hill bearing N., and the E. end of Long cay N. 73° 07' W. The best outside anchorage is in 6 fathoms with the E. end of Cove cay in line with the flagstaff on Government hill. Abreast of

Cockburn harbor the bank of soundings should be cautiously approached.

The United States is represented by a consular agent.

Long Cay anchorage.—From the S. end of Long cay a reef extends a short distance. Between the W. side of the cay and a cay about a mile to the westward of it, is a small but sheltered anchorage. A good berth is with the S. point of Long cay bearing S. 67° 30′ E.

Little Ambergris cay is very narrow, and so low as to be with difficulty distinguished from seaward.

The **Swimmer rock** is a dangerous rocky ledge, having less than 2 fathoms upon it. It is bold on the eastern side, but the SE. point of the Caicos bank terminates about 2 miles from it. The edge of the bank on the eastern and southern sides being covered with dark-colored seaweed, it is difficult to distinguish.

For 17 miles from the S. point of the bank the edge is quite clear, but thence to the West Caicos it is very dangerous. All this part of the bank is of a light-green color, presenting a strong contrast to the deep blue of the sea outside. Capt. Richard Owen, R. N., remarks that on this edge of the bank the luminous reflection known as the bank blink may frequently be seen on the horizon and upon the edges of the clouds. To the northward of the W. sand-spit the edge of the Caicos bank is clear for about 5 miles. From here the coasters and wreckers leave the bank, crossing from the eastward and passing to the southward of Long cay.

French cay is small, low, and covered with bushes. It is the resort of great numbers of sea-birds, whose eggs are gathered by the fishermen from April to July.

In 1881 the Caicos bank was crossed from Long cay to French cay, when not less than 14 feet of water was obtained and there were no dangers that could not be seen.

Turk islands.—The nine islands of the group are composed of sand and sand-stone partially clothed with stunted bushes and a peculiar species of cactus somewhat in the form of a Turkish cap, hence, probably, their name. There are no wells, and the inhabitants who reside on Grand Turk island and Salt cay depend upon rain-water caught in tanks. The Caicos islands furnish them with ground provisions; Santo Domingo with cattle; other supplies are generally obtained from the United States; so that strangers must not depend upon finding resources here.

These islands belong to Great Britain and are attached to the government of Jamaica.

Grand Turk island is low, except on the E. side, which is formed by a narrow ridge of sand hills about 70 feet high. A dangerous reef extends from the northern point, and a narrow ledge of the bank, on which there are from 6 to 40 fathoms, runs off 6 miles farther. The reef skirts the eastern shore at the distance of about 1½ miles and connects itself to the small islets lying to the SE. as far as East cay. The reef is broken here and there, but there is no safe passage through for strangers. The town, which is the seat of government, stands on the western shore and in front of an extensive salt pond.

The population is about 2,000.

The Clyde line from New York call every three weeks.¹ A branch of the Cunard line from Halifax to Kingston, Jamaica, touching at Bermuda and Turk islands, call both ways, one steamer a month.

Pilots.—There are 6 or 7 regularly appointed who are efficient. Half pilotage is paid by vessels refusing to take a pilot.

Imports are provisions, manufactured articles, and dry goods, the greater part of which comes from the United States.

Exports.—The principal one is salt; about 75,000 bushels are annually exported, two-thirds of which goes to the United States.

There are no export duties. Salt manufacturers pay a royalty of 10 per cent. to the government. Import duties are specific, certain commodities being free.

The United States is represented by a consul, vice consul, and deputy-consul.

There is a volunteer company, and in case of necessity salutes can be fired.

Anchorage.—When making Grand Turk island from the NW. a square house at the E. extreme of East Caicos island forms a good mark. Philips reef generally breaks and is steep-to on the northern side. The anchorage off the town on the W. side of Grand Turk island is not recommended, as the bottom has been rendered foul by the discharge of ballast.

An anchorage can be had off the town, both northward and southward of the ballast ground; that to the northward is not recommended to sailing vessels.

Man-of-war anchorage, so called by the pilots, is on the edge of the bank, which shows white, in from 6 to 9 fathoms water, with the president's flag-staff (1½ or 2 miles southward of the town) bearing S. 39° 22′ E., and the light-house N. 19° 41′ E. But should the vessel swing inshore, she will tail on to or near a rocky patch, with not more than 17 feet water on it. Vessels must therefore be prepared to weigh or slip the moment the wind threatens a change, but between the months of April and August it never shifts from the eastward without ample warning. Those merely wishing to communicate should remain under sail. It is better for strangers to take a pilot. The difficulty in using these anchorages is in shooting in, which requires great judgment; in a sailing vessel, the better way will be to keep the topsails at the masthead ready to throw all aback. This, however, must depend upon the strength of the wind, for care must be taken not to bring up too short, or the vessel will drag off, or hook her anchor under a rock and probably lose it.

Riding place, a little southward of Government house, also affords better anchorage than that off the town, and there is less surf for landing.

Beacons are placed on Penniston and East cays and Toney rocks as guides, but a stranger would run considerable risk in making use of them without the assistance of a pilot, and vessels drawing over 17 feet should not attempt it at all.

For Hawk's Nest, the best channel is round the SW. end of the southwest reef, as there will then be room to beat up. In this case should the wind be well to the northward a vessel may haul round the reef, with the beacon on East cay just touching the E. end of Cotton cay, and this mark will lead between it and Southwest bank, about half a mile to the SW., on which there are only 12 feet water close to the edge. Or she may pass to the southward of Southwest bank with Toney rock beacon in one with the SW. end of Cotton cay. The whole space is studded with numerous small rocky heads distinctly seen, and in beating up the eye must be the guide. The most convenient anchorage will be found between Dunbar shoals and a small dry sand-bore on the southwest reef.

Salt cay is almost triangular in form. The NW. end forms a bold bluff, and on the summit there is a small lookout house and a flag-staff. The town stands on the W. side toward the NW. end of the cay, between the beach and a valuable salt-pond. There is anchorage before it of precisely the same character as that at Grand Turk, and the same precautions must be observed.

The United States is represented by a consular agent.

The space between Salt and Cotton cays is full of dangers, and should not be navigated except in case of necessity, when the eye must be the guide.

Sand cay is nearly divided at the center by a small neck of low, bushy land, so that at a distance, in an E. or W. direction, it has the appearance of being two islets.

It is clear on all sides but N. A coral reef runs off in that direction and the sea breaks heavily over it, except after very fine weather. There are several small black rocks from 10 to 16 feet high on the reef. The edge of the bank runs almost on a straight line between the reef and the S. end of Salt cay, and this space is quite clear, with regular soundings right across the eastward, of from 9 to 11 fathoms white sand and fans.

From the eastward do not come upon the bank, which extends 4 miles eastward of both cays, until the S. end of Salt cay bears N. 67° 30′ W., for the ground to the northward of this line is very foul. Moderate depths extend 1½ miles westward from Sand cay, and anchorage will be found in 6 fathoms water about a mile off, with the gap bearing N. 67° 30′ E. A vessel can weigh with any wind, and run off the bank on a south course clear of all danger.

Endymion rock is composed of seven or eight rocky heads, upon several of which there are from 13 to 23 feet of water, with from 7 to 8 fathoms between them.

The shoalest spot frequently breaks with a fresh breeze, but in smooth weather, when no breakers can be seen, the rock becomes exceedingly dangerous, as over it the water is so dark that it cannot be seen at any distance.

To avoid and pass to the westward of this danger it is necessary to steer clear of the white sandy bottom till the beacon at the N. end of Sand cay bears N. 53° 26′ E. By keeping the beacon on this bearing, the anchorage previously mentioned may be reached. Although no other dangers seem to exist in this region, it will be prudent to keep outside of the sand bank lying S. of Salt cay.

Swimmer rock and Endymion rock mark, to a certain degree, the E. and W. sides of the southern entrance to Turk's Island passage. A ship wind-bound in this passage can anchor to the westward of Sand cay and wait for a fair wind.

Directions for Turk's Island passage.—This passage is much frequented by vessels bound to the southern ports of the West Indies, but the Mona passage is much safer.

If it is intended to use this passage, it will be well, especially if at all doubtful of the ship's position, to reach the parallel of 21° 40′ N. (9 miles northward of the latitude of the light), 60 miles to the eastward of it.

Having arrived at this position, and no land being in sight, the ship is sure to be to the eastward of the island, and should then be kept W. to pass 8 or 9 miles to the northward of the light. Being visible from deck at a distance of 15 miles, it will almost certainly be seen. Every opportunity must be used by night or day to verify the latitude. This is the more necessary as frequently to the northward of these passages the current runs strongly to the N., and if the vessel should pass the light without its having been seen a serious disaster might occur. After making the Grand Turk light every precaution must be taken in rounding the N. point of the island.

From a position 3 miles W. of the light-house, a S. 25° 10′ W. course for 26 miles will carry the navigator 4 miles to the westward of Endymion rock, and 8 miles E. of the Swimmer rock.

The current in Turk's Island passage is said to be very feeble, and the tides not felt, but strong currents have been met running through the passage. The local pilots state that they run very strong, but always through the channel in a NE. or a SW. direction. The tides are very strong sometimes, having a strength of 3 knots.

In this region, during the winter months, if the wind hauls from SE. to S. it is an almost certain indication of a sudden change to the NW. Under these circumstances, it would be better to remain under short sail to the northward of the islets, keeping the light in sight till the change of wind has taken place.

If, after having entered the passage, the wind dies away and hauls to the southward, it would be advisable, instead of trying to beat to the southward, to anchor in some one of the places which have been pointed out to the westward of the cays.

Caution.—If, before recognizing the entrance to Turk's Island passage, the navigator has passed to leeward of it and the Caicos are in sight, care must be taken to pass them well to the northward at a distance of at least 8 or 9 miles. It is dangerous, especially with light winds, to pass nearer to them, for the tides which run in the channels between the islands of the group are very strong and make themselves felt at a distance of 5 or 6 miles.

Mouchoir bank or **Mouchoir carré** (square handkerchief) is irregular in breadth. The southern edge, with the exception of a shallow patch 4 miles within it, appears to be free of danger. The eastern side terminates in a long point or narrow spit; about $1\frac{1}{2}$ miles within the extreme end of the spit there is a small breaker. The outline of the N. side is irregular and extremely dangerous to within about 9 miles of the W. end, where there is a patch of 6 fathoms. The rocky heads at the NW. extreme of the bank lie about S. 36° 34' E., 21 miles from East cay of the Turk Islands group.

Silver bank.—It will be better not to venture on any part of this bank, for it is dangerous. As the water on the bank is not discolored, except over the shoals, where it has a white appearance, the lead must be well attended when approaching it from any quarter.

Currents.—Irregular currents have been experienced on and near Silver bank, the general set being to the westward, the current being strongest near the edge of the bank.

Navidad bank.—The water is not sufficiently discolored to render this bank visible.

Between the Navidad and Silver banks there are three small detached knolls, steep-to, with 10, 12, and 17 fathoms water on them.

The passages between these cays and banks afford clear and convenient channels, especially for vessels voyaging between ports in the United States and the western part of the Caribbean sea.

Great Inagua island.—There are several small elevations on the S. side, generally about 30 feet high, appearing from the southward like separate islands. Salt-Pond hill, the highest of them, is, in the evening, sometimes taken for the SW. point of the island when coming from the southward. Several wrecks have, from this cause, taken place. The island can not generally be seen from a distance on account of fogs and mist which frequently hide it.

The western coast of Great Inagua is mostly composed of low bluffs, and is generally clear, with, however, a few rocky dangers at from 200 to 400 yards from shore.

Mathew Town road lies abreast of the small settlement from which the anchorage takes its name. The village is scattered along the shore, with large salt ponds behind it. On a small rocky point near the northern end of the village is Henrietta fort.

With the usual trade-wind the only safe anchorage is off the village in $4\frac{1}{2}$ and 5 fathoms water, about 600 yards off shore, and near the edge of the bank of soundings.

For a man-of-war the best anchorage is with Fort Henrietta bearing N. 78° 45′ E.

Stand in slowly and be ready to anchor as soon as white water is reached, which may be recognized from aloft. If the weather threatens a change the vessel must leave at once and run around to *Molasses road*, E. of the SW. point of the island, as soon as the wind is to the northward of W. Before such change of weather the barometer usually falls to about 29.80.

Vessels coming here for salt may anchor off Salt-Pond canal, $1\frac{1}{2}$ miles S. of the town, but the swell coming around the SW. point of the island makes it a rough anchorage.

Water can only be procured from a well in Man-of-war bay, unless, which seldom happens, the inhabitants can spare any from their tanks.

Caution.—Vessels approaching the light must pay careful attention to its bearing, as it can be seen over the land where not intercepted by objects.

Tides.—Along the W. coast the flood runs to the southward at the rate of about one-half a knot, and meets the flood from the eastward off SW. point.

Man-of-war bay is a bight 6 miles wide between Middle point and Northwest point. The anchorage extends about one-third of a mile from shore all around the bay except the S. shore, and is sheltered from all but westerly winds.

With northerly winds, the best berth is in the northern part of the bay with the outer point bearing N. 67° 30′ W., with southerly winds, off the sandy beach in the SE. part of the bay.

The same precautions must be observed as in anchoring in Mathew Town road, and care taken to pick out a clear, sandy spot.

The NW. point of Great Inagua is low, the tops of the palmetto-trees on it being only about 20 feet above the sea.

Alfred sound.—A reef nearly dry at low water, and steep to, skirts this bay at the distance of about $1\frac{1}{2}$ miles from the shore, and within it there is a snug anchorage for a small craft drawing 6 feet, over white coral sand and patches distinctly seen, called Alfred sound. The entrance lies between Northwest point and the W. end of the reef; there is also a narrow intricate cut through the barrier, NE. about $1\frac{1}{4}$ miles from the point. With the wind to the southward of E., a vessel of 12 feet draught may anchor in the opening to the westward, named

Alfred road, taking care not to bring Northwest point westward of S. 22° 30′ W.; but it is by no means a desirable anchorage.

The flood stream in Alfred sound sets eastward, the ebb westward, at the rate of about a knot.

From Saline point, which is low and rocky, the northern shore of Great Inagua takes a NE. direction to Palmetto point. The reef which protects Alfred sound comes gradually home to this point, and N. 73° 30′ E. about 5 miles from Northwest point there is on the edge a small cay about half a mile long. At three-quarters of a mile eastward of the cay, and N. 2° 49′ W. from a black isolated rock on the beach, there is a small cut through the reef, in which there are 8 or 9 feet water; the reef runs quite straight and is steep-to.

James hill, about 90 feet high, is remarkable as being the only elevated ground on the N. side of the island westward of Carmichael point.

The eastern side of the island is skirted by a reef the whole way, from 200 yards to half a mile from the beach, with soundings outside it to the distance of about half a mile. Toward the NE. point there are some sand hills rather higher than the rest of the coast, off which the reef extends nearly a mile, falling into the NE. point in a curve.

Statira shoal.—From the SE. point of Great Inagua a spit or tongue of the bank runs off for a distance of 6 miles, and on it is a rocky patch. It is about half a mile long, with as little as 6 feet of water on it, and breaks in heavy weather. The water on the bank being of dark color, it is difficult to distinguish the shoal, except in heavy weather, when the sea always breaks.

To the eastward of the head from Lagoon hill there is an opening through the reef capable of admitting small coasters to a snug anchorage within. The interior, however, is so completely studded with small coral heads that the eye alone must be depended upon as a guide. The bay on the W. side of the head is only safe with the prevailing trade-wind, which is here more regular than at the islands to the NW. From abreast Salt Pond hill, at about 4 miles eastward of the SW. point of the island, the land bends to the northwestward and round to the SSW., forming a bay, very foul.

Molasses reef is a rocky ledge 2 miles from the SW. point of Great Inagua; it is steep-to and the sea breaks on it with easterly winds. There is a clear spot eastward of the reef named Molasses road, where vessels driven from the anchorage on the W. side of the island may ride out NW. and N. winds in safety. The ground, however, is flat and rocky, and they must weigh the moment the wind draws round to the usual quarter. The best berth will be in 8 or 9 fathoms, just within the edge of soundings, and about a mile eastward of the reef, with Salt Pond hill N. 11° 15′ E., and the SW. point just open to the southward of the reef, S. 87° 11′ E.

Caution.—Great care must be taken in approaching the reef, for with the wind off shore the reef does not show itself, and the discolored water is not easily seen at even a short distance; care must also be taken not to shoot too far in, and be prepared to anchor the moment soundings are obtained.

Clarion shoal.—This shoal has been repeatedly searched for and has not been found. H. B. M. S. *Argus* in 1879 shaped a course to pass directly over this shoal and when about 3 miles S. 23° W. of its assigned position a depth of 10 fathoms was found with the hand lead. The ship was immediately stopped and backed when bottom was found at a depth of 157 fathoms with the deep sea lead.

Little Inagua island is somewhat quadrangular in form and in the center of the NW. side there is a flat hill, which is the only rising ground on the northern part of the island, and on the S. side there are several hills of about the same height. A dangerous reef, steep-to, runs off three-quarters of a mile from the E. end, and there are generally heavy breakers on it.

The NE. and NW. sides of the island present a bold rocky shore, with soundings on a clear bottom to the distance of about one-third of a mile. The SW. side appears also to be free of danger.

The SE. side is about 8 miles long, and eastward of the S. point there is a small bay, and in front of it snug anchorage for small craft, protected by the reef, which terminates near the middle of this shore. The entrance to this anchorage is through a break in the reef about 2½ miles eastward of the point. There are no inhabitants, but there is said to be wild hogs on the island, and consequently water.

Hogsty reef or **Los Corrales** is shaped like a horseshoe. The highest rock is about 20 feet above sea level. The reef forms a good harbor, with a depth of from 3½ to 5 fathoms; there are a few black rocky patches on the clear white sand, but they may be easily seen and avoided.

At both ends of the horseshoe there is a small low sandy cay, nearly devoid of vegetation. There is a tank for rain-water on NW. cay. A good anchorage is just inside the edge of soundings, in 6 fathoms, to the southward of NW. cay, but there is plenty of room to work up the horseshoe, if necessary.

Vessels bound through the Crooked Island passage and being so far to windward are recommended by some navigators to use the anchorage at the Hogsty reef for the night, in preference to that under Great Inagua; it will, however, be far more prudent to avoid so dangerous a bank altogether. It is seldom that any weather-current will be found here, and the run should be regulated so as to make Castle island soon after daylight, to enable the vessel to get through the passage before dark.

Ciudado reef was in vain sought for in 1832 by Capt. Richard Owen, R. N., and in 1873 by Commander Phythian, U. S. Navy, also by H. B. M. S. *Argus*, in 1879. The wreckers who are continually passing over this region state that they have never seen discolored water. The navigator should therefore exercise the greatest care in passing in the vicinity of this and other dangers, the position of which are still doubtful.

Brown shoal is composed of sand and coral, has from 9¾ to 17 fathoms of water on it, and can be seen only under very favorable circumstances.

GREAT BAHAMA BANK, SOUTH SIDE.

St. Domingo cay is a barren rock, 17 feet high. There is a little eminence in the center with bushes on it, and having the appearance, from a short distance, of a ship bottom up. A reef extends 1 mile from the cay N. 56° 15' E., and in the same direction, 3 miles from the cay, is a ledge on which the sea usually breaks.

From here the edge of the bank for the first 12 miles is quite clear. The soundings near the edge are quite irregular, but a short distance within the depths are 8 and 9 fathoms, with a clear sandy bottom.

From the above position to Verde cay it is foul and dangerous.

For a space of 7 miles to the NW. of St. Vincent rocks the bank is full of small rocky heads, with deep water between them.

Verde cay is covered with low sea-grape trees and prickly-pear bushes, and inhabited by large flocks of boobies and man-of-war birds. The N. end is low, but the S. point rises to a hill 72 feet high. On the W. side there is a projecting sandy beach, skirted by a ledge of rocks, dry at low water, which makes landing difficult. There is anchorage under this side in 7 fathoms of water, but not to be recommended, as a heavy swell rolls round both ends of the cay in strong breezes.

Little Ragged island is low, and separated from Great Ragged island by a little opening nearly blocked up by small cays and rocks, under the lee of which there is an excellent boat-harbor. It is entered from the westward.

The Brothers are two small black rocks about 5 feet high. On the S. side they may be approached within half a mile, but a dangerous coral ledge extends 4 miles to the northward of them, leaving a clear channel between it and Hobson breaker 1½ miles wide. It will always be better, however, to pass to the northward of the breaker, between it and the shallow sand-spit which runs off about 2 miles to the S. 67° 30' W. of Little Ragged island.

Anchorage.—There is a good anchorage under the W. side of this latter spit in 3 fathoms water, with the S end of Little Ragged island bearing E., and the SW. point of Great Ragged island in one with the beacon. In standing in, however, take care to avoid several small coral heads, which are easily seen from aloft.

Great Ragged Island beacon.—Near the S. end a large, woody hill rises to the height of 95 feet above high water, and on the summit there has been heaped up a rough pile of stones 20 feet high, which is a valuable land-mark. The island contains about 100 inhabitants, and possesses a valuable salt-pond, but supplies are scarce.

The S. end of Great Ragged island forms a sandy bay, and near the center, not far from the shore, there is a well of good water. There is a more convenient well, and with better water, in a small bay about half-way along the W. side of the island.

Ragged Island harbor.—At the N. end of Great Ragged island, between it and Hog cay, there is a small harbor capable of receiving vessels not over 13 feet draught. The entrance lies close to the southward of a small black rock off the SE. rocky headland of Hog cay, named Black Rock point, between it and Outer Bar reef, lying in the center of the opening. The channel is, however, only 100 yards wide, with a depth of 13 feet across the bar at low water. The ebb runs out with great force, but with the usual winds blowing strong there will be great risk in attempting to beat out, except in a handy fore-and-aft rigged vessel that can insure staying.

In a case of necessity a vessel may run in by the eye with the assistance of the plan, by bringing the Black rock on a S. 45° W. bearing; or bring the beacon 30 feet high (the base and upper part *red* and the middle portion *white*) standing on Pig point, the SE. extreme of Hog cay, to bear S. 59° 04' W. and steer for it, passing between Black rock and Outer Bar reef, until Pig point and the N. end of Pigeon cay are in one, then steer so as to pass 100 yards from the point.

Strangers should take a pilot, who will be at hand by making the usual signal in time. Small coasters find their way out over the bank to the westward.

Jumentos.—These islands are generally called the Jumentos, but the pilots and wreckers give this name only to those lying to the eastward of Water cay. These are much smaller and lower than the others; indeed, most of them are only a few feet above the sea. There are several wide openings between them navigable for vessels of light draught, and which might be used most advantageously by those capable of crossing the bank; but the islets are so much alike that until they are distinctly pointed out by beacons it would be extremely rash for a stranger to attempt to pass through without a thorough knowledge of the locality and experience in the navigation of these banks.

Raccoon cut is so narrow and winding as to be difficult of access for all but small vessels, as the channel S. of the sand spit, extending a mile westward from the S. end of Raccoon cay, carries only 12 feet water.

Raccoon cay has about 25 inhabitants on it, and possesses good water and a valuable salt-pond, the salt being conveniently shipped from an anchorage close under the W. side. Vessels bound here for this purpose, drawing over 12 feet, had better take the route round the S. end of Ragged island and haul in round Darvill spit.

Nurse Channel cay has a beacon on it. For the best track in bring the beacon to bear W. three-quarters of a mile distant, which will be as soon as a depth of 10 fathoms is reached, and steer S. 70° 19' W. till the beacon bears N. Then steer N. 84° 22′ W. till it bears N. 84° 22′ E. From this point a course S. 84° 22′ W. should be kept till a distance of 14 miles from Nurse Channel cay is reached. Another channel, though not so good, lies to the northward of the cay.

Man-of-war cay is on the N. side of the entrance to Man-of-war channel.

Directions.—Vessels drawing not more than 18 feet may cross the southern part of the bank. To do this the navigator should have local experience of this peculiar navigation or the assistance of a pilot. In coming from the N. or NE. with this view, the Crooked Island passage should be taken, and, having verified the ship's position by sighting Bird Rock light-house, a course should be shaped for the entrance of the channel which is to be used. These channels are Ragged Island channel, Nurse channel, and Man-of-war channel.

Great care must be taken in approaching the bank.

If the Ragged Island channel be used a course should be shaped from Bird rock for the hill near the S. end of Ragged island. Having made this land, which must be done by daylight, the bank may be entered upon about 7 or 8 miles E. of Ragged island. The edge at this part is easily seen from aloft.

A slight current will probably be found here setting either to SW. or NW. Should the vessel be set to the northward Ragged island will be readily distinguished by its superior height.

Having entered upon the bank South rock should be rounded at half a mile distance. From this point the course is S. 78° 45′ W., 8 miles, leaving the Hobson breaker on the port hand. When the beacon on Ragged hill bears N. 50° 37′ E. haul up N. 33° 45′ W., 18 miles. If, after running 9 or 10 miles on this course, there should be less than 3¼ fathoms, the vessel will be a little to the E. of her course on the tail of the Darvill sand-spit, and should be kept more to the westward till these soundings are reached, and then hauled up again.

Having run the above distance 18 miles, the course will be N. 45° W., 25 miles, which will lead through the narrowest and worst part of the channel, between the Cochinos and the Nurse sand-banks, and a good lookout must be kept for small, black, rocky patches. In running this course the depths ought to be from 4 to 4½ fathoms at *low* water; if less is obtained the vessel will be too far to the eastward; if more, to the westward; but remember that the E. side is always the safest, and take the precaution to measure the lead-line (when wet) *to feet* between 3 or 4 fathoms, for the soundings on the chart may be fully relied on.

Caution.—Should darkness overtake the vessel before having reached thus far, it will be better to anchor, which may be done anywhere in safety. It would not be prudent to attempt to beat through this part of the channel. At the end of the above course the vessel will be off the N. extreme of the Cochinos on the parallel of 22° 42′ N., and a S. 84° 22′ W. course will lead off the western edge of the bank to the southward of Guinchos cay, clear of danger, and in from 4½ to 5 fathoms water all the way. Care, however, must be taken to keep on the above parallel by checking the latitude as often as possible.

Through Nurse channel 3 fathoms may be carried, taking care to steer clear of the rocky heads. After reaching a point 14 miles S. 84° 22′ W. of Nurse Channel Cay beacon the course is N. 45° W. to the parallel of 22° 42′ N.

Man-of-war channel, 16 miles further N., is the best of all these passes. Here a depth of 4 to 5 fathoms may be carried on to the fairway of the bank.

A constant lookout must be kept from aloft for coral patches. When running with the wind aft, and the small clouds, called by the pilots "flyers," moving slowly, the navigator will be very apt to be deceived by their reflection on the water over the clear, sandy bottom, having the appearance of a rocky shoal. It will always, however, be prudent to avoid a dark spot. A vessel may anchor anywhere on the bank, only looking out for a clear spot.

If approaching the bank from the SE., St. Domingo cay may be sighted and the bank entered on to the NW. of it; but this requires more than ordinary care. In this case, having rounded the SW. end of the cay within the distance of about half a mile, steer N. 11° 15′ W. for 20 miles, which will bring the vessel to a clear space on the edge of soundings, where she can enter, and 6 miles further upon this course Ragged island will be sighted bearing NE., when the route can be taken described above. Great care must, however, be taken when passing the parallel of the Brothers to avoid the two shoals, for these rocks will scarcely be seen from aloft; and the run should not be made without clear daylight.

The bank may also be entered upon at Verde cay, and perhaps with less risk. In taking this route, having rounded the S. end of the cay, steer N. 45° W. 10 miles and then W. 20 miles, when the vessel will be up to Little Ragged island; but on all occasions, when among the shoals, the mariner must endeavor not to steer with the sun directly in his face, which will completely blind him from seeing them even at a very short distance.

Pear cut is only fit for small coasters, which find a passage from thence along the S. side of Exuma and through the sand-bore channels into the Tongue of the Ocean.

Diamond point is the SW. extreme of the Mucaras reef, and forms the NE. point of the entrance to the old Bahama channel. It is extremely dangerous, being very steep-to.

Mucaras reef is very dangerous, from the fact that its dark color and sea weed upon it give the water over it nearly the same color as that in mid-channel, and being steep-to the lead gives no warning of its vicinity.

From Diamond point to Lavanderas reef the bank is quite clear, and a vessel may run in on it and anchor anywhere in 5½ or 6 fathoms of water with clear sandy bottom, as far as 4 miles within the edge of soundings.

Lobos cay is a small rocky islet about 200 yards in diameter and only 6 feet above the sea. Anchorage will be found to leeward of it in 5 fathoms water, with the cay bearing S. 61° 52′ E. from half a mile to a mile distant; but care must be taken to avoid the shallow sand-bores which will be seen from aloft about 2 miles to the NW. of it. A vessel may also run round the W. end of these ridges by the eye, and anchor anywhere within them.

From Lobos cay to Guinchos cay the bank is steep-to all the way.

Guinchos cay is only about 200 yards in diameter and 6 feet high. It is formed of sand and dead bleached coral, and has a few stunted bushes upon it.

Anchorage may be found in 4 fathoms water in a small, clear space about half a mile W. of the cay.

From Guinchos cay the SW. edge of the bank trends to the NW. about 92 miles. All this distance is clear, with only a few rocky heads, which may easily be seen. The edge of the SW. bank then gradually inclines to the N. of. W. for 42 miles to the parallel of 24° 35′ N. and is foul all the way.

Salt Cay bank is somewhat in the shape of a pear, and is skirted by islets on all sides but the S. Between it and the coast of Florida to the NW. lies the Florida channel, on the eastern side lies the Santaren channel, and south of it is the Nicholas channel. To the SE. these two last channels unite to form the Old Bahama channel.

The **Double-head Shot cays** are on the northwestern edge of the bank. They are from 20 to 40 feet high, and lie so close to each other that there is scarcely a safe boat channel between them, and consequently form a complete breakwater to a good anchorage between them.

Water cay is the easternmost and largest of them. Near the center, on the S. side, there is a natural well of excellent water, and opposite to it, on the same side of the island, is a good landing place.

Salt cay, so named from its possessing a valuable salt-pond, is in the shape of a triangle. The NE. side is formed by a narrow ridge of sand-hills; the other parts are very low and sandy, and partially clothed with brushwood. During the season for raking the salt it is inhabited. There is temporary anchorage close under the W. side, in about 7 fathoms, on the edge of soundings, but it is not good. The tides set around it with great strength, and are sometimes influenced by the Florida stream running to the SE.

The **Lavanderas** is a small rocky ledge, awash. Between this and the Anguila islets there does not appear to be any danger along the southern limits of the bank; this part, however, has not been satisfactorily examined, and there is reason to believe many rocky heads may be found near the edge. The center of the bank is foul in many places, and had better be avoided.

1018—No. 85——5

In beating across the bank a vessel should keep within 7 or 8 miles of the northern edge of the bank.

Anguila, the largest of the islets on Cay Sal bank, is partially wooded, and from 40 to 50 feet high. It is cut through in several places, but there is no opening fit even for a boat; it may, therefore, be described as one island. It lies at the SE. extreme of the bank, and its NE. side is close to the edge of soundings.

Good anchorage will be found in 6 or seven fathoms water, off the SW. side. There are some wells of good water on it, but very difficult to find.

Between Anguila and the Dog rocks to the NW. are several clusters of small, low rocks, with deep water between, but most of the openings are dangerous.

Dog rocks.—The northeasternmost islets on Cay Sal bank are barren and rocky. They are separated near the center by a narrow but deep navigable cut, and the eastern edge of soundings is about 2 miles outside them. Vessels crossing over from the Great Bahama bank in the night by proper attention to the lead will escape danger; and it may be observed that accidents frequently happen here by neglecting this safeguard. The opening between these islets and the nearest rocks to the SE. is 7 miles wide, and although the soundings are irregular and the bottom dark and alarming, it appears to be quite clear, and is frequently used by vessels crossing inside the cays.

Muertos or Deadmen's cays lie about 3 miles within the edge of the bank, but great care must be taken in the night, as they are steep-to, and the soundings do not indicate the distance from them, and they are likewise not in sight of the Elbow Cay light. Several of the rocks are a considerable distance apart, but it would not be prudent to cross the ledges between them.

Tides.—The direction and height of the tides are much influenced by the wind, but generally the flood tides run from all sides on to the bank and the ebb off. At the Double-headed Shot cays the tides have a gyratory course from N. through E. to S.

Directions.—It has been the almost universal custom for vessels proceeding westward from the Great Bahama bank to endeavor to strike soundings on the NE. end of Salt Cay bank or to make Elbow Cay light.

With light winds or in thick weather this course is still preferable, but with reasonably clear weather and a good breeze the distance will be much shortened by crossing over at once to the Florida shore, making Alligator Reef light, and by bearings of this light with the ones on Sombrero and Sand keys running along inside the Gulf Stream.

If the Salt Cay bank route be taken and the wind be scant from the westward vessels may run in on the bank on either side of the Dog rocks and pass off to the southward of the Elbow; or should the wind be light and tending to calm they may anchor within, to avoid being set to the northward, otherwise it will be better to run down outside, especially in the night, paying great attention to the lead.

Having passed Elbow Cay light, the course should be S. 47° 49′ W. until close over to the Cuba shore, to avoid the strength of the current. This course should lead direct toward the Pan of Matanzas, and within about 12 miles NW. of the light on cay Piedras, but this will depend upon the set of the current, which is very uncertain and sometimes strong, into the Nicholas channel.

If bound to the SW. ports of the Southern States of America it will be advisable to run along the Cuba shore as far westward as Mariel, and then shape a NW. course, so as to pass at a proper distance westward of the Tortugas. Should the Cuba shore be left in the daytime, an occasional bearing of the high land will enable the mariner to estimate the strength of the stream and to regulate his course accordingly. He may depend upon finding the current right across, and probably with increased strength, as he advances to the northward.

Remarks.—The Old Bahama channel has been considered as dangerous and difficult to navigate, but since the establishment of lights on various points on the N. coast of Cuba and that on Lobos cay it need not be so considered. As is the case everywhere in the vicinity of these banks, the navigator needs to exercise vigilance, caution, and judgment, but with ordinary care this channel presents no special difficulties.

There is seldom any perceptible current in mid-channel; when there is any it appears to depend upon the wind.

Winds.—In the winter season, from November to March, northers prevail, and sometimes the wind will veer round to this quarter after intervals of only a few days. A short time previous to the change the trade-wind will generally fall light, or a calm ensue for a few hours, and the land will be seen with unusual distinctness, but the barometer will scarcely give any warning. Dark clouds will be seen gradually rising to the WNW., and in a short time the wind will rush suddenly down from that direction with the strength of a double or close-reefed topsail breeze. It will probably blow steady at NW. for a day or two, and then draw gradually around to the N. and NE., accompanied by heavy squalls and rain, and wear itself out with the wind at E.

As the wind veers from the westward the barometer will rise, and the mariner may be sure of the wind never backing. Should the weather indicate this change before he has entered the channel it will be better for a sailing vessel to remain outside, and maintain a good offing to the northward of the Maternillos light-house, which will be a good guide, until the wind veers to the eastward of N. Should the vessel have entered the narrows, it will be better at once to seek an anchorage on the Bahama bank, through either of the openings between Diamond point and Guinchos cay, or run back and take up a position as pointed out above. During the remaining portion of the year the wind prevails from the E. and SE., and a vessel will not be exposed to this interruption and risk, except in the case of a hurricane, which, however, seldom occurs in this locality.

CHAPTER V.

THE ISLAND OF CUBA.

The coast is very much indented, and the greater portion of the shores very foul and bordered with numerous cays and reefs. The harbors are numerous and excellent. A range of mountains, highest at the eastern end, where an elevation of 7,000 feet is attained, extends through the island from E. to W. The land along the shore is generally low and flat.

The coast from Cape Maysi to Cape Cruz on the S. and to Point Maternillos on the N. is bold and free of danger, as is the coast-line between Havana and Matanzas; the rest of the coast-line is foul and difficult to approach.

The climate is hot and dry during the greater part of the year. The warmest months are July and August, with a mean temperature of 82° to 84° Fahrenheit, and the coldest December and January, with a mean temperature of 68° to 70°. The seasons are spoken of as the rainy and the dry, but the line of demarkation can not be exactly drawn. Rain often falls in torrents from July to September, and occasional showers fall for a month or two before and after these periods. Fevers, more or less malignant, prevail from May to November, and to a greater or less extent throughout the year. Of these, the yellow fever, to which all the sea-ports are subject, is the most fatal.

Hurricanes are less frequent than in the islands more to the eastward. In the neighborhood of Santiago de Cuba earthquakes of moderate force are sometimes felt.

In 1883 the population amounted to 1,521,684, of whom 509,143 were blacks, only 365,000 being slaves. Slavery ceases in 1890.

No connected survey of the shores of Cuba has ever been made.

A large portion of the coast is very imperfectly known, and the navigator must bear in mind that the charts are only approximately correct.

In 1875 the positions of Havana and Santiago de Cuba were established with very great care under the direction of the United States Hydrographic Office, but the latitudes and longitudes of many points on the island are known to be very seriously in error.

Cape Maysi is the eastern extremity of the island of Cuba. When seen from the southward the cape has the appearance of a long low point. This part of the coast is low and covered with brush-wood.

One or 2 miles W. of Cape Maysi the land begins to rise, and seen from the northward forms three steps, the upper one 1,850 feet high, gradually sloping upward to the eastern summit of the Cobre mountains. Strangers coming from the northward have mistaken the lower termination of the slope for Cape Maysi, and keeping away too soon have fallen to leeward.

In approaching the eastern end of Cuba from the NE., some of the peaks of the Cobre mountains form good landmarks. The most remarkable is called *El Yunque*, or the Anvil, from its shape. It is 27 miles from Cape Maysi and 4 miles from Puerto Baracoa, for which it is a good guide. In rounding Cape Maysi it should be remembered that the current frequently sets to the westward with considerable strength, especially during the winter months.

A large cave, within which the sea breaks, lies nearly a mile S. of Pintado point. There is a spring of good water 300 yards N. of Negra point.

Pintado bank is between Points Pintado and Quemada. Near the shore there are from 4 to 8 fathoms of water, with a bottom of fine white sand. The edge of the bank is steep-to, there being 18 to 28 fathoms 200 yards from its edge, and a quarter of a mile farther off no bottom at 90 fathoms.

The coast from Quemada to Point Negra is steep-to and exposed to wind and sea.

Point Negra is a dark-colored, salient point, steep, barren, and easily distinguished. Sixty yards SW. of the point there is a precipice, with a small cove at its foot, called the Salto de la Punta Negra, where the sea breaks heavily.

This portion of the coast is composed of inaccessible white cliffs of dead coral and hard sand, more or less covered with trees, the high land rising close to the shore.

From Point Caleta the Soboruco cliffs extend nearly a mile to the beach, called the Playa de Caleta, about 90 yards wide. A river flowing through a cut in the high land empties about the middle of the beach. Its mouth is generally choked up, except during the rainy season, and the water near the beach is salt. A little higher up, however, it will be found to be fresh and good.

From this beach the Soboruco cliffs continue one-half a mile to a white sandy beach called Playa Blanca. In the middle of this beach is a rocky point, just eastward of which and near the shore is a spring of excellent water.

Jauco river is half a mile from the Playa Blanca, emptying over a sandy beach, and navigable for boats during the rainy season. Near the mouth of the river is a rocky point, having a cavern in it called the Cneva de Jauco.

All along this part of the coast the mountain range is close to the shore. The three cuts or ravines of Caleta, Caletilla, and Jauco are very conspicuous. The land is thickly wooded, especially near the river Jauco.

A rocky ledge commences near Caleta beach and skirts the shore at an average distance of 300 yards as far W. as Muertos beach. A little outside of it, or about 400 yards from the shore, the depths are 9 or 10 fathoms; but off the point and cave of Jauco this depth is found at a third of a mile off.

The **anchorage** of Caleta is on a bank of fine white sand, with a few spots of rock and gravel in the indentation between Caleta point and the western extremity of the Playa Blanca. It is sheltered by high land from ESE. round by N. to W. Although heavy squalls sometimes cause ships to drag here, this anchorage is very useful, as it is the only one in the vicinity.

In approaching this anchorage a vessel should steer in for the beach till within one-fourth of a mile of the shore, and let go the anchor in 10 fathoms of water.

This locality may be known by two small hills on the slope of the high mountain toward Caleta point. With the wind from S. or SE., a vessel should not anchor here. A rocky head with less than 3 fathoms on it and 5 fathoms around it lies on the line between the beach and the point of Caleta at a distance of nearly 400 yards from the former.

Water can be obtained at low tide from a spring at Playa Blanca. Wood also can be obtained.

The **Rio Seco** is only open during the rainy season, and during the remainder of the year closed by two bars, one of stone, and the other, farther in, of sand. The water is hardly fit to drink, and is difficult to obtain by boats on account of the bars. In case of necessity the best place to water will be to the leeward of the mouth.

Llana point, composed of Soboruco, projects a little at the western termination of the beach.

Salto de Joho point is high, salient, and white, and can be seen at a great distance.

Jojo point is of black, rugged rock, of moderate height, and at its inner part is an isolated elevation like a sugar loaf.

Jojo bay lies between Jojo point on the E. and Tintorero point on the W. These two points are two-thirds of a mile apart, and between them is an anchorage for small vessels.

Jojo river empties into this bay, and from it and the ponds near its mouth good water may be procured.

Tintorero point is low and sandy; a mile to the westward of it is the mouth of the river Tacre, and half a mile farther on is Puerta point, flat and sandy.

All along this part of the coast the high land rises abruptly from the shore, with breaks or ravines abreast of the Rio Seco, Rio Tacre, and Puerta point. The mountains are covered with trees, with the exception of Salta de Jojo, which is arid and barren.

The coast is bordered by a reef, broken in places, at an average distance of 200 yards from the shore. Everywhere along this part of the coast at three-fourths of a mile from the land there are more than 90 fathoms of water.

Small vessels may anchor on the bank in Jojo bay, sheltered from E. by N., round by N. to W. by S., but it is not a place to be recommended, as the sea rolls in heavily. In standing in for it keep closer to Jojo point than to the other side, to avoid a sunken rock, and anchor just inside of the line joining the two points in 9 or 10 fathoms of water, sandy bottom about 300 yards off shore. Vessels anchoring farther out, in 13 or 14 fathoms, will be much more exposed to wind and sea.

The **Sombrero rock**, above water, lies about 60 yards off the eastern side of the beach.

As there are a few small houses and some cultivated ground in the neighborhood, a small amount of fresh provisions and water may be obtained.

Caution.—This anchorage should not be approached with southerly or SE. winds.

The **Beach of Imia** is about two-thirds of a mile long, and near its eastern end is the mouth of the river of the same name. To obtain water from the Imia river, the shore will be approached most easily N. 67° 30′ W. of the small bay of Caoba, where it is clear of reefs. The mountains rise abruptly from the shore and are covered with trees. A broken reef skirts the shore at the distance of 70 yards.

The **anchorage** off Imia beach is only available with northerly winds. The only good position is about 400 yards off the eastern part of the beach, in 9 or 10 fathoms of water, with a bottom of sand and weeds. Wood, water, and fresh provisions may be obtained here.

Piedras Gordas point is so called on account of the large bowlders upon it. To the westward of this point the shore forms a bay, at the head of which is a beach 600 yards long. The shore is clear, except a rock near the eastern end of the beach, near which is a spring of fresh water, easier of access and more sheltered than the stream farther to the westward.

Guarda-Raya point is the western limit of this bay, and the next indentation in the coast to the westward is a small cove called the Guarda-Raya de Yacabo, which is skirted by a flat reef and is almost unapproachable. The high land is here also very near the coast, with a break, through which runs the Yacabo river, emptying into the bay of the same name.

In this bay there is an anchorage entirely open to the southward. Vessels anchoring here should do so at the eastern edge of the beach to avoid the rocky heads off the western end.

Fresh provisions may be obtained from the neighboring houses.

To the westward of the Guarda-Raya de Yacabo the coast is rocky for about half a mile, followed by a beach one-fourth of a mile long, with the mouth of the river Ocampo at its western end.

Savana-la-Mar point is farther to the westward at a distance of about 4 miles; it is a remarkable projection, steep and moderately high, with a rock on its summit, and is 25 miles W. of Caleta point.

Between this point and Jaba point, 1½ miles to the eastward, the shore forms the bay and beach of Savana-la-Mar, where the river of the same name empties. This bay affords temporary anchorage, entirely open, however, to the southward.

As good a berth as any will be found one-quarter of a mile off the eastern part of the beach in 8 or 9 fathoms of water, with sandy bottom, and near a rocky, projecting point. Farther to the westward the bottom is of gravel and rock.

This locality may be easily known from a distance by the Pan de Azucar, visible 30 miles. It lies about three-quarters of a mile N. 22° 30' E. of the eastern end of Savana-la-Mar beach, and, seen from the westward, has the appearance of a sugar-loaf, but from the eastward looks like the roof of a house.

Water is abundant, and fresh provisions are easily obtained from the neighboring houses.

The edge of soundings here is steep-to and close to the shore, there being generally no bottom at 90 fathoms half a mile off the land.

The **coast** is skirted here and there with reefs at from 50 to 100 yards from the shore.

Baitiqueri is sheltered from all winds, and has a good holding ground, but from the extreme narrowness of a portion of the entrance it can only be used by very small vessels.

Port Baitiqueri can be readily recognized by the Azucar Pan, which is about 5 miles from the entrance. Vessels bound to Baitiqueri from the southward or from well off shore, should steer in with the Azucar Pan on a N. bearing. When within a mile of the shore the mouth of the harbor will be plainly seen bearing W., opening between the high hills or coast mountains, sloping down to rocky points on both the E. and W. sides, with an inner point of green trees and bushes on the W. side. The reefs on both sides of the channel can be seen when close in to the land or when 400 yards off shore.

Supplies can be had. The water is good, and may be obtained a short distance from the river mouth. Wood can also be obtained, and cattle, pigs, and provisions from the houses. Game is abundant.

The river Baitiqueri empties at the head of the harbor, but is obstructed by mangrove trees.

The land-winds blow regularly all the year round at night, but do not reach far to seaward, and, as the coast may be approached within 1 mile without danger from Santiago de Cuba to Guanos point, these land-winds are of much service to vessels endeavoring to get to the eastward.

A short distance off shore the flood tide sets to the westward and the ebb tide to the eastward. Farther out the current runs constantly to the westward during the months of July, August, and September, with a velocity depending upon the strength of the winds producing it.

W. of Malano point, at a distance of 3 miles, is the entrance to Puerto Escondido, just to the eastward of which are two isolated hills.

Puerto Escondido or Hidden harbor is, as its name indicates, difficult to discover, but its locality may be known by the two hummocks to the eastward of the entrance. The entrance lies between two rocky points. Beyond the entrance the harbor widens into an irregular shape, affording anchorage sheltered from all winds. There are several projecting mangrove points and many small shoals, but they are easily seen and avoided.

No trustworthy directions can be given for entering Puerto Escondido. The best way will be to buoy the edge of the weather reef with a boat, and the harbor may then be entered without much difficulty.

No fresh water is to be had here, and, as there are no dwellings in the vicinity, there are no pilots.

Port Guantánamo is a spacious and excellent harbor, easy of access for vessels of the largest draught. This port may be said to form two ports, separated by numerous cays and projecting points. The inner harbor, called Joa bay, has, however, a depth of only 12 or 15 feet, and the channel leading to it, although deep, is very narrow.

There is a narrow rocky ledge, with 18 feet of water on it, about half a mile within the outer points of the entrance. The various accounts of its location do not agree, but its most projecting point is believed to be half a mile from the western shore and E. of the mouth of the river Guantánamo.

From here a low sandy shore bends round to the NE., forming the N. side of the outer port. Near the center of it there is a remarkable light-brown cliff. A shallow bank or reef borders this western and northern shore at the distance of about 400 yards.

Water may be obtained from the Guantánamo river, but boats will have to go 11 or 12 miles up the river for it. It is also to be had from a small stream in the NW. part of the inner harbor. The stream, though only 16 or 18 feet wide, is deep enough for launches inside the bar, but on the bar at low water there is only 2 feet.

In approaching Guantánamo from the southward, on about the meridian of 75° 10′ W., a remarkable conical mountain will be seen to the NNW., about 15 miles westward of the harbor. As the land is approached this mountain will assume a saddle shape, and a small isolated hill, with two small paps or hummocks near it, will be seen to the westward. The E. side of the entrance is a round hilly bluff, barren but of green color; the western point is low and woody. The coast is bold and steep-to, and no soundings will be obtained until within the points. The eastern point can be rounded at 400 yards distance, and when abreast of it steer N. 11° 15′ W. for the brown bluff above mentioned on the northern shore. When Fisherman point is open haul up

N. 22° 30′ E., and when it bears S. 78° 55′ E. haul up N. 45° E. or N. 56° 15′ E., and anchor as convenient with Fisherman point bearing from S. 11° 15′ E. to S. 22° E.

The eastern shore is quite clear and a vessel may stand farther in if desired. It will be well for a sailing vessel to wait for the sea-breeze to enter and for the land-breeze to go out. Should it be necessary to beat in or out, do not stand inside the depth of 6 fathoms, and in standing to the eastward do not bring the *brown* cliff to the westward of N. 16° 52′ W. to avoid the Fisherman ledge. A series of beacons have been established in the harbor of Guantánamo from Point Hicacal to the inner anchorage. Each beacon bears on its upper part a board 4½ feet long and 1 foot wide, on which is marked in black letters the number of feet of water in which the beacon stands.

Fresh provisions, fruits, and vegetables can generally be obtained here.

There is a telegraph line to Santiago de Cuba; also semi-weekly steamers to the same place.

The United States is represented by a consular agent.

Berracos point may be recognized by a remarkable conical hill upon it.

To leeward of the bay of Cape Bajo are three small sandy bays, separated from each other by high, steep bluffs called Los Altares, or the Altars, from the remarkable flattened summit of the eastern one.

To eastward of Santiago de Cuba are the mouths of the rivers Sardinero and Aguadores, and near them are some small houses on the shore.

At 7 or 8 miles E. of the entrance of Santiago de Cuba a vessel may anchor in 17 fathoms of water, on the edge of the bank, abreast of a valley or ravine, and about 1½ miles off shore. With the Morro Castle bearing from N. 45° E. to N. 11° 15′ E., distant 1 mile, there are 4 fathoms rocky bottom, and there is the same depth 400 yards off shore.

Santiago de Cuba will admit vessels of the largest draught, entirely sheltered from all winds. Its locality is indicated from a distance by a remarkable valley, separating the eastern from the western spur of the Cobre mountains.

The lofty mountain of Turquino is 56 miles W. of Santiago, and in clear weather may be seen from the N. coast of Jamaica.

The Morro Castle, on the eastern side of the entrance, is a rather large fortification, standing on the western extremity of a flat ridge about 200 feet high.

The entrance to the harbor is about 200 yards wide. After passing Smith cay the channel widens, and, although the course is crooked, the sea-breeze is generally a fair wind up to the city.

Steam tugs are in readiness to tow sailing-vessels in or out of the port if required.

SANTIAGO DE CUBA.

The city is quite large, and is the oldest in the island, and is built on the NE. side of the harbor. Population, 45,000.

An iron pier 375 feet long has been built on wooden piles on the northern side of La Cruz point. There are 29 feet at the end of the pier and 23 feet in the middle of it. A railway connects the iron ore mines, 16 miles distant, with the pier, and vessels can load 2,000 tons a day.

A telegraph cable connects Santiago de Cuba with Jamaica and the Windward islands, and another laid along the S. coast affords communication via Havana with the United States and Europe. A line also connects with all the principal ports on the island.

Coal in large quantities can be had at from $8 to $9 per ton, brought off in lighters.

There is one good shop where ordinary repairs to steamers may be made.

Provisions of all kinds can be had at moderate prices.

Water.—Pipes are laid into the city from a reservoir of excellent water supplied from streams on the hills. Cost, 50 cents per ton.

The authorities to be visited are governor of the department and the captain of the port.

There is a battery of nine guns, and salutes are returned.

Imports.—Ice, coal, cooperage stock, petroleum, machinery, provisions.

Exports.—Sugar, molasses, rum, coffee, tobacco, copper, honey, wax, fustic, iron, mahogany.

Compagnie Translantique (Spanish) from Havana, Neuvitas, Gibara, Santiago de Cuba, Ponce, Mayaguez, San Juan, arrive 5th each month; returning 15th each month. Lines Campo (Spanish) from Havana and other ports, 10th, 20th, 30th each month; returns 5 days later. Another line to Kingston from Havana leave Havana 5th of each month, returning each month. New York and Cuba Steamship Company (Ward's line) leave New York every fourth Tuesday, also return. Time from New York, 5 days. A coasting steamer for Guantánamo semi-weekly. A coasting line (Spanish) for Trinidad, Cienfuegos, etc., semi-weekly.

Pilots are efficient but not necessary for a man-of-war; compulsory for merchant vessels. Fees: 3-masted vessels, entry and departure, $32 gold; two masted vessels $20, gold; one mast vessel $10, gold. Light dues, $2.50; health dues, $4.25; interpreting fees, $4.25; wharfage, $5 per day; custom-house fees, $10; bill of health, $2.50; labor, $2 per day; ballast, discharging, 50 cents per ton.

The place is healthy, but in summer yellow fever occurs. During the winter the temperature varies from 65° to 85°. The mornings and afternoons are pleasant.

The United States is represented by a consul and vice-consul.

Diamante de Afuera shoal, just to the W. of the entrance, is probably laid down a little too far off shore. The pilots state that the sea in heavy weather breaks upon it. After passing the shoals a vessel may haul up for the city and anchor as convenient. The depth gradually decreases toward the northern part of the harbor.

A sailing vessel may enter the port as far as the outer anchorage with the wind from ESE., but to proceed to the city she must have the wind as far to the southward as SE. by E., in order to weather the Colorado shoal. To leave the port, as she will have to haul up as high as SE. by E. between Smith cay and Gaspar point, the wind should be as far to the northward as NE. With very light winds vessels should not attempt to enter or leave the port under sail. In winter when NE. winds prevail, some days may elapse when vessels can not enter under sail, but there is generally during the day-time a breeze from SE.

During the rainy season the current in the channel at the entrance is very strong.

Within the port squalls are frequent between May and October, bringing much rain and wind, especially if they come from the NE.; they appear to rise in a great measure from local circumstances, inasmuch as off the coast, and even in the channel they are less frequent. The land-winds are constant during the night, weak from May until October, but fresh in the dry months and northerly winds; sometimes they begin to blow at 9 p. m., at other times they do not commence until early morning, yet they almost always last until a little before the sea-breeze sets in, between 9 and 10 a. m.; between the two winds there is an interval of calm.

Sailing vessels should avoid running into the calm near the Morro, especially if there be much sea outside. From May till October storms from the SE. take place all along the coast, when the weather is so thick and dirty as to completely obscure it; during which it is dangerous to endeavor to make the port, as it is then difficult to recognize, and the sea is so heavy at the entrance as occasionally to close it.

Cape Cruz.—From Santiago de Cuba to Cape Cruz, a distance of 110 miles, the coast takes a westerly direction and is steep-to, bold, and thickly wooded. The mountain range decreases in height, falling by steps to the cape, which is low and covered with trees, and near the end of the sandy point there are some small huts and a flag-staff.

Pilots can be obtained at the cape.

At 4 miles eastward of the cape the shore is composed of scarfed cliffs about 90 feet high, having horizontal strata, but near the cape they are copper-colored with perpendicular strata.

Soundings appear to extend all along this coast, a short distance from shore, and there are several boat harbors, and small partially sheltered bights, where very small coasters may find temporary anchorage. In good weather a vessel may anchor in 6 or 7 fathoms of water abreast of the beach at the foot of Mount Tarquino.

El Portillo, 24 miles E. of Cape Cruz, is a harbor said to be accessible to vessels of large size. Good temporary anchorage will be found here

CAPE CRUZ REEF. 77

for vessels of the heaviest draught. The locality may be known by three perpendicular white cliffs on the western side of the harbor, while the land on the eastern side is low and marshy. Both points of entrance are foul to a short distance, but the reefs which skirt them are steep-to and the sea breaks upon them. The interior of the harbor is obstructed by sand-banks, which are generally marked out by stakes.

In mid-channel there is a depth of 7 fathoms. A good berth will be found, with the eastern point S. 67° E., one-quarter of a mile distant, in $5\frac{1}{2}$ or 6 fathoms of water. Good water can be obtained here.

To the westward of this harbor there are from 6 to 12 fathoms at from 2 to 4 miles off shore.

The depths are irregular, often changing suddenly from 4 to 7 fathoms, but the water is clear, and there is no difficulty in selecting a sandy spot for anchoring.

About 12 miles westward from Portillo there is said to be an excellent reef harbor for vessels of any size, with no dangers that are not apparent and easily avoided. It is at the foot of the Ojo del Toro mountain, and, although no precise directions can be given for it, the knowledge of its existence might, in emergency, be useful.

Cape Cruz reef, on which the sea breaks heavily, commences $1\frac{3}{8}$ miles E. of the cape, and extending to the westward terminates 1 mile SW. of it. There are often a number of fishing stakes on the reef, and its western extremity is frequently marked by a staff with a bunch of palm leaves upon it, placed there by the pilots. To the westward of the reef a bank with from 4 to 7 fathoms of water on it extends 3 miles farther W.

Good anchorage will be found to the northward of the reef in 4 fathoms of water, with sandy bottom, with Cape Cruz bearing S. 50° 37′ E., Mount Ojo del Toro N. 78° 45′ E., and the extremity of the reef S. 11° 15′ E.

In coming from the eastward do not bring Ingles point, 8 miles E. of Cape Cruz, to the eastward of N. 78° 45′ E. till Colorado point, the second point N. of the cape, and of dark green color, comes open of Cacimba point, to avoid the reef.

Pilots reside at Cape Cruz, but as they are not numerous it frequently happens that a vessel has to wait till one arrives in an outward-bound ship. In this case good anchorage will be found, as above stated.

Caution.—Navigators must bear in mind that even the best charts give but an incorrect idea of the chain of cays, reefs, and shoals which extend 150 miles to the NW. from Cape Cruz. No good survey of this part of the coast has ever been made, and no materials exist for describing it correctly. A vast number of the cays are precisely alike, and the channels, when marked at all, are only marked by small bushes placed by the pilots, and which the first rough weather will wash away. There are doubtless deep navigable channels between the shoals, but they are only known to the pilots, who are very reticent and unwilling to communicate any information regarding them.

Limones river is navigable for boats to a distance of 3 miles, as far as the landing stage, known as Marca de Limones. There is an anchorage in 4 fathoms to the southward of Limones cay, which lies N. 33° 45' W. about 3½ miles from the entrance to the river, and is the largest and most westerly of the cays in the immediate neighborhood. There are two farms on Limones cay.

Manzanillo.—From Cape Cruz the coast takes a NE. direction for 45 miles to the anchorage of Manzanillo, the sea-port of Bayamo, a large town 18 miles inland. The population is 6,000. The United States is represented by a consular agent.

Manzanillo bay lies between the mouth of the river Yara on the N. and Caimanera point on the S., 3 miles apart. The shores are low and covered with mangrove trees, and the water is shallow.

Gua cays.—N. 22° W. of Gua point are three cays of the same name, and between them and Gua point there is a channel over a mud flat with a depth of 11 feet.

The Manzanillo cays are a group of low islets, most of them covered with mangrove trees, affording a sheltered anchorage for large vessels, with deep water. In the middle of them there is a passage about 85 yards wide, with a depth of 7 to 11 fathoms.

Perla cay is a short distance S. 45° W. of these cays, and is a small islet which forms with the Gua cays a channel about 200 yards wide, with 7 fathoms of water; muddy bottom.

The great chain of shoals, cays, and reefs which skirt this part of the coast commences about 15 miles N. 45° E. of Cape Cruz, with the great bank of Buena Esperanza, and extends to the westward as far as Maria Aguila point, near Trinidad de Cuba.

The usual approach to Manzanillo is by the Balandras channel, a narrow passage carrying from 17 to 22 feet of water between the small cays off the SE. part of the Buena Esperanza bank and the cays close to the Cuba shore.

Proceeding to the NE. from the Balandras channel, in 7 to 8 fathoms of water, the Manzanillo and Gua cays will be seen, and the passage between them should be steered for.

Barcos channel is a passage farther to the westward, leading to the anchorage of Manzanillo, but it is not well known except to the pilots.

Cauto river is 12 miles to the northward of Manzanillo. It is one of the deepest rivers in Cuba, and navigable for a distance of 60 miles, although the bar can only be crossed at high water by boats.

The channels leading to Manzanillo, although not very well known, may be navigated by vessels drawing not more than 15 feet by carefully following these directions.

From the end of the reef off Cape Cruz the course is N. 22° W., passing within three-quarters of a mile of Cacimba point, but taking care not to go within a depth of 3½ fathoms to avoid a shoal making off from it. When abreast of Cacimba point, haul up N. 5° 37′ E., passing about 3 miles off Colorados point, with a depth of water of 4½ to 6 fathoms.

From Colorados point a reef runs off, its extremity being generally marked by a stake. Give this stake a berth of 400 yards, and when abreast of it haul up N. 56° 15′ E. for Nigüero point, the extremity of the land now visible, and on the port bow will be seen the Huevos cays, 7 miles distant. The next stake, which is 1 mile N. 45° E. of the first, should be left on the port hand, and from it steer N. 73° 07′ E. with a depth of about 11 fathoms.

Between Points Colorados and Nigüero will be seen Limones point, 6 miles NE. of the former, with a small cay off it. Steering on as directed, the course lies between a shoal to seaward and some sunken rocks in shore, and after running about 1½ miles two pairs of stakes will be seen. The channel lies between them, the least water being 5 fathoms. Each beacon is composed of two stakes, with a board nailed across the head of the one nearest the channel.

A stake will be seen planted in 11 feet of water on the edge of the bank extending from Point Limones, and one-half mile farther off shore will be seen another stake on the Limones shoal. The channel with 8 to 9 fathoms of water lies between them. Each one of these beacons is a cross-headed stake. From here the course is N. 22° 30′ E. toward the most salient of the Balandras cays, which may be seen open of the Huevos cays.

The next narrow place is between the extremity of the reef extending from the Huevos cays, marked by a stake about 1 mile off the cays and a shoal about one-half mile farther out, marked by a pair of stakes. In mid-channel the depth of water is 9 fathoms, with the Huevos cays bearing S. 67° 30′ E. and the most projecting of the Balandras cays N. 16° 52′ E.

From here through the Balandras channel the course is N. 22° 30′ E., the water gradually shoaling to 2¾ fathoms between the Balandras cays and the main-land. There are two stakes in this channel, both of which are to be left on the starboard hand. After passing these stakes a N. 45° E. course will lead up to Manzanillo cays, and from here the channel between the bank of Buena Esperanza and the main-land is perfectly clear and 6 miles wide, with a depth of 7 to 10 fathoms. The W. I. Pilot states that in 1868 H. M. S. *Niobe* was piloted through a channel westward of the Balandras, called the Balamina, which if properly marked would be navigable for the largest class ships.

Pass to the westward of the Gua cays, and as soon as the vessels at anchor in Manzanillo bay bear N. 67° 30′ E. steer toward them, passing between Gua and Perla cays at 1 mile distant from each, and carrying a depth of between 4 and 5 fathoms, which gradually decreases to 2 fathoms at three-fourths of a mile from the town, off the northern part of which is the best anchorage, with a bottom of soft mud.

The greatest rise of the tide is in the months of September and October with the winds from S. or SW.

Bank.—The bank of soundings lying between Cape Cruz and the eastern end of the Doce Leguas cays, 55 miles to the NW., is clear of danger, and vessels may stand in to 7 fathoms anywhere except from about 8 miles N. 22° 30′ W. of the cape to the cay on the southern extremity of the bank Buena Esperanza; within these limits it is not safe for vessels to go within the depth of 10 fathoms, as the ground is intersected with numerous rocky ridges, some of them nearly awash.

Caution.—There are very material errors in all the published charts of the S. coast Cuba, and the positions of but few of the points on the coasts can be entirely depended upon.

From the Balandras channel the edge of the Buena Esperanza bank trends to the westward for 10 miles to a small cay lying about N. 11° 15′ W., 17 miles from Cape Cruz. Thence it takes a northerly direction for 18 miles, then bending to the N. 67° 30′ W. 15 miles to the Cuarto Reales channel, the eastern passage to Santa Cruz, forming also the Bracos and Pitajaya channels.

The entrance to Cuarto Reales channel bears N. 22° 30′ W. from Cape Cruz.

Santa Cruz.—The anchorage of Santa Cruz is accessible only to vessels of light draught. Vessels bound here should from the western edge of the reef off Cape Cruz steer a N. 11° 15′ W. course, which will lead up to a group of eleven small cays extending E. and W., the two most westerly of which are separated by a channel 6 miles wide, called Cuarto Reales channel. The eastern cay is called Coiba, and is distinguished by some round-topped trees in its center. Immediately to windward of Coiba cay is a remarkable sandy cay, and near it is another where the pilots reside.

The least depth of water in the Cuarto Reales channel is 16 feet. The channel leading to Santa Cruz is narrow and crooked, but the water is so clear and the shoals so steep-to that the vessel may be easily guided by the eye.

Media Luna cays.—After passing Coiba cay the course is N. 11° 15′ W., leaving on the starboard hand the Media Luna cay and on the port hand the cluster called the Mordazo cays, and on arriving abreast of the N. point of these latter cays, steer to the westward, passing between the Mordazo cays and the Carenero cays near the coast, and carrying a depth of 3½ to 5¼ fathoms of water over variable bottom.

The Carenero cays, two in number, lie E. of the entrance to the anchorage, and to the westward are two others, called Pinipiniche. From the anchorage the houses of the town bear from N. 45° E. to N. 45° W.

The **Eastern channel** lies between the easternmost of the Doce Leguas cays and an extensive bank, on the western part of which are the Uvero cays.

To enter this channel from outside steer N., giving a berth of 1 mile to the reef which forms the eastern side of the channel. When abreast of the white sand-bank, haul up N. 22° 30′ E. and pass through a group of three cays, leaving two of them to the eastward, and carrying a depth of 11 to 12 fathoms of water. After passing these three cays steer toward the easternmost of the Pilon, a group of four islets extending WNW., and ESE. When within 1 mile of this latter cay the Mate channel will be seen, to enter which bring the N. point of the easternmost Pilon cay to bear N. 53° 26′ W., and steer S. 53° 26′ E.

A better, because easier, course is to pass between the eastern Pilon cay and the Mate cays, and, rounding the latter to the northward, pass between them and the coast of Cuba. In both of these channels the depth is 16 feet.

To the eastward of the Mate cays keep the coast aboard, carrying about 5½ fathoms of water till about one-half a mile to the southward of the Pinipiniche cays, when the town will be seen and anchorage will be found, as before stated.

Tides.—The tides rise and fall about 4 feet, but are greatly affected by the winds.

The United States is represented by a consular agent.

Outside the cays the soundings are regular, and vary from 8 to 20 fathoms. On the edge of the bank the bottom is generally rocky, but inside of a depth of 10 fathoms vessels may anchor temporarily on sandy bottom.

The **Doce Leguas cays** form a chain of low islets, generally covered with brushwood and surrounded by sand-banks. As they are steep-to, the lead will give no warning of their proximity, and a good berth should be given them during the night-time. The white sand-bank lying between this chain of cays and the shore is studded with numerous small islets and reefs with deep channels between them.

There are various channels through these cays for vessels drawing not more than 15 feet of water, but a pilot should be taken. Pilots can be obtained at Cape Cruz, at the entrance to the Cuatro Reales channel, or from one of the numerous fishing vessels from the Grand Caiman which frequent this vicinity.

The principle passages are, the eastern channel just described, the Caballones, and the Boca Grande. All these are wide and easily recognized.

Caballones channel, or **Boca de Caballones**, is the easternmost of the channels through the Doce Leguas cays for vessels larger than boats. It is easily recognized, being 2 miles wide, while none of the openings to the eastward have a greater width than half a mile. At a distance of 1 mile to the westward of this channel is a cocoa-nut tree. Most of the trees on these cays are a sort of dwarf palm; the cocoa-nut is seldom seen. There are only 2¼ fathoms of water in this channel, and the same depth is found to the SW. of the entrance, from each side of which reefs extend, narrowing the channel to 400 yards in width. No good marks can be given, and the eye will be the best guide.

After passing this narrow place the depth of water increases to 10 and 12 fathoms.

The inside western point of the channel is called Mangle Prieto point, and bears N. from Practicos point, the outer eastern one. This channel is one of the best fishing grounds on the S. side of Cuba. An abundance of fish can be caught either by trolling or bottom fishing or by hauling a seine. The beach on the western side is also frequented by turtle. Fishermen, whose services are always available as pilots, live about half a mile east of Practicos point.

Directions.—After entering, a N. course will lead between Bergantin and Manuel Gomez cays. The first of these lies 6 miles N. of the E. end of Caballones or Llana cay, which forms the western side of the channel. From these cays a N. 11° 15′ W. course for 18 miles will carry the vessel up to the NE. end of the Yagua shoal, and from here a N. 45° W. course for 18 miles farther leads to the mouth of the river Jatibonico. The aid of a pilot will be necessary for a stranger.

The best anchorage for small craft is 1 mile N. of Practicos point, with a depth of 2¼ fathoms, sheltered from all winds except those from S. to WNW., which are very rare. Should the wind come out from these unusual directions, a vessel can easily find shelter under one of the cays.

The **Boca Grande** is the most convenient channel of approach to the river Jatibonico. It is 4 miles wide and its depth is 2¼ fathoms, except within half a mile of either shore. Cay Grande should be given a berth of 2 miles on account of a reef extending for 1½ miles to the southward off its western shore. This reef can be easily seen.

Having entered between the cays, the course is N. 28° 07′ E., which leads to windward of Rabihorcado and Burgado cays. The depth in the channel ranges from 10½ to 13 fathoms. The course lies to the westward of numerous coral heads, steep-to and easily seen from aloft. After passing Burgado cay the course is N. 5° 37′ W. to the mouth of the Jatibonico river, where mahogany and cedar timber is shipped in large quantities. When the water is smooth the Boca Grande is a safe passage for vessels of 15 feet draught. The best track is W. of the middle of the channel.

There are two anchorages at the entrance to the Boca Grande, neither of them very good. The first one, with a depth of 4 to 7 fathoms of water, is in a bight formed by the reef in the eastern part of the channel, and lies 1 mile S. 14° 04′ W. from the western end of Cay Grande.

Here a vessel is better sheltered from the usual easterly winds than in any other part of the entrance, and the tide is not felt so strongly, but with the wind from the southward or westward it would not be a safe berth, and, moreover, a sailing-vessel with these winds and a flood tide could not leave.

CAY BRETON—ZARZA DE FUERA CAY. 83

The other anchorage, with a depth of 2½ fathoms, is sheltered from W. and NW. winds. It lies in the western part of the channel, about N. 67° 30′ E. from the S. end of the Cinco Bolas cays, and S. 5° 37′ W. from their NE. point. This anchorage is exposed to the entire force of the NE. wind and the sea, and a vessel lying here with these winds will have a dangerous reef right astern.

The **tides** in these channels are strong and irregular, and vessels should therefore anchor at night, which they can do safely almost anywhere. The currents set in and out of the Boca Grande with a velocity of from 1 to 2½ miles.

Cay Breton should be rounded carefully on account of a reef extending from it 3½ miles to the SW. This reef is steep-to, and the sea generally breaks on it. Off the western end of the cay there is anchorage in 4½ fathoms, with the NW. end of the cay bearing N. 47° 49′ E., and the SE. end S. 78° 45′ E. In standing in to a less depth than 4 fathoms keep a good lookout for rocky heads.

Sailing-vessels generally have to beat up to this anchorage, and in this case, after rounding the western end of the reef, the NW. end of the cay should not be brought to the southward of S. 67° 30′ E., nor on the other tack should the same point be brought to the northward of N. 56° 15′ E. This anchorage is sheltered from N. by E. to SW.

Caution.—As the reef already mentioned off the western end of Cay Breton does not always break, vessels are apt to haul too close round it, and consequently this reef is seldom without a wreck upon it.

The **reef** begins again 3½ miles N. 45° W. of Cay Breton, and in the opening is the entrance to a narrow, crooked channel, leading onto the interior of the bank, but it is only well known to the Cayman fishermen, who navigate through it by the eye.

Zarza de Fuera cay is a low, sandy islet covered with trees, distant about 8 miles from the nearest point of the Cuban shore, and about 3 miles eastward of the NW. portion of the reef. The reef is steep-to on all sides, having 10 fathoms of water close to its edge. There are no cays or islets upon it, except here and there a patch of dry sand.

The positions of the edge of the reef, as laid down on the charts, are not at all to be depended upon. The Medanos de Manati cays are also inaccurately laid down, their position being about latitude 21° 27′ N., longitude 79° 16′ W. The neighboring coast of Cuba is also laid down 7 miles to the S. as far E. as Pasabanao point. The channel separating the coast of Cuba from Zarza de Fuera and the Mendanos de Manati cays is clear and affords excellent anchorage.

A vessel should pass 3 miles westward of Zarza de Fuera cay, and when it bears E., if wishing to enter upon the bank, the vessel may be hauled up N. 45° E., the edge of the bank being quite clear for 12 miles, or within 2 miles of Machos de Fuera cay. After striking soundings the water will shoal almost immediately to 5 fathoms, and then deepen to 10 and 12 fathoms, with occasional patches of 5 fathoms as the vessel advances along the channel.

This part of the coast affords good shelter and holding ground and is without danger as long as the beach is in sight. Abreast of the Doce Leguas cays the coast is low and marshy, producing quantities of tobacco, honey, wax, and mahogany, exported in vessels of not more than 15 feet draught from Santa Cruz and the river Jatibonico, the mouth of which lies 30 miles to the northward of the Boca Grande.

There is an inside channel between the ports of Santa Cruz and Trinidad, which is smooth and well sheltered, with numerous excellent anchorages. The assistance of a pilot is, however, indispensable.

The extensive bank inside the cays has generally depths of 10 fathoms on the western side and 13 fathoms on the eastern, over a very soft white marly bottom, the mud from which discolors the water and adds to the dangers of the navigation. The whole space is covered with groups of low cays and reefs, very inaccurately laid down on all charts, and their names are in much confusion. There are many excellent anchorages among these cays where vessels could ride securely in the heaviest weather. The assistance of a pilot would be necessary to reach them.

Palomas or **Brigand Cay anchorage** is one of the best of the anchorages in this vicinity. It is 15 miles N. 11° 15′ W. from the Boca de Caballones. The outside anchorage is in a large bay formed by a semicircular chain of reefs and cays, and which may be entered from the N. or W. without danger. It is well sheltered from SW., round by S., to NNE.

A good berth will be found three-fourths of a mile N. 14° 04′ W. from a small sandy cay on the reef which joins the most western of the cays with the rest of the group. There are 7 fathoms of water, with good holding ground. If, however, a more sheltered anchorage is desired, it will be found in the lagoon inside, having an entrance open to the eastward, through which a depth of 3 fathoms may be carried. This inner anchorage is completely surrounded by reefs and cays, and lies in latitude 21° 06′ N., longitude 78° 56′ W. As the charts of this region are not at all trustworthy, the cays surrounding this anchorage may or may not be the Palomas group.

In many portions of this bank there are shoals of branch coral rising to the surface of the water from a depth of from 5 to 12 fathoms. By sending a boat ahead to sound a steamer may be navigated among them, but not without risk. From a point 5 miles N. of the Boca Grande to within 10 miles of the Cuban coast these dangers are very thick. The channel E. of ¦Burgado cay is so full of these coral shoals as not to be fit for use.

The **tides** run off and on this bank with great force.

Close in to the Cuban shore the wind draws more to the northward in the early morning than at any other time of the day, hauling to the eastward as the sun rises. The land-breeze commences shortly after sunset.

MEDANOS DE MANATI BANK TO BLANCO ZARZA CAY. 85

A short distance W. of the mouth of the river Jatibonico is the point of the same name, and from here to point Pasabano the coast is swampy and covered with mangroves. Between these two points is a bay with a depth of 2¾ fathoms of water.

Medanos de Manati Bank is S. of Manati point, and is the northern extremity of an extensive bank separated from the mainland by a channel with from 6½ to 8½ fathoms of water in the middle of it, the depth diminishing toward the sides.

The **Zarza river**, which empties a short distance E. of the point of the same name, is navigable for boats for a considerable distance. Its water is not fit to drink.

The **town of Sancti Spiritu** is on its bank, 26 miles from the mouth. Four-hundred yards south of Zarza point are two small cays, from which a reef extends 1 mile to the eastward. Between these cays and the shore there is a snug well sheltered anchorage for small vessels, with a depth of 3 fathoms, clay bottom.

Port Tunas, between Zarza point and Caney point, is a small bay with a depth of from 2¾ to 4½ fathoms, with a bottom of clay and weeds. Port Tunas is the seaport of the city of Sancti Spiritu, with which it is connected by a railroad.

Vessels bound to Tunas will find the Trinidad range of mountains, which can be seen for a distance of 30 miles, a good landmark; also, the range of mountains to the eastward, separated from the Trinidad range by low land.

When the eastern mountain, known as Loma de Banao, bears N. 11° 15′ E. it may be steered for, and the bank entered upon in 6 fathoms of water, 5 miles from Zarza de Fuera cay and 8 miles from Marchas de Fuera cay.

These cays are on the bank, are both low and covered with small trees and mangroves, and can be seen 8 or 10 miles.

The bank is clear of danger to within 3 miles of the southern or Zarza de Fuera cay, and to within 2 miles of Marchas de Fuera cay. Entering upon the bank with Loma de Banao bearing N. 71° 15′ E. the course to Tunas is N. 50° 37′ E. 6 miles, leading to the entrance of the harbor.

The **soundings** on the bank will be at first 6 and 7 fathoms, and then 5, 4, 6, 8, and 10 fathoms will be obtained, followed by a decrease to 5 and 4 fathoms until the port is reached. As the land is neared, the harbor will be recognized by Blanco Zarza cay, which lies to the westward of it.

Blanco Zarza cay is a small island with a lagoon in the center, covered with trees, and having a white sandy beach. A few huts are on the eastern end, where it is said pilots may be procured. Another good mark is given by the tall chimneys of the sugar-mills, situated on the coast to the eastward of the port.

Blanco Zarza cay makes two channels, both of which appear to be easy to navigate. The one to the northward of the island is the better, the deepest water being midway between the island and the mainland. Boats sounding in this channel got no less than 3 fathoms, and information was obtained from the captain of the port and from the captains of trading-vessels that this depth is carried by all who know the channel.

If pilots cannot be obtained, strangers will find it advisable to send boats ahead to sound the channel.

Embarcadero Del Mangle is to the westward of Caney point and is frequented only by smugglers; 6 miles farther to the westward is Ciego point. In the bight between these two points there are from 3 to $4\frac{1}{2}$ fathoms of water. At the head of the bight is the mouth of the river Tallabacoa, dry except during the rainy season. From Iguanojo point, one-half a mile W. of Ciego point, a reef extends one-half a mile to seaward.

Good water may be obtained from a brook running through a ravine a short distance W. of the Tallabacoa river, and also from a small water-course which empties just to the westward of Ciego point. The river Iguanojo, which empties near the point of the same name, furnishes excellent water about 3 miles from its mouth.

From **Agabama point** a narrow reef runs off 6 miles S. 45° E., forming with Iguanojo point, a deep bight, called San Pedro bay, having a depth of $3\frac{1}{2}$ to $5\frac{1}{2}$ fathoms, with muddy bottom.

On the reef stretching off from Agabama point is a cluster of small islets, called the Tierra cays, with another small islet, called Machos de Afuera cay, $2\frac{1}{4}$ miles from the edge of the reef, and $2\frac{3}{4}$ miles S. 22° 30′ E. of the Tierra cays. From Machos de Afuera cay a reef stretches off nearly 2 miles to the eastward.

Agabama river is near the point of the same name; its water is brackish 18 miles from the mouth.

From Agabama point to Point Casilda the coast is a mangrove swamp; from the latter point to Point Guaurabo it is of sand and steep rocks.

Sierras de Sancti Spiritu are some high mountains 10 miles inland. Two of the peaks higher than the rest serve as useful landmarks; the northeasterly of these is called the Pan de Azucar and may be recognized easily by its flattened summit. Loma de Banao, the other peak, lies 4 miles SW. of the Pan de Azucar. Four miles N. 22° 30′ W. of the city of Trinidad is another remarkable peak called Pico del Potrerillo, which is visible 60 miles, also an excellent landmark.

The **City of Trinidad** is one of the most important on the S. side of Cuba, having a population of 13,000. It is situated on high land, 3 miles from the sea, and about half a mile from the left bank of the river Guarabo, which is navigable only for boats. Imports and exports are landed and shipped at the harbors of Casilda and Masio, the former lying $2\frac{1}{2}$ miles and the latter $4\frac{1}{2}$ miles from the town.

The town lies on the slope of a remarkable saddle-shaped mountain, and in approaching from seaward a church, 700 feet above the sea, is a conspicuous object. When the mountain behind the town is seen from the W. or SW. it has the shape of a gun-quoin, and can be seen at a distance of 30 miles.

There are no tug boats; the cargo is landed by lighters.

Port charges.—The pilotage depends on size and rig. Bark or three-masted schooner, $32; brig or schooner, $26; custom-house fees, in and out, about $8; interpreter's fees, about $4; bill of health, $2.50; lighterage on coal, $1 per ton; discharging ballast, 75 cents per ton; labor, $1.50 per day; tonnage dues and general regulations are the same for all ports of Cuba. Coal can be had for $8.50 to $9 per ton; there is generally about 900 tons on hand.

The United States is represented by a consular agent.

Point Maria Aguila lies about 10 miles N. 67° 30′ W. from Point Agabama, and between them the shore-line is deeply indented, forming four small bays, of which the easternmost, called Jobabo, is fit only for small coasters. Port Masio has the deepest water, and Port Casilda has a depth of 21 feet. There are numerous cays, reefs, and banks lying from 2 to 3 miles off shore, and the channels separating them, although deep, are intricate and require the assistance of a pilot.

Cayo Blanco.—The shores of this cay, as its name imports, are formed of white rock and sand. It is a small low islet, 22 feet high, covered with trees and with a lagoon in its center. When seen from the southwestward this cay seems wedge-shaped, the higher part being to the southeastward. In case of having to wait for a pilot, as is probable, anchorage in 9¼ fathoms may be had with the city of Trinidad bearing N. 33° 45′ W. and Blanco cay bearing N. 45° E., distant 1 mile. Before anchoring a clear spot should be selected.

If bound for Trinidad, after passing Zarza de Fuera cay, instead of entering on the bank of soundings, steer about N. 22° 30′ W., and after sighting Machos de Fuera cay, keep away N. 67° 30′ W. for Blanco cay. When the Pan de Azucar is on with the Loma de Banao, Machos de Fuera cay will bear N. The knowledge of this fact may assist a stranger to recognize the land.

Port Masio, of the ports of Trinidad, will be found the most convenient for a sailing-vessel, as it can be entered and left with any wind. Neither this harbor or port Casilda is suitable for vessels drawing more than 15 or 16 feet. For larger vessels the best anchorage will be found in from 3 to 4 fathoms of water, with Blanco cay bearing S. 78° 45′ W. and Puga cay S. 11° 15′ E.

In entering either port the shoals, in clear weather, can generally be seen from aloft. To enter Port Masio take the channel 1 mile wide between Blanco cay and the reef off Puga cay. The eastern end of the former cay should be passed at one-quarter of a mile distance. After passing these cays, if obliged to wait for a pilot, good anchorage will be found, with Blanco cay bearing W., in 3 or 4 fathoms of water.

If intending to proceed without a pilot bring the southern end of Blanco cay to bear W. and the middle of Puga cay to bear S. 33° 45' E., and from this point steer N. 45° W. This will lead between the ledge off the NE. end of Blanco cay, on the port hand, and Cascajal reef nearly awash on the starboard hand.

Jobabo point may be known by a sandy beach on it, and as soon as it bears N. haul up N. 22° 30' W., steering for the western point of entrance of Puerto Masio, avoiding by the eye the shoals on either side. In standing in toward the middle of the harbor it is only necessary to keep clear of a shoal extending from the landing place on the W side. In standing in for Puerto Masio, the small bays of Jobabo and Caballones will be left on the starboard hand. To enter these bays it is only necessary to keep half way between the points of entrance, anchoring in 2½ or 3 fathoms of water, mud bottom.

Port Casilda.—There are three channels: The first, E. of Blanco cay; second, W. of the same cay; and the third, the Mulatas channel, close to the eastward reef of that name.

Merchant vessels are obliged to take a pilot at Blanco cay. If not able to obtain a pilot, the following directions may be of service. A boat sounding ahead will afford assistance.

Until within a mile to the southeastward of the entrance to port Masio the channel to port Casilda is the same. From this point steer one-quarter of a mile N. 67° 30' W. through the narrowest part of the channel, carrying 16 feet of water, leaving, about 200 yards off on the port hand, a stake planted in 10 feet of water on the end of a reef; then steer S. 56° 15' W. 2 miles, passing on the S. side of Guayos cay, when port Casilda will be well open; then steer N. 22° 30' W. for 2 miles, to the entrance of the harbor, keeping the western shore aboard to avoid the long sand-spit making out from the eastern side of the entrance.

The anchorage is in from 16 to 25 feet of water, mud bottom.

Caution.—The stakes marking the channel are frequently changed by the pilots, to keep strangers from learning the pilotage.

Mulatas channel is shorter than the one just described, and it is said to have a depth of 15 feet, but the aid of a pilot is necessary.

Casilda harbor is only 800 yards wide, and although it is 2 miles nearer Trinidad than Port Masio, a vessel will have to send to the Guarabo river for water. There are other channels leading to Casilda, but they are somewhat foul, and there are no good leading marks for them. The assistance of a pilot is therefore necessary.

A vessel proceeding to this port should obtain a pilot at Blanco cay, as the approaches from seaward are narrow and tortuous. If it should be necessary to heave-to outside for a pilot, the port should not be brought to the eastward of N. 67° 30' E. in order to avoid the Mulatas reefs, extending to the westward of the port.

Tug-boats can generally be obtained to assist vessels in calms and light head-winds.

Coal.—A small supply may be obtained at times.

The tides in the channels run to the SW. and NE., with a strength of half a mile an hour, rising and falling 1½ feet, but after a SE. wind the rise and fall is 3 feet.

Guarabo anchorage.—If it is only desired to communicate with the town of Trinidad, a conveniently accessible anchorage will be found at the mouth of the river Guarabo, 3 miles to the westward of the town. This anchorage is, however, entirely open to the SW. To enter it, keep on to the NW., past the entrance of the Mulatas channel, and, after hauling around point Maria Aguilar, keep close along the shore till the town bears E., when the bay will open out. Cirioles point, the southern limit of the bay, should be passed at a distance of 300 yards, and a good berth will be found in 8 fathoms with this point bearing S.

Although the bay appears roomy, there is only room for one vessel, the bottom being strewed with rocks, on some of which there is only 6 feet of water. This place will be found a convenient anchorage for communicating with Trinidad, as it will be only necessary to pull 3 miles up the river as far as a bridge which lies only three-quarters of a mile from town.

Along this part of the coast are the rivers Guanayara, Cubagan, Hondo, Yoguanabo, and San Juan, navigable for a short distance for coasters drawing 6 feet of water. Three miles from the mouth the water of these rivers is drinkable.

The harbor of Cienfuegos or Xagua is spacious and deep enough for the largest ships, but the entrance is narrow and crooked. The bank fringing the coast on the western side of the entrance to this port is reported to extend farther from the shore than was formerly supposed, midway between Punta de la Sabanilla and Angeles Castle. The SE. point of Cayo de Carenas can be passed as near as 50 yards.

The shoal of 1¾ fathoms to the northward of Cayo de Carenas is marked by a square black buoy, which may be passed within 100 yards on either side. This is the only buoy in the harbor, and can not be depended on to be always in position.

Caution.—As the current runs about 3 knots, vessels going with the tide must be particularly careful in rounding Point de Pasa Caballos, as they are apt to be swept on the opposite shore.

The town of Ferdinanda de Xagua or Cienfuegos is built on a peninsula on the eastern side of the bay. Population, 23,000. This peninsula separates two large bays, each affording excellent anchorage.

Vessels discharge into lighters till their draught is reduced to 10 feet, when they can haul alongside of the wharf.

There is an extensive coal yard where a large supply of coal is kept at a cost of $8 to $8.75 per ton. Small vessels can coal at the wharf, large vessels lie almost one-half a mile off. There are two slips where vessels 200 feet long drawing 8 feet forward, 12 feet aft, may be hauled up. Also two machine shops; where steamers may repair.

CIENFUEGOS—DIRECTIONS AND REGULATIONS.

The market for fresh provisions is good and the price fair, large quantities of salt provisions being kept on hand.

River-water can be obtained from water boats, 1¼ cents a gallon. There are pipes at the wharves where water can be obtained by boats.

The sanitary condition is good, the city being clean. There is a health officer who boards all vessels. Quarantine is not very strict and rarely lasts more than a day or two. The public hospital is under government control, and accommodates 250 patients. Foreigners are charged $2 per day. A doctor is in charge assisted by a corps of trained nurses. There is also a small private hospital.

The principal trade is with the United States.

Exports.—Sugar, molasses, and small amount of tobacco.

Imports.—Lumber, coal, machinery, flour, provisions.

Steamers.—Ward's line from United States call twice a month during the busy season, and once a month during the rest of the year. Atkins line from Boston call once a month, only during the busy season; also coast line, Spanish.

Telegraph.—A land line to Havana, also a cable—the West India Telegraph Company.

Mail is received twice a month by steamer and twice a week by rail from Havana. A railroad runs between this place and Havana.

Pilots are under the control of the captain of the port and are reliable. Pilotage is compulsory except to vessels under 80 tons. Vessels coming into port or going out at night pay double pilotage. Pilotage fees on foreign vessels: 80 tons is 60 pesetas; 80 to 100 tons is 70 pesetas; 100 to 150 tons is 80 pesetas; 150 to 200 tons is 90 pesetas; 200 to 300 tons is 100 pesetas; 300 to 400 tons, 110 pesetas; 400 to 500 tons is 120 pesetas; 500 to 1,000 tons is 135 pesetas; 1,000 tons and over is 150 pesetas.

Port charges for a vessel of 368 tons are: Custom-house fees, $5.50; pilotage in and out, $88.25; interpreter, $4; harbor master, $25; towage out, $50; light dues, $24; reporting and passport, $1.25; charter party and stamps, $10.

Authorities to visit are the military governor and captain of the port. The United States is represented by a consul and a vice-consul.

Directions.—In entering the harbor of Cienfuegos give the shore E. of Colorados point a berth of 1 mile, but the point itself may be passed within 50 yards. Then keep in mid-channel all the way to where the shores separate to form the bay. The eastern interior point is called Point Mizpa, and off it a spit extends for a quarter of a mile with 8 feet of water on it. N. of Point Mizpa is the bank of the same name, to avoid which steer for the SE. end of Carenas cay as soon as Mizpa point is abeam. When the N. point of Alcatraz cay bears E., Mizpa bank is passed, and the vessel may anchor, if desirable, in 7 or 10 fathoms of water.

If intending to proceed farther, Carenas cay should be passed on the starboard hand, as a long spit connects it with the northern shore. The assistance of a pilot will be necessary, as, although the edges of the banks and shoals are generally marked by stakes or beacons, they are liable to be changed and cannot be depended upon.

Xagua bank is a coral formation with a shoal spot on its NE. end on which there is only 13 feet of water. The northern edge of the bank is steep-to, but on the southern side the depths shoal more gradually, and the navigator is warned by the change in the color of the water. From the shoalest spot San Juan peak bears N. 39° 22' E.

Cochinos bay.—The eastern shore is formed by Soboruco rocks and steep-to. Half a mile from the northern extremity of the bay there are 14½ fathoms of water, with a bottom of rock and sand, the depth rapidly diminishing toward the beach. On the western shore there are sand-beaches with a narrow bank of soundings and rocky bottom. In the northern part of the bay there is a landing-place, but no good anchorage, as the bottom is rocky.

The Gulf of Batabano, between Padre point and Mangles point, a distance of 160 miles, is bordered on the S. side by the Jardinillos bank, the isle of Pines, and the islands known as the Mangles, Indian, and San Felipe groups. To the northward of these groups are almost innumerable cays and sand-banks, as yet very imperfectly known and forming numerous and intricate channels. To navigate these channels and to identify the cays used as land-marks local knowledge is positively necessary. The principal channels leading to the road of Batabano are: From the eastward, the Gorda channel, between the mainland and the Juan Luis cays; from the southward, the Rosario channel, along the western edge of the Jardinillos bank; and from the SW. the channels between the Isle of Pines and the Indian cays, between the Indian and San Felipe cays, and between the latter group and the mainland.

Pilots and masters of steamships running constantly to Batabano have asserted that vessels drawing 11 feet can go there with safety.

Pilots may be obtained at Cienfuegos or at the isle of Pines.

Piedras Cay reef.—Padre point is low and sandy, and from it a reef extends to cay Piedras, which is low and small. The reef is steep-to and intersected by several narrow cuts, through which depths of 16 to 22 feet may be carried. The best one is close to the northward of the cay.

The coast to the westward of Padre point as far as Cristobal point, a distance of 36 miles, is very low, swampy, and bordered by cays covered with mangroves. On the eastern end of Blanco cay good water may be obtained by digging wells in the sand. To the westward of Blanco cay the shore inclines to the northward, forming the bay of Cazones. The water is shallow, and the western shore is formed by a line of low mangrove cays, terminating in Diego Perez cay. There are some natural wells of good water on the northern end of this cay. Fish and game are said to abound here.

Jardinillos bank is perfectly steep-to, showing only one or two sandbanks above water, and, although the edge of the bank is nearly awash, the sea does not always break on it.

Caution.—The bank forms the SW. side of the gulf of Cazones and is to be avoided by sailing-vessels on account of its frequent calms and strong currents.

To the westward of Diego Perez cay a chain of low mangrove cays, only a few of which are laid down on the chart, extends for 15 miles. The larger of these, called the Flamenco, Bonito, Palanca, and Fabrica cays, make the N. side of a channel between them and the Jardinillos bank, through which at least 10 feet of water, and probably a little more, may be carried.

Juan Luis cays are to the westward of this chain of cays. To the eastward of these the channel leads.

From Cazones bay to the westward the shore is low, marshy, and much indented, forming several small bays and points of no importance. There are numerous channels for small vessels among the numerous cays along the coast and between them and the shore, but there are no leading marks which a stranger could recognize, nor does any intelligible and accurate information regarding them exist. The numerous large steamers running along the S. coast of Cuba from Batabano to Cienfuegos and Santiago de Cuba are all furnished with skillful pilots, but no general information can be procured from them respecting the navigation.

Broa bay.—The shores are covered with mangrove swamps, through which the river Jatibonico and numerous other small streams empty.

The general depth of water in the bay is from 3 to 4 fathoms. At Rosario and Caimito, piers have been built to facilitate the loading of coasters.

From the Mayabeque river, 1½ miles to the NW. of the point of the same name, good water may be easily obtained.

Batabano is 9 miles to the westward of the river Mayabeque and is a place of constantly-growing importance, as the port through which nearly all the communication of Havana with the southern coast of the island takes place. A railway runs to Havana, time two hours, and the submarine telegraph cable is here connected with Havana by land lines.

The channels leading to this port only admit the passage of vessels drawing 12 or 13 feet of water, and the anchorage is entirely exposed to SE. winds. There are but few scattered buildings on the shore, the town of Batabano lying 3 miles inland.

From Batabano the coast is low and irregular in outline, taking a general westerly direction for 24 miles, when it trends to the SW., forming Majana bay. It is marshy as far to the westward as the mouth of the river Guanima, 20 miles from Batabano.

From Majana the coast is somewhat indented by bays and lagoons to Fisga point. Access to this part of the shore is much impeded by banks and shoals, which in some places extend off as far as 7 miles. Numerous rivers of no special importance empty into the sea, affording shelter within their mouths to droghers and fishing boats.

From Fisga point the coast is low, swampy, and much indented by lagoons and small coves to the mouth of the river Galafre. It then sweeps round forming Cortes bay, where there are 3 to 3½ fathoms of water.

In Cortes or Pirate's lagoon there are 15 feet of water, but only 6 or 7 feet between the cays at the entrance. Fish and turtle are said to be abundant in this vicinity.

Piedras point is to the southward of this lagoon; the coast then sweeps round to Mangles point, which is low and only to be distinguished by the sudden elbow which the coast makes in turning to the westward. All this part of the coast is foul and bordered by a reef.

Before proceeding farther with the description of the coast we will give a general description of the shoals, cays, etc., lying S. of Batabano.

It is but very seldom that a man of-war or a merchant vessel needs any description of this neighborhood, and it must be remembered that no correct and complete survey has ever been made here.

The **current** in the gulf of Cazones is uncertain both as to direction and strength, and the navigator cannot be too careful.

East Guano cay is a small islet, 40 feet high, covered with grass, dwarf cactus, and shrubs.

From Trabuco cay there is a chain of high, rocky cays lying near the edge of the bank, which is bordered by a reef.

Largo cay is thickly wooded, and bordered by a reef which extends 3 miles off from the SE. side of the cay.

This reef extends from the SE. end of cay Largo about 12 miles, and then trends to the southward for six miles, forming a narrow sand-spit.

Jack Taylor reef, on which the water breaks, is of coral, and 1 mile S. of it there are 12½ fathoms of water, coral and sandy bottom. On the sand-spit connecting this reef with the bank there are 5 or 6 fathoms of water.

Jardine cays, on the southern edge of the bank, extend from the Isle of Pines to Cay Largo.

Rosario cay, when first seen from the southward, looks like three islets, the largest one in the middle. It may be known by some sandy cliffs upon it. It is said to be frequented by fishermen who resort to it for water and for the cabbage-palm. Water is obtained by digging wells in the sand.

Rosario channel leads into the Gulf of Batabano, and has 3 fathoms at the entrance, but is said to be only 9 feet at 7 miles from the entrance.

Cantille cay, just W. of Rosario channel is wooded.

Dry Shingle or Cascajo bank is bordered by a very dangerous reef and many vessels have been lost on it. Just N. of the Dry Shingle is a reef called the Calapatch Mehagan, a mass of coral just awash, where many vessels have been wrecked.

Anchorage may be had in 5 fathoms of water, sandy bottom, with the Dry Shingle bearing S. 56° 45′ E., 1 mile distant. There are soundings about 1 mile outside, in from 5 to 14 fathoms.

There is also anchorage under some of the cays to the eastward of Isle of Pines, but in the absence of trustworthy charts local knowledge only can be depended upon, and no trustworthy directions can be given.

The Isle of Pines is of irregular shape with a deep bay on the western side, sheltered on the SW. by a projecting tongue of land.

The southern half of the island is low and swampy, but the northern part is more elevated and in some places mountainous. Very many water-courses and lagoons along the shore are navigable for vessels drawing 7 or 8 feet of water. The island is covered with trees, affording, as its name indicates, pine spars and masts for vessels.

Most of the inhabitants, about 800 in number, live in the northern part of the island, where the capital, Nueva Gerona, is situated. Cattle are raised here to a considerable extent.

In making the land from the southward three mountains first come in sight. Of these, the westernmost and highest, called Dolphin Head, or Mount José, appears from the S. as one peak, but from the westward three peaks are seen. It can be seen 45 miles off.

There is good anchorage at Port Frances in from 6 to 8 fathoms, with sandy bottom. There are wells of good water here, but the ground is rocky. Wild cattle may be found and plenty of fish.

From Bush cay, just off Point Frances, a reef is said to extend for three-fourths of a mile.

Siguanea bay.—The shores are generally low and lined with mangrove cays. A bar with only 16 feet of water on it runs across from Frances point to the S. end of the Indian cays, but inside the depths are from $3\frac{1}{2}$ to 6 fathoms, and the anchorage excellent. Water may be obtained from springs at the foot of the Siguanea hills.

Indian river.—Good anchorage, but exposed to the westward, will be found in $2\frac{1}{2}$ fathoms about 1 mile off shore. The mouth is nearly closed by a mud bar, but inside depths of from 1 to 3 fathoms will be carried for 4 miles. Two and a half miles inside the bar the mangrove trees give way to the pines, and a short distance farther up excellent pine spars as large as a frigate's topmast or smaller may be cut so as to fall into the river. At first they are so heavy as to sink, but soon become dry and much lighter. On the banks of the river crocodiles abound, and in the woods will be found wild pigs.

Rio Casa.—The mouth of the Casa river forms the port through which all the business of the seat of government, *Nueva Gerona*, is transacted with the Island of Cuba. The river is navigable for boats for a short distance, and the water is drinkable about 4 miles from the mouth. On the left bank are the Casas hills. From the settlements beef and pork may be procured, but vegetables are scarce.

On this part of the coast are the Caballos hills, of moderate height, and the shore becomes firmer and less marshy than it is to the westward.

The eastern coast of the island is low and marshy.

The numerous cays, islets, and sand-banks lying N. of the Isle of Pines, and extending from its N. shore to the mainland of Cuba, are only imperfectly known, and are now only important as obstructing navigation.

These cays have few if any distinguishing features by which the navigator may know them, being for the most part covered with mangrove trees and surrounded by reefs.

The **Mangles group** is the most extensive and numerous. Northward of them are the Petatillos sand-banks, and still farther N. and close to the Cuban coast are numerous cays very much alike.

The **Indian cays**, are low, wooded, and separated by narrow channels. They are surrounded by reefs, which extend nearly 2 miles off shore.

San Felipe cays form a group lying about midway between the Indian cays and the mainland of Cuba. They are low, marshy, and surrounded by reefs. On the S. point of the eastern cay there is a well of good water near the beach. Fish and turtle abound.

The high tide appears to take place in the morning and the low tide at night. The flood sets strongly to the NE.

The coast from Mangle point to Cape Corrientes is probably laid down erroneously on the chart, a part of it, at least, being represented 7 miles too far S. It is formed of low white bluffs, thickly wooded, and, as far as is known, is clear of danger.

Cape Corrientes is low and sandy, with a depth of 5 fathoms three-fourths of a mile off shore. Before the establishment of the light on Cape San Antonio it is said that Cape Corrientes was sometimes mistaken for the western extremity of Cuba, but that error could hardly occur now. Temporary anchorage may be found in 9 fathoms of water, with Cape Corrientes bearing N. 84° 22′ E., 1¼ miles distant.

The **current** off the S. side of Cuba has the same general characteristics as elsewhere in the West Indies, viz, generally setting to the westward, but being seriously influenced, both as to strength and direction, by the prevailing winds. Just before and during northers, which blow during the winter months, the current frequently sets to the eastward. From October to May the NE. trade-winds blow freshly along the S. coast of Cuba, but are temporarily interrupted at times by winds from NW. and N.

From May to October, however, the prevailing winds are light, and show an inclination to haul round with the sun every day, commencing in the evening with a northerly wind off the land, by daybreak veering to ENE., then by noon through E. to ESE., and by 4 p. m. arriving at SW., where it continues till it falls calm, and is succeeded in the evening by the land wind. The strong currents and untrustworthy character of the charts make it incumbent on the navigator to exercise even more than ordinary caution and vigilance while near the land on the coast of Cuba.

Cape San Antonio, the western extremity of Cuba is low, and covered with trees 70 to 80 feet high. The shore is formed by sandy beaches, separated from each other by low, white cliffs. There is no salient point to the westward, the land bending round for 4 miles very gradually. Two or three miles S. of the light-house a bank commences, which sweeps round the cape about 1 mile off shore and connects with the Colorados reefs.

Temporary anchorage will be found under the W. end of Cuba, with the N. extreme of the land bearing N. 22° 30′ E. and the S. extreme bearing S. 45° E. This anchorage must be approached carefully, as it shoals quickly and the bottom is foul.

Lieutenant Pillsbury, U. S. Navy, considers the following to be a better temporary anchorage, and reports: "I anchor in 10 or 11 fathoms, sandy bottom, and no coral heads, the light bearing NE. by E. A coral reef extends about a mile off shore, its outer end bearing N. from the anchorage about half a mile distant."

The **Antonio knoll** is a coral bank, 10 fathoms being the least depth found. Discolored water may be seen in clear weather.

Although several shoals have been reported in the vicinity, it is evident from the examinations made by the U. S. S. *Tallapoosa* in 1883, and the U. S. Fish Commission steamer *Albatross* in 1884, that there is no danger to navigation outside of the Colorado reefs. The discolored water seen over the 10-fathom spot in Antonio's knoll doubtless being the only ground for supposing that any shoal existed.

Commander A. G. Kellogg, U. S. N., commanding *Tallapoosa*, reports as follows, viz:

MARCH 27, 1883.—I steered in for the reef for the purpose of making an examination, but the heavy sea and wind prevented my attempting it. Twice I went in and anchored on the reefs, neither time being able to carry more than 3¼ fathoms. In my judgment no ship drawing over 15 feet should attempt it. After passing the reef from 4 to 5 fathoms can be carried to within 1 mile of the cays. The reefs extend fully 1¼ miles to the westward of the position laid down on the chart.

Currents in the vicinity of the reef set with the prevailing wind, close to the reef to the southward.

On the morning of March 25, while steaming out over the reef, we experienced the most severe squall I have ever known, lasting nearly one hour.

As there is deep water close to all these shoals, great caution must be exercised while in their neighborhood.

The edge of the great bank from which the Colorados reefs rise, commencing 2 miles W. of Cajon point, takes a general northeasterly direction for 120 miles to Bahia Honda.

All the coast from a short distance N. of Cajon point is skirted by dangerous, broken reefs. Coasters of 10 or 11 feet draught pass through the numerous cuts and among the cays inside. The land abreast of the western end of the reef is quite low and can not be seen from the edge of the reefs. The sea seldom breaks upon them, and the bank of soundings outside is seldom more than a mile wide.

The lead will, therefore, give but little warning, and as the currents are strong and variable this part of the coast should be navigated with great care.

Colorados reef.—The SW. point of the reef begins 15 miles from Cajon point, and between them is a bank of soundings with from 3 to 6 fathoms on it, sandy and rocky bottom. The reef here is from 2 to 3 miles wide and from 7 to 14 miles off shore, with several detached heads on both its eastern and western sides.

The Lena or **Mangles cay**, a group of four small islets, are low and covered with mangrove trees. They are separated from each other by narrow channels, shallow at the entrance but deep inside. The largest of these cays, called Punta de Afuera, is low and marshy. It is separated from the coast by a bay, nearly land-locked, being protected to the eastward by a salient point. This point forms, with the eastern end of Punta de Afuera Cay, the Barcos channel, where vessels drawing not more than 15 feet may find sheltered anchorage.

Barcos channel.—The points at the entrance lie E. and W. of each other, a small reef extending from each, so as to leave a clear channel 200 yards wide, with a depth of 2 fathoms, muddy bottom, at the entrance. Inside, the channel deepens to $4\frac{1}{2}$ fathoms, widening at the same place to 500 yards, again narrowing and shoaling as a small submerged cay is approached.

This small cay forms a channel about 6 feet deep, by which small vessels may reach the bay above mentioned. To enter it a sailing-vessel needs a fair wind, but the entrance has no danger, and inside a vessel may anchor as convenient, there being 5 fathoms of water close to the mangroves.

There are several small cays, having only boat-channels between them, in the bay to which the Barcos channel leads. The general depth is from 6 to 9 feet.

Lena and **Rebellines cays.**—To the westward of Punta de Afuera cay are three other small mangrove cays, the northern and smallest of which is called Lena cay, the others the Rebellines. The latter, lying about a quarter of a mile off the coast, have a small reef running off the southern side.

Anchorage can be found to the southward of the Rebellines, sheltered from northers, in about 2 to $2\frac{1}{2}$ fathoms of water, muddy bottom.

Near the shore there are some rocky heads.

Between Caravela Chica and Plumajes points, 10 miles apart, there are several small coves of little consequence.

Plumajes point is a bluff. Although not high as, compared with the land in its vicinity, it is easily distinguished. From the western end a reef extends three-quarters of a mile to the N. 67° 30′ E., and rocky ground extends 2 miles farther in the same direction.

Tolete point is E. of Plumajes point; farther in the same direction is Guadiana point, forming, with Algodonal point, three-quarters of a mile to the northward, the entrance to the bay of Guadiana. This entrance is narrowed by mud banks, extending from both sides toward the middle of the channel and contracting its navigable portion.

An excellent anchorage, sheltered from all winds, will be found in the center of the bay, with a depth of 3½ to 4 fathoms. Just inside of a beach on the northern shore is a lagoon affording good drinking water.

The **River Guane Guamas** or **Guadiana** empties into the NE. part near its mouth. On the northern shore is Geronimo point, off which a reef extends one-quarter of a mile to the SE. The river has a depth of about 7 feet. but is so narrow and crooked that boats only can navigate it. The towns of Guane and Paso Real export from here hides, wax, and tobacco.

Between Algodonal and Pinalillo points the coast is of moderate height, and covered with pine trees.

Garanacha bay, although exposed to westerly winds, affords good anchorage, gales of wind from that quarter rarely blowing. The holding ground is good, the bottom being muddy. In the center of the bay, 1½ miles off shore, there is a depth of 1½ fathoms at high water. There are only 6 feet of water at low tides 400 yards off shore, so that lighter can not reach the landing-place at that time. On the shore is a small beach, with roads leading from it towards the towns of Mantua, Guane, and Pinar del Rio.

During the rainy season water may be had from a lagoon near the beach; in the dry season it is procured from the Santa Lucia river, which empties into the bay.

Avalo point is a low, narrow tongue of land extending more than 1 mile to seaward. Under its shelter is a good anchorage, protected from northers. Between Pinalillo and Avalo points is a bay 2 miles deep, with an inner arm or cove, on which is situated the landing-place of San Francisco.

The **Pass of Buena Vista** has only 2 fathoms of water in some places, and is only 200 yards wide. To enter it, bring the western point of Buena Vista cay to bear S. 45° E., and steer for it, carrying a depth of from 2 to 4 fathoms of water as far as a bank of whitish clay with hardly 2 fathoms of water on it. After passing this bank, haul up E. till the eastern point of the cay bears S. 45° E., when a palm-tree beacon will be seen on the edge of the Buena Vista bank. The beacon should be left on the starboard hand, and after passing it a vessel may steer for Arroyos anchorage without danger.

Buena Vista cay is low and swampy, and divided in the middle by a creek navigable for boats. A mud-bank extends 200 yards off its NW. point, on the extremity of which is planted the beacon above mentioned.

The channel between the cay and the Cuban coast has a depth of a little more than 6 feet, and forms a short cut for small steamers and coasters of that draught. The channel is marked by beacons, but no definite instructions can be given for it.

Between the mouth of the Buena Vista river and Ingleses point, farther to the southward, is the anchorage of Arroyos, having a depth of 3 fathoms, gradually diminishing toward the shore, and sheltered from all winds from NW. round by E. to SW.

This is the principal port of the town of Mantua, 9 miles inland, and has a wooden wharf where coasting vessels load and discharge their cargoes. To enter this channel, run along outside the reef till abreast the middle of a small sandy beach on the NE. end of Rapado cay, when haul up directly for the beach. The channel may be known by the dark color of the water.

Rapado cay is mostly covered with a mangrove swamp. Three miles S. of it is a place called Canas, where coasters load and discharge cargoes. The passage between the cay and the coast is navigable only by vessels of very light draught—4 feet or less.

Vinagera reef.—The passage of the same name lies between Rapado Grande and Epllabado cays, and leads to the small anchorages of Cana, Santa Isabel, and Santa Maria. From these landings coasters carry to Havana considerable quantities of tobacco, lumber, wax, and honey. This passage is 200 yards wide, with a depth of 10 to 11 feet.

Rapado Chicos cays.—The passages N. and S. of these cays have from 1½ to 2 fathoms of water.

Beacons.—The channels between the cays and banks leading to the anchorages in this vicinity have been marked with palm-tree beacons, but these marks are not so permanently placed as to make it worth while to describe their present location.

From Tobasco point a reef runs 350 yards to the NW., marked by a barrel-shaped buoy moored in 8 feet of water. One hundred yards outside of this buoy there are 13 feet of water.

Roncadora pass.—To enter it, coast along the edge of the reef until the town of Bajas, on rising ground 2 miles inland, is in sight, then bringing the tower of the church on with the little hill of Acostas; this mark will lead through mid-channel with depths of from 16 to 26 feet after passing the reef.

Baja bay is a secure anchorage, being only open to NW. winds. In this direction the reefs are at no great distance and prevent any heavy seas from rolling in. At the head of the bay there is a landing-place, serving as a port for the town of Baja, about 3 miles inland. Vessels of light draught lie one-third of a mile off the landing in 8 feet of water.

Galera pass lies 2 miles W. of Jutias cay, and is marked by a beacon of branches. The pass is rather more than 400 yards in width, with a depth of 13 feet, rocky bottom.

Jutias cay is swampy in the southern part, with drier land in the northern portion. It is separated from the mainland by a narrow channel, only navigable for boats.

Nombre de Dios bay is between the western point of Jutias cay and Jaguey point. The entrances are nearly closed by an extensive mud bank. There are two channels of entrance to the bay, both marked out by beacons. One of these is within 200 yards of the shore of Jutias cay and the other is 400 yards farther to the westward. Each of these channels is 100 yards wide and carries a depth of from 11 to 16 feet of water.

Jutias pass is formed by the reef to the eastward, and to the westward by a ledge of rocks almost awash, extending from the NE. point of Jutias cay.

This pass is divided into 2 channels by a shoal on which there is very little water. Temporary beacons, in the form of stakes, mark out the various channels.

Pan de Azucar.—Half a mile within the mouth of this river good drinking water, said to be the best on this part of the coast, can be obtained.

Inez de Soto cay seen from the northward appears to be divided by a narrow channel in two parts. This channel is, however, only a small inlet 300 yards in extent. The cay is represented on the charts erroneously as in two parts. The southern portion of the cay is swampy.

San Cayetano bay.—In the middle of the shore of the bay are several huts, a storehouse for copper ore, and a wooden wharf. In this bay the bottom is of mud and the anchorage is sheltered from E. to W. round by S.

In standing in for this anchorage care must be taken to avoid a reef extending half a mile to the S. 56° 15′ E. from the eastern point of Inez de Soto cay. The best berth is in 11 feet of water with the eastern point of Inez de Soto cay bearing N. 39° 22′ W., and Lavandera point N. 28° 07′ E.

Lavandera point, is 1½ miles E. of the eastern point of Inez de Soto cay, apparently on the mainland, but really the northern point of a cay, 3 miles long, separated from the Cuban shore by a narrow channel uniting San Cayetano and Berracos bays. The northern part of this cay is of dry land, but all the rest, except a small beach on the western side, is swampy and covered with mangroves.

The Berracos are two small, low cays, joined to the coast by a reef preventing the passage of boats and sheltering the anchorage of Berracos bay. The channel leading to this anchorage has a depth of from 9 to 16 feet, gradually diminishing toward the shore. This channel is situated between the easternmost of the Uvas cays and the westernmost of the Berracos cays.

Arenas cay, N. of the Berracos, is separated from the reefs outside by a channel 500 yards in width, navigable for boats only; its southern portion is swampy. There is a short reef extending from its SW. point.

The **Dios cays** are two small swampy islets lying E. ¼ mile from Point Purgatorio and very near the coast.

Leviza cay is divided in two by a narrow creek navigable for boats. Its southern part is swampy. Between the cay and the Colorados reefs, 1 mile outside, there is a channel fit only for small coasters.

Two miles from the eastern part of Leviza cay is the mouth of the Puercos river, the water of which is not fit to drink.

Alacranes cay lies a short distance eastward of the pass of the same name, and is separated from the outside reefs by the Reduan channel, 1 mile wide and 7 to 8 feet deep. The southern part of the cay is a mangrove swamp, and is separated from the Cuban coast by a canoe channel leading to the Casigua cays.

Leviza pass.—The outer limit of the reef passes 1½ miles to the northward of Leviza cay, after forming to the westward the pass of the same name, in which there is very little water, then continues to Alacranes pass, then to Blanco Cay pass.

The greatest depth of water in Alacranes pass is 8 feet. It is only used by small coasting vessels.

Off the western part of Blanco cay there there is anchorage in 3½ to 4½ fathoms of water, muddy bottom.

The reef terminates at Pescadores point, on the W. side of the entrance to Bahia Honda. Vessels of not more than 8 feet draught can navigate inside the Colorados reefs. The Alacranes pass is not safe when the weather is at all rough. The Galera pass is better.

In passing Diego and Rapado cays care must be taken to avoid the shoals near them. Near the reefs are many detached coral heads, and the bottom is rocky. Near the Cuban shore it is of mud and sand. Between the Colorados reefs and Cajon point vessels may easily leave or approach the channels inside the reef. Here the chart will be the best guide.

The **harbor of Bahia Honda** is well sheltered, and will admit vessels of any draught of water. The points forming the entrance as well as the sides of the channel are bordered with reefs and shoals, making the assistance of a pilot necessary to a stranger. The town is 6 miles from the bay, and contains about 1,000 inhabitants, and is now a closed port, no foreign trade being permitted. It has a fort, which is a good mark for entering. There are no pilots. The health of the place is good except in the sickly season, which commences in April and lasts through the summer.

To enter the harbor, bring the entrance to bear S. and steer for it. When within the distance of 1 mile Difuntos point will be seen between the sandy points on either side of the entrance, and beyond it a remarkable hill, with a square top, back of a sugar estate. By keeping the eastern end of this hill on with Difuntos point a depth of 10 to 5 fathoms will be carried in. The eastern side of the entrance should be kept close aboard, and when abreast of Carenero point a vessel may anchor in 6 fathoms of water, or, if it is desired to proceed farther in, she may stand on the SW. and anchor just within Difuntos and Mangles points. Placer point should be given a good berth, as a sand shoal just awash lies ¼ of a mile off it. Sailing-vessels must wait for the seabreeze to enter, and for the land-breeze to leave, Bahia Honda. Although several streams empty into the harbor, good water can not be obtained in great quantity.

From Bahia Honda to Cabanas the shore should not be approached nearer than 2 miles.

Reef.—The American schooner *Hattie Weston* struck on a reef in latitude 23° 06′ N., longitude 83° 04′ W., at an estimated distance of 5 to 7 miles off shore. This shoal had been searched for without success, but as the *Hattie Weston* had to discharge cargo in order to get off, there can be no doubt of the existence of a shoal in this vicinity, though the position given may be wrong.

The harbor of Cabanas is a good and well-sheltered anchorage and vessels of the largest draught may safely enter it. South of the port, 5 miles inland, there is a range of mountains 1,400 feet high at the western part, sloping gradually toward the eastward to a large plain extending as far as the table-land of Mariel. At the eastern end of the heights there is a remarkable peak bearing S. 45° E. from the entrance to the harbor, and about the middle of the range there is a remarkable gap.

On the eastern side of the entrance there are two small hills, on the western part of which are the buildings of a sugar estate. The entrance is 1¼ miles wide, and when it bears S. a guard-house or tower with several adjacent buildings will be seen 2 miles inside. This tower is on the extreme of an islet called Don Juan Tomas cay, which divides the harbor into two large arms. The eastern of these is only fit for coasters; the western one affords anchorage for vessels of 15 feet draught.

Having opened the entrance to the port, bring the tower to bear S. 8° 26′ E., when it will be in line with the gap in the mountain above mentioned, and also in line with Pescadores point inside the harbor. This course will lead toward the entrance, with depths of 16, 12, and 9 fathoms, sandy bottom. When the first point on the western side, called Point Arbalatos, bears N. 87° 11′ W. the vessel will be in the mouth of the entrance in 7 or 8 fathoms of water. Then steer S. 39° 22′ E. till Point Pescadores, the western inner point, bears S., then a course S. 5° 37′ W., with a depth of 5 fathoms, will lead between the banks of rock and sand till the water deepens to 13 fathoms.

Having passed the inner point on the W. side of the channel, haul up and anchor close under the weather-shore in 8 or 9 fathoms mud, near the entrance of the SE. arm, or keep away and come to in the SW. arm under the lee of the tower. In doing this, however, be careful to avoid a patch of rocks and sand, which extends 200 yards N. and S., and on which there are $2\frac{1}{2}$ fathoms water; it lies nearly half a mile N. 11° 15' W. from the tower, and may be seen from aloft.

Caution.—In leaving the harbor it will be desirable for a sailing-vessel to weigh with the early land wind, to insure its carrying the vessel well out before it fails, as there is generally a very heavy swell in the offing, and frequently a strong SW. eddy, which might set her on the reef skirting the shore.

The town contains about 700 inhabitants and is closed to foreign commerce. There is telegraphic and postal communication with Havana by land. There are several streams of fresh water, but not very good. Salutes can be returned by the fort. The authorities to visit are the commandant of the fort and the alcalde.

The district is rich and fertile and occupied principally by sugar estates.

Between Puerto Cabanas and Puerto del Mariel, 12 miles to the eastward, the coast is, in places, bordered by a reef half a mile off shore. The edge of the reef is steep-to, and, as there is frequently a strong eddy to the SW., vessels must take care not to get becalmed in this vicinity.

Port Mariel.—The shore in its vicinity becomes a little more elevated, and a short distance inland, to the eastward of the port, there is a remarkable long flat ridge of table land of moderate height, with a notch or step at its E. end, called the Table of Mariel, which can not be mistaken, and a little westward of it will be seen a remarkable cliff, facing westward in the harbor. The entrance lies N. 45° W. from the W. end of the table, and on its eastern side there is a martello tower and some huts, and when the tower bears S. 11° 15' E. a church and several buildings will open out in the interior.

The port is well sheltered, but its entrance is only 50 yards wide. The least depth is 4 fathoms. The eye will be the best guide in entering, and when within the narrowest part keep the weather shore aboard until abreast of Gorda point on the W. shore, on which there is a small fort, when the vessel may anchor in 5 or 6 fathoms in safety.

The port is closed to foreign commerce. Cattle can be obtained at the sugar estates, but no provisions. Water can be obtained from the fresh water streams. It is generally healthy, the sickly season being from April to September. The battery at the fort can return salutes. There is telegraphic communication, also a railroad, to Havana. There is a small police force. Pilots are not necessary.

Coast.—The shore eastward of the Table of Mariel, which is steep-to, becomes rather low and flat until within a mile or two of Havana, when it rises into a few small fortified hills.

The shore is composed of dark-colored bluffs, clear of danger, and steep to. Between Mariel and Havana are the mouths of the small rivers Mosquito, Guajaibon, Banes, Barracoa, and Banta.

Reef.—Abreast the mouth of the river Jaimanita, 9 miles W. of Havana, a reef extends 1 mile off Mangles point.

The harbor of Chorrera is 4 miles W. of the entrance to Havana, at the mouth of the Almendaraz river. It is quite open to the northward, and has no bar or other obstruction at its entrance. The anchorage in 3 to 5 fathoms would scarcely accommodate half a dozen vessels, and the holding ground is only coral sand.

Telegraph cable.—At this place the end of one of the telegraph cables between Cuba and Key West is landed.

The rather low coast in the vicinity of the entrance to Chorrera is very ragged, the blackened coral rock being honey-combed by the sea.

Havana.—The entrance to the port of Havana may be easily recognized by the Morro castle and light-house, with the extensive line of fortifications on the eastern side of the entrance. The land to the eastward of the city, until near the Jaruco or Iron mountains, 18 miles distant, is about 200 feet high and the shore bold and steep-to.

Nine miles S. of the Morro there is a remarkable isolated hill 732 feet high, with two round hummocks, called the Tetas de Managua or Managua paps. This hill is not only an excellent guide for Havana when coming from the northward, but useful also as a point of departure.

The channel for about half a mile is not more than 200 yards wide; farther in it widens, opening into a basin of irregular shape, $2\frac{1}{4}$ miles long and from a half to 1 mile wide.

Morro point is steep-to and vessels of large draught may pass close to it. Soundings extend off from the point half a mile. The northern shore of the channel is bordered by the Cabrestante bank, which, at the outer part, extends off more than 100 yards.

Both sides of the channel are marked by buoys, which are, however, frequently out of place. All the buoys can be used in good weather for warping except that planted on the Apostles' shoal on the N. edge of the channel. Men-of-war can generally, by applying to the captain of the port, obtain a mooring buoy to lie at. There is a line of buoys for this purpose laid down, extending from the Maguina landing to the dock-yard in the southern part of the harbor.

Within the harbor the western shore is bold and vessels lie alongside the wharves. The arsenal is in the SW. angle of the harbor.

The population is about 205,000, being the largest and most important city on the island. It is strongly fortified, there being several forts and castles. The streets are narrow and dirty, there being no sewerage. Yellow fever is endemic. The sickly season is from June to October. The average temperature in summer is 87°, in winter 85°. As there is little ebb and flow of the tide in the harbor the water is filthy and foul-smelling. As a sanitary precaution, it is advisable to anchor as far from the southern light of the harbor as possible. The water should not be used for washing decks or clothing.

Hospitals are: Military, leprous, charity, lying-in; also insane asylum. Police are efficient and numerous.

Provisions of all kinds can be obtained in abundance. Water can be had from water-boats which come alongside; it is poor in quality, especially after the rainy season. An aqueduct from the ruins supplies the city, cost 1¼ cents per gallon.

Docks.—At the naval arsenal are ways capable of taking up vessels not over 500 tons. In the NE. part of the harbor is an iron dock, open ended, 302 feet long, 80 feet wide, capable of taking a vessel of 3,000 tons, 20 feet draught; charges, 75 cents per register ton first day, 25 cents per ton for any succeeding day.

There are several machine shops where steamers may repair.

The usual supply of coal on hand is about 90,000 tons; cost, $8.50 to $10 per ton. Vessels can coal alongside the coal dock.

There is telegraphic communication with all parts of the world. There are many steamer lines to the United States and Europe.

A railroad runs to the principal places on the island.

The authorities are: Captain-general, comandante de la marina, a vice-admiral, captain of the port (naval officer).

Salutes will be returned.

The United States is represented by a consul-general and a vice consul-general.

Imports.—Breadstuffs, provisions, petroleum, coal, cooperage stock.

Exports.—Sugar, molasses, coffee, tobacco, tropical fruits, etc.

	Pilotage.	
	Inward.	Outward.
80 tons	$13.00	$7.00
81 to 100 tons	14.00	8.00
101 to 125 tons	14.50	8.50
126 to 150 tons	15.00	9.00
151 to 175 tons	15.50	9.50
176 to 200 tons	16.00	10.00
For each 50 tons increase, to 500 tons	.50	.50
500 tons and upwards	18.50	12.50

Inward pilotage is compulsory; outward is optional except when a tug-boat is taken, then it is compulsory; custom-house fees, $10 to $15 inward, $25 outward; tug-boat, as per agreement, $10 to $45; harbor tonnage, $10 to $20; interpreters' fees, $4; ballast, discharging, 50 cents per ton. Commission, for collecting freights, 2½ per cent.; on delinquents, 2½ per cent.; on procuring freight, 5 per cent.

Vessels bound to Europe pay lighterage; bound to the United States is paid by cargo, cargo to be hoisted by the vessel's crew; labor and board of men $2.50 per day.

Stores of all kinds being imported are from 50 to 75 per cent. higher than in the United States.

Mooring charges.—From 101 to 150 tons, $3; from 151 to 200 tons, $3.25; and 25 cents additional for each 100 tons over 200.

There is no regular ebb and flow of the tide, but with the land breeze a slight current usually runs out.

Vessels bound to Havana from the westward, having rounded Cape San Antonio, with the usual trade-wind at E., should not steer higher than N. for 15 miles, when they may haul to the wind, and the chart must be their guide along the Colorados. Here, however, the current generally sets to the SW. on the edge of the bank. It will, therefore, be better to stand to the northward, as far, at least, as the parallel of 24°, before tacking.

Gulf Stream.—Nothing is more uncertain than the point where the great Florida stream is first met with. Sometimes it will be found 50 miles to the SW. of the Tortugas islands; the vessels position, by chronometer, should therefore be ascertained as frequently as possible. Under any circumstances, it will be better to avoid the Cuba shore until the vessel is well to the eastward, when it may be necessary to sight the high lands in order to check the reckoning. In approaching the Cuba shore the easterly stream will seldom be met with until nearly on the meridian of Havana, or on the line between there and the Tortugas. It generally runs at the rate of from 2 to 3 knots close off the mouth of the harbor, and from thence in a NE. direction right across the Florida strait.

It frequently happens that having arrived at a position S. of the Tortugas without feeling the influence of the stream, it is perhaps entered soon after the reckoning has been checked in the evening, and in making the land on the following morning the vessel will be found far to windward of the port. The features of the land to eastward, however, differ so considerably from those to the westward that there will be no difficulty in making out the position. The land eastward of the Morro is about 200 feet high and rather flat, but about 18 miles to windward it rises into a remarkable ridge of irregular hills of moderate height, about 3 miles in length E. and W. and a short distance from the shore, called the Jaruco or Iron hills.

The Pan de Matanzas can be seen from a distance of 36 to 40 miles. When seen from the NW. its summit forms three hummocks, the center one being much the highest, rising from behind a flat rocky ridge of land of moderate elevation. From the NE. it appears as a prominent rounded mountain standing out by itself, and becomes a valuable point of departure. Should the vessel be found in a position thus far to windward, or less, it will be better to stand in and run down within about 2 miles of the shore to avoid the current, taking care, however, to steer clear of the Jaruco bank, on which there are only 11 feet of water, and which lies about 1½ miles from the shore, midway between

Havana and Guanos point, off the Iron hills. The discolored water on this bank, which is of some extent, may be seen from aloft in clear weather, and soundings appear to extend for a short distance all along the shore.

Several small streams empty into the sea between Havana and Guanas point, among which are the rivers Bacanagua, Puerto, Escondido, Canasi, Jibacoa, Santa Cruz, Jaruco, Bacuranao, Guanabo, and Cojimar. Generally speaking, these rivers, excepting the Jaruco, can not be entered even by boats. The mouth of the Jaruco river is open to the N. and only admits very small coasters.

The river Cojimar, empties into the cove of the same name about 3 miles E. of the Morro Castle. This cove is clear of danger and the shores are steep to. The water, except very close in shore, is too deep for vessels to anchor. At this place English troops landed in 1763 to attack Havana.

Telegraph cable.—The end of one of the cables connecting Havana and Key West is landed here.

The coast is generally clear of danger except the bank of Jaruco, on which are only 11 feet of water.

Maya point is low, with a few huts on it. These huts mark the point when abeam, otherwise it can not be distinguished from the surrounding country. From this point a rocky ledge extends northward about 1 mile, and on a narrow bank of soundings W. of this ledge temporary anchorage will be found in 7 to 15 fathoms water. The land on the western side of the entrance is bold and steep-to. S. of Sabanilla the western shore of the bay is bordered by a 2-fathom bank extending off nearly one-fourth of a mile.

Matanzas, the second in point of commercial importance in the island of Cuba, is situated at the head of the bay. Population, 36,000. The town is triangular in shape, the apex being at the water front. The land rises from the water to quite high ground in the rear of the city. On the summit of the ridge to the northward stands the church of Mont Serrat, overlooking the famous valley of the Yumuri. This, surrounded by trees and facing the harbor, forms a conspicuous land-mark. There are several suburbs to the city proper. The only other prominent marks along the western shore of the bay are fort or castle Severino, barracks, and hospital. The bridges and warehouses mark the two rivers running through the town, San Juan being the one to the southward. The celebrated caves of Bellamar are under a low ridge, the highest point of which is Penas Altas. The railroad connecting Matanzas and Havana runs along the above-mentioned ridge. The depot is in Pueblo Nuevo. It is built of red brick with French roof. It is just to the southward of the large sugar factory situated on the southern bank of the San Juan river at its mouth.

Boats can either run into the San Juan river or alongside the dock, which runs to the northward from its mouth to the captain of the port's office. The market is one-half a mile up the San Juan river, convenient to boat landings.

Water for ship's use can be obtained up this same river. It is also brought off in a water boat at 1 cent per gallon. It is strongly impregnated with lime.

Coal may be procured in moderate quantities from $9 to $10 per ton.

Freight is towed off to vessels in lighters.

Port charges are about the same as Havana.

Hospitals.—There are three—government, private, and woman's. The government is the largest; it has an efficient staff; sick mariners are admitted at a stipulated price. The woman's hospital is for women exclusively. The private hospital is supported by the best and wealthiest people in the city, and is for their own sick; patrons pay $5 per day.

Imports.—Provisions, coal, petroleum, and cooperage stock.

Exports.—Sugar, molasses, honey, etc.

Steamers.—Ward's line of steamers from New York frequently stop here, also tramps for sugar cargoes.

There is telegraphic communication with Havana and a mail daily from Havana by railroad.

Salutes can be returned.

Pilots are not necessary, but can be obtained.

The United States is represented by a consul and vice-consul.

The longitude as given on the charts at present is thought to be about 2' too far W. The shoals are supposed to be buoyed, but the buoys cannot be depended upon. The shoals, however, as laid down on the chart can easily be avoided by a careful lookout and following the soundings as given in U. S. Hydrographic Office charts. The bottom is stiff clay. But little difficulty will be experienced in picking out an anchorage, except in the sugar season, when the harbor may be more or less crowded; anchorage may be found in 10 fathoms outside of the reefs to the northward of Baja Nuevo, the spot generally occupied by merchant steamers. It will be smoother, however, and more convenient to anchor inside Laja bank, and as the latter is plainly visible at all times for its entire length, no trouble will be experienced in rounding either end, even if the buoys should be out of place.

The river Canimar is in the SE. part of the bay. On the western point of its entrance is the battery and town of San Felipe. The river is navigable for 9 miles from its mouth, having a depth of from 6 to 15 feet. On the bar at the entrance there are only from 6 to 9 feet, and a heavy sea breaks there during northers.

A large number of small vessels load with fruit in this river for Havana and Matanzas.

The rivers Yumuri and San Juan also empty into the bay, flowing through the city of Matanzas, and by the deposits of the sand and mud which their waters bring down, form shoals and banks, which narrow the limit and depth of the anchorage.

A shallow mud-flat runs off in front of the city, preventing vessels from coming nearer to the wharf than one-half a mile.

Winds.—The sea-breeze is regular, but it is sometimes interrupted for a day or two by a fresh southwesterly breeze that finally hauls to the NW. and dies away to be followed by the regular sea-breeze. As the bay is open to the ENE. a heavy swell sets in with fresh trade-winds. The northers which frequently blow from September to February interrupt the land-breezes, and the departure of a sailing vessel may be hindered on this account.

In approaching Matanzas from the eastward give Maya point a berth of 1¼ miles, steering between W. and S. 67° 30′ W. till the bay is well open, then haul up S. 45° W., taking care to avoid the bank of sand and stones having 2¾ fathoms of water on its edge and which extends nearly 1 mile to the NW.

Icacos or Ycacos Point is the northern extremity of the long and narrow peninsula which shelters Cardenas bay to the northward. The point is low and has a few huts upon it. The shore from Maya point to this point is steep-to and may be approached within 1 mile, but is low, sandy, and covered with brush-wood, the beaches being here and there interrupted by low bluffs.

Eight miles west of Icacos point is a small cove called Varadero bay. Four miles farther to the WSW. is the point and landing of Camacho, low and sandy. Five and one-half miles eastward of Maya point is the mouth of the river Camaricoa, on the left bank of which is the town of the same name.

The coast is steep-to and clear of danger, the bank of soundings extending only one-half mile off-shore.

Cárdenas bay is bounded on the N. side by a very narrow strip of low, sandy, wooded land, which terminates to the eastward of Icacos point; the entrance to this bay is so blocked up by small cays and shoals that it is only navigable for vessels of from 11 to 14 feet, according to different authorities, to the anchorages of Cárdenas and Signapa.

The best channel for entering this bay is that between Buba or Mangle cay and Diana cay. The bottom in the channel between Chalupa cay and Diana cay is very irregular, and in the center of the passage are some rocks, over which there is a depth of 8 feet. This channel is only frequented by small vessels. Even the most recent charts of this locality are not to be strictly depended upon. It is reported by the local authorities and captains of vessels visiting Cárdenas that 15 feet can be carried into the anchorage off the city at high water. The reefs are said to be growing in ridges to the northward and eastward. In 1881 a channel was projected and buoyed by private enterprise. The buoys are spars with anchors at the heel, painted black on the W. side of the channel and red on the E. side, but are so time-worn as to be hardly distinguishable.

The town of Cárdenas stands on the swampy shore at the SW. side of the bay, and is a place of considerable commerce, and communicates by means of a railroad with Havana and Matanzas. The town of Siguapa is westward of Cárdenas and they contain together some 11,000 inhabitants.

Supplies.—There is about 1,500 tons of coal on hand; cost $11 to $12 per ton, United States gold, and $1.80 per day for laborers. The coaling is slow, about 40 tons per day. There is only a moderate supply of provisions on hand and the prices are high. Water can be obtained from San Autin river.

Sanitary condition is good, streets are well laid out, broad and clean. The city is lighted by gas.

Imports are breadstuffs, provisions, coal, cooperage stock.

Exports.—Sugar, molasses, coffee, rum.

Steamers.—One line small steamers inside the cays weekly to Caibarien, also a line from Havana every ten days to Caibarien, stopping at Cárdenas each way.

There is telegraphic communication with all parts of the world. The government reserves the right to demand a translation of all messages.

Pilots are not necessary unless going up to the city, when they are necessary.

There is one machine shop where repairs to machinery and iron vessels can be made.

The authorities to visit are the governor and captain of the port, who is a Spanish naval officer.

The United States is represented by a consular agent and vice-consular agent.

From Icacos point as far E. as Maternillos point, a distance of about 250 miles, the coast is bordered with low mangrove cays and reefs to the distance in some places of 20 miles from the mainland. The greater part to the westward of Paredon point is but imperfectly represented on present charts, and being studded with dangers steep-to, should be most cautiously approached.

From the mouth of the Rio Juearo the coast runs in an easterly direction for 25 miles, its outline is broken, the land is apparently low and swampy. There are a vast number of cays extending from 11 to 17 miles off this part of the coast. They form the southern edge of the Nicolas channel along here and inclose the bay of Santa Clara, which affords good anchorage for small craft, and is reached by a number of narrow, intricate, shallow channels between the cays.

Bahia de Cadiz cay is small and low, with some fishermen's huts and a flag staff on its NE. point. To the westward is an anchorage sheltered from the usual NE. winds, but exposed to northerly winds. In hauling around the W. end of the cay vessels drawing not more than 15 feet may bring the Tetas de la Bella to bear S. or S. 5° 37' E., and steer for them till the center of Bahia de Cadiz cay bears N. 84° 22'

E., or N. 78° 45′ E., when the anchor may be let go in 4 fathoms of water, sandy bottom. Vessels drawing more than 15 feet should bring the same peaks to bear S. 16° 52′ E., till the center of the cay bears E., then anchor in 5 fathoms. In standing in the depths will be 4, 4½, and 5 fathoms, with a dark-colored bottom, it being sand covered with weeds.

Supplies.—Wood and fish are easily procurable, but there is no water to be had.

This part of the coast is little known and inaccurately laid down on the charts.

The following land-marks will be found useful in determining the ship's position: About 21 miles inland from the Nicolao reef and the Medina islet are the Sierras Morenas, extending NW. and SE. for a considerable distance and having several prominent peaks.

A little to the westward of the Sierra Morena is a chain of mountains presenting three peaks, called the La Bella paps, the central one being the highest and bearing S. 22° 30′ W. from the Nicolao reef. This peak bears directly S. from Bahia de Cadiz cay, consequently when it is on that bearing a vessel will be to the westward of the Alcatraces and Nicalao reefs. S. 14° 04′ W., 6½ miles from Nicolao reef, is the eastern extremity of the Alcatraces cays, and 9 miles S. 42° 11′ W. of the Medano, the western extremity. Between these cays and a chain named Falcones is the Boca de Alcatraces, where vessels of 9 feet draught will find shelter from all winds.

From Verde cay a chain of rocky heads, bordering the cays, extends as far as the western point of the Bocadde, Sagua la Grande. On this reef the sea breaks constantly.

The entrance of the river Sauga la Grande has several channels of approach.

The Boca de Marvillas or Marillanes is the best and deepest entrance to the harbor of Sagua la Grande, being capable of admitting vessels drawing 16½ feet.

At the eastern end of Christo cay are some huts occupied by pilots, and near them a flag-staff, from which is displayed a blue flag, on which is the letter P in white.

In approaching the harbor of Sagua la Grande all vessels of more than 8½ feet draught should take the Boca de Marillanes. To do this, if intending to take a pilot, bring the pilot-station on Cay Cristo to bear about from one-half a mile to 1 mile distant, and heave to till his arrival.

The buoys are liable to be washed away and cannot be implicitly depended upon.

The land is low all around the harbor, affording no leading marks, but with attention to the soundings and the aid of the chart there need be no difficulty.

The harbor of Sagua la Grande is of very irregular shape. The land surrounding it is so low that but little shelter from the wind is found, and in threatening weather, particularly during the months of September and October, precautions should be taken against dragging or parting.

The population is 17,000, the city being about 14 miles from the river mouth, having communication with the harbor by river boats and a railroad. Vessels quarantined are sent to Carahattas a mile along shore away from the fleet.

There are two tug-boats in the harbor.

Pilotage.—In and out, vessel of 250 tons, $32; of 400 tons, $42. To and from wharf, vessels of 250 tons, $10.66; 400 tons, $14. Vessels of smaller or larger class pay in proportion. Interpreter, $4. Ballast master, $2 per day. Discharging ballast, $1 per ton. Labor, $3 per day. Lighterage from 75 cents to $1 per hogshead. Rate of entry, $4.25. Clearance, $8.50. Wharfage, 1¼ cents per ton per day. Bill of health, $2.50. Stevedore, $5 per day. Stamp paper and registry, $9.50.

Coal can be obtained here.

Imports.—Coal, provisions, ice, lumber, cooperage, and manufactured goods.

Exports.—Sugar and molasses.

The United States is represented by a consular agent and vice-consular agent.

For entering the anchorage the eye and the chart are the best guides in the absence of a pilot, who may be obtained generally without difficulty.

La Vela cay.—There is an anchorage S. 45° W. of this cay for vessels of 10 feet draught, sheltered from E. and NE. winds, but open to the NW. To reach it haul round the western end of La Vela cay, anchor as convenient.

The Boca de Lanzanillo is a channel between the cay of the same name and Carenero cay one-half a mile wide and 1¾ fathoms deep, and leading to Lanzanillo anchorage, of which Lieut. Don Rafael de Aragon, commanding the Spanish steamship *Don Juan de Austria*, gives the following description:

This anchorage is a commodious and secure harbor for vessels drawing less than 11 feet. It lies between Lanzanillo and Carenero cays, and is completely land-locked by them and other cays adjacent, so as to be sheltered from all winds. It is clear of hidden dangers, and has a depth of 11 feet of water, with excellent muddy holding-ground. Lying between Caibarien and Sagua la Grande, its shelter may be reached when there is not time to reach either of these other ports. The channel leading to it, between Lanzanillo and Carenero cays, is bordered with reefs on either side and has also a hidden shoal in its center, dividing the channel in two, of which the leeward or western one is preferable, being the deeper. Although this channel is short, it is somewhat difficult, as the reefs on the sides as well as the shoal in the center can seldom be seen. A beacon has therefore been planted in 9 feet of water at low tide on the most salient part of the reef, on the western side of the lee or western channel.

In approaching this anchorage from the offing, steer for a fisherman's hut, of white color and easily seen, situated on the beach of Lanzanillo cay. Leave La Vela cay on the port hand, skirting the bank extending off its western end. When the channel is well open the beacon will be seen, and should be passed close-to, leaving it on the starboard hand. In this way the shoal in the center of the channel will be avoided.

After passing the beacon, Carenero cay and reef should be carefully rounded, anchoring under their shelter as convenient in 11 feet of water muddy bottom.

Cay Frances is of regular height. On its northern shore, which is clear of danger, are three small round hills; two of them close together and the third somewhat apart. These are called the Tetas de la Vinda. To the SW. on the Cuban shore the paps of Buena Vista and Mount Guajabana will also be seen.

Cay Frances anchorage is, however, only a narrow vein of deeper water about one-third of a mile wide and running E. and W. In standing in keep the paps of Buena Vista well open to the westward of Herradura cays and Cay Cobos (lying S. of Cay Frances) till the SW. end of Cay Frances bears S. 78° 45′ E. Then haul round the sand-bank and anchor with the flag-staff bearing N. and a small white cliff on the W. side of the cay bearing N. 78° 45′ E.

In beating in for the anchorage do not stand to the northward into less than 3½ fathoms, as the bank is steep-to. To the southward toward Cobos cay a vessel may safely go into 3 fathoms. Around Cay Frances there is an abundance of excellent oysters.

There are some good wells at the S. end of Cobos cay, and water will be found at the port of Coco cay.

From the mouth of the Rio Sagua la Grande to Caibarien the coast is very much indented and very little known to strangers. The channel leading to it through the numerous outlying cays are intricate, shallow, and almost entirely unknown.

Puerto de Caibarien, on the mainland about 15 miles from Cay Frances, is the port of San Juan de los Remedios, about 5 miles in the interior, the communication being by railroad. The channel to this port lies between Boca Chica, a small flat cay 4 miles S. 56° 15′ W. of the western part of Cay Frances and the W. end of Cobos cay. Vessels drawing under 9 feet can anchor off the town of Caibarien, but those of heavier draught load at Cay Frances.

Pilotage.—Tariff of pilotage free outside the banks and obligatory among them for foreign vessels not assimilated, approved by His Majesty the King in the royal decree of March 24, 1881.

Inwards or outwards.

Under 80 tons	$9.00
From 81 to 120 tons	11.50
From 121 to 150 tons	14.60
From 151 to 175 tons	16.50
From 176 to 200 tons	19.00

From 201 to 300 tons	$23.50
From 301 to 500 tons	28.50
From 501 to 1,000 tons	32.25
Over 1,000 tons	38.50

Tariff of pilotage free outside the banks and obligatory among them for Spanish and foreign vessels assimilated.

Under 80 tons	$7.00
From 81 to 120 tons	9.00
From 121 to 150 tons	11.00
From 151 to 175 tons	13.00
From 176 to 200 tons	15.00
From 201 to 300 tons	19.00
From 301 to 500 tons	23.00
From 501 to 1,000 tons	26.00
Over 1,000 tons	31.00

NOTICES.

(1) According to the orders in force, the vessels not obliged to take pilot are those registering less than 80 tons and those employed exclusively in coasting trade, whatever be their tonnage, as well as those foreign vessels which by international treaty are assimilated in this case to the Spanish ones.

(2) The steamships that come in or go out the port employing their engines, excepting those employed in foreign trade of more than 500 horse-power, will pay for pilotage, when they use it, one-third less than is established in the respective tariff, according to their tonnage and flag; it is understood that said deduction is to be made from the net amount remaining after discounting the amount for the pilot's boat.

(3) The sum established in the tariff is for pilotage inwards or outwards.

(4) Vessels that change place in the wharves for loading or unloading, or those that remove from one place to another between Key Frances and Caibarien, will pay the fourth of the pilotage marked out in the tariff for coming in, according to tonnage and flag.

(5) Vessels for moving to any other anchoring place on the coast inside Key Frances will pay two-thirds of the corresponding pilotage, according to their tonnage and flag.

(6) The pilotage fixed for coming in or going out is the same whether the vessel remains in Key Frances or proceeds to Caibarien.

(7) Pilotage will be calculated upon the total tonnage of the vessel.

(8) Vessels coming in or going out during the night will pay one-third more than is fixed in the tariff.

(9) If a vessel takes on board a pilot during the night and does not employ him until day, she will pay for his sojourn on board $4.

The city contains about 4,000 inhabitants, and San Juan de las Remedios about 13,000.

Imports.—Coal, machinery, cooperage stock.

Exports.—Sugar and molasses.

Water costs 2 cents per gallon.

Of the coast from Caibarien to Boca de Caravelos very little is known, but apparently it is low and sandy, backed by numerous lagoons and swamps. At a distance of 15 miles off shore is a string of rather large cays, separated from the Cuban coast by an immense shallow lagoon with here and there a group of small cays. Outside of the large cays and bordering on Old Bahama channel, a dangerous reef extends the entire distance from Cay Frances to Boca de Caravela.

The whole of this vicinity is very imperfectly laid down on the present charts, and urgently needs resurveying. It is consequently dangerous to approach, and only affords anchorage and shelter to coasters of light draught, the masters of which have an intimate knowledge of the localities. Immediately adjacent to and to the eastward of Cay Frances are several cays of moderate size, the principal ones being Cay Cobos and Santa Maria.

Media Luna cay is flat and bordered with reefs on its southern and western sides. N. 78° 45′ W. from the cay, and lying on the edge of the bank of soundings, are two shoals. S. of these shoals and of San Felipe, Media Luna, and Santa Maria cays, there is a channel from Port Coco to the anchorage of Cay Frances for vessels drawing not more than 9 feet.

S. of Guillermo cay, and extending from the W. end of Cay Coco, is a group of 13 cays laid down on the charts, the names of which are not given. From Cay Coco they curve around to the S. and W., the curve being open to the eastward.

Coco cay is low. On the northern part are several sandy places. The southern part is covered with mangroves.

Paredon Grande cay is rocky, wooded, and about 40 feet high.

Between Cay Confites and Paredon del Medion there is no anchorage as the space is full of shoals not sufficiently large to afford shelter. The bank should not be entered upon without some specific purpose.

Caiman cay is somewhat higher than the cays near it.

The edge of the bank between the Tributarios de Minerva and Confites shows itself distinctly just within the line of soundings, which is very steep-to. This part is extremely dangerous, and should be approached very cautiously, as there is no safe anchorage whatever.

Cay Confites is a low cay, and lies close on the edge of soundings. On its S. end there is a pile of stones, and near the N. end a solitary tree, which is the first object seen when coming from the SE. Off the N. end a dry reef extends to the distance of 1 mile, leaving a small channel 12 feet deep between it and the cay. A dry reef also extends from the S. end.

Between this latter dry reef and the reef running off to the northward of Cay Verde there is a clear channel carrying a depth of 5 fathoms, and leading into anchorage under Cay Confites in from 2 to 4 fathoms of white sand. The best sheltered berth is with the cay bearing N. 45° E. about a mile off, or nearer, according to the vessel's draught. It should be observed, however, that with the wind to the southward of E. a heavy roll of the sea sets in round the S. end of the cay. This is the only anchorage on this side of the Bahama channel, between Nuevitas and Paredon Grande cay, where a vessel drawing more than 12 feet can ride out a norther in safety.

In passing through the channel between Cay Verde and Cay Confites keep a little closer to the latter than the former. When the middle of Confites cay bears N. 45° W., and Cay Verde S. 11° 15′ W., a vessel will be on the edge of the bank of soundings, or nearly so. Then steer N. 68° W. till the S. end of Cay Confites bears N.; thence the course is about N. 22° 30′ W. till the southern end of Confites cay bears N. 45° E., where the anchor may be let go in 3 to 4 fathoms of water, sandy bottom.

In quitting this anchorage, if the wind does not permit a vessel to leave by the SE. channel, steer to the NW. until clear of the reef extending from the N. end of the cay.

Cay Verde is a small, low islet, of a circular form, and 200 yards in diameter, covered with bushes to the height of 10 feet above high water, and inside the reef, N. 11° 15′ E. of the river Guajaba, there is an opening through which 10 feet of water may be carried, and one-half a mile SW. of Cay Verde there is shelter for vessels of this draught against northers. The best channel to take is that round the N. end of the reef, about 1½ miles from the cay; but it requires good local knowledge of the place to enable a vessel to thread her way safely through the shoals.

The reef continues from Cay Verde to the southward and eastward within a distance of from 1 to 2 miles off the islands. Between Cay Verde and Boca de Caravela there are several breaks which afford anchorage for small vessels of not more than 7 feet draught.

The only good water to be obtained at any of these cays is from a few springs or wells. In some places by digging in the sand it may be found, but is generally brackish.

The tidal streams set right on and off the bank at the rate of about one-half a knot an hour, but in the openings between the cays they run from 2 to 3 knots. Between the cays and the main the rise and fall is not more than 1 foot, and the stream is scarcely perceptible.

Romano cay is inside the chain of cays and reefs just described, and separated from the Cuban shore by a sort of shallow lagoon. It is mostly covered with a mangrove swamp and divided in two by a narrow inlet.

On the eastern end of Romano cay is a remarkable hill. At the foot of this hill, called the Silla de Romano, on the beach will be seen two fishing stations.

There is a smaller hill 16 miles to the NW., and only 100 feet high, called the Alto de Asi. Another similar hill, near the NW. extremity of the cay, is called Juan Saez.

The bottom between Cay Romano and the Cuban shore is of olive colored mud covered with weeds.

Cay Romano harbor.—In the northern part of the cay is the harbor of the same name, sheltered from NE. to E. by Jaula cay and a small reef uniting it to Coco cay. This anchorage is entirely exposed to northers, and is only fit for coasters.

Guajaba island.—From Boca Guajaba the NE. side of the island trends nearly SE. for 10 miles to Boca Caravela. For the first 6 miles there is a sandy beach; the remainder is a low mangrove shore. The reef along here is about 1¼ miles off shore. On this island are two small hills. The SE. hill is about a mile in extent NW. and SE., and 90 feet high; the other is a smaller round lump and a little less elevated. When first seen from the eastward they have the appearance of four small hummocks, and serve as guides to this part of the coast.

The Boca de Caravelos is a narrow opening between Cay Sabinal and Guajaba island. There is a depth of 1 fathom on its bar, and about the same depth may be carried through a crooked channel between the mangrove cays as far as the town and river of Guanaja, 22 miles to the westward. This village is on the great bay of the same name, bounded by the coast of Cuba and the cays of Guajaba and Romano.

At the entrance of the Boca de Caravelos the tide runs at the rate of 3 knots.

Cay Sabinal.—The shore is very low and sandy, backed by numerous lagoons and swamps, and skirted by a broken reef 1 to 1½ miles, with soundings about one-third of a mile outside of it.

Between this reef and the coast there are anchorages for vessels whose draught does not exceed 9 feet, such as Tortuguilla, Cruces, and Caravelas, where there is shelter from the ordinary winds, but not from the northward. These anchorages are entered through the openings in the reef which are shown by the sea breaking, and a vessel may steer in by the lead and eye and anchor, when sheltered as convenient.

The only remarkable object on this coast is a large clump of mangrove trees about 10 miles to the westward of Maternillos point called the Alto de Juan Danue. Very near it is a small cay 30 feet high.

Maternillos point is 4½ miles from the entrance to Port Nuevitas. The coast between is low, but free of danger.

Nuevitas is the port of the city of Principe, 25 miles inland, the two places being connected by a railway. The land is low and swampy for a considerable distance inland. The entrance of the harbor may be recognized by the Maternillo light-house, by three small hills on the S. side of the harbor, and by three islets in the harbor called Los Ballenatos, a little higher than the surrounding land. Also on the E. side of the entrance is a quadrangular building, painted yellow, surmounted by a white mast, from which is shown a light.

The harbor is large, completely sheltered, and capable of admitting vessels of the largest draught. The entrance is through a crooked narrow channel, nearly 6 miles long, so that the assistance of a pilot is desirable, although there are no hidden dangers. The outer points of the entrance are low and about half a mile apart. In entering without a pilot the eye and chart are the best guides. Care must be taken to avoid a dry sand-spit near the end of the eastern reef, and bearing N. 56° 15' E. 1 mile from the flag-staff on the point.

If it is only desired to communicate with the town, anchorage will be found off the fort about 1¼ miles within the entrance. The town of San Fernando de Nuevitas is nearly 11 miles from the entrance, on the point of a peninsula which separates the southern part of the harbor from Marinavo bay.

At the entrance of the port the tidal stream is said to have a strength of 3 miles an hour, but inside the tides are felt but slightly.

The population is about 2,200. The health of the city is good, the sickly season being from April to September. Only a small stock of provisions is kept on hand; prices are high. Rain-water can be had from a large cistern, also from a small stream on the west side of the harbor, but it is difficult to get to the boats on account of the bar at the mouth of the stream.

Trade is mostly with the United States.

Imports.—Provisions, machinery, lumber.

Exports.—Sugar, molasses, tobacco, honey, and woods of the island.

Steamers.—Compania Transatlantica (Spanish) from Havana to Santander, monthly, touch here. Lines Campo (Spanish) from Havana to St. Thomas, tri-monthly, touch here each way. Herreras West Indian line, from Havana to St. Thomas, monthly. Telegraph lines to Havana via Puerto Principe. Postal by steamer to Havana. Authorities to visit, comandant de la marina (captain of the port).

The United States is represented by a consular agent.

Nuevas Grandes is merely a small, tortuous inlet, in some parts only 100 yards wide, and only navigable for vessels under 12 feet draught. All this part of the coast is bordered by a reef, and should not be approached nearer than 2½ miles.

Puerto de Manati has a depth of 4½ to 5½ fathoms. It is merely a long, narrow, crooked channel, bordered by shoal banks on both sides, and leading into a shallow lagoon surrounded by low marshy land. The place is only fit for small coasters. On its western side is a conical hill called el Mañusco, and a little beyond it another, not quite so high, called the Pardo or Mesa de Manati. These elevations may be seen 15 or 20 miles and are good guides for the offing; when seen nearly in a line they somewhat resemble the Saddle of Gibara, and if mistaken for it the error might lead to accidents. All this part of the shore is foul, the reef extending off about two-thirds of a mile from the entrance of the inlet, through which a channel is formed leading to the port.

At Piedra point there is a small opening leading into the bay or port of Malagueta, an extensive unnavigable lagoon. The land around is low and swampy.

All this coast is skirted by a reef to the distance of about 2 miles.

Port Padre is a secure and capacious basin, with a depth of at least 4 fathoms in the greater part of it. The western side of this bay is steep-to. To enter the port it is only necessary to keep well off the reef which terminates off Point Jarro, and when this point bears about S. 45° E., stand into the bay, keeping near the western shore. Steer in mid-channel; with the aid of the chart no difficulty will be found, as there are no hidden dangers. There is a village on the western side of the entrance.

The harbor is nearly divided in two parts. The easternmost anchorage will be found the most convenient for leaving with a sailing-vessel. The channel leading to it is between the two islands just inside the entrance.

The shores of the harbor are low and swampy.

Gibara is merely a small bay open to the northward, having a depth of 3¼ fathoms just inside the points of the entrance.

Three small hills to the southward of the port, and which from the offing resemble islands, serve as landmarks for this vicinity. The easternmost of these is called the Saddle of Gibara, the middle one is shaped like a sugar-loaf, and the westernmost is called Mount Candelaria. The town is on the W. side of the bay, and can be seen at a distance of 9 miles.

To enter the harbor it is only necessary to bring the entrance well open and steer in half way between the points of entrance.

There is said to be a bank near the middle of the bay called the Casco de San Vicente, but no definite information can be given as to its exact location or depth of water. It may, however, be avoided by keeping the eastern shore aboard. Although there is no shelter from northerly winds and the harbor is only fit for small vessels, it is the port of Holguin, a large town about 15 miles inland in a highly productive part of the country.

The river Gibara, navigable for a short distance by boats, empties into the head of the bay. Coast pilots for the N. coast of Cuba and the old Bahama channel may be obtained here.

The United States is represented by a consular agent.

Puerto de Jururu is completely sheltered, with a depth of 4 fathoms. The entrance is narrow and somewhat crooked, but can be easily navigated by a steamer of moderate length by the aid of the chart.

Port Bariay is open to the northward, and, therefore, not safe in the winter months, but there is good temporary anchorage close under the weather shore of the second sandy beach from the entrance. Farther in the channel is partially obstructed by a shoal on which there is as little as 6 feet of water.

Port Vita is a small irregularly shaped inlet, easily entered and left by vessels of not more than 18 feet, with the aid of the chart. This part of the coast is low, sandy, and steep-to, with no hidden dangers.

Port Naranjo is a basin of irregular shape, having depth and capacity enough for vessels of any size, which are sheltered entirely from wind and sea, and can be entered or left by sailing vessels with the usual trade-winds.

Care must be taken to avoid the bank which also borders the western shore, and which extends nearly 400 yards northward from the outer point. Having steered through the entrance by the eye, a good berth will be found in 9 fathoms of water, off a small sandy cove one-half a mile inside of the outer points. If it is desired to proceed farther in, it can be done with safety, as there are believed to be no hidden dangers, and the water shoals gradually towards the head of the harbor.

Wood and water may be obtained here. A road leads from this harbor to Holguin, a town of considerable importance 50 miles inland.

Port Sama is a small inlet only fit for vessels drawing not more than 11 feet of water. The entrance may be readily found by the Pan de Sama, which rises S. of it. To the westward of the port there is also the table-land, or flat-topped ridge of mountains running NW. and SE. Its W. end is bold, scarped, and of a whitish appearance.

Port Banes is open to the eastward, and is situated at the head of a bay lying between Point Canones on the N. and Point Palmas on the S., 2 miles apart. The shores of the bay gradually approach toward the entrance, which is only 300 yards wide. The chart will give a better idea of it than any description. The anchorage is fit for vessels of any description, but it is difficult for a sailing vessel to leave. A vessel depending on the land breeze must be well off shore before it fails, as otherwise she will be becalmed with the swell and current setting directly on a dangerous lee shore.

Port Nipe is quite secure against all winds, and will admit vessels of the largest draught without difficulty. All that is necessary in entering is to keep in mid-channel. After passing the inner points of the entrance keep the northern shore aboard for about 1 mile till within Mangle point, from which a shoal extends to the N. 22° 30′ E. three-fourths of a mile, when anchor as most convenient, in 6 or 7 fathoms water.

It is perfectly easy to enter with the prevailing wind, but more difficult for a sailing-vessel to leave, as she must wait for the land wind, which is sometimes interrupted for some days at a time.

The land in this neighborhood is remarkable. At about 10 miles inland the Sierras del Christal, a continuation of the Baracoa chain, rise to a great height. To the NW. of Port Nipe there is also a lofty ridge of mountains, rising from the shore at Mulas point to Pan de Sama, with some long table-land close to the westward and a peaked hill to the E. of it. It can not well be mistaken, and may be seen at a distance of 20 miles. The two ranges are separated by an extensive valley, which also serves as a good guide.

Ports Cabonico and **Livisa** are entered through a narrow deep channel about a cable wide. At about half a mile within the entrance a narrow neck of land divides the interior into two channels, the eastermost leading into Cabonico, the other into Livisa. Both are very crooked and intricate, but have sufficient water for vessels of the largest draught. Most of the dangers are visible, and by referring to the chart the eye will guide in mid-channel.

The locality of the entrance to Ports Cabonico and Livisa may be recognized by the Christal mountains, of which the highest peak is directly S. of the entrance, 13 miles inland.

Port Tanamo is of considerable extent, and studded with small islets, between which are channels deep enough for the largest vessels. The cut through the reef and the channel into the port are, however, both very narrow, but the dangers are easily seen, and the eye will be the best guide.

Port Cebollas is difficult of access and only fit for coasters. The shore is low and sandy, and the reef about half a mile distant.

Port Cananova.—It is a small narrow inlet of similar character, and is entered through an intricate opening in the reef N. of it, which is here only half a mile from the shore.

Yaguaneque harbor is only fit for very small vessels, being small and shallow. Its entrance is through an opening in the reef, narrow and intricate. To enter the harbor, the best way is to coast along the reef from the eastward till abreast of the opening in the reef, which bears three-fourths of a mile N. 45° W. of Arenas cay, then steer to the southward, keeping close to the edge of the eastern reef. The chart will be the best guide.

Port Cayo Moa anchorage is protected on its northern side by a group of small islands, nearly joined, called Cayos de Moa.

The anchorage is about 1 mile long and a half mile wide, and is approached through an opening called the Quebrado de Moa, about 600 yards wide in its narrowest part and having a depth of 21 to 24 fathoms, sandy bottom.

Punta Gorda, a small bluff from which a hill slopes inland, lies S. 22° 30′ E., 2¾ miles from this opening.

N. 56° 15′ W., three-fourths of a mile from Punta Gorda, is a small bluff called Punta Yagrumaje, the coast between them forming a small bay called the Ensenada de Yagrumaje, at the head of which empties the small river of the same name, not navigable even for boats. From Punta Yagrumage to the mouth of the river Moa the coast, partly of sandy beach and partly of mangrove swamp, trends N. 78° 45′ W. for half a mile, then turns sharply to the northward for about the same distance to the Punta del Rio Moa, where there is a fisherman's hut.

The mouth of the river is close to this point, and is 160 yards wide. At high tide the bar at its mouth may be passed by boats, and it is navigable for them for 1 or 2 miles inland.

The river Moa, one of the largest in Cuba, has a fall of more than 300 feet a short distance from the mouth. The entrance is shallow and only 30 yards wide, but the river deepens inside. About 12 miles inland are some mountains called the Sierras de Moa, which are good landmarks. From the mouth of the river to Punta Yaguasey, 1½ miles to the westward, the coast is low and formed by sandy beaches alternating with mangrove swamps, through which the creeks or esteros of Fabrica and Yaguasay empty. Another creek empties at Yaguasey point, which is low, and from which the coast, also low and covered with mangroves, trends S. 67° 30′ W. for 1½ miles to the mouth of the Estero de Moa, where there are three or four fishermen's huts, the remains of a former settlement.

From the Estero de Moa the coast trends N. 50° 37′ W. for 2 miles to Cabañas or Cavagan point, is low and sandy, with a few rocky bluffs, and three-fourths of a mile from Estero de Moa is a spot where good water may be obtained.

The bay between Yaguasey and Cabañas points is called the Ensenada de Moa.

Cayos de Moa are two islets lying just inside the reef, 1 mile westward of the opening. The larger one of the two is 1½ miles long, from one-fourth to one-third of a mile wide, of rectangular shape, and has a projecting point at its SE. angle. The smaller cay lies NW. of the larger, from which it is separated by a narrow creek, is one-fourth of a mile in diameter, and both cays are low and covered with mangroves.

Shoals.—Just within the opening in the reef and on a line between it and the mouth of the river Moa is a bank of sand and rock called the Bajo Grande, about one-fourth of a mile in diameter, from the northern edge of which the southern extreme of Cayo Grande de Moa bears N. 73° 07′ E. In some places on this shoal there are less than 2 fathoms of water. One mile W. of the Bajo Grande and one-half a mile S. of Cayo Grande de Moa is another shoal, of small extent, called the Yaguasey shoal, the least water on which is 9 feet. Another small shoal spot, one-fourth of a mile farther to the northward, called Palancos shoal, is generally marked by a stake.

The eastern or weather reef at the entrance to this anchorage is distinctly marked, even in fine weather, by broken water, and the rocks are rather above water than awash. But on the lee or western side of entrance there is nothing to mark the danger for at least ⅜ of a mile from the eastern reef. The general body of the shoal extending from Cayo Moa is coral covered with dark weed, which, even with 9 feet of water over it, looks deep; but the SE. end of it is white sand and the bottom can be seen. In standing for this anchorage bring the mouth of the Rio de Moa to bear S. 11° 15′ W., on which bearing the opening in the reef will present a fair channel-way and the eastern side of the reef be easily distinguished. Or, coast along the weather reef from the eastward, keeping off about 100 yards, or less, if necessary, as 7 to 9 fathoms will be found 30 yards off.

The course through the opening is S. 11° 15′ W., keeping near the weather side. As soon as the SE. point of Cayo Moa, called Pajaros point, bears N. 81° 34′ W., steer S. 70° 19′ W., leaving the Bajo Grande on the port hand, till the mouth of the Rio Moa bears S. 19° 41′ E., then haul up a little more to the westward and anchor in from 11 to 12 fathoms, muddy bottom, with Pajaros point bearing about N. 28° 07′ W., one-half a mile distant.

At the eastern end of Cayo Moa the flood sets to the SW. about 1 mile an hour and the ebb to the northward.

Cañete bay is between Guarico point and Jaragua point. The shores are entirely exposed to wind and sea and are skirted by a reef which starts from Jaragua point and extends 2 miles seaward. The river Yamaniguey empties at the head of the bay. Cañete and Yamaniguey anchorages are in this bay, fit only for coasters.

Jaragua is a small anchorage where small vessels may lie under shelter of the reef. The break or opening is about 200 feet wide and its edges on both sides are marked by breakers. Just inside the reef, abreast of the opening, are three small islets.

To enter the anchorage, coast along outside of the reef till the eastern point of the southern and largest of these three islets bears S. 50° 37′ E. Then steer for this point and anchor according to the vessel's draught of water.

Abreast of the middle islet there are 5½ fathoms of water, decreasing farther in.

This vicinity should be avoided, and when near it the latitude should be frequently and carefully ascertained, especially at night, as a strong indraught is said to have caused many disasters.

Port Taco.—The anchorage is well sheltered, but limited in extent, the space outside of the 2-fathom line being only one-fourth of a mile in diameter. Although at the anchorage and in places in the channel there are from 6 to 7 fathoms, it should not be attempted, except in case of emergency, by vessels drawing more than 15 feet, as the points of the banks on either side of the entrance project so as to make the turns very short and are not easily seen, although there is at least 19 feet in the channel. To enter the harbor of Taco a pilot should be taken. If one cannot be obtained the chart will give a good idea of how to run in.

Wood, water, and a limited supply of provisions may be obtained.

Port Navas is open to the N., but well sheltered from the prevailing NE. winds. The depth varies from 11 fathoms at the entrance to 5¼ and 4 fathoms inside the harbor. With the assistance of the chart it is perfectly easy to enter and depart from.

At the distance of 1 mile S., 45° E., from the port is the bay of Naguarage, only fit for boats and into which the river of the same name enters.

Bay point is 1 mile farther to the eastward. It is rather low and almost separated from the coast, having on its lee side an inlet fit for boats. This point is often named Vaez, but the pilots and seamen of the coasters call it Bay. All this part of the coast is thickly wooded, and a short distance inshore the land is high.

The coast from Bay point to Baracoa is also backed by high land covered with vegetation to very near the shore. Between Duaba point and Baracoa the mount or hill of Jaitecico rises about 600 yards inland, is about one-half a mile in extent, of little elevation, covered with trees, and is useful in recognizing the port of Baracoa. There are 92 fathoms of water at about one-half a mile from the coast, and 13 to 23 fathoms, sand and rock, 400 yards from it, except off the beaches of Duaba and Toar, where there are 92 fathoms at the distance of three-quarters of a mile, and 14 to 46 fathoms at one-half a mile.

Port Bay lies half a mile to the eastward of Bay point, is small, and only fit for coasters.

Port Cueva is about the same as Port Bay.

Port Aguacate, three-quarters of a mile to the eastward, is only a small inlet capable of admitting very small coasters.

Port Maravi.—Its shores are of soboruco, but on the W. there are three sandy beaches. At the head of the port the land is marshy, with mangroves, and here the river of the same name empties. A bank of sand, gravel, and rock borders the shore, contracting the entrance to about 50 yards, and the anchorage to less than 150 yards in breadth. Therefore, although the water is deep, there being from 9 to 15 fathoms, mud and rock, the port is only fit for small vessels, and in entering the eye will be the best guide. A sailing vessel should leave with the land wind in the morning. This port is, however, exposed to the NE. and not a safe anchorage except under favorable circumstances.

Supplies.—Water may be had from the river, but it is very shallow in the vicinity of its mouth and dry at low tide. Wood and small supplies of provisions may be obtained.

From Puerto de Maravi to Puerto de Baracoa the shore is clear of danger, and is formed partly of soboruco cliffs and partly by a sandy beach. As this part of the coast is directly exposed to the wind and sea, a good berth had better be given it.

Port Ligua is one-half mile eastward of Puerto de Maravi. It can only be used by very small vessels and only in fine weather.

Port Baracoa may be readily found by the Yunque de Baracoa or Anvil 4 miles S. 78° 45′ W. from the entrance, and is a remarkable isolated steep and flat-topped mountain, rising to 1,824 feet; may be seen at a distance of 40 miles. It is partly covered with vegetation, and there are some white and red spots in the break or opening in the rock of which it is composed, visible at some distance. It is a most useful landmark, and its shape, resembling an anvil, prevents its being mistaken for any other mountain.

Its shores are bordered by a sand-bank, which considerably contracts the anchorage. At about 35 yards to the NW. of the inner point

PORT BARACOA—DESCRIPTION AND SUPPLIES—PORT MATA. 125

on the SE. side of the entrance, is an isolated rock called the Buren, which uncovers at low tide; the sea always breaks on it, it is steep-to, and the only danger. It is exposed to the prevailing winds, which throw in a heavy sea. Vessels generally anchor close up to town in 3¾ to 5 fathoms of water, mud, and sand. It can only be left, except in a small vessel, with the land wind; consequently, in the season of the northers, a sailing vessel will be liable to some days' detention. The bottom in general is loose, and during fresh northerly winds the port offers but little shelter.

Winds.—From March to September squalls from S. to SW. are experienced, but the most violent are in July and August. These squalls are of short duration, but a vessel should ride by a fair scope of cable. Remittent fever is at times prevalent at Baracoa, and the place should be avoided during the summer months.

Supplies.—Near the pier at Baracoa the river Macaguanigua runs into the sea, where water may be obtained. Fresh meat is not easily procured. Large quantities of fruit are exported to the Bahamas and United States.

The population is about 5,500. The houses are well built and have fine gardens around them. It is very sickly from April to November. There is a hospital on the hill. Salutes can be returned by a battery of four guns on the point. The port is the center of a large fruit trade.

Steamers.—Lines: Campo (Spanish) line from Havana to St. Thomas call here each way three times a month; Herreras line (Spanish) once a month each way between Havana and St. Thomas.

Telegraph.—There is telegraphic communication to Havana and Santiago.

Postal communication is by steamer.

The authorities to be visited are the military governor (this place being the capital of the district) and the captain of the port.

The United States is represented by a consular agent and vice-consular agent.

Playa de Miel.—To reach the anchorage, being about half a mile W. of point Rama, steer to the southward till the mouth of the river Miel bears about S. 59° E, then anchor in 5 or 6 fathoms of water, with a bottom of black sand, about 400 yards from the rocky coast to the windward and the same distance from the beach. This is the best berth. The anchorage is exposed to northerly winds.

Water may be obtained from the river Miel.

Port Boma.—This harbor is only the mouth of the river of the same name, forming an inlet three-quarters of a mile long and hardly 200 yards wide. The shore at the entrance is of rock, but farther in it becomes a mangrove swamp. The harbor is only fit for coasters seeking temporary anchorage or to load with the products of the neighboring farms. It is open to the northward, and fresh breezes cause a heavy sea to roll in.

Port Mata.—Is only fit, from its limited size and shallow water, for small vessels.

The banks which border the shores leave only a space 300 yards in diameter in the middle of the harbor, having a depth of 15 feet.

The entrance is open to the NE., and in the winter months a heavy swell sets into the entrance.

A bank borders each side of the entrance, and a vessel in entering has only to keep in mid-channel, carrying a depth of 4 to 6 fathoms.

Supplies.—Several small streams of good water empty into the harbor and wood is plenty. Fresh provisions may be obtained from the people in the neighborhood.

Winds and currents.—All this part of the coast, from cape Maysi to Baracoa, is exposed during the winter months to the N. and NE. winds, which prevail at this season. During the summer squalls off the land are experienced. The land winds are regular, and spring up fresh generally at daylight, but do not extend far from the coast.

The direction of the current to a short distance from the land is westward with the flood tide and eastward with the ebb.

Yumuri anchorage is in 11 fathoms of water, with a bottom of sand and mud, just W. of Silencio point. It is open to the northward and full of dangers.

From near the mouth of the river Yumuri a high range of mountains runs along the coast to the eastward, diminishing in height near Baga point, and ending a short distance S. of it.

The river Yumuri runs through a deep ravine in the mountains, emptying into the sea nearly half a mile to the westward of Silencio point.

Bank.—Outside the Maysi reef there is a rocky bank, with about 9 fathoms water on it at the distance of 500 to 700 yards, and at a mile from it there are from 73 to 90 fathoms, sand, gravel, and rock.

Caution.—Vessels from the northward, bound to the southern coast, should be careful to steer sufficiently eastward to clear the reef; and in rounding the cape from the southward, the light should be brought well westward before steering northward.

Currents.—Near the land off cape Maysi the flood runs westward and the ebb eastward. During the summer months, with southerly winds, easterly currents will be experienced, and with northerly winds southerly currents.

CHAPTER VI.

THE WINDWARD CHANNEL AND JAMAICA, WITH THE NEIGHBORING BANKS AND CAYS.

Windward channel.—The northern part is perfectly clear, with no dangers; but the southern part is somewhat obstructed by several banks and cays, among which are the Formigas bank, Navassa island, and Morant cays.

The currents in the channel generally set to the SW., attaining a strength of 1 to 2 knots between Cuba and San Domingo. S. of Cuba and Jamaica the set is more to the westward.

Navassa island is 28 miles from Cape Tiburon. Its surface is nearly level, with steep, sloping sides, terminating all round in bold perpendicular white cliffs about 20 feet high. It is inaccessible, except at the landing platform on the NW. side, which is used for the shipment of guano.

The island is of volcanic origin, composed of limestone, interspersed with veins of sharp, honey-combed rocks of iron pyrites.

The spaces between the rocks are filled up with guano, which in some places is 14 feet deep.

With the exception of the NW. extreme, a prominent bluff, a narrow ridge about 15 feet high above the cliffs and 200 yards broad, extends all around the island. The summit is clothed with stunted palm-trees and cactus, and is inhabited by iguanas and numerous flocks of seabirds.

Formigas bank.—The SW. end is about 39 miles from Morant point light-house, and when on the center the fall in the high land of Jamaica will be seen to the northward of Plantain Garden river. It is steep-to. The body of the bank is rocky. With strong breezes the position of the bank may be recognized by the heavy swell which rolls over it.

Albatross bank lies S. 61° 52′ E. from point Morant, distant 30 miles.

Morant cays are a group of three small islets from 7 to 10 feet high, which, with the adjacent reefs, form a crescent, convex to the southeastward. They are known as Northeast, Southeast, and Southwest cays.

A reef, on which the sea constantly breaks, surrounds them. There is only one opening through this reef, situated between Southeast cay and Southwest cay, with from 18 to 20 feet in it. This opening should not be used except in cases of emergency.

Sea-birds arrive at these cays in great numbers during March, and in April the islets are covered with their eggs, which are collected and conveyed in schooners to Jamaica. Later in the summer turtle are caught, but the supply is becoming scarcer every year.

The supply of guano is abundant but of poor quality. Several wrecks lie on the reefs round these cays, which are occasionally broken up by the sea and drift into the anchorage. In clear weather the high land of Jamaica is visible; Blue Mountain peak, bearing N. 41° W. from Southwest cay, is distant 52 miles.

Northeast cay is at times divided into three portions, the sea washing over the connecting sand-spits. A conspicuous cocoa-nut tree stands in the center of the cay with some smaller trees and bushes southward of it, and at the north extremity of the islet are two isolated trees. On the southern portion of the cay are one or two houses and a small pier, also a pond of brackish water.

Southeast cay is covered with bushes and trees, among which one cocoa nut tree rises considerably higher than the others. There are two houses on the cay and a pier on the west side. The sand-spits, extending from the extremities of this islet, alter in shape at different seasons of the year; in summer the southwest spit is washed away and the sand deposited on the western shore of the cay.

Southwest cay.—There is one house on this cay which can be seen from a distance of about 8 miles; a rocky ledge is used as a pier for shipping guano. Landing is seldom practicable at Southwest cay, but at the other islets, especially at their Southwest extremes, an opportunity of doing so can generally be found; it is not advisable to land at the piers on the islets on account of the submerged reefs in the vicinity.

Anchorage.—On the west side of Morant cays the bank slopes gradually off to the depth of 10 fathoms, and anchorage may be taken up by the lead, carefully avoiding the irregular ground extending NW. of Northeast cay; the bottom is composed of dead coral with patches of small brown weed growing over it.

When approaching from the northwestward the water shoals suddenly after passing the 100-fathom line, but a vessel may safely stand in, Southeast cay bearing S. 45° E. until in the required depth for anchoring.

Small vessels drawing not more than 12 feet will find smooth water at half a mile westward of the south extreme of Northeast cay, but with strong northerly winds this is not a safe anchorage as the sea then breaks in 3 fathoms.

Water may be procured by digging wells near the center of either Northeast or Southeast cay, taking care, however, not to dig as deep as the level.

The drift current sets towards W. and NNW., with a velocity of three-quarters of a knot an hour after the trade-wind has been blowing freshly for a day or two. When the trade is lighter a current setting to NE. or E. is frequently experienced.

Vessels having occasion to pass near Morant cays at night should keep northward of them.

In standing in for the E. end of Jamaica from the SE., Yallahs hill, which bears from the Morant cays about N. 50° 37′ W. 45 miles, will be a useful guide in clear weather; and in working up to the northward of the cays, the NE. end of Jamaica, kept open of Morant point, will lead to the windward of them.

Jamaica is the largest and most valuable of the British West India islands. The general appearance is extremely beautiful. On the N. it rises into hills of gentle ascent, covered with pimento groves and intersected by valleys, while on the S. it presents abrupt precipices and inaccessible cliffs.

The coast-line is 500 miles long. The northern shore is free of dangers and generally steep to, but the S. side, particularly near the middle, is deeply indented and fringed with reefs and cays, which must be cautiously approached. The principal ports are Kingston, Port Royal, Port Morant, Black river, and Savannah-la-Mar on the S. coast, and Lucea and Montego bay, Falmouth, St. Ann, ports Maria Antonio, and Annotto bay on the N.

The Blue mountains, a lofty range, run through the whole length of the island from E. to W., attaining a height of 7,300 feet, but the highest peaks are generally hidden by clouds. Other shorter ranges branch off in every direction. The valleys are all very narrow, not more than the twentieth part of the island being level ground. The principal rivers are the Minho, Black river, and Cobre, all emptying on the S. coast, but none of them are navigable except for boats.

The land and sea breezes are regular, except for a short time before the rainy season. The temperature of the year near Kingston ranges between 70° and 80°, but a difference of elevation affects the temperature very sensibly; at 4,200 feet above the sea it usually ranges between 55° and 65°. The year is divided into a short wet season, beginning in April or May and lasting about six weeks; a short dry season, from June to August; a long wet season, comprising September, October, and November, and a long dry season, occupying the remaining four months, during which the weather is serene, pleasant, and comparatively cool.

Earthquakes are frequent, and sometimes violent.

Hurricanes are not so frequent as in the Windward islands, coming generally between July and October.

The principal exports are coffee, rum, sugar, logwood, and tropical fruits.

Population in 1881 was 580,804—14,433 white, and the remainder colored and blacks.

The island called Xaymaca by the Caribs was discovered by Columbus in 1495, and was settled by the Spaniards in 1510, and in 1655 was taken by the English, to whom it has since belonged.

Morant point, the E. end of Jamaica, is formed by a strip of low, swampy, wooded land, extending about 2½ miles from a low range of hills about 800 feet high, running parallel to the S. coast at the foot of the Blue mountains. It is about 2½ miles broad at the inner part, and thence gradually diminishes to the point, which is sharp and well defined when seen from the N. and S.

Reef.—The point is skirted by a reef, which extends off to the distance of nearly one-quarter of a mile. There are 22 fathoms water at 1¾ miles off, close to the edge of the bank; and as the land is not more than 20 feet high, should the weather be thick or the light obscured the greatest caution must be observed when nearing it. Overfalls are generally seen eastward of the point, near the edge of soundings, and the stream runs at from 1 to 3 knots.

Caution.—In approaching Jamaica from the eastward, as in many other localities in the West Indies, great advantage will be gained from observing meridian altitudes of stars N. and S. at morning and evening twilight, after losing sight of Alta Vela, until Morant Point light or Yallahs hill is sighted.

Yallahs hill is about 19 miles westward of the point and can not be easily mistaken, being a remarkable mountain, rising rather abruptly on its N. side from the valley between it and the Blue Mountain range, and falling with a long, gradual slope to the sea on the S. side, and its rounded summit is seldom clouded.

Approaching from the NE. through the Windward channel, the Blue Mountain mass will generally come first in sight, and strangers are apt to keep away too soon, which should not be done until the vessel's position is correctly ascertained, lest they may not be able to weather Morant point. It is advisable to keep well to windward until the lighthouse bears northward of W., as the current generally sets strong to the westward.

Within the reef at Rocky point is a secure anchorage for coasters and a good landing wharf.

Port Morant is a small, secure bight. The approach to the harbor is easily distinguished. The hills on the western side, between 400 and 500 feet high, slope gradually to the shore, and are higher than those on the eastern side, which rise abruptly from the sea. At the head of the harbor is a remarkable red cliff, and 2 miles inland, at an elevation of about 500 feet and between two palm trees will be seen Kelly house. Palm point, on the western side of the entrance, may be known by the conspicuous cluster of trees on it.

Buoys.—The harbor is buoyed, but their position can not always be depended upon. In entering Port Morant great attention must be paid to the leading mark, for in strong trades and misty weather some difficulty may be experienced in distinguishing Kelly house. When Pero point shuts in the low point south of it, haul a little to the eastward of the leading mark and anchor in 5 or 6 fathoms with Bowder pier bearing N. 39° 22' E. As a rule vessels can enter or leave with the usual trade-winds and they seldom wait for the land-wind in the morning.

Good water may be obtained from the pier off the village.

The United States is represented by a consular agent.

Morant bay.—From Port Morant the shore bends in to the town of Morant, and then to Belvidere point, forming the bay. The reef still skirts the shore to the distance of about half a mile, but becomes more broken, with a better channel within, and terminates altogether S. of the wharf at Morant.

The sea breaks on this extreme end, and under the lee of it there is anchorage for large vessels in 5 or 6 fathoms water, with the court-house bearing about N. 11° 15' E. A short distance westward of Port Morant there is a narrow opening through the reef leading into Fisherman bay, in which the soundings are from 3 to 2 fathoms, but it is only fit for coasters. Within the reef to the westward are other anchorages of the same character.

The English church and the court-house, both a little northward of the principal wharf, are the most conspicuous buildings in the town.

Large ships standing into the bay should not bring the court-house to bear northward of N. 22° 30' E. to clear Galatea rock with $2\frac{3}{4}$ fathoms on it.

Cow Bay point is low, rounded, and wooded, and its extreme is nearly 2 miles from the foot of the hills. Small craft find shelter under Yallahs point from the strong trade-wind, which sometimes continues for three or four days. Large vessels might also anchor here, but care must be taken to avoid an 18-foot patch from which the point bears S. 67° 30' E., distant nearly one-third of a mile.

In Yallahs bay vessels of considerable size load logwood. The best anchorage is S. of the center of the bay, in 10 fathoms, about one-third of a mile from the beach, but it would be prudent to weigh on the first signs of a southerly wind, as a very heavy sea sets into the bay, and ships have been wrecked here.

Land and sea breezes are generally regular between Port Morant and Port Royal. As far as Yallahs point the land-wind is felt but a short way from the shore; westward it extends to a greater distance. Working off Point Morant in the early morning, the sea-breeze is almost invariably met with, the land-wind being only of sufficient strength to carry a vessel clear of the harbor. Off Port Royal ships frequently carry it some distance to sea. In the early months of the year, when the trade-wind is not very strong, the land-wind may come down with considerable, but never with dangerous, strength. Its approach will be known by a strong earthy or dusty smell. The strongest sea-breezes appear to be in June and July, and freshening as they advance westward, attain their greatest force off Port Royal. The time of commencement of the sea-breeze varies from 9 a. m. to noon, and generally lasts until 5 or 6 p. m., but in some cases it may blow continually for three or four days. The beginning of the land-wind is equally uncertain. In the summer or hurricane months the breezes are sometimes interrupted by calms and light southerly winds, with heavy rains and an exceedingly oppressive atmosphere. The sea-breeze will rush in with violent squalls from the SE., and last but a short time.

Currents.—Between Point Morant and Port Royal, at an average distance of 3 miles from the shore, the current setting to the westward is seldom found to exceed 1 mile per hour, depending upon the strength of the wind. East of Point Morant it sets in a S. and SE. direction at the rate of between 2 and 3 knots, causing a heavy sea. Two or three days of southwesterly or westerly winds will cause a slight current in an opposite direction. After heavy rains, the discharge from the rivers will for a short time cause a slight local set.

Port Royal.—From about 1 mile S. of the Martello tower, a low, narrow, sandy flat projects to the westward, terminating in Port Royal point. This peculiar tongue of land is more or less overrun with low mangrove bushes, particularly on its inner side, and is in part planted with cocoa-nut trees. It forms the spacious harbors of Port Royal and Kingston, and is called the Palisados. Near its western extremity is Fort Charles, and within it is the town of Port Royal, naval hospital, and dock-yard.

The east channel to the harbor is formed on the N. by the Palisados and on the S. by numerous low cays and banks, which extend off shore to the distance of 3 miles. The outer danger at the entrance of the channel is called the East Middle ground.

East Middle ground is a rocky bank composed of two knolls, occupying a space of about half a mile, and separated by a narrow cut of deep water in a N. and S. direction.

Maiden rock lies westward of East Middle ground, and it is a low barren rock. It is connected with Maiden cay by a rocky ledge, dry in places, which extends also 200 yards northward of the beacon, and to the westward for about 800 yards.

Lime cay is partially covered with bushes. In case of necessity a vessel will find anchorage close under its lee in 10 fathoms, muddy bottom, taking care, however, to avoid the Lime cay shoal.

Rackum cay is very small, low, and barren, and from its N. end a ledge of small, dry rocks extends out 200 yards in that direction. The cay is also foul on the S. and W. to the distance of nearly one-quarter of a mile, but steep-to on the E. side.

Gun cay is sandy, and, being wooded, is visible from a considerable distance, but Rackum cay, now about 2 feet above water, can only be seen on nearing the harbor.

As the turning at Gun cay is rather sharp for long vessels in a strong sea-breeze, they may pass through between Gun and Rackum cays. Vessels should not pass between the New and Beacon shoals. In a heavy ship it would probably be advisable to pass northward of Gun cay and southward of Beacon shoal.

The most convenient berth for merchant-vessels will be found outside Port Royal spit; they should therefore shorten sail in time after passing the point. English ships-of-war secure to mooring buoys off the dock-yard, the buoys being numbered from S. northward.

At night, when about 3 miles off Cow Bay point, the red light on Plum point will generally be seen, and it may be steered for. Running for the channel, its western limit should not be passed or the white light brought in sight until at about 1 mile from it, in order to clear the East Middle ground, then steer for Gun cay, as before.

If the land-breeze is likely to overtake the vessel before getting through the east channel it will be better for a sailing vessel not to proceed farther to leeward than the Upper White Horses, but to stand off and on until the sea-breeze comes down in the morning. It will be advisable not to be too hasty in bearing up until the sea-breeze is observed to have firmly established itself in the harbor, for the crew will only be worried in bracing about the yards to the conflicting winds.

Kingston harbor is a large, spacious inlet, formed by the Palisados, and capable of containing many vessels of the largest size. Shoals extend westward and northwestward from Gallows point, and eastward, bordering the northern shore of the Palisados as far as abreast the city, which with the shallow ground on the northwestern shore of the harbor contracts the ship-channel to a very narrow breadth.

This channel lies along by Fort Augusta, an extensive fortification on the extremity of a low, sandy spit of swampy land on the northwestern side of Port Royal harbor, and is pointed out by pile-beacons on either side. Vessels of large draught lie alongside the wharves of the town.

Kingston, the capital of the island, stands on a gentle slope, the population being 32,000. The streets are regular and straight, and the public buildings large. The residences of the upper classes are fine, with large grounds around many of them. The city is healthy, the range of the thermometer being from 71° to 86°. The island is divided into medical districts, under the head of the superintending medical officer.

Quarantine is strict, all vessels being boarded by a health officer. There is one public hospital.

Supplies.—Provisions are plentiful and moderate in price. Water can be had from water boats which come alongside. It is charged by weight; from 70 to 150 tons, $3; from 151 to 250 tons, about $7.

Coal can be had in any quantity. There is about 3,000 tons on hand; price from $7.20 to $8.16 per ton. Vessels coal alongside the wharf. The government and steamer lines have their own coal.

Repairs can be made to vessels. There is a large government dockyard, and the men-of-war of this station make large repairs here.

Steamer lines.—West India and Pacific line to Liverpool; French line to Havre; Atlas line to New York; Cunard line from Halifax; Glasgow line (monthly) to London; Spanish mail line from Havana and Santiago de Cuba.

Telegraph.—There is a cable to Havana and thence to all parts of the world.

Pilots are numerous and efficient. Pilotage, 150 tons, £4; 200 tons, £5; 250 tons, £6; 350 tons, £7; 500 tons, £8; 800 tons, £9; over 800 tons, £10.

Port charges.—Manifest, 2s. 6d. to 10s.; advertising, etc., 5s.; ballast costs 2s. per ton; health officer's fees, ship or bark, 12s.; brig, 9s.; schooner or sloop, 6s.; hospital tax, 4d. per ton; Kingston harbor duties, ship or bark, £1 12s.; brig, £1 4s.; schooner, 16s.

The authorities to be visited are the governor of the island and commodore of the naval station.

Salutes will be returned.

The United States is represented by a consul and vice-consul.

When leaving Kingston, having passed the pile off Creek pond, a bushy cay (just N. of Fort Augusta) in line with a large cotton tree on the low land westward of it leads to the narrows. Sailing vessels will find it advantageous to shift to the fairway at Port Royal the day previous to departure, so as to quit with the land-wind at early dawn, and to get out well clear of the shoals before the sea-breeze sets in.

East channel.—If bound to windward the E. channel will of course be the best, being clear, and can readily be followed in thick weather, avoiding only the shoal off Plum point, the range marks in the S. channel being often obscured.

Turning marks.—Should the sea-breeze overtake a vessel after getting to the eastward of Gun cay, she may stand toward the Palisados till the flag-staff of the Apostles battery is in one with the belfry of Port Royal church, until near Rocky point, when the staff must be kept open to the southward of the belfry to avoid the reef off the point.

Eastward of that point, use the same turning mark until near midway between Middle and Little Plum points, when the staff of the Apostles battery must not be brought to the northward of the N. part of Fort Charles to clear the shoals off the latter point. When Kingston church bears N. 2° 49′ W., do not stand farther to the northward than the flag-staff of the Apostles battery, in line with that of Fort Charles, to avoid the foul ground off Plum point.

Standing to the southward toward Lime Cay shoal, do not approach it nearer than to bring the flag-staff at Port Henderson just touching Port Royal point; and when standing toward Lime cay, do not come within 400 yards of the N. end. When eastward of it, the high bluff point at the N. part of Green bay, kept open of the N. part of Lime cay, will clear the foul ground to the northward of Maiden rock, and approaching the East Middle shoals, keep the high cliffs at the S. part of Green bay open to the northward of Lime cay until clear of them. It is seldom large ships work through this channel; the capabilities of the vessel and the force of wind and swell should be considered.

South channel is a narrow vein of deep water through the close mass of shoals which lie S. and W. of Port Royal. It is nearly always used by sailing vessels leaving at daylight with the land-wind; the buoys on the E. side are red, and those on the W. white.

West Middle rock is a very small head, with 22 feet water on it, lying directly at the entrance of the channel. On it there is a floating beacon, forming with the beacon on Fort Augusta the leading mark for this channel.

West Middle shoal is a coral bank partially covered with a thin layer of sand, and near the center has as little as 2 feet of water on it, steep-to, particularly on the west side. There is a patch with 5 fathoms water on it S. 22° 30′ W., 600 yards from the spindle.

Turtle heads are numerous detached rocky shoals, some nearly awash, which extend to the eastward from Small point. The leading mark carries just eastward of a shoal with 4¾ fathoms water on it. Should the buoy be adrift, the dock-yard clock-tower on with the eastern angle of Fort Charles will lead half way between the shoals and the nearest 27-feet knolls.

Drunkenman's cay is a small low islet of stones and sand, on which there are a few bushes. A short distance to the northward of it there is a dry sand-bore, and from thence it is nearly connected to the S. end of the West Middle shoal by a rocky ledge, in some parts dry.

South knolls.—Nearly midway between Drunkenman's cay and the Turtle heads, on the line of the leading mark, are four small detached heads of hard sand, called the South knolls, on which there are 27 and 30 feet of water.

Portuguese shoals are two small banks at the SE. side of the entrance of the S. channel. There are only 6 feet water on the easternmost, 17 to 23 feet on the other, and a red buoy with a staff and vane is moored in 5 fathoms water on the western edge. The channel is here half a mile wide, and the W. side is formed by Bush reef, on which the sea generally breaks.

Three-fathom banks are two detached banks lying off the SE. end of Bush reef, at the SW. side of the entrance to the South channel; the outer is S. 30° 56′ W., 1,500 yards from the Portuguese buoy. The least water on the inner bank is 19 feet. Vessels after passing Portuguese shoals should steer well to the eastward and take care not to get to leeward on these banks, or Wreck reef. There are other patches southward of these; the shoalest has 5 fathoms water on it.

Wreck reef.—Should the vessel be drifted to leeward and unable to weather this reef, she may run round its S. end and anchor close to leeward of it, to await the land-wind to carry her out again. A shoal, with a depth of 4¼ fathoms, lies N. 53° 26′ E., 1½ miles from Wreck reef.

Directions.—A vessel leaving by the S. channel should be under sail with the land-wind at dawn. If, however, she has good sailing qualities she may leave with the sea-breeze, provided she can lie up S. by E. Having passed close to the westward of West Middle Rock beacon, keep it in line with the black beacon at the SE. angle of Fort Augusta, and a notch in the Liguanea mountain, N. 5° 37′ E.; the latter, however, is difficult for a stranger to recognize, and is frequently obscured.

If of heavy draught, on approaching the South knolls, when a gap in the distant hills comes on with the S. extreme of Small point (which is conspicuous) N. 67° 30′ W., keep a little to the westward until the dock-yard clock-tower comes just open of the E. angle of Fort Charles, and keep it so till the high or southern end of Drunkenman's cay bears E., when haul up again on the leading mark. When Healthshire beacon, which is white and close to the beach in Half Moon bay, is just open to the northward of Healthshire hummock the vessel will be clear of Portuguese shoals, and may be hauled to the wind, or, if bound westward, continue on the same course clear of the outer shoals of Wreck reef, taking care to keep the Apostles battery well open eastward of Small point until well to the southward.

A vessel will generally have the assistance of a strong outset as far as Drunkenman's cay, when she will meet the usual westerly stream and heavy swell; therefore should the land-wind fail at this point she had better anchor under the S. end of the cay during the calm which intervenes, sometimes for several hours, between the breezes, in order to avoid being set on the shoals to leeward. By no means run the risk of having to bring up outside the Portuguese shoals. Should the seabreeze set in before she has cleared the channel, and she should be obliged to work out, which is a very hazardous undertaking, except under most favorable circumstances, do not stand farther to the westward than to bring the notch in the mountain on with the center of a low house in Fort Augusta, nor to the eastward than to bring the notch on with the E. end of that fort.

Navigators well acquainted with the locality may venture in a case of necessity to enter by this channel; but it will be attended with some risk, especially if the mountains are clouded.

Soundings extend for 4 miles to the southward of the cays, and the edge is very steep, there being in places only 14 fathoms of water 200 yards within the 100-fathom line. In the fairway of the channel the bottom is generally composed of mud and sand, and occasionally clay, but near the reefs it is sand, with portions of broken coral.

Tides.—There is no regular tidal stream, but in general there is an outset from the harbor and through the S. channel at the rate of one-quarter to 1 knot an hour until as far as Drunkenman's cay, where it takes a more westerly direction, and generally increases in strength. Sometimes it will be found running in this direction at the rate of 2½ knots. A good offing should therefore always be obtained before shaping a course to the westward.

When the land-breezes have been strong, and light southerly winds have prevailed during the day for a short period it often occurs that the current is running to the eastward in the morning even as far as the East Middle shoals, when it takes a more southerly direction, and to the southward of the shoals it will be found setting to the SW. or WSW., the strengt hquite depending on the force of the wind that has been blowing.

California bank, with from 21 to 27 fathoms on it, lies S. 9 miles from Plum Point light-house.

Portland bight.—The high land of Healthshire terminates at Polink point. Thence the coast trends to the NW. and sweeps around to the southward, forming between it and Portland point an extensive bight. The shore is skirted by small islets and detached reefs, within which are several excellent anchorages for vessels of moderate draught. The outer part of the bight is also protected by numerous reefs and small, low, wooden cays, with channels between them capable of admitting vessels of the largest draught. The best channel to enter by is between Pelican and Bare Bush cays, through which a vessel will carry from 6 to 8 fathoms of water.

Pelican cays are two small, low, bushy islets which lie near the center of a rocky ledge. The ledge generally shows itself, and the W. end is dry and steep-to.

Bare Bush cay is nearly dry and steep-to.

Morris shoal is a coral knoll, steep-to, with a clear channel about three-quarters of a mile wide between it and Bare Bush bank.

Portland reefs are 3½ miles in length and about 2 miles in breadth. The inner or SW. edge lies about a mile eastward of Portlan dpoint, but in the channel between there is a depth of only 2 fathoms. Half a mile within the SW. end of the reef is Portland cay, a small, bushy islet, and about 2 miles N. 22° 30' E. of it are two more similar cays, called the Half-Moon cays, within the NE. point of the bank, which generally breaks in most parts.

Pigeon island is low and steep-to on its E. and S. sides. The NW. side forms a small bay, off which there is an anchorage in 7 or 8 fathoms water.

White shoal is a small detached knoll.

Directions.—Vessels bound into Portland bight should have the assistance of a pilot. In coming from Port Royal, having passed well to the southward of Wreck reef, edge to the westward until the N. peak of Erazaletta hill bears N. 73° 07' W. This hill can not well be mistaken, being the northernmost of two remarkable elevations on the western range of mountains, about 890 feet high, with a deep gap or valley between. Steer in upon this course, and, as the vessel advances, Pigeon island will be seen from aloft on the same line of bearing.

If bound to Old harbor, which is the northernmost anchorage in the bight for vessels of moderate draught, being between Pelican and Bare Bush cays, a remarkable hummock will be seen on the northern ridge of mountains, something in the form of a jockey's cap, called Cudjoe hill. When this hummock comes in line with the base of the western slope of the hill at the E. end of Goat island, N. 50° 37' W., haul up with this mark, and it will lead to leeward of the dry reef at the W. end of the Pelican bank, and between it and White shoal, in 5½ to 6½ fathoms water. When the Northern Pelican cay bears S. 84° 22' E., steer N. 33° 45' W., so as to pass about half a mile to the SW. of Careening cay. When abreast the latter cay the wharves of Old harbor will come in sight and will direct a vessel to an anchorage off them in 4½ or 4 fathoms, between Careening island and the NE. end of the reef which fronts the western shore and generally shows itself.

If bound to Long's wharf, having entered the channel as before and brought the S. side of Round hill (the southernmost of the two hills mentioned before) just open of Brazaletta hill, which mark leads on the White shoal, round the latter gradually to the northward, and bring the upper house at Long's wharf in one with the N. end of the gap or flat open space in the mountains, N. 39° 22' W. This mark will lead through the best opening in the reef in 4 fathoms, which is here a mile from the shore, and when within it anchor, as most convenient, in 3½ or 3 fathoms water.

Salt river.—The entrance to the anchorage lies between Long and Salt islands. Having entered the Pelican channel and being abreast the cays, it will be better to shape a course so as to pass around the S. end of Pigeon island, which is steep-to. Thence a N. 45° W. course 3½ miles will lead to abreast of Salt island. Round its N. end at the distance of about 400 yards, steer for the entrance of the river, and anchor off it in 3 fathoms water, with the S. side of Pigeon island just in sight to the southward of Salt island. Pigeon island, however, is so low that in a small vessel this mark must be watched from aloft. Large vessels will find a well-sheltered anchorage in 5 fathoms, close up under the NW. side of Salt island.

Peake bay being open to the eastward, with strong sea-breezes, a heavy swell rolls in. The best holding ground will be found in 3½ or 4 fathoms water, under the northern sandy shore, about a mile within the outer part of the reefs. The entrance bears N. 84° 22' W., 3½ miles from Pigeon island.

West harbor.—The only anchorage for vessels of large draught is just to the westward of the northern reefs in from 5½ to 4 fathoms water, where the holding ground is good.

Directions.—Vessels should leave either of these anchorages with the land-wind at early dawn, in order to get clear of the outer reefs before the sea-breeze arrives; should it, however, overtake them before they get to the eastward of Pigeon island they may work out in moderate weather either to the northward or southward of it; the former will be the best route, as the water will be smoother. In this case do not stand too far to the southward, and attend to the mark already given for White shoal.

Goat island and Cabrietta point may be approached by the lead, not coming within the depth of 4½ or 5 fathoms. Should it blow hard it will be better to anchor under the lee of Pelican reef until the breeze lulls or the land-wind comes off; but if intending to proceed on, pass out between Bare Bush reef and Morris shoal, and the leading mark for the Northern channel answers the purpose here, viz. Cudjoe hill on with the fall of Goat Island hill. It leads, however, so close to the W. side of the reef, that when the Half-Moon cays come in one (which is the mark for the SE. end of Morris shoal) it will be better to edge a little to the westward, bringing Cudjoe hill open of the fall of Goat Island hill, until the vessel is to the southward of the reef, or the southern Half-Moon bears W., when she may be hauled to the wind.

If unable to lay through and the sea is smooth enough to allow of working out of the Pelican channel, in standing toward Morris shoal do not bring Bare Bush cay to the southward of S. 67° 30′ E.; and in approaching the Pelican reef do not open the fall of Brazaletta hill to the northward of Pigeon island. A vessel may stand toward the white water off Bare Bush cay to the depth of 5 fathoms, remembering the 4½ fathoms patch between Bare Bush and Pelican cays.

Portland ridge is flat wooded land, of moderate height, and when seen from the eastward has the appearance of an island. The 100 fathom line is 11 miles from this part of the shore, and it may be approached in the day-time to the depth of 6½ fathoms, at 1¼ miles off.

Caution.—A vessel bound to leeward, however, must be careful to keep the land of Portland to the northward of W. to avoid the cays and reefs just described, which are somewhat hidden by the eastern point.

The current generally sets strong to the westward, and although the soundings are regular a vessel at night should not come within the depth of 12 fathoms.

Robertson shoal.—The sea breaks heavily upon it in strong trades.

Carlisle bay lies immediately to the northward of Rocky point, and for small vessels is sheltered with the usual breezes as far round as SE. Anchorage will be found off the wharf.

Milk river.—Vessels loading here call first at Port Royal, where they pay light dues.

The United States is represented by a consular agent.

Between Milk river and Alligator hole, 2¼ miles to the westward, the shore is composed of red and white cliffs 50 feet high, thence to Alligator point there is a sandy beach.

Brane bank is about 1 mile in extent and rocky.

Alligator reef is dry in places. It should be given a wide berth at night, as 9 and 10 fathoms near its outer edge (which is steep-to) are the uniform depths at that distance from the coast.

Alligator Pond bay is between Alligator point and Little Pedro point. The shore, westward of Alligator point, is rocky, with low cliffs, thence to Little Pedro point sandy beach, the land behind rising precipitously to 800 feet.

The **anchorage** in Alligator Pond bay is near the center of the bay. It is sheltered from the eastward by Alligator reef, but with westerly and southwesterly winds a heavy swell rolls in, when the shore should be cautiously approached on landing, so as to pass close to leeward of some rocks that lie in the same line of direction as the wharf, at a distance of 100 yards.

Little Pedro point is a rocky ledge projecting 200 yards from the shore, the land behind rising suddenly 909 feet, thence gradually to 1,670 feet at a distance of 2 miles N.

The **coast** from Little Pedro point forms a small bay to the westward, in which there is an indifferent landing.

White Horses.—About 3 miles W. of Little Pedro point lies Cutlass point, and midway between them there is a large, whitish, triangular spot (named the White Horses), at a height of 600 feet, on the cliffs, which rise 1,000 feet nearly perpendicular from the sea; half a mile westward of the White Horses there is a remarkable white spot 500 feet above the sea.

Pedro bay.—There is occasionally a heavy swell in this bay, especially after a continuation of easterly or southeasterly winds, when the depth of water in the bay decreases 2 or 3 feet. Landing is not at all times good.

The coast from Pedro bay to Black Spring point has several indentations, the largest of which is Frenchman bay. This part of the coast is reef-bound, with the exception of one or two passes known to fishermen and to the pilots residing along the coast, who look out for vessels making the pilot signal.

Starve Gut bay.—A ledge of reefs awash extends around the shore of this bay, except in the NE. part, where there is a small sandy beach, from which a morass commences and extends between the sand-hills that fringe the coast-line and Sand Hill range to beyond Black river.

The bay affords a temporary anchorage in 4 fathoms half a mile from the shore, and is used occasionally by small vessels bound to the eastward, when unable to work against the current, which, after a continuation of easterly winds, sets from 1 to 1½ knots an hour to the westward.

Parattee, or Sand Hill point, is low, having on it a few palm-trees. The coast-reef projects three-quarters of a mile westward from this point, and extends in a northerly direction as far as the line of reefs that protects the anchorage off Black river.

Black river flows from the N. and E., through a large morass, and is navigable for 30 miles of its course; beyond are rapids and falls. There is a bar close to the mouth, the depth varying with the strength of the outpour. The water is fresh 3 to 5 miles up the river, according to the season of the year. The river abounds with fish and alligators.

The town of Black river stands on the west side of the river, facing the bay, its church, court-house, and hospital being conspicuous from seaward. It has a population of about 1,200, and, as a shipping port, it ranks third after Kingston. Poultry and yams are plentiful; fresh meat on Saturdays only.

Moco point is formed of large mangrove trees, 25 to 30 feet in height. Between this and Malcolm point is Hunts bay, fringed with mangrove trees.

Commencing at the beach under the court-house—a large two-storied building with portico in front and wings connected by archways—and gradually extending its distance to a quarter of a mile off Moco point, extends a reef, which thence follows the coast-line into Hunt bay. Malcolm point has also a small fringing reef.

Malcolm bay, between Malcolm point and Long Acre point, has good temporary anchorage for vessels waiting for a pilot.

From Long Acre to Burnt Ship point, 1 mile west, is a sandy beach off which Doctor reef and other foul ground extends seaward half a mile. Thence to Luana point are sandy beaches and rocky ledges alternately.

Shoals and reefs.—Off Parattee point the foul ground gradually increases its distance from the shore from a quarter of a mile to $1\frac{1}{4}$ miles, where the bay commences to trend to the NE. Thence the foul ground, including Barrack and Ravient reefs, which have several patches and sharp heads of rock, extends to the N. 67° 30′ W., 2 miles; according to local information these are rapidly growing. In shore off Barrack reef extend the Inner Barrack reefs, having 2 and $2\frac{1}{4}$ fathoms, to within 1,600 yards of the hospital, which was formerly used as barracks.

Pilots take schooners of light draught and occasionally larger vessels in ballast to Black River anchorage by passing close to the eastward of the barrack and inner barrack reefs.

Ballast ground lies to the west of a north and south line drawn through a large white house midway between the church and courthouse, and in less than 10 feet of water.

Seals' cove, a small but well-sheltered loading place for cargo boats, lies about midway between Luana and White House points. The entrance is not easily recognized by strangers. There is a limited anchorage off the entrance in 7 fathoms, sand and rock, with the large trees on mount Edgecumbe open of White House point. This anchorage is not recommended, and should not be taken up without a pilot.

Anchorage.—Vessels may anchor off White House point in 7 fathoms, mud, with that point bearing E. distant 400 yards. The soundings decrease rapidly from the edge of the bank, but the holding-ground is better than that off Seals' cove.

A pilot should be employed, as the anchoring ground is of small extent. Vessels occasionally load at this anchorage, but their cargoes are more usually conveyed in cargo boats to Black river or Savanna la-Mar for shipment.

Parker bay affords good anchorage for small vessels within the outer reefs, the channel through which, though not long, is narrow and carries a depth of $2\frac{1}{2}$ fathoms; the basin inside deepens to $3\frac{1}{4}$ fathoms over sandy bottom.

Leading marks.—To proceed through the channel between the outer reefs, bring the east extreme of Wharf house in line with western of two towers (which stand on a grassy slope half a mile inland) bearing N. 5° 37′ E.

Blewfields bay.—The soundings in this bay are irregular, over sand, rock, and weed.

Anchorage.—The best is in 5 fathoms, with the Wesleyan chapel on Friar's Cap bearing N. 8° 26′ E., and the overseer's house bearing N. 78° 45′ E.

The overseer's house (which has a veranda) is situated on a hill about 150 feet high and a quarter of a mile inland.

Water may be obtained at a small stream in Blewfields bay, but a more convenient place will be found round the bluff at the N. end of the bay.

Savannah-la-Mar may be readily distinguished by the town, which stands on the shore of a low and flat plain of considerable extent. The ridge of hills bounding this plain on the N. is very remarkable, and one of the peaks, called the Dolphin head, also serves as a guide to the locality. The anchorage is formed by a line of reefs running along shore and abreast the town, about $1\frac{1}{2}$ miles off, with channels between them. The most conspicuous object in this town is a ruined fort at its southern extremity.

A beacon is on the shore at the edge of the mangroves, 700 yards eastward of the fort.

A stranger should take a pilot.

If a berth is taken up outside the reef, be very careful in approaching, as it is steep-to. With a strong trade this anchorage is by no means desirable, and risk will be run of losing an anchor. The extreme elbow of the weather reef does not show itself; has 3 fathoms on it; is steep-to; lies S. 10° 52′ W., 2 miles from the center of the town, and S. 84° 22′ W., $4\frac{1}{2}$ miles from St. John's point.

Supplies.—Provisions can be obtained at Savannah-la-Mar, but the best watering places are those situated in Blewfields bay.

The United States is represented by a consular agent.

Vessels, when approaching this part of the coast, should on no account get into soundings, unless intending to anchor off Hope wharf, situated

1¾ miles eastward of St. John's point, which should not be done without the aid of a local pilot.

Between St. John's point and West point, the only places where landing can be effected are at Little bay and Homer's cove, situated 2¼ and 3 miles, respectively, northwest of St. John's point.

Banks.—There are at least two outlying banks on the SW. coast of Jamaica, but their limits have not been accurately traced.

Blossom bank lies W. about 11 miles from Pedro bluff, and has from 16 to 24 fathoms on it over sand and coral.

New bank lies about 20 miles from the bluff, and has from 12 to 20 fathoms water on it.

South Negril point, the extreme W. of Jamaica, is bold, round, rocky, and steep-to. Long bay lies between it and North Negril point.

Anchorage.—Vessels can anchor in Long bay in 4 to 5 fathoms, sand and rock, with South Negril point bearing S. 16° 52′ W., distant 1¼ miles, and the westernmost houses on the beach, situated nearly 1 mile within that point, bearing S. 11° 15′ E.

Booby cay lies one fourth of a mile off shore, about 1½ miles to the southward of North Negril point, and the coast between forms a small bay, called Negril harbor, which, however, is seldom visited even by droghers, and can not be recommended as a safe anchorage. The ground both northward and westward of the cay for half a mile is foul with rocky heads.

Orange bay is too shallow to afford anchorage. The entrance to the bay is foul.

Orange islet is a small islet lying close to the coast at half a mile eastward of Orange point; foul ground extends from it to the eastward.

Green island harbor.—During north and northwest winds a heavy sea rolls into this harbor, rendering loading or unloading impossible.

St. Lucea harbor, although of small dimensions, is one of the best harbors on the N. side of Jamaica. Its entrance is about 600 yards wide, but, within, it sweeps round into a most picturesque basin capable of receiving vessels of the largest size. Its position may be readily recognized by the fort, church, and barracks, which stand near each other on the western side of the entrance. From an offing it will be found by bringing the Dolphin head to bear about S. 5° 03′ E.

To pass eastward of the reef extending eastward from Antonio point, the west point of entrance being a detached house about 100 feet above the level of the sea and situated a quarter of a mile west of Thorn hill, in line with Dolphin head, bearing S. 5° 03′ E., a good berth for a heavy ship is with the fort bearing N. 22° 30′ W., and the court-house in line with the Baptist chapel S. 78° 45′ W., in 5¼ fathoms water. Farther eastward a vessel will be exposed to northers, which at times send in a heavy sea. Vessels loading may go as far in as to bring the fort N. 11° E. in 3½ or 4 fathoms water. The bottom is mud. Should a vessel have to work out in standing toward the eastward shore, do not go farther than to bring the house on Barbara hill in line with a house above it on Thorn hill, but tack short of this line, especially near Cane point, as it leads close to the coral bank.

Supplies are good, and water may be procured from the town or at a well to the northward of Georgia river, on the S. side of the harbor, at from 4 to 2 shillings per ton.

Between Lucea point and Mosquito cove the coast is low and composed alternately of sand and rock, with a bank of soundings extending to seaward for a distance of about half a mile.

Mosquito cove is a narrow, well-sheltered inlet, capable of receiving vessels of large draught. A vessel will sail in with the sea-breeze, but as no marks can be given, and the cove being so narrow, the assistance of a pilot will be required. In approaching, avoid the Buckner reef. A vessel may pass around either end of this reef, and soundings will be found half a mile outside of it.

Round Hill bluff is a remarkable, bold, wooded headland. Reefs extend about half a mile from the shore between Mosquito cove and Round Hill bluff, and when working along this part of the coast a vessel should tack before striking soundings.

Great river discharges itself into a small bay at about a mile to the eastward of Round Hill bluff, and may be recognized from the offing by a red bridge which spans it. The anchorage is used as a quarantine station for Montego bay. It is protected on the N. by a reef, within which there is anchorage for two or three vessels of moderate draught. In the event of being caught by a norther in the bight of Montego bay, and not able to fetch that anchorage or weather Round Hill bluff, which is foul for nearly half a mile off, a vessel may run for this place as a last resource by observing the following directions:

Directions.—Being off the anchorage, steer in for it on about a S. 22° 30' W. bearing, and having made out the point of the reef, which shows itself, pass close round it, leaving it on the port hand; then luff up, shorten sail, and anchor immediately the vessel is head to wind, as near the reef as possible, as there will be only room to veer out 100 fathoms, and be in 3 fathoms. It will perhaps be safer to drop both anchors at once, to prevent dragging. The river is navigable for flat-bottomed boats to a considerable distance.

Winds and weather.—When seeking an anchorage off the north coast of Jamaica the possibility of a gale from the northward should always be borne in mind. These storms are most prevalent during the autumn and winter months, and are invariably accompanied by thick rain, squalls, and heavy seas.

Montego bay.—The head of this bight is filled with low mangrove cays, skirted by reefs to the distance of a quarter of a mile, almost wall-sided, with 20 fathoms water at about 100 yards off.

The Marine hospital, situated on Old Fort point, one-third of a mile south of Sandy point, is a conspicuous object. Between the town of Montego and Sandy point the coast is formed by a rocky cliff about 20 feet high.

On the eastern edge of the harbor, northward of the town, are the remains of a former breakwater, part of which is above water.

The ballast ground is situated in the southwest part of the bay.

The anchorage in the bay is quite safe during the period of the ordinary land and sea breezes, which range from NNE. to SE.; but between November and March, when northers sometimes blow in, accompanied by a heavy sea, a second anchor may have to be dropped, and accidents have occurred.

Directions.—Montego bay being an open roadstead there is no difficulty in getting to the anchorage, except from its generally crowded state, especially from December to June. Anchor as most convenient, with Sandy point, which is a little northward of Old Fort point, shut in. Sandy point just open of Old Fort point leads along the edge of the bank, which is steep-to. A good berth will be with the church from E. to N. 78° 45′ E. and Old Fort point N. 5° 37′ W., in $10\frac{1}{2}$ fathoms water. In winter the farther to the northward the berth is taken the better, as the vessel will get the protection of the reef, but the holding-ground is not so good. In anchoring be prepared to veer out a good scope of cable at once, or the vessel may drag off the bank.

Water and provisions of all kinds can be readily obtained at Montego. Population is about 6,000.

The United States is represented by a consular agent.

Between Sandy point and Falmouth harbor the bank of soundings to the depth of 100 fathoms extends about half a mile from the shore. Numerous wharves have been built on this part of the coast from which produce is conveyed by cargo boats to either Montego bay or Falmouth harbor.

Directions.—In beating up from Montego bay the set of the current should in the first place be found, and taken advantage of accordingly. Should there be none, keep the shore aboard during the evening, which may be done without fear, to catch the land-wind. If it is found more advantageous to seek an offing, the mariner will find a good guide as to his progress to windward in the peak of Turquino, the highest and most remarkable mountain on the S. side of Cuba, and generally visible.

Falmouth is a reef harbor capable of receiving a small number of vessels not drawing over 16 feet, moored head and stern, and may be readily known by the public buildings of the town, which fringe the beach and is of considerable extent; the channel, however, although buoyed, is so extremely narrow and intricate that, for a vessel of over 10 feet draught, a pilot (who may always be found in the offing) is indispensable. The buoys on the bar frequently break adrift; some of the inner shoals are marked by beacons; the reefs will be known by the color of the water. Another evil is, that a vessel can only leave with the land-wind, and in the winter season this is frequently interrupted for many days.

Directions.—In entering the harbor carry small sail and con from the masthead. Bring the beacon on the coast line eastward of the town, bearing S. 20° 05′ W., in line with the northeast side of a house 1 mile inland, and proceed until the southeast corner of the courthouse, bearing S. 59° 28′ W., opens north of the memorial stone of the Baptist chapel behind it, when immediately keep away on that mark and enter the anchorage by the most convenient of the three passages, selecting a good berth in one of the tiers in which vessels are placed. The passage to leeward of Inner shoal should be avoided unless the wind is well to the northward, or a vessel will not shoot far enough to windward to be well clear of Spider reef on taking her cable. If arriving late in the afternoon (when the land-wind may be expected at any moment), be prepared with stern moorings or a kedge.

Current.—When the sea-breezes blow continuously for some days without the intermission of the land-wind, there is at times, owing to the constant beat on the reefs and the amount of water forced into the harbor, a current induced which sets to windward through the anchorage and is strongest with the strongest winds. It is often the case that vessels are riding entirely by their stern moorings with their bower cables hanging up and down, the current being stronger than the wind.

Supplies.—Provisions are plentiful. A water pipe is laid out in the harbor, alongside which two boats can fill at a time. A water rate, according to tonnage, is levied on all vessels entering the harbor.

Ballast and quarantine ground.—The ballast ground lies off Fort point, to which it must be sent in boats for discharge. The quarantine ground being at Great river (the same as for Montego bay), renders it necessary to obtain *pratique* before entering the reefs. Departure in a sailing vessel being impossible during the sea-breeze.

The United States is represented by a consular agent.

Rio Bueno, once an important shipping roadstead, may be recognized by some remarkable slate-colored bare patches on the face of bluff table-topped cliffs of from 100 to 150 feet elevation, lying 1 mile eastward of it; or by the church and houses in the southwest corner of the bay.

Anchorage.—It is not advisable to attempt this anchorage without a pilot or having previously sent in a boat to mark spots for each anchor. Mooring is recommended as the only protection against northers or severe weather, and is necessary at all times with more than two vessels on the bank, in addition to a kedge astern. The best anchorage is with the E. extreme of the sandy beach bearing S. 78° 45′ E., and the mouth of Rio Bueno bearing S. 45° W.

Water.—A plentiful supply of good water can be obtained at a short distance up the river. The port of entry for Rio Bueno is Falmouth.

Dry harbor.—The conspicuous cliffs eastward of Rio Bueno serve to indicate the position of this harbor, it being situated 2 miles eastward of them. Across the mouth of the harbor stretches a coral reef, for the most part nearly awash; but at two-thirds of the distance across from the W. side of the harbor is a narrow channel carrying 2¾ fathoms on the leading mark, with coral heads and shoal water close-to on either side of it. The only leading marks are, unfortunately, not at a sufficient distance from each other to be good. The channel is marked by two spar-buoys, but little reliance can be placed upon them, and a stranger visiting the port for the first time should take a pilot. After crossing the bar the water rapidly deepens to 25 and 30 fathoms, but there is a shoal spit 700 yards south of the bar and close eastward of the course to the best anchorage.

Directions.—The best time for entering or leaving Dry harbor is soon after daylight, before the sea breeze sets in, which causes a heavy swell to set across the bar, especially with the wind from the NE., and would altogether prevent a vessel of more than 13-feet draught crossing at those times.

To enter, bring the E. side of the western of two store-houses on Knox wharf, bearing S. 24° 51′ E., in line with the W. side of the green veranda porch of the house close above and behind (Beverland house). This will lead between the two spar-buoys if in place. Should one be adrift, great care must be exercised in determining which, for the channel lies only on the line of the leading mark and there is a depth of 1¾ fathoms close-to on either hand.

Anchorage.—A flat extends from the eastern shore of the harbor a distance of 300 yards with depths decreasing from 18 feet, but the ground is rocky and foul, rendering it an undesirable anchorage even for small craft. In the S. and SW. parts of the harbor, close to the shore, are three reefs awash with several rocky heads; this portion of the harbor has foul ground and the depth is too great to admit of convenient anchorage. The best anchorage is in the SE. corner of the bay, opposite Knox pier.

Provisions are plentiful and the harbor abounds with fish, but water can only be obtained at 2¾ miles eastward of the harbor, from Pear Tree bottom, which boats can not approach during severe weather.

Runaway bay is a small open roadstead with a wharf. An unprotected anchorage may be obtained in 10 fathoms with the wharf bearing S. 30° E., distant 600 yards, and Flag point, the eastern extreme of the bay, bearing N. 69° 22′ E.

Coast.—From Flag point the shore takes an easterly direction to the entrance of St. Ann's bay. Along this extent of coast many small streams and rivulets empty themselves into the sea. The western part is sandy.

St. Ann's bay may be recognized by the buildings of the town, situated on a gradually rising hill; by a large waterfall 3 miles to the eastward of the town and only visible when seen from the eastward; or by its position with regard to St. Ann peak or the Camel's Hump.

Anchorage.—Vessels require to moor head and stern, and should select a berth toward the western side of the harbor to obtain during northers the full protection of the reef. On the western side of the anchorage and detached from the main reef is a heap of ballast, over which there is only 1 fathom water. To the southwestward of this anchorage there is a small arm suitable for small coasting vessels. During heavy weather a similar current, attributable to the same cause as that at Falmouth, is here experienced.

Provisions are plentiful, and water may be obtained from Drax Hall river.

Land-wind.—The continuous blowing of the sea-breeze at times prevents sailing vessels leaving the port for some days, a wind off the land being necessary.

The United States is represented by a consular agent.

From St. Ann bay the coast curves gradually round into Mammee bay, and thence to Ocho Rios. Mammee bay has a fringing reef extending from the shore and some prominent red cliffs at its eastern extreme, near which a river falls into the sea. The falls of this river, at a short distance inland, are plainly visible from seaward, and are of some extent.

Ocho Rios is situated at the bottom of a bay, from the eastern entrance point of which a plainly visible reef extends to the westward, affording partial shelter. The inner part of the bay is to some extent narrowed by a reef that runs out from the S. side of the anchorage. It is easy of approach, the best berth being in $3\frac{1}{2}$ fathoms, with the only wharf (which extends from a zinc circular-roofed warehouse) bearing S. 52° 30′ E. and the western extremity of the reef awash, bearing N. 20° 37′ E.

Bull point, at the W. end of the bay, is a remarkable rocky knob, 30 feet high.

Supplies.—Provisions are plentiful, and water is obtainable from any of the springs that discharge themselves into the harbor.

Ora Cabeza is a better anchorage, having a depth of 10 fathoms, mud, with the NW. extreme of a small islet at its eastern part bearing N. 71° 15′ E., distant 400 yards. It is, however, open and exposed to the N. and W. Its vicinity is found by bringing the western ridge of the Blue mountains to bear S. 22° 80′ E., which will lead up to the point.

Port Maria is divided into two portions by Cabrita island. The town is situated on the shores of the western part, in which is the best anchorage, the other portion being at present seldom used on account of the decrease in sugar cultivation. The shore between Galina point and the town forms a shoal bay, and is covered with a forest of cocoa-nut trees, which serves to indicate its position from a distance.

Directions.—To enter, a vessel should carry easy sail and steer midway between Fort point and Cabrita island, with the westernmost wharf bearing S. 26° 15′ W., and anchor shortly after Pagee point (the eastern entrance point) is shut in by Cabrita island. Cabrita island is fringed for a distance of 150 to 200 yards from the shore with reefs and foul ground, which must be borne in mind when shooting up after rounding to.

Supplies.—Provisions are easily obtainable; good water may also be procured from Pagee river, in the SE. corner of the bay.

The quarantine ground of port Maria is at Oro Cabeza.

Pilots are generally to be found some miles outside.

Sheerness bay is small, with a coral-fringed harbor for droghers and lighters, open to the NE.

Annatto bay.—The town in this bay is situated close to the beach, and is easily recognizable by its stores and the church in the NE. corner, within a mile of Free point. At the SW. end of the town is situated Gray's Inn wharf, with an estate at the back; close to Annatto Bay church is situated Gibraltar wharf.

Schoolmaster shoal runs to the northwestward from Gibraltar wharf and turns to the eastward towards Free point, affording to some extent protection to the anchorage during the usual sea-breeze, but none from northers.

Anchorage.—The best anchorage is as close to the northeastward and to Schoolmaster shoal as possible, with Gibraltar wharf bearing S. 71° 15′ E., distant 550 yards. This position is a good one from which to leave for sea on the approach of a norther. There is good holding-ground along the E. side of the bay, but its extent rapidly narrows to the southwestward.

Directions.—If entering from a position to windward, do not run down within 1 mile of the shore nor haul to the southward until Gray's Inn house is open westward of Gray's Inn wharf, bearing S. 45° 56′ W. A vessel is then clear of the extreme of Schoolmaster shoal and may run S. 48° 45′ W. until abreast the proposed anchorage. The bank shoals very rapidly, and as vessels should invariably moor, the port anchor must be dropped in about 15 fathoms with plenty of cable ready, and the other anchor let go in about 5 fathoms, while the kedge should be ready for running out astern to hold during land-winds.

Free point.—Approaching from the eastward, this point makes as a long, low, bluff point, over which the masts of the vessels at anchor inside may be seen. Palmetto point, to the eastward, resembles Free point, and off it a breaking shoal extends half a mile.

Buff bay.—The western part and bottom of this bay are very foul and break in 5 and 6 fathoms at a quarter of a mile off shore, the bottom being composed of rocky pinnacles.

Roadstead.—Off Spring Garden wharf, situated 2¼ miles W. of Savannah point, a vessel would find anchorage in 12 fathoms, mud, at 300 yards N. 26° 15′ E. of the wharf. This anchorage can not, however, be recommended, being on a lee shore during northers and unprotected from the sea raised by the ordinary sea-breeze. The bank is very steep to and rapidly shoals from the anchorage, the quality of bottom changing from mud to stones and gravel. It is, in fact, only suitable for droghers, as is also a small spot off Orange bay close to Savannah point.

To the eastward of Wag Water river, at Annatto bay, the land rises very rapidly from the coast into well defined hills that inland form the spurs of the Blue Mountain range. The intervening ravines are deep, with small, fertile plains at their coast termination; they contain rivulets and streams which, during heavy rains, deepen into rivers and torrents, preventing communication and sweeping away the shingle barriers on the beach that are thrown up by the surf.

Between Savannah point and Ship rock there are two bights, forming Hope and St. Margaret's bays, in the bottoms of both of which there are anchorages for droghers and boats only. The Coast range rises in places to a height of about 800 feet. Between these hills and the Blue Mountain range is a fine valley, formerly cultivated with sugar, but now rapidly growing into bush again. The Rio Grande rises to the eastward of the Blue mountains, and flowing NW. through a deep valley, empties itself into St. Margaret bay.

Ship head is a prominent bluff point with a small islet to the westward of it, called Ship rock.

Port Antonio.—Is divided into two harbors by a narrow peninsula which takes a northerly direction nearly half a mile from the main, with a curve to the NE. The town of Titchfield stands upon it, and at the N. end there is a fort and barracks, which are conspicuous objects from the offing.

Western harbor.—It is approached from the eastward through a narrow but deep channel about 100 yards wide, which is marked by three iron can-buoys, between Navy island and the main, and there is also a narrow outlet to the northward through a tortuous channel with 2 fathoms water in it, but useless for any but small cargo boats; this harbor can only be left with a land-wind.

Beacons.—Two truncated pyramidal beacons, painted white, are on the western side of West harbor. The west beacon is about 100 feet above the level of the sea; the east beacon is situated close to the beach. These beacons in line lead through the channel between Navy island and Titchfield peninsula. Lights are placed on these beacons when the mail steamer is expected.

Eastern harbor.—Divided from the western harbor by Titchfield peninsula, can be left with either a land or sea-breeze. It has good holding-ground in from 10 to 6 fathoms for large vessels; but being open to northers, which send in a heavy sea, it is not so much frequented as the inner harbor.

Rock.—A small rock lies 50 yards off Rover point, which is situated 134 yards S. of Folly point. With this rock in line with Folly point and Titchfield point bearing N. 41° W., anchorage will be obtained in 9 fathoms of water.

Directions.—Eastern harbor; there is no danger in entering, and the eastern or weather point is bold-to. Keep in mid-channel between Folly point and Navy island and then haul over toward the fort on the N. end of Titchfield peninsula to avoid the shoal ground on the E. side of the harbor, and approach the anchorage under easy sail, as there is no room to shoot far in. As a heavy swell sets into this port, sailing-vessels ought not to weigh for the purpose of proceeding to sea without being well satisfied that the land-breeze extends to a sufficient distance, for the depth of water at the entrance is so great as to render anchorage quite unsafe should the breeze fail.

To enter the West harbor, run in under easy sail, and when within or abreast Folly point, edge away gradually until the beacons are in line and stand in on that line until the harbor is opened, when haul up and anchor in 6 or 7 fathoms. There is a slight set from the eastern harbor towards the reef off Navy island, on which is a depth of 7 and 8 feet—this must be borne in mind when proceeding either way through this channel in light winds.

Supplies.—Provisions are plentiful, and good water is obtainable from either a well or Annatto river, both situated in the western harbor.

The United States is represented by a consular agent.

The general nature of the coast from Port Antonio to South Booby point is cliffy, with little sandy coves interspersed, off which rocky and foul ground generally extends. But from South Booby point the land commences to fall and trends into Plantain Garden bay, then sweeping round SE. again towards Morant point.

From Port Antonio a range of hills commences to rise gradually towards the direction of Morant point, attaining on the bearing of WSW. from Manchioneal harbor and at 4 miles inland a height of about 3,000 feet and running almost parallel to the coast towards which by degrees they fall. From the summit they fall more rapidly to the southward and terminate at Plantain Garden river, then thence to Morant point, being an almost level plain.

The **Northeast end of Jamaica** is a remarkable, bold, rounded headland rising almost perpendicularly from the sea to a considerable height.

Priestman's River bay and Long bay are both steep-to; neither of these bays are available as an anchorage; the cliffs that fringe them rise perpendicularly from the water to 20, 30, and 40 feet in height.

From the NE. end the rocky shore trends to another prominent bluff point called South Booby point with some remarkable red cliffs. The land is here also very elevated, sloping steeply down to the edge of the cliffs.

Manchioneal harbor is situated at the S. extreme of a cocoanut plantation 2 miles long on the coast, is very small; a reef extending from Nettle point on its N. side narrows the entrance to a width of 100 yards, which leads to an anchorage close off Shipton's point, barely exceeding 200 yards in diameter. From this anchorage to the northward is a narrow, well protected haven for small craft; it is 100 yards wide at the entrance, with 5 fathoms, and gradually shoals inwards.

Caution.—Vessels should moor in the southern anchorage in about 7 fathoms, and as, from its small size, the placing of the anchors is of great importance a pilot should be taken.

Supplies.—Provisions are plentiful, and water is obtainable a short distance up the Drift river, which during heavy rains swells and causes a strong off-set through the harbor and entrance.

Plantain Garden bay.—To the southward of the red cliffs the shore bends in to the SW. and forms a deep bay, skirted by a reef, at the head of which is Plantain Garden river, 3½ miles N. 69° 30′ W. of Morant point.

Anchorage.—Between the reefs off the mouth of the river and the shore there is a roadstead, where the telegraph-cables from Santiago de Cuba and from St. Thomas are landed. This bay can not be recommended as an anchorage on account of its exposed position and the difficulty of getting away on the setting in of a norther, or NE. wind; caused by the rapidity with which the bottom shoals from deep water to the broken and foul ground fringing the coast.

Current.—Along the N. coast of Jamaica the prevailing current is to the westward with the trade-wind, varying from half a knot to 1½ knots an hour with the strength of the wind; this prevailing current is occasionally replaced by a slight easterly set, most observable, but not always so, during the moon's second quarter.

Pedro bank lies SW. from the island of Jamaica, and is about 100 miles long and 55 miles broad at its western extremity. The northeastern extremity lies 35 miles SW. of Portland point. The soundings on the bank vary from 6 to 20 fathoms, except near the southern edge, which is dangerous of approach and where there are numerous rocks, cays, and shoals.

The bottom is generally of white sand and dead coral, but occasionally of mud and live coral; on the NE. part the bottom is of a reddish color. On the eastern extreme of the bank, even in moderate weather, the sea is generally rough with overfalls; over other portions the sea is not higher than in deep water.

Shoals having less than 3½ fathoms can be seen from aloft as discolored water, unless the sun is in line with them or the sea rough. From Portland rock for 50 miles along the SE. edge, the bank is studded with dangers. The cays on the bank are dependencies of Jamaica.

In rounding the E. end of the Pedro bank a good berth must be given to it, as the current generally sets strongly to the westward.

Portland rock has a double summit; it is 290 yards long and appears double when bearing either east or west. A ridge, over which there are irregular soundings, extends half a mile N. 26° 20′ W. from the rock.

Vessels seeking temporary anchorage may slowly approach the western side of Portland rock, and anchor in 8 fathoms, clear sand, within a distance of 400 yards from it; westward of this position the depths increase to 10 and 12 fathoms.

Landing on Portland rock is very difficult to effect.

Blower rock.—In ordinary weather the sea breaks heavily on Blower rock, and the column of water sent up can be seen from a considerable distance.

Caution.—Vessels should not cross the Pedro bank between Portland rock and Shannon shoal without having local knowledge, nor under any circumstances should they do so at night.

In crossing Pedro bank, through the channel eastward of Blower rock, vessels should pass within 3 miles of Portland rock.

If crossing westward of Blower rock, unless the breakers on that rock are clearly seen, it is advisable to sight Shannon shoal.

Shannon shoal in calm weather uncovers about $1\frac{1}{2}$ feet for a length of 50 yards near the western extremity, but during rough weather, or even in a moderate sea, the shoal is covered with breakers. If approaching from the southward the soundings would not give sufficient warning of approaching this danger.

In 1875 the royal mail steam-vessel *Shannon* was wrecked near the eastern extremity of this shoal, and in October, 1880, a portion of the machinery was still to be seen rising over 20 feet above the sea, and forming an excellent beacon, which on a clear day was visible from a distance of 7 miles.

Caution.—The edge of the bank between Shannon shoal and NE. cay forms a remarkable curve inwards. No attempt should be made to cross this part of Pedro bank.

Pedro cays.—These four cays, known respectively as NE., Middle, SW., and South cays (of which SW. cay is the largest), are dependencies of Jamaica, and are rented by merchants in Kingston for the purpose of collecting guano. Temporary huts have been erected on them, close to which the best landing places will be found.

Cocoa-nut trees have been planted on NE. and SW. cays but they do not yet rise above the bushes.

Northeast cay.—The large cocoa-nut tree formerly standing on this cay has been blown down. From the southeast extreme of the cay, a reef, which breaks, extends to the southwestward for a distance of one-third of a mile.

Vessels can anchor in 5 fathoms over sandy bottom, with the northwest extreme of NE. cay bearing N. 71° 20′ W., but there is generally an uneasy swell at this anchorage.

The east extreme of SW. cay (seen from aloft), open the apparent length of that cay west of Middle cay, bearing S. 20° 42′ W., leads northwest of these dangers.

Vessels approaching from the northward, and having cleared the shoals may pass between NE. cay and Middle cay into deep water.

Middle cay is covered with brush-wood; from the southeast extreme a reef, which generally breaks, extends to the southward, and is continued as a rocky ridge in the direction of SW. cay, forming a protection to the anchorage.

Anchorage will be found in 5 fathoms, bad holding ground, with the west extreme of Middle cay bearing S. 86° 10′ E., distant one-third of a mile.

Southwest cay is partly covered with bushes which attain a height of 12 feet above the sea.

A reef awash fringes the eastern side of this cay, and foul ground extends from it for a distance of two thirds of a mile towards Middle cay. Good anchorage may be obtained westward of SW. cay in any required depth, but small vessels desirous of anchoring close in should carefully avoid the spit extending from the north side of this cay. The center of SW. cay is slightly depressed, and water may be procured by sinking a cask, but it is brackish.

Vessels leaving the anchorage off SW. cay and intending to proceed to the southward should pass east of South cay.

South cay.—There is clear ground both eastward and southward of South cay, but shoal water extends about a mile northward and westward from it. There is no anchorage off South cay, and landing can seldom be effected on it. The channel between South cay and SW. cay is available for vessels, provided that South cay is not approached within a distance of 1¼ miles.

Shoals.—A shoal bank, which, within a depth of 5 fathoms, is about 3 miles long, lies about half a mile within the southern edge of Pedro bank, at 4 miles westward of South cay.

Two shoal heads are situated upon this bank at a distance of 1½ miles from each other; the eastern of these (at half a mile within the eastern edge of the bank), with 6 feet of water upon it, breaks in moderate weather, but the western shoal head with 12 feet over it (lying nearly 1 mile within the western edge of the bank), seldom breaks; between these shoal heads there is a general depth of 4 and 4½ fathoms.

A dangerous reef, over the center of which there is a depth of 6 feet, lies about 10 miles S. 68° 31′ W. from South cay and 5 miles N. 71° 20′ E. from Banner reef, N. extreme. This reef, within a depth of 5 fathoms, is 1½ miles long, and probably breaks in heavy weather, but not in a moderate sea.

In the center of the channel between this reef and Banner reef there is a depth of 8 fathoms.

A depth of 100 fathoms is found 1¼ miles SE. of this reef.

Banner reef is just awash, and in a smooth sea might show no indication of its existence; during a fresh breeze the sea breaks over a space extending about 1½ miles in a NNE. and SSW. direction.

Numerous shoal heads, with sandy bottom between them, lie within a distance of 1 mile northward and westward from Banner reef, and this part of Pedro bank should not be approached under any circumstances.

The bark *Banner* was wrecked on this reef, and portions are still visible above water, but she is fast breaking up.

Southwest rock is very dangerous, as in fine weather the vicinity is only indicated by ripplings.

Current.—The general set of the current over the eastern part of Pedro bank is to NW., attaining its greatest velocity when the trade-wind is strongest, but seldom exceeding the rate of 1 knot an hour.

In calm weather the flood tidal stream sets to SSE., but is easily overcome by a slight breeze.

The ebb stream apparently sets to NW. as soon as the moon has passed the meridian.

In moderate weather a slight southerly set may therefore be expected for five hours preceding the moon's upper or lower transit, and a strong set to NW. for the next seven hours.

Over the western part of the bank the current sets to NNW. and to SW., having a tendency to the northward on the N. edge of the bank, and to the southward on the S. edge; the velocity, which varied from half a knot to 1½ knots an hour, was affected by the wind.

Bajo Nuevo or New Bore, about 95 miles S. 33° 45' W. of Portland rock, is oval-shaped, about 14 miles in extent and 5 miles in breadth. Two extensive reefs rise from the bank; the eastern one, close to its edge, is a solid semicircular reef, convex to the eastward, dry in places, with its horns curving along on the N. and S. sides of the bank for about 2½ miles, and at the southern termination is a dry sand-bore. It is steep-to, the edge of soundings being about one-quarter of a mile off, except at the northeastern end, where it is about 1 mile off.

The southwestern reef, somewhat similarly formed, is separated from the eastern reef by an opening about 1 mile wide, and it trends along the southeastern edge of the bank for 7½ miles from the southwestern extremity of the eastern reef, and near its termination is a sand-bore. A shallow ledge, with 10 fathoms water close to it, runs off to the westward of the bore for about 1½ miles to within 2 miles of the SW. end of the bank, which makes this termination of the reef, if possible, more dangerous than the other. Small ridges of sand occasionally form on other parts of the reef, but they disappear in strong breezes.

Low cay.—On the northern point of this leeward reef, which is nearly in the middle of the bank, there is a barren cay, composed of sand, broken coral, and drift-wood, thrown up by the sea to the height of 5 feet. It is 300 yards long, about 50 yards wide, and lies in latitude 15° 53' 00" N., longitude 78° 39' 04" W. On it there is a small pond which is resorted to by seals, and in the months of March and April the bank is visited by fishing vessels from St. Andrew and Old Providence for the purpose of taking them.

To the westward of the eastern reef the N. side of the bank is clean for about a mile within its edge, as far as about 2 miles westward of the cay. There is also a clear space of about 3 miles on the western side of the bank. The depths vary from 8 to 17 fathoms of water over coral and sand. Care should be taken when standing toward the broken ground on the N. side of the leeward bank, as a coral head lies S. 70° 19′ W., 2 miles from the cay. The northern edge of the bank is also so steep that the first cast of the lead may be 12 or 15 fathoms. The bottom is visible. The current in the vicinity of this reef sets strongly to the westward, at times as much as 2 miles an hour.

Anchorage may be taken up in moderate weather in 8 fathoms water with the cay bearing S. 78° 45′ E., distance about 1½ miles, but it is exposed to the winter breezes.

Grand Cayman island is low and irregular, and can only be seen from the deck of a moderate-sized vessel about 12 miles. Its SE. end forms a rounded bluff cliff, topped with trees to the height of about 40 feet above the sea. The SW. end is low and sandy, and at 400 yards southward of it is a small sandy cay, about 2 or 3 feet out of water, from which a reef which generally breaks on the greater part runs off half a mile; it therefore requires great caution when rounding this end of the island, especially at night, as the lead will give but short warning. The NW. extreme is similar to the SE.; the NE. end is somewhat lower.

The island is almost everywhere thickly wooded, and on all sides but the W., is skirted by a reef, which is steep-to. At the E. end it forms a solid barrier to the distance of 1 mile, and the sea breaks on it heavily at all times. There are several small cuts through the reef on the S. side which admit the small vessels of the island into shelter within. The largest opening is on the N. shore near the NW. end, and it leads into North sound, which is shallow and of considerable extent. There is a church, and a small village is scattered along the shore of the bay at the SW. end of the island, but the principal settlement is at Bodden town. In 1875 the island contained about 3,000 people.

Anchorage.—The only anchorage for large vessels at the Grand cayman is under the W. end, about 1¼ miles northward of the SW. point. Care, however, should be taken to pick out a clear sandy spot, which can be easily done by the eye, and shoot in under easy sail, for the soundings do not extend more than about 400 yards from the shore, and the edge is very steep. A clear berth will be found with the church S. 81° 22′ E., and the SW. point S. 5° 37′ W. in 7 or 8 fathoms, but if it is merely to communicate, a vessel had better remain under sail.

Caution.—As before stated, great care must be taken in rounding Southwest point to give it a berth of at least a mile, until it is brought to the eastward of N. In leaving the anchorage with the usual trade-wind, it will be better to heave the anchor up before making sail, to prevent dragging at a short stay, for the holding-ground is not good, and the anchor in tripping might catch under a shelf of rock and be lost or broken.

This anchorage is a convenient place for obtaining wood and stock, except cattle, which are not always to be had at the moment; turtle are generally abundant and form the chief product of the island. Strangers approaching are met off the south side, at a considerable distance, by canoes having them for sale. Water is obtained from wells at about 100 yards from the beach, but it is scarce.

Cayman bank is a remarkable ridge of coral and sand, and barely in sight from the deck of a moderate-sized vessel. By keeping a good lookout the discolored water may be seen, and sometimes it may be detected by a strong current-ripple.

Little Cayman.—The southern coast is sandy and skirted by a reef which extends for about half a mile from the shore, and is steep-to; both the E. and W. ends are foul to the same distance, and soundings will be found about 1 mile distant from them. There is a well in a small cove called Bloody bay, near the NW. end, and a house and flagstaff on the western part of the island. The village is on the S. side, about 2 miles from the W. end; here a passage through the reef is used by coasters.

Cayman Brac is woody, and partially cultivated by two or three families, whose chief occupation is catching turtle. All its shores appear to be foul to a short distance, and the rocky ledge is steep-too. Anchorage is off the W. end in about 13 fathoms water, with a dark-green clump of trees bearing N. 45° E.

Caution.—Approach with care, as the bank shoals suddenly, and pick out a clear spot for anchoring. The village is on the NW. side of the island.

Pickle bank is of an irregular shape. The outer edge of the shoal is clearly marked when immediately over it, and is plainly visible from a boat running along it. On the edge there are from 13 to 20 fathoms of water, and one boat's length outside of the bank there is no bottom at 35 fathoms.

When directly over the bank the white coral with the dark spots of grass can be plainly seen, but 20 yards away the water has the appearance of the rest of the sea.

CHAPTER VII.

SANTO DOMINGO, OR HAYTI.

Santo Domingo, or Hayti, is a rich and beautiful island, the second in size of the West India islands.

It is very irregular in form, being deeply indented with bays and inlets and having corresponding projections, the most remarkable of which forms the southwestern extremity.

Three connected chains of mountains intersect the island from W. to E., and between these ranges are extensive plains and savannas. The principal range of mountains, called the Cibao, runs in an E. and W. direction from Cape Nicolas to Cape Engaño.

Mount Yaque is its highest peak, near the center of the island. Almost parallel with this chain another, commencing near Monte Christi, runs in an easterly direction, skirting the N. coast, and terminating abruptly on approaching the peninsula of Samaná. To the eastward of this range are low, marshy grounds, interlaced by estuaries and channels which formerly separated Samaná from the main-land and afforded communication from the gulf of that name to the sea on the N. shore of the island; the heights, however, reappear on the opposite side of the low ground and terminate in Cape Samaná.

La Vega Real lies between these two mountain ranges, affording rich and extensive pasture lands.

The third and most southerly mountain range commences at Cape Tiburon, and extends to the eastward, terminating at the river Neiva, about 80 miles west of the city of Santo Domingo.

All the streams of Hayti of any importance originate in the great central mountain chain. The principal rivers are the Artibonite, flowing W.; the Monte Christi, or North Yacki, NW.; the Yuma, flowing SE.; and the Neiva, or South Yacki, the Nisao, and the Ozama, flowing S. The mouths of all these rivers are obstructed by sand bars, and hence few of them are navigable. The Ozama, however, admits vessels drawing 10 feet.

Mineral springs of various kinds exist in different parts of the island.

The mineral products are various and very rich, including gold, platinum, silver, quicksilver, copper, iron, tin, sulphur, manganese, antimony, and rock-salt.

All tropical fruits and vegetables grow in abundance, and coffee, sugar, cotton, indigo, and tobacco can be plentifully raised.

Timber of all kinds is abundant, including pine, mahogany, oak, satin-wood, lignum-vitæ, and many other species.

The sea-ports are all or nearly all very unhealthy, yellow fever being a constant attendant during the hot season.

The island was discovered by Columbus on the 5th of December, 1492. It is now divided into two nominal republics. The eastern one is called Santo Domingo and the western one Hayti. The boundary-line is very irregular and is in dispute, but is generally considered to run from the mouth of the river Massacre, in Manzanillo Bay, on the N., to the creek Anse-a-Pitres, or Pedernales, on the S. coast, in about longitude 71° 50′ W.

The people are almost entirely of the negro race, and speak a Spanish dialect in Santo Domingo and a barbarous French patois in Hayti.

The winds in the island vary according to the trend of the different parts of the coast.

The rainy season continues from the end of May until November. In this season gusts and storms are frequent; at the same period strong SE. winds are experienced in the bay of Gonaives and in the channel of St. Marc. In November, December, January, and February the winds are from the NE., variable to NW., blow with force, principally on the northern coast of the island.

On the southern coast frequent storms occur in June, July, and August, in which the winds come from the S., and are violent principally from that direction.

On the entire coast of this island the sea-breezes blow, their direction varying according to the trending of the land. The sea-breeze commences from 8 to 9 a. m., increases until midday or 4 p. m., when it diminishes and gives place to the land-breeze, which lasts until 4 or 6 o'clock in the morning.

The general track of hurricanes lies to the northward of this island, occasionally, however, during the hurricane season, from July to October, they blow with terrific force.

The coasts of this island are imperfectly surveyed. Many of the ports at which vessels call for cargo are not chartered, and masters of vessels are compelled to rely on the pilots, who for the most part are ignorant, and know little of the English language. The ports of entry for imports and exports are San Domingo, Puerta de Plata, Azua, and Samana. Monte Christi is a port for export only. Vessels taking cargo on the S. and E. coasts enter and clear at San Domingo and take a pilot, also a number of laborers to assist in handling cargo. The pilot acts as stevedore and is paid from $1.50 to $1.75 per day, Sundays and fast days included. The laborers receive from 75 to 87½ cents per day, all being subsisted by the vessel while they are on board. The pilot directs the laborers, who work the lighters, and by his experience knows better how to bring them alongside the ship. Europeans, not accustomed to work in the water, frequently take sick, and vessels will meet with quicker dispatch by employing laborers and not exposing their crews, little accustomed to work in the tropics. The port charges are moderate. Vessels that enter under the following circumstances are free from port charges, unless they take water or a pilot, for which they pay as is stipulated, viz:

(1) Vessels of war, foreign or domestic; vessels that arrive with emigrants, and those that enter to repair damages, or to sell part of their cargo to supply their wants, without doing any other business.

(2) Those that enter and clear in ballast, or to procure provisions, to try the market, or on account of bad weather, to make repairs, or other causes, on condition that they do not discharge or take cargo on board.

(3) Vessels that on account of damages discharge a part or whole of their cargo, which if it was sold according to law would have to pay the same port charges as other vessels, but if the cargo is re-exported in the same vessel, without any part being sold, they would pay only 2 per cent. storage on the value of the cargo as determined by the appraisers. They would also pay the "derecho de muelle," also pilotage and water if they are taken.

Cape Samaná is the eastern point of the peninsula of the same name and forms a bold, double cliff of moderate elevation, the upper one rising a short distance within the summit of the lower. These cliffs extend about 2 miles to the southward of the cape, are of a reddish color, and steep to. A small reef on which the sea breaks extends off Cape Samaná.

Samaná bay has been thoroughly surveyed. Navigators, by consulting the chart and keeping a good lookout from aloft for the coral heads, will have no difficulty in entering it. The best entrance is along the northern coast where the least depth is 5 fathoms, except on Jean Bart reef with $3\frac{3}{4}$ fathoms and a rocky patch to the southward of Carenero cay with $4\frac{1}{2}$ fathoms, but these places can easily be avoided and a depth of 6 fathoms carried to the head of the bay. There are numerous channels through the Barco Perdido shoals, but as they are not buoyed or marked it is not recommended to use them.

Vaca point.—About one-third of a mile southward of this point is a remarkable spout resembling jets of steam, occasioned by the rush of water into a subterranean cavern. This spout can be seen 7 miles.

Marks.—At the S. end of a small sandy bay, called Frances bay, is a remarkable cliff with three large fissures in it.

Shoal.—To the southward of Canandaigua bank a shoal with $5\frac{1}{2}$ fathoms on it has been discovered; its extent has not been ascertained but is supposed to connect with the bank extending from the S. shore of Samaná bay.

Balandra Point is a remarkable red cliff lying at the foot of Mt. Diablo. Between this point and Santa Barbara are numerous huts and cultivated patches of ground.

Levantado cay is the largest of the group and is thickly wooded.
Chinchilline cay is a low rock.
Pascual cay is a small round islet, steep-to on its northern side, partly covered with trees.
Arenas cay is SW. of the others. These cays are joined by a reef, on which there are from 3 to 7 feet of water. The best anchorage is E. of the reef. In entering, haul close around Punta de las Heches and anchor in 6 fathoms, the point bearing S. 61° 52' E.
Clara bay is perfectly clear, and affords good anchorage. The bay is half a mile wide between Lirio and Gorda points, both of which may be approached within 200 yards. A good berth will be found, with from 9 to 11 fathoms of water, in the middle of the bay and just within a line drawn between the two points.
Gorda point is on the western side of Clara bay, and from this point the shore trends NW. for 1¼ miles, and then turning to the southward as far as Escondido point, forms a bay, sheltered to the southward by a chain of reefs and cays extending about a mile from Escondido Point.
Santa Barbara bay.—The entrance to the harbor lies between Gorda point and Poloma cay. A village of the same name stands at the head of the bay, at the base and on the sides of some small hills which are almost hidden from the eastward by a headland.
Paloma cay is the most easterly of the chain extending from Point Escondido, and is about 70 feet high, with steep sides, the summit being covered with bushes. From the E. end a shallow ledge runs off 500 yards in a southeasterly direction. Its extreme end, with a depth of 25 feet, lies S. 30° 56' W., one-third of a mile from Gorda point, leaving the entrance to the channel between it and the point less than one-quarter of a mile wide.
North of the western extremity of Paloma cay and nearly in mid-channel there is a bank with 4 fathoms of water on it, with a narrow channel on either side.
Carenero cay has a hill at each end about 100 feet high and well wooded. A wooden pier about 40 feet long, with a depth of 18 feet at low water at the extremity, extends from the N. side of the eastern part of this cay. The American mail packets use it as a coaling pier. Between this cay and Tamiso cay the ground is foul, with only a boat passage.
Aguada bay is a small cove in which anchorage may be found for small vessels. Off the N. side of Carenero cay a narrow ledge extends off nearly 300 yards and is steep-to. To the northward and in mid-channel are two patches having only 3 fathoms on them.
Gomère bank.—The western limit of Aguada bay is called Punta de la Cruz. Immediately S. of it, at about 150 yards distance, is a rocky shoal, nearly awash, called the Gomère bank, with deep water on either side, and between it and the head of the bay is the inner anchorage, sheltered from all winds and having a depth of from 3½ to 5 fathoms.

A small bank with from 8 to 10 feet of water on it lies S. 22° 30′ E. from Castillo point, at the eastern end of the town, and about 200 yards **distant.**

Castillo point, on which Fort Barbara stood, is a steep bare cliff of reddish color, about 40 feet high, with an old wooden house on the summit.

Directions.—Being at a distance of 3 or 4 miles E. of Balandra head, there will be no difficulty in recognizing it by its red color and the detached rock lying at its base. This headland should be rounded at a distance of from a quarter to half a mile, and a course steered along shore to the westward, taking care not to shut Balandra head in with Cocoa point until past the Chico shoals. The buoys and beacons formerly marking the limits of this reef and the Levantados reef have all disappeared. As soon as the Chico cay bears N. 33° 45′ E., the reef of that name will have been passed when, if bound to Santa Barbara de Samana (or Samana), the vessel may be hauled up toward Gorda point, taking care in passing to the westward of it to keep the eastern hill of Carenero cay open to the northward of Paloma cay, in order to avoid the ledge to the eastward of the latter.

The shoals may often be seen from aloft.

Having passed Gorda point, the deepest water will be found on the S. side of the channel, along by the edge of the reef until abreast of the W. end of Paloma, when haul-in N. 39° 22′ W. toward Aguada bay to avoid the shoal off Carenero cay. When the W. end of that cay bears S. 53° 26′ W., bear away to the westward for the inner anchorage. Keep the southern side again aboard to clear the Gomère bank, southward of the W. point of Aguada bay, and anchor in 5 fathoms water, muddy bottom, with Castillo point bearing N. 30° 36′ E., W. end of Great Carenero cay S. 42° 11′ E. and W. end of Tamiso cay S. 30° 56′ W.

Caution.—As the land and sea breezes are quite regular here, except for short periods in the winter when strong NE. trades prevail, a sailing-vessel should only attempt to leave Port Santa Barbara with the land-wind.

Should the sea-breeze spring up before the vessel reaches Balandra head, great care must be taken, if to the eastward of the Levantados cays, not to bring them to the northward of W. until abreast of Balandra head, in order to avoid the reefs which stretch to the SE. across the mouth of the Gulf of Samaná, and on which many vessels have been wrecked.

Tides at Santa Barbara de Samana frequently run at the rate of 1¼ miles an hour, and during the rainy season a velocity of 3 miles is sometimes attained. In leaving the harbor with a sailing-vessel, attention must therefore be paid to the time of the tide.

The town of Santa Barbara de Samaná (or Samaná) contains about 1,000 inhabitants.

SUPPLIES—COMMUNICATION—PORT CHARGES, ETC. 163

Supplies.—Fresh meat, vegetables, fruit, and bread can be readily procured at moderate prices. Water can be obtained at Aguada bay and is said to be wholesome. There is a small quantity of coal kept on hand for the use of the Clyde steamers. Coaling is rapid, by baskets, with no interruption on account of the weather.

Steamers.—An English steamer connecting with the Royal Mail steamers at St. Thomas calls twice a month; an American steamer once a month.

Port charges for ports in Samaná bay.

Vessels which do not receive or discharge cargo are not required to pay ship's dues, but pay harbor-master's fees at the rate of 3 cents per ton. Regular steamers pay ship's dues only at the rate of 30 cents per ton on cargo delivered and received.

Vessels bringing coal only and leaving in ballast are only required to pay half these dues.

	Per American ton.	
	Ship's dues.	Harbor-master's dues.
Vessels of more than 100 American tons, other than regular steamers, are required to pay on their entire burthen, if discharging or receiving:		
One-half or more of their burthen	$0.30	$0.05
One-quarter and up to one-half	.20	.04
Less than a quarter	.10	.03
Less than 1 ton		.03
Vessels of only 100 tons, which receive or discharge 1 ton or more of cargo, without regard to amount of cargo, are required to pay their entire burthen:		
Above 75 and up to 100 tons	.25	.05
Above 60 and up to 75 tons	.20	.05
Above 45 and up to 60 tons	.16	.05
Above 30 and up to 45 tons	.13	.05
Above 15 and up to 30 tons	.10	.05
Above 15 tons or less	.06	.05

Fees of health officer and fort fees.

	Fort fees.	Health officer.
A ship	$2.50	$5.00
A brig	1.25	5.00
A top-sail schooner	.60	3.00
Any other schooner	.30	3.00
A boat	.12	3.00

The United States is represented by a commercial agent and vice-consular agent.

If bound into the bay, after passing Chico cay steer S. 87° 11′ W., and stand on until Point Seballo bears N., then a S. 75° 56′ W. course will carry 6 fathoms through the coral patches S. of Point Corozos. There are only a few small ports in the western part of the bay where coasters load with mahogany.

The Yuna river, which empties into the western part of Samaná gulf, is obstructed at its mouth by a sand-bar, with only 2 feet of water on it. Boats may ascend it to within a few miles of Cotuy, 40 miles in the interior.

Barracota river empties into the southwestern part of the bay. The mouth is obstructed by a bar with from 2 to 5 feet on it. This river is navigable for boats 5 or 6 miles from its mouth.

The **Bay of San Lorenzo** is well sheltered and sometimes visited by coasters.

Savana la Mar, on the S. side of the gulf, is a scanty collection of huts. Landing, even from a small boat, is difficult, on account of the mud-flats which reach off from the shore.

Port Colorado.—No directions can be given for this port. The river Capitan empties into it, and the coast between it and Port Jicaco is obstructed everywhere with reefs, on which are several cays and islets. Two rivers, called the Culebras and the Magua, empty into the gulf between Jicaco and Colorado.

Port Jicaco, or English port, lies on the S. shore of Samaná gulf and 11 miles W. of Cape Rafael.

The harbor lies between Jicaco point on the E. and Manati point on the W. The rivers Yeguada, Guanabo, Real, and Jayan empty into the harbor, which is principally resorted to by coasters to load logwood and mahogany.

There is a small rocky islet, called Jicaco, near the entrance, for which it is an excellent landmark, as well as for the leeward and windward channels into the port. To enter the harbor bring this islet between the peaks of a high mountain inland, and steer in on this bearing S. 11° 15' W. Good anchorage will be found in 5½ or 6 fathoms of water inside the reef, about half a mile from shore.

Caution.—A stranger should not attempt to enter Port Jicaco without a pilot, nor, indeed, should he run inshore to leeward of Cape Rafael without one.

Cape Rafael, the southern point of the great gulf of Samana, is quite low; but 2 miles inland from it there is a remarkable conical hill, called Mount Redondo, which, at a distance from NW. and SE. has the appearance of an island. The coast in the vicinity of Cape Rafael is low and foul, and should not be approached nearer than 3 miles.

From Cape Rafael to Cape Eugaño the coast runs in nearly a straight line S. 45° E. This part of the island abounds in mahogany and logwood, and there are several small ports and bays where small vessels load with these woods, but as the shore is skirted by a broken reef and exposed to the wind and sea these small anchorages are not only difficult to approach, but are dangerous even in the fine season.

There are several small cuts in the reef through which vessels of 6 feet draught may pass, but larger vessels must lie 1 mile or more off shore.

Frequent accidents occur, and communication with the shore is sometimes interrupted for weeks at a time.

There is no opening in the reef or safe anchorage between Cape Rafael and Port Macao.

Port Macao.—To the northward it is protected by a reef which joins two remarkable rocky islets. The eastern or windward one, called Cabezote Barlovento, lies close off Macao point, with a boat-channel between them; the other, Cabezote Sotavento, or el Infiernito, lies about half a mile from the shore and to the eastward of the entrance of the river Anamuya, where there is said to be an excellent oyster-bed. The anchorage for coasters is about half a mile to the northward of the reef, and their cargoes are brought off by boats from the Anamuya river.

Mahogany and logwood are also loaded here from the rivers Maymon and Nisibon, the first 5 miles and the second 14 miles NW. of Port Macao.

Arena Gorda.—This anchorage is the first one to the SE. of Port Macao. There are three small cuts in the reef here through which a small vessel not drawing more than 5 feet may pass to the inner anchorage. Larger vessels lie from 1 to 1½ miles off shore in 10 to 12 fathoms of water.

Ranchitos bay, 2 miles SE. of Arena Gorda, has two small cuts in the reef, with 4 or 5 feet of water in them. The anchorage is 2 miles off shore in a depth of from 11 to 12 fathoms.

Babaro, 9 miles SE. of Los Ranchitos, is one of the best of these anchorages, as the reef lies near the shore and the sea is smoother. The anchorage for large vessels is 1½ miles off shore in 10 or 12 fathoms of water.

Cabeza de Toro is the first anchorage to the westward of Cape Engaño.

Through the reef in front of this port there are two passages, and in the lee one, called la Nayba, a depth of 10 or 12 feet may be carried. Large vessels anchor in 10 or 12 fathoms of water, outside, with a bottom of sand and rock. This place is much frequented by wood-droghers, and large quantities of mahogany are shipped.

Cape Engaño, the eastern extreme of the island of Santo Domingo, is a long low point from which a ridge of rocks runs 3 miles in a north-easterly direction.

A short distance inland there are two small hills which, seen from a W. by S. direction, at a distance of 17 or 18 miles, present the shape of a wedge.

Between Cape Engaño and Point Espada the coast is low, and soundings extend some distance off shore, with a white sandy bottom.

There are several small cuts through the reef which skirts this part of the shore and some small sandy bays, where mahogany is shipped, but, like similar places between Capes Rafael and Engaño, large vessels are obliged to anchor 2 miles off shore, exposed to wind and sea.

Punta Cana is the first anchorage south of Cape Engaño. The shore is inclosed by a reef, which obliges vessels to anchor, according to their draught, from a mile to a mile and a half from the shore. There are two openings in the reef, through which the boats pass to carry cargo to the sandy beach. These openings have 6 feet of water in them, are narrow and obstructed by coral rocks, requiring great care in navigating them. The surf is heavy on this coast and with a N. wind prevents communication with the shore.

Puntanal and Guayacanes are ports similar to Punta Cana. Upon the shore of these ports are some houses; they are inhabited by laborers employed in cutting mahogany from the adjacent forests. Puntanal is 3 miles S. of Punta Cana.

Point Espada, the SE. extreme of the island, is a remarkable bold cliff of moderate height. Its extreme point is low and prolonged by a bank or reef which gives the water a whitish color. Banks of this nature are frequently met with in different places off the coast of Santo Domingo and are called Placeres blancas, or white grounds. They are very often strewn with sharp-pointed rocks.

Tides.—At the anchorages outside of the reefs on the southeastern coast of Santo Domingo the flood-tides generally run to the S. 22° 30' W. for 9 hours, with a strength of $3\frac{1}{4}$ miles an hour, and the ebb-tide, for $2\frac{1}{2}$ or 3 hours, runs N. 33° 45' E. The tides in this vicinity are, however, very variable in their strength, duration, and direction; sometimes ebb and flood each last six hours. Sometimes again the ebb lasts longer than the flood, and in this case the NE. current is stronger than that running to the SE.

Yuma Bay anchorage is good but of limited extent, exposed to the NE. winds, and is in front of a little sandy beach called "Playita," near the windward point of the mouth of the river, in 12 fathoms of water. The mouth of the river is obstructed by a bar with 8 or 9 feet of water on it, but inside there is a depth of 12 feet.

Fresh water is obtained by ascending the river as far as Derrumbadero, but this can only be done in small boats.

Anchorages.—Vessels will find good anchorages between Port Yuma and False cape in 9 to 12 fathoms of water, but they will be exposed to NE. winds.

The tide runs with great velocity, especially about Point Cnevita, where it has a velocity of 4 or 5 miles.

False cape.—The land about this cape is formed by precipices of coral rocks, in the form of walls with a height of 150 to 200 feet. False cape is the southern point of this high land, and seen from the northward presents the profile of a grotesque figure.

Granchora anchorage.—Vessels are compelled to anchor several miles off either to the leeward of Catalinita or to the leeward of the reef which extends from Granchora to that island. The surf is generally so great on the beach at this place that weeks may elapse before cargo can be taken on board.

Puerta Martel is a port similar to Granchora.

Vessels about to visit any of the numerous small places on the E. coast or between Point Espada and the city of Santo Domingo generally take a pilot at the latter place, which is the port of entry for all these places.

Saona island may be justly said to form the southeastern extreme of the island of Santo Domingo, for the space between them is so filled with reefs and shoals as to leave only a boat-passage. It is covered with trees. Its NE. point is formed of steep bluffs; its SE. point is quite low, and a dangerous ledge extends a distance of 3 miles in the same direction. The sea breaks on this ledge 1½ miles off shore; farther out the depths are 4 and 5 fathoms.

At a distance of 5 miles off the southern shore of Saona there are from 7 to 10 fathoms of water, and a ship should keep at least this distance when to the southward and eastward of the island.

Bahia Caballo.—Three miles to the westward of the SE. point of Saona there is good anchorage off a sandy beach.

Alert bank.—In approaching this anchorage great care must be taken to avoid a dangerous rocky head called the Alert bank. This rock has only 4 feet of water on it, and the sea breaks in heavy weather. N. 45° W. of Alert rock there is another rocky head, with from 9 to 18 feet of water on it, with a deep channel between the two dangers.

Supplies.—Wood and water can be obtained here.

The western coast of Saona Island is lined with reefs and dangers, especially toward the northwestern point and near Palmillas point on the mainland.

Catuano pass.—There is only 7 feet of water in its shoalest part and is narrowed by a bank of mud and coral rocks.

A reef extends from the W. point of Saona towards the coast, and care should be taken when approaching the land.

Kurea reef is from 1,000 to 2,000 yards long, 200 yards wide, and nearly awash at low water. This may be a continuation of the Alert rock mentioned above. Until more accurately defined, navigators should give the island a good berth.

Catalinita island.—Between this island and Saona a dangerous reef extends, called the Horseshoe. Near Saona there is a cut in this reef through which a depth of 6 fathoms may be carried into a sheltered anchorage with muddy bottom, having Catalinita island bearing N. 11° 15′ E.

Caution.—The N. shore of Saona is steep-to till this reef is approached, but the sea is so heavy and the currents so strong and irregular that this part of the island had better be avoided; indeed, Saona island should not be approached from any direction nearer than 6 miles, except in cases of necessity.

Bank.—The captain of the Spanish brig *Arina*, whose draught was 10 feet, reports having touched five times in three minutes when 9 or 10 miles southward of Saona island.

Guaraguao is an anchorage 8 miles to the southeastward of the Quiabon river, and is seldom visited.

Bayahibe is a few miles to the northwestward of Palmilla point. A vessel can anchor in 6 or 7 fathoms of water about 1 mile off shore, well sheltered from the SE. by Saona island and Palmilla point.

Quiabon river is obstructed by a bar, sometimes dry and rarely having more than 3 feet of water on it. The anchorage off the mouth of this river is only an open roadstead, but with good holding-ground. The best berth will be found with the two points of Minos and Aguila in one, the latter being the eastern point of entrance to the Romana river, and with two cocoa-nut trees on shore in front of the largest house in the village bearing N.

The ground to the eastward of this bearing is rocky, and there is said also to be in that direction a rocky shoal with only 13 feet of water on it. In the rainy season good water can be obtained by going 2 miles up the river.

Between the mouth of the Quiabon and the Romana river, a short distance to the westward, there are three small loading-places, called Minos, Burgado, and Caleton. The first two are only fit for small vessels, and the latter is entirely unsheltered. The anchorage for large vessels off Minos has 19 fathoms of water.

Romana river.—The entrance may be known by the village on the hills on the right bank, 180 feet above the sea. It empties into the sea between bold limestone bluffs, and its entrance is only about 200 yards wide. Large vessels, however, can enter it, and it is one of the best and most sheltered anchorages on the southern coast of Santo Domingo.

The only danger to be avoided is a small rock, with 6 feet of water on it, lying about 75 yards S. 45° E. of the western point. A short distance E. of Aguila point, the eastern point of the entrance, is a reef which breaks and is easily seen.

Directions.—The entrance to the river Romana is too narrow to beat in. On standing in toward the entrance two prominent points will be seen, one on each side of the river. When in line they lead directly on the rock just spoken of. They should therefore be kept just open of each other, bearing about N. 16° 52′ W. Steer in on this line, and when inside the mouth of the river keep the eastern shore aboard. Upon entering the river two small rocks, 6 or 7 feet out of the water, will be seen on the eastern shore a short distance S. of the inner salient points just mentioned.

Anchorage.—With the northern of these rocks in one with Aguila point a vessel may anchor in 5 fathoms of water. The ship should be steadied by a hawser to the rocks. Small vessels of 10 or 11 feet draught may, with the assistance of a pilot, go 2 miles farther up the river, or they may anchor just within the inner western point. Off the eastern inner point there is a bank with only 6 feet of water on it.

Good water may be conveniently obtained by sending a boat up the river as far as the rapids.

Catalina island is small and low. The channel between it and Santo Domingo is navigable for large vessels. The Santo Domingo shore should, however, be kept aboard to avoid a reef which generally breaks off the NW. point of Santa Catalina.

There is a good anchorage in 3½ fathoms of water in the NW. part of a bay, where vessels are well protected by the two prominent points of the island.

Cumayasa river is nearly abreast of the western end of Catalina island and is said to be broad and deep enough to afford shelter to large vessels. Those drawing 18 feet or more should anchor about 300 yards inside the entrance, in 4 fathoms of water, and a little to the southward of the smaller of two coves on the eastern bank. This berth is near a small dry-dock.

Small vessels of 6 or 8 feet draught may take the channel close to the western bank and ascend the river as high as San Pedro rock, 1¾ miles from the mouth. Beyond this rock there are three islands. Higher up the river becomes so narrow that it is only navigable for boats to the embarcadero of San Juan, 2 miles above San Pedro.

A short distance above San Juan good water may be obtained from a basin called Agua Dulce. Boats can not approach it nearer than 200 yards.

Soco river.—Although one of the largest of the rivers flowing S. from the Cibao mountains, it is not navigable except for boats, as a shallow bar obstructs its mouth, inside of which the channel is blocked up by sand-banks, covered with drift-wood.

Anchorage.—Vessels sometimes anchor about 3 miles off shore in 5 fathoms of water, with the entrance bearing N. 11° 15′ E. or N. 22° 30′ E., but this anchorage is entirely unprotected. Small vessels lie closer in, in 3 or 4 fathoms, exposed to southerly winds and hardly sheltered to the eastward by Mortero point.

The landing place is 200 yards inside the mouth of the river, on the western bank.

Santa Cruz del Ceibo lies on the bank of the river of the same name, which is one of the branches of the Soco, about 15 miles from the sea.

Port Macoris is formed by the river of the same name. It will admit vessels drawing 10 feet of water. The entrance is about half a mile wide between the S. point and Point Tibiz, N. and W. of it. Nearly abreast of the entrance there is a small cay, called Isleta, having a reef extending off its NE. point. On the western side of this cay there is a mud-flat, and the channel, with from 15 to 17 feet of water, runs close along the eastern shore. Care must be taken to avoid a small rocky head called Edward shoal, with 6 feet of water on it, which lies about 100 yards N. of the S. point.

The mark to clear Edward shoal is the second cocoa-nut tree, near the house of the captain of the port, in the village on the eastern bank, in one with the N. point. After passing the Isleta reef the cocoa-nut trees should be kept just open till the vessel is within the Edward shoal, when haul in and anchor in 11 feet of water, just inside the N. point.

Caution.—A sailing-vessel can only leave the river with a fresh land-breeze; and as the current sets towards the Edward shoal, care must be taken to avoid it.

The United States is represented by a consular agent.

Guayacanes anchorage is 9 miles W. of the Macoris river. It is an open roadstead. The anchorage is 1½ miles off shore, in 8 or 9 fathoms, with good holding ground. There is a small opening in the reef skirting the shore through which boats may reach the landing place.

Juan d'Olio is also an open roadstead, and the anchorage is some distance from the land. There are a few houses on the shore.

Andres bay is formed between Caucedo and Magdalena points. The other part of this bay is not safe, but off Agua del Rey, in the inner or eastern part, about 4 miles from Magdalena point, there is a fair anchorage off the beach in 5 fathoms water, but a heavy swell rolls in. A vessel will lie sheltered as far round as SE., but it is open to the southward. There is another spot in the bay called Playa de Andres, where wood is shipped; but the anchorage is 3 miles from the shore, outside an extensive reef, which forms with the coast a channel with 9 feet water. This place is famed for the prodigious number of pigeons which visit it in May and October, when they may be killed with sticks.

La Caleta is a small bay close to the westward of Caucedo point, where temporary anchorage will be found in from 3 to 7 fathoms water, sheltered round to SE. Near the point there is an embarking place for mahogany, but large vessels are obliged to load under sail.

Santo Domingo city.—The bar at the mouth of the river, which is shoaling, prevents vessels of a greater draught than 10 feet from entering, there being generally 12 feet on the bar at low water and 18 feet inside; all others are obliged to anchor in the open roadstead. The city is surrounded by a wall, which, with the fort at the entrance of the river, the outworks, bastions, and many of the principal buildings in the town, is in a more or less ruinous state. The town is now the capital of the Dominican republic.

The roadstead can only be considered as a temporary and unsafe anchorage.

Estudios bank is composed of rock with a thin covering of sand and mud, not at all trustworthy holding-ground. A vessel lying here in the season of rollers or tidal waves (November to March) or in the hurricane season (July to October) would be very likely to drag her anchors, and in such a case on this rocky shore, where the sea beats with such fury, there would be little chance of saving either ship or crew. With any appearance of bad weather ships lying in this roadstead should immediately seek an offing.

In approaching this anchorage the lead should be kept going, as the bank is steep-to. Comparatively good holding-ground will be found in 8 fathoms of water, bottom of mud and sand, on the following bearings: Torrecilla point, N. 50° 37' E.; signal-tower, N. 2° 48' W. With these bearings some houses on the eastern side of the Ozama will be open off the citadel. With these shut in, the bottom is rocky.

The difference in the nature of the coast is a good indication of a vessel's position in this neighborhood.

The shore to the eastward of Torrecilla point is almost entirely composed of rock; there is scarcely a sandy beach to be seen, and the sea generally breaks against it with great violence.

Torrecilla point is low, sandy, and skirted by a bank on which the sea breaks heavily with a southerly swell.

Arenas point is low and salient, contracting the river to a width of about 100 yards.

On the W. side of the river, a little to the northward of Homenaje point, there are several rocks close inshore on which the sea breaks. In calm weather sometimes they can not be easily distinguished, and are dangerous for boats. The outer part of the bar commences a short distance northward of Torrecilla point and takes a direction toward the light-house.

To enter the river Ozama, a pilot should be taken, and it should be borne in mind that, the bar being composed of rocks, a smooth time and high water should be chosen, as a vessel drawing 10 feet would receive serious damage by even touching on the bar. Extensive works are in progress with a view to deepening the water at the entrance. A jetty has been partially constructed on each side of the river, which is narrowed at the mouth to 400 or 500 feet.

As the current in the middle of the river is sometimes very strong, a vessel had better moor head and stern close inshore.

The stream out of the river Ozama runs with great velocity.

Tides.—The rise and fall of the tide is about 2 feet, and the time of high water is uncertain. During the rainy season the depth of water on the bar somewhat increases.

When steering from seaward for the anchorage off Santo Domingo city it will be useful to remember that a few miles to the eastward of the Cibao range of mountains two small hillocks rise to a height of 200 or 300 feet above the plain; these appear as two islets long before the low shore is seen, and if kept on a N. 11° 15′ W. bearing will lead up to the anchorage.

Winds.—During the winter months, and especially in the spring, the land and sea breezes succeed each other with tolerable regularity; but during the remainder of the year they undergo some interruption, particularly in the summer season. Frequently the fresh north winds on the S. coast of Santo Domingo completely overcome the sea-breeze. Within the Ozama the land wind blows from NNE. to NE., and the sea-breeze from S. to SSW. The first begins soon after sunset, and continues until 8 or 9 in the morning.

Between Beata point and Saona island, when the moon's age increases, the ebb-tide sets twelve hours eastward and the flood twelve hours westward. The ebb begins at 9 or 10 in the morning and runs at the rate of 1¾ miles an hour. The rise of tide is a little more than 3 feet in Agujero Chico, and 1½ feet at Nisao point. When the moon's age decreases the waters run invariably to the westward during the twenty-four hours at from 1 to 2½ miles an hour. The weather is then changeable, and at times strong squalls are experienced. Off this part of the coast of Santo Domingo, after fresh northerly or southerly winds, the current often sets eastward, and occasionally at other times. The westerly current strikes the coast between Beata point and the mouth of the Neiva, then turns to the NE. as far as that river, and thence eastward, trending with the coast. The city contains about 15,000 inhabitants.

Provisions can be obtained, also water.

The exports are mahogany, fustic, logwood, coffee, sugar, wax, molasses, tobacco, hides, etc.

The imports, machinery, dry goods, petroleum, lard, earthenware, cooperage, stock, etc.

There are four regular lines of steamers: French transatlantic line; German line from St. Thomas, Jacmel, Puerto Plata; Spanish line from Rico, terminating at Havana, and English line from St. Thomas to La Guayra. The Clyde line from New York is the most important, running steamers twice a month.

The Clyde Steamship Company has a small quantity of coal here.

Port regulations.—ART. 1. All masters of vessels coming from a foreign port must deliver to the pilot who goes on board all the letters and papers destined for the port, excepting the letters to his consignee. The master can engage or not the pilot to anchor his vessel in the road or to take it into the port.

ART. 2. Upon the visit of the health officer the master will deliver the bill of health and will have visible all of his crew and passengers.

ART. 3. After the vessel is anchored the custom officials will visit the vessel, to whom the master must deliver his ship's papers and the manifest of the cargo; he will, without any concealment, state the places where seals ought to be placed, and will permit a watchman to remain on board until the cargo is discharged.

ART. 4. The vessel, either with cargo or in ballast, will be placed in the proper place for discharging by the pilot that anchors it, and in no case can the vessel move from one place to another without having obtained the permission of the captain of the port.

ART. 5. It is prohibited to throw overboard ballast and slops either in the road or in the port. The captain of the port will designate the place for their discharge.

ART. 6. In order to obtain coast pilots and laborers for vessels that are going to load on the coast the master and his consignee will present themselves to the captain of the port, who will facilitate it, and in order that the contract shall be made in his presence.

ART. 7. Upon clearing, masters of vessels must present to the captain of the port the passports of the passengers that he has on board, and before making sail will send his permit to leave to the man-of-war on the station.

Port charges.—Tonnage, 50 cents per ton; anchorage, $6; pilotage, $6; bill of health, $2; interpreter, $2; entering, $2; gangway (if taken), $4; water, $2 (paper) per pipe; light-house dues, 6¼ cents per ton.

There is also a charge of one-fourth per cent. upon the total value of the imports and exports called "derecho de muelle;" this latter is paid by the merchants. The coasting trade is reserved by the Government to the Dominican vessels, but as these are not sufficient in number for the trade, foreign vessels are allowed to load in any port where there is no custom-house, on payment of a license fee of 50 cents per ton.

The United States is represented by a consul and vice-consul.

Jaina river is about 5 miles W. of Santo Domingo city.

Mahogany is shipped from here, but, as there is no shelter, and bad holding-ground, vessels are obliged to lie a long way off shore, and can only receive cargo during calms or northerly winds.

Nigua river.—On its S. bank, a short distance from the mouth, is the village of the same name. Although numerous vessels load here, the loading presents many difficulties. The bank of soundings is so narrow that vessels lie close inshore in 12 to 14 fathoms of water. The anchorage is entirely unsheltered, and strong breezes cause the sea to rise 13 to 15 feet above the ordinary level.

Caution.—Vessels can only load during northerly winds, and, indeed, a vessel's safety would be seriously endangered by remaining at anchor off the Nigua river with the wind from any other quarter. The place has the reputation of being very unhealthy.

Najallo river empties into the sea a short distance S. of the Nigua river, and the anchorage is equally inconvenient and unsafe.

Port Palenque affords sheltered anchorage, but very confined, with a depth of 23 feet of water over a gravelly bottom. The shore is very steep to, with 3 fathoms close in shore.

In entering or leaving this anchorage, be careful to avoid a reef which extends SE. and NW. from the weather-point.

Nisao point is low, and descends to the sea by a gentle slope. Off the point is a reef, inside which fishing-boats find shelter. From here the coast takes a westerly direction to Salinas point, which is low and sandy, and may be recognized by the sea breaking over it.

Nisao roadstead.—To the westward of Point Nisao there is an open roadstead where vessels load with mahogany. Here the river Nisao empties into the sea, and vessels may anchor 1½ or 2 miles off its mouth in from 7 to 9 fathoms. The bar is almost impassable, even for boats, on account of the rapidity of the stream, and the sea breaks at a distance from shore, making landing difficult.

Water of the river is good at one-fourth of a mile from the mouth.

Port Viejo is an open roadstead. The anchorage is 1½ miles off shore in about 7 fathoms of water. This anchorage and that of Nisao road lie in a deep bight, between Point Palenque on the E. and Point Catalina on the W.

Catalina bay is but little frequented. There is no anchorage in its eastern part. In its western part small vessels only can anchor in 3 fathoms of water. A mile S. of Catalina point there is a shoal with 12 feet of water on it.

Sabana bay affords good anchorage in 5 or 6 fathoms, sheltered by the latter point as far round as ESE.

The roadsteads of Pava, Agua de la Estancia (the port of the village of Bani, 5 miles inland), and Estancia Colorado lie between Sabana and Salinas bays, and are all open and unprotected. Vessels lie from 2 to 3 miles off shore.

Salinas bay.—The best anchorage is with two hills, covered with palm-trees, on with a clump of the same species of trees near the shore, in the eastern part of the bay, and bearing between E. and N. 78° 45′ E. Small vessels anchor in 5 fathoms, and, as the bottom is so steep, they are obliged to run a hawser on shore to hold the ship in case the anchors drag.

The gulf of Ocoa is open to the southward, and the heavy sea which is caused by the prevailing winds when they blow strong renders the western shore dangerous to approach. The coast of the gulf is bordered by a sand-bank, generally narrow, but in places it extends off 1½ miles; the western shore is also skirted by a reef and the eastern shore partly so. At the head of the gulf there are two large bays; the Neiva or Juliana, in the western part, and the Ocoa, which occupies all the northern and eastern shore.

In these bays are various ports and anchorages, some of which are formed by reefs; those in Neiva afford but moderate shelter; those in Ocoa bay are very good. The hill of Baburuco on the W., and the mountain of Busu to the NW. of the gulf, are conspicuous objects. To the eastward of the gulf are the plains or flats of Bani, backed at the distance of 4 or 5 miles inland by the chain of the Cerro Gordo.

The **coast** from Salinas point to Caldera point is sandy, and free from danger. Half-way between the two points the coast projects a little and forms Ranchos point, which is bordered at 100 yards' distance by a bank of coral and sand with 10 to 12 feet of water on it.

Caldera bay.—Banks extend nearly across the bay, from N. to S., dividing it into two parts, called the eastern and western anchorages. The eastern anchorage is about three-quarters of a mile in diameter, with from 5 to 7 fathoms of water, diminishing toward the shore, with muddy bottom. This anchorage is perfectly clear after passing the banks which divide it from the western anchorage. These in smooth weather can be easily seen, but with a breeze from SE. or ESE. the sea breaks everywhere, and the channels are not easily distinguished. A stranger should take a pilot.

The western anchorage is only about 500 yards in diameter, with depths of 3¼ to 7 fathoms of water over gravelly and sandy bottom.

These two anchorages are sheltered from all winds, but a sailing vessel would be obliged to tow or warp in.

Both of these banks can be easily distinguished from aloft by the discolored water above them. From the western anchorage a depth of 3 fathoms may be carried into the eastern anchorage. For this the eye from aloft will be the best guide.

Water may be obtained from a small spring in the eastern part of the bay.

The **tides** in the bay are much affected by the wind.

Playa Vieja.—The establishment of the port is uncertain.

Anchorage outside of Caldera point. The best berth is with Caldera point bearing S. 78° 45′ E., 400 yards distant, in from 11 to 14 fathoms. This is a safe anchorage except during the hurricane months.

Caution.—In approaching Caldera, or any of the ports in the gulf of Ocoa, from the westward, a vessel, after weathering that part of the coast between Beata island and Avarena point, should make northing, as the current which runs to the westward near Alta Vela sets to the eastward in approaching the gulf of Ocoa. It is, however, advisable to keep clear of the western shore of the gulf. If bound to port Caldera work well to windward, but do not stand to the southward of latitude 18° N.

Ocoa road is in the NE. part of Ocoa bay. The anchorages are well sheltered from the usual trade-wind, but the holding-ground, of sand and loose stones, is not good, and anchors easily drag.

The usual anchorage off the entrance of the river is confined to a narrow ledge of sand, with rocky patches, very steep to, and so close to the shore that a cable must be carried to the nearest palm-trees, keeping an anchor to the westward to check the vessel against the landwind at night, which blows from the W. and WNW. The N. side of the river is the best. A large number of ships may, however, anchor here in safety; and at the beginning of the present century it was much resorted to by ships of war. The anchorage should not be approached before the sea-breeze is established, at about 10 a. m., and preparation must be made to meet the sudden and violent gusts which rush off the land after passing Ocoa point, the S. extreme of the bay.

Anchorage of Caracoles lies immediately to the northward of Ocoa road and abreast the mouth of the river Caracoles. As good a berth as any may be found 1½ miles off shore, with a depth of 5 or 6 fathoms of water. Landing on the beach is not difficult, but with southerly winds a heavy swell sets into the bay.

Azua bay, into which the river Via empties, is open to the sea, which sets in heavily. While the sea-breeze blows vessels ride very uneasily. Vessel can seldom tow wood to the ships after 11 a. m. There is not room to beat, and vessels are obliged to leave with the land-breeze.

There is a reef off the western point of the bay, and near the eastern point the bottom is very uneven.

Tortuguero, the port of Azua, is a fair anchorage.

The United States is represented by a consular agent.

The mountains in the neighborhood are covered with trees furnishing a wood of yellow color, fit for cabinet work.

Port Escondido is about 15 miles to the northwestward of Salinas point. The entrance to this harbor is half a mile wide, and its western point is clear and steep-to. The eastern point, lying more to the northward than the western one, is foul to the distance of 200 yards. Half a mile inside the entrance there is a rocky shoal 400 yards long N. and S. and 200 yards wide.

Directions.—In entering the harbor the southwestern shore must be kept aboard, at a distance of 400 yards, to avoid the rocky bank just mentioned, and large vessels should not go farther than one-third of a mile inside the entrance. One-fourth of a mile inside of this there is a depth of only 2¼ fathoms.

Anchorage can be found in 4 or 5 fathoms to the northward of the rocky bank, 600 yards from the entrance, but it is more exposed than the other. Small vessels drawing 13 or 14 feet may proceed farther in; for them port Escondido is an excellent harbor. Large vessels are exposed to winds from the S. or SE., which cause a heavy swell.

Puerto Viejo de Azua is the first anchorage in Ocoa bay, coming from the westward. It is a short distance N. of Martin Garcia point, and affords excellent and secure shelter to small vessels. Having a depth of only 12 to 15 feet at the entrance, it is inaccessible to large vessels, which may lie outside in good weather in from 3 to 9 fathoms, but this outside anchorage is entirely exposed to the sea-breeze.

Reef.—The entrance to the harbor is quite narrow, and a reef lies off the N. point.

In entering, avoid the SE. point, which is distinguished by high and towering rocks. Anchor in 5 fathoms midway between this point and the point of the reef; or having passed the entrance, steer N. 22° 30′ W., and anchor in 3 fathoms, the end of the reef bearing S. 22° 30′ E.

Tavora or **Tabara** river lies E. of Puerto Viejo de Azua, 1 mile distant.

Rancho del Cuba anchorage is half a mile NW. from the white bluffs of Martin Garcia. A good berth will be found, with a depth of 5 fathoms of water, 400 yards off shore and sheltered from the prevailing winds by Point Martin Garcia.

Alejandro bay.—This anchorage is separated by a point remarkable for its red bluffs from a small cove called Alejandro bay. This bay is bounded on the W. by the mouth of the river Neiva. It affords no good anchorage, and there are several rocks and shoals in it.

Barahona harbor lies on the W. side of Neiva bay. It is a reef-harbor, and vessels require the assistance of a pilot to enter it. It is not a suitable place for large vessels. The reef is very steep-to, and at a distance of 800 yards there is no bottom with 118 fathoms, then suddenly the depth decreases to 5 fathoms, shoaling soon after to 10 feet.

The village of Barahona can be seen at a distance of 2 miles, and above it two ranges of hills, one above the other, each range having a saddle bearing S. 67° 30′ W. from the village.

Baburuco anchorage is a short distance S. of Avarena point; it lies between two reefs, and is dangerous and contracted. Small vessels only can anchor there, with a depth of 12 to 15 fathoms of water 1½ miles from shore.

Mala-Pasa anchorage is easily distinguished by some white cliffs on shore. This anchorage is off the mouth of the river Nisaito, and like the anchorages of Nisaito and Naranjal, a little farther N., is a dangerous place for vessels.

Riocito anchorage.—The shore is so steep-to here that vessels are obliged to lie in dangerous proximity to it. It is exposed to wind and sea, and, although vessels load here in fine weather, it can by no means be considered a safe anchorage.

Petit Trou is extremely difficult to enter, and should not be attempted by any vessel drawing more than 10½ feet, or without the assistance of a pilot. The holding-ground is rocky, and not to be trusted. The anchorage is sheltered toward the eastward by a reef 3 miles long, having two cuts in it. The eastern one is 400 yards wide, with several sunken rocks in it, on one of which there are only 10½ feet of water. The western passage has from 18 to 20 feet, but the part of the anchorage to which it leads is strewn with dangerous sunken rocks.

To enter either of these passages, as before said, a vessel should not draw more than 10½ feet, and should be guided by the eye from the bowsprit end. The best time for entering is between 11 a. m. and 1 p. m., when the various dangers may be more easily seen.

During the increase of the moon the tides set twelve hours each way, the ebb to the E. and the flood to the W., at the rate of about 1 mile an hour. On the decrease there is no ebb at all, and the current increases to 1¼ knots. The rise and fall is about 3 feet.

The sea-breeze at Agujero-Chico sets in at 2 a. m. and blows till 7 or 8 p. m., when it veers to E. and E. by S. till near midnight. There is consequently little or no land-wind. The river Agujero-Chico empties into the harbor.

All this part of the coast abounds in game.

Cape Mongon is a high promontory, which from a distance of 15 or 18 miles appears like an island.

Beata point is the southern extreme of the island of Santo Domingo and terminates to the southward by two salient points forming a small bay.

There is a rocky, quoin-shaped hillock 2 miles NE. of the S. extreme of the point. When seen from the southward it resembles Alta Vela, though apparently much smaller.

Beata island is covered with trees and brush-wood. The southern part is the highest; the northern point is long and low. From the northwestern point a bank with from 10 to 13 feet of water upon it extends 2½ miles; on its outer edge are five small rocks called the Islets and the Table. The eastern shore is bluff and steep to, rising toward the S., with very deep water off it in some places. The SE. point is a steep bluff, having some small rocks off it. The S. coast is also formed of bluffs, and from the SW. point a ledge stretches off some distance. The western shore is clear and steep-to, and is skirted by a bank.

To the northward and westward of Beata island are five small rocky islets.

There is a breaker N. 11° 15' E. from the island, but its exact distance can not be given.

There is a heavy swell and variable current in the channel between Beata island and the main-land, and the depth is somewhat less than than 3 fathoms.

The channel between Alta Vela and Beata island is quite clear, but the currents are strong and irregular, and it will, therefore, be more prudent to pass to the southward, on which side it may be approached within 1½ miles.

Frayle rock from a distance appears like a group of a sharp-pointed white-topped rocks.

The current in this vicinity generally sets strongly to the westward. In January H. M. S. *Druid* experienced a current of 1½ knots setting to the southeastward against the wind. Commander Woodward, U. S. Navy, reports that he found a current of over a knot an hour setting to the eastward on the S. coast of Hayti.

From Beata point, and as far as Cape Rojo, the coast is formed by vertical bluffs, which give a peculiar character to the small bays along the shore. These bays lie between the points of the cliffs, and are bordered by a narrow sand-beach, from which it is necessary to climb the bluffs or seek a ravine in them if it is desired to go farther inland. The coves or small bays of Rousselle, Sin Fondo, Thomas, Burgados, Truyes, and Vases, afford examples of this singular conformation, particularly remarkable immediately to the westward of Beata point. The old descriptions of the coast of Santo Domingo give the name of *acculs* to the bays of this description. From the shores of the bays the summit of the cliffs is frequently very difficult of access.

Between Point Beata and Cape False there are three small bays, only affording suitable anchorage for small vessels in from 8 to 11 feet of water. East of Burgados or Agujero Azul bay, the western of the three, a white sand-bank commences, which, bordering the coast to Beata point, connects it with Beata island by a narrow ridge, on which there are from 2½ to 2¾ fathoms of water.

Thomas bay.—Anchorage, sheltered from S. and southwesterly winds, may be found in the middle of this bay, in from 5½ to 8 fathoms of water.

Sin Fondo or **Aguilas bay** is skirted by a beach of coarse sand and gravel, with steep bluffs behind it. The depth varies from 12 to 8 fathoms, diminishing to 2½ fathoms as the beach is approached. Good anchorage is found here, unsheltered, however, from westerly winds. A good berth is half-way between the two points and a little within a line drawn between them, in 7½ or 8 fathoms.

Rousselle bay is like the bay just described, a beach of sand and gravel at the base of high cliffs. Vessels may anchor 1½ miles off shore, in 8 to 11 fathoms of water, sheltered from N. round by E. to S. A river of the same name runs into the bay.

Cape Rojo.—To the northward of Rousselle bay is a cliff 40 feet high, and 2 miles long, called Trou Jacob cliff, the northern extremity of which is Cape Roxo.

Trou Jacob bay is between Cape Rojo on the S. and Platform point on the N., into which empties the river of the same name. Anchorage, sheltered from the usual winds, may be found in this bay in from 3 to 7 fathoms, with a bottom of coral or sand, with Cape Rojo bearing S. 33° 45′ E. or S. 22° 30′ E., 2½ miles distant.

Platform point is a moderately high bluff with a flat top. To the northward and between it and Point Pedernales or Pitre are two bays also called Pedernales or Pitre. The river of the same name, which empties into the northern bay, is a considerable stream and forms in part the boundary between the republics of Hayti and Santo Domingo.

Anchorage may be found abreast the lowland of the northern bay or to the southward of the western point of the mouth of the river. The anchorage is easy of access and without danger. The coast in this neighborhood is formed of chalky cliffs with a few gravelly beaches.

From Pedernales point the coast takes a NW. direction to the village of Sale-Trou; between are the small bays of Piéges, Raccroc, Cochon, Grand-Gosiers, and Boeuf.

A remarkable range of red rocks 3 miles long lies immediately NW. of Point Pedernales, terminating at Point Piéges, the southern limit of the little bay of the same name. This point may be known by a remarkable white triangular cliff, 220 feet high.

All the coast here is formed by white cliffs above a stony beach; soundings extend off for 2 miles.

The **anchorage of Sale-Trou** is limited to the westward of Bocachica point, formed of high white cliffs which extend for 3 miles to the westward. Behind these cliffs the land rises rapidly to the mountains of La Hotte. On the E. the anchorage is bounded by Point Predicador, a low point to the eastward of which, half a mile distant, is a small islet near the coast, not easily distinguished.

In the NW. angle of the bay is the village of the same name. There is a beach of coarse gravel, terminated by a red bluff called Tapion, easily distinguished from a distance. Half a mile to the eastward of this cliff the river Sale-Trou empties into the bay. Small vessels may anchor abreast of the village with from 17 to 20 feet of water, sand, and mud. Large vessels must anchor 1 mile off shore in 7 or 8 fathoms, but the holding-ground is not so good. The anchorage is entirely open to the southward and is dangerous during the summer months.

Jacmel bay.—At the head of this bay is the town of Jacmel, on the eastern bank of the Gauche river, which formerly flowed through several mouths into the bay.

From the offing to the eastward of Jacmel an excellent landmark for its locality is a deep cut in the mountain range back of Cape Marechaux. Should this notch be hidden by clouds, as it frequently is, a remarkable point, called Belle-Roche, situated to the eastward of Cape Marechaux, and off which there is a white rock of the same name, which, being overgrown with bushes in the center, appears like two rocks, will be a good guide toward the bay.

As the bank of soundings where anchorage is practicable is very steep-to, the ship should be under easy sail or steam, ready to anchor at once on striking soundings. Steamers calling here frequently remain underweigh and do not anchor.

The anchorage space is limited and when more than one vessel is lying off the town it is necessary to lay out a kedge to avoid fouling when the land-wind comes off. A small pier or boat jetty has been built close-to, westward of the wharf.

The population is about 7,000.

Steamers.—The steamers of the West India Mail Company call here twice a month. The French Transatlantic line and a German line also call here.

Coal can not be depended upon, but other supplies are plentiful. The watering-place is on the W. side of the bay, at a dark spot between two cliffs.

Land and sea breezes are generally very regular in Jacmel bay. A heavy swell rolls into the bay, and care must be taken to avoid being becalmed near the shore. With a land-breeze this may be avoided by keeping the valley open.

Pilots are very slow to board vessels, and their services are not necessary.

Exports.—Sugar, molasses, coffee, rum, fruits, etc.

Imports.—Breadstuffs, provisions, petroleum, and cooperage stock.

BAINET BAY TO DIAMOND ISLAND.

Pilot charges.

[Haytian currency.]

Inwards:
Vessels below 300 tons	$80
Vessels above 300 tons	120
Vessels below 100 tons	10

Outwards:
Vessels above 100 to 200 tons	20
Vessels above 200 to 300 tons	30
Vessels above 300 tons	40

Interpreter's fees, vessel under 100 tons, $25; 100 to 200 tons, $50; above 200 tons, $100, Haytian currency.

Tonnage dues, $1 per ton. The weight in use is the old French pound livre.

Anchorage dues.—Vessels entering and leaving port again within twenty-four hours pay $25—Spanish dollars; for the right of proceeding to a second port in Hayti vessels under 150 tons pay $200; above 150 tons and below 200, $250; above 200 tons, $300—Haytian currency.

The United States is represented by a consular agent.

Bainet bay is open to the eastward and is clear of dangers. Under very favorable circumstances a vessel might anchor temporarily in 20 fathoms of water off the southern part of the sandy beach. There is a small village at the head of the bay, but no regular landing, and the sea sets in heavily.

Morne Rouge point is of considerable elevation, and at some distance off appears a bold headland, but as it is approached it becomes known by five remarkable white hummocks near its extremity. The mountains near it rise to the height of about 1,000 feet. In a small bay on the E. side of the point there is a small rock called the False Diamond. At a short distance from the point there are 10 and 11 fathoms water.

Aquin and **English bays** are partially protected to the southward by a chain of reefs and cays lying from 1 to 3 miles off shore, with clear channels leading into the bay between most of them.

In Aquin bay there is secure anchorage for vessels of light draught in 3½ and 4 fathoms of water. In English bay the water is deeper and the holding-ground is good, but the anchorage is not so well sheltered.

Grosse or **Aquin cay** can be recognized by two remarkable white hills, from 300 to 500 feet high, and four white cliffs on its southern side. It is bold and steep-to on all sides.

Diamond island is a small white rocky islet nearly in the middle of the eastern channel into Aquin bay. The rock is bold on all sides except the N., whence a long narrow ledge runs off.

Kansas reef.—The depths on it are very irregular. The edge is very steep-to, the soundings decreasing suddenly from 10 fathoms to 3 fathoms. The sea generally breaks on it except in very smooth weather.

The channels leading between the cays into English and Aquin bays are deep and clear. That between Morne Rouge point and Diamond cay is not to be recommended for a sailing vessel, as the wind is apt to be baffling under Morne Rouge, and the ledge N. of the Diamond is to leeward. The channel between Diamond and Grosse cays is to be preferred. The channel between Grosse cay on the E. and Regalle and Anguille cays on the W. is clear and good. The passage between Ramier and Anguille cays is to be avoided, as it leads too near the Kansas reef. Between Ramier and Regalle cays vessels drawing more than 10 feet should not pass on account of a ridge of rocks extending to the westward of the latter islet. Between Cape St. George and Ramier cay the channel is free of danger, but care must be taken to keep clear of the ledge W. of Ramier cay. Entering the bay by any of these channels the best anchorage will be found on the N. side of Grosse cay in 5 or 5½ fathoms of water, keeping closer to the cay than to the Santo Domingo shore, on account of a bank with 9 feet of water on it which makes out half a mile to the southward from the main-land, taking care not to get south of a line joining the two points of the northern side of Grosse cay to avoid Dryad shoal.

St. Louis bay.—In entering, keep Pascal point, on the western shore, close aboard to avoid a sand-bank lying off it, nearly in mid-channel. Having cleared this, stand up the bay, and a good berth will be found in 7 fathoms of water, 3 cables W. of the old fort of St. Louis. Small vessels may pass to the northward of the fort for an inshore-berth.

In case of necessity a vessel may enter St. Louis bay by passing in NE. of Mosquito cay and close to the northward of Rat cay, between the latter and Taignense cay. The channel is narrow, however, and there are said to be several shoals between Rat island and Bonita point.

The winds from March to September are from SE.; from September to March, from ENE. Near the coast, to the W. of St. Louis, the wind is NE. or E., while at the same time N. of Cape Tiburon it blows from SE.

Mella Bank is at a distance of 1½ miles from the coast and to the northward of the cays and sand-banks which border the N. coast of Vache island, consisting of four shoals lying between the meridian of Toulan point (the eastern point of the entrance to Flamand bay) and that of Boyet point (the eastern point of the entrance to Meste bay). They are all of small extent, steep-to, and when the sun is shining brightly may be seen from aloft. It is probable that the bank is still changing. The outer shoal is about 1¼ miles from the shore.

Flamand bay.—During the fine-weather season good anchorage will be found just inside the entrance, but in the hurricane season a vessel should proceed farther up the bay.

The heat and the mosquitoes are said to be almost unbearable here during the summer season.

The bottom is everywhere mud.

Trou de Forban is on the western shore close to the little village of Renou. It is a completely sheltered cove, with from 1½ to 2 fathoms of water, called the Trou de Forban.

On going to sea from Flamand bay vessels pass to the westward of Vache island, as hereafter directed, and generally take a pilot, upon whom, however, but little dependence can be placed, and a vigilant lookout will be necessary.

Aux Cayes.—One and a half miles SW. of the town is the village of Vieux Bourg, off which is the road of Chateaudin, and still farther to the SW. is the little village of Torbec. Numerous small streams empty into the bay, the largest being the Acul river, 3 miles SW. of Torbec. Many reefs and dangers lie off the coast and on the N. side o Vache island.

The various charts of the bay of Cayes differ very much, and the hydrography of this vicinity, like that of the greater part of the coast of Santo Domingo, is exceedingly defective. It becomes, consequently, difficult to reconcile the different authorities from which this work is compiled.

Vache island affords a good landmark in approaching Aux Cayes.

Diamond islet is not easily distinguished, being of the same color as Diamond point, from which it is only distant 20 feet, and is not easily recognized more than 1 mile distant.

Diamond point is the central one of three detached white cliffs in the northwestern part of Vache island.

Latanier's point, the SW. extreme of Vache island, is low and thickly wooded.

Agua bay.—Between Diamond point and the NW. point of Vache island there are two coves, the northern of which is called Agua bay.

Temporary anchorage may be found about 1 mile off this part of the island in 5 or 5½ fathoms of water, sandy bottom.

Feret bay is about three-quarters of a mile eastward of the NW. point of Vache island, and at its eastern point of entrance is the high white islet of Raquette, connected to it by a reef. The bay is small. Small vessels in entering the bay should keep midway between the points, and anchor in the middle of the bay, avoiding the white sand-bank with 1¼ fathoms on it, easily seen, and which borders the salient points of the bay.

East cay is small and low, but well marked by a grove of cocoa-nut trees and some fishermen's huts.

East reef.—The edge extending from the E. point of Vache island round the adjacent cays to the NW. is tolerably well defined by an almost constant break or ripple, as also by several small rocks above water. By day the reef may be approached with safety, provided a good lookout be kept, but at night the utmost caution is requisite. No outlying dangers are apparent.

Great reef is an extensive white sand-bank southward of Aux Cayes, upon which at the NW. and SE. parts are two heads of coral partly uncovered. These banks, extending from abreast Cayes to nearly half way toward the island of Vache and along the shore for 1 mile SW. of Torbec, shelter the anchorages of Chateaudin.

The **inner anchorage of Cayes** is very limited—has only about 13 feet water—and difficult to enter or leave. That of Chateaudin is separated from it by a narrow tongue of white sand, which leaves the shore and joins the northern end of the Great reef; small vessels pass over it from one anchorage to the other. The Chateaudin anchorage is well sheltered, and extends from Principe point, W. of the village of Torbec, as far as Chateaudin point.

The entrance to Chateaudin road between the W. end of Great reef and Maho point, is about half a mile in breadth and carries 15 feet water. Vessels anchor in about 17 feet, sand and mud, at half a mile from shore off the village of Torbec or that of Vieux Bourg. Those of large tonnage anchor in 7 or 8 fathoms southward of Compania islet.

To reach Aux Cayes anchorage, steamers can use the S. passage, but sailing-vessels must use the E. passage.

Several shoal heads have been reported in Cayes anchorage. Many of the discolored patches are, however, caused by dark weeds growing on the bottom. It will, however, be prudent to avoid the dark patches as much as possible.

Battery point is readily distinguished by its fortification, and is well clear of the houses in the eastern part of the town and having a hut on it. There is also a hut on the western side of the entrance to L'Ilet river.

The population is about 11,000.

Provisions can be obtained.

Steamers.—The Atlas line of steamers from New York, Diamond line from Boston once a month. French and German lines call here.

Exports.—Coffee, sugar, rum, dyewoods, etc.

Imports.—Manufactured goods, hardware, coal, lumber.

Port charges.—Pilotage, $5 inwards and outwards; health visits, $5; tonnage dues, $1 per ton register; stevedores, 20 cents per ton stowing cargo; bill of health, $1.

The United States is represented by a consular agent.

East channel.—In proceeding to the eastward from Cayes anchorage, steer S. 75° 56′ E., and when East cay bears S., a course to the southward and eastward may be steered.

South channel.—Steer S. 67° 30′ E. for Great Cay a l'Eau until the western point of Vache island bears S. 22° 30′ W., when steer S. 50° 32′ W. with Boyet point astern until Diamond rock is opened, and then steer S. 2° 24′ W.

Chateaudin road.—If this anchorage is preferred, bring Diamond rock opened from Diamond point as before directed, then steer N. 64° 41′ W., which course will lead about a mile northward of Étron-du-Porc, and toward Maho point, in from 5 to 8 fathoms water; on nearing the latter a beacon with a white flag on it, at the SW. end of Great reef should be sighted, which must be left to the eastward.* Having rounded the reef which is easily seen, haul up along-shore, keeping in from 3½ to 4½ fathoms of water, and anchor a little eastward of Vieux Bourg. In approaching any of the anchorages in Cayes bay a stranger should have the assistance of a pilot; but it must be remembered that implicit confidence is not to be placed in them.

The **Winds in Cayes bay** are quite regular. The land-wind comes off from the NW. and veers round gradually to the NE. until about noon, when the sea-breeze sets in from the SE. and veers to the S. toward evening.

Tides.—The ebb stream sets strongly to the southeastward over the shoals northward of Vache island.

A **current** of over a knot an hour to the eastward has been met with off this coast.

Abacou point is low and skirted by a reef, said by some authorities to extend off nearly 1 mile, but Captain Owen, R. N., says only 200 yards. Commander Haxton, U. S. Navy, reports a small reef stretching off shore between Gravois and Abacou points, and extending 1½ miles off shore, but with deep water inshore of it. Until a more thorough examination is made the shore between these two points should not be approached.

Diablo bay.—Between Point Abacou and Gravois point there are two small bays, called Port Nonnettes and Diablo bay. The latter is immediately W. of Abacou point, and has a small sandy beach at the head of the bay, over which a brook empties. The western point is bluff, and skirted by a reef to the distance of 400 yards.

Port Nonnettes is a little inlet open to the southward, and, like Diablo bay, has a sandy beach and the mouth of a small stream at its head. Both points of the entrance are bordered by reefs to the distance of 400 yards. Coasters find temporary shelter from the prevailing winds in these two bays. Port Nonnettes is 3½ miles E. of Point Gravois.

Gravois point is thickly wooded and is 60 feet high. It is steep-to, there being 45 to 50 fathoms water one-third of a mile off shore.

From Gravois point to Burgos point the coast is very imperfectly known. It affords several unsheltered anchorages, all of which open to the heavy swell, and very unsafe with the wind from SE. and southward.

Port Salut.—In this small bay three rivers empty, and a small village of the same name is situated on its shore. NW. of this village there is a remarkable white bluff, abreast of which small vessels anchor. There is also said to be a coral patch with 12 feet of water on it, abreast of the village, and about 1 mile off shore.

---

* This beacon can not always be depended upon.

The low point on the N. side of Port Salut separates it from Drick bay, a small cove surrounded by high land. A small stream empties into the bay, and it is separated from Juif bay on the N. by a large, broad point composed of high cliffs and overlooked by high land. The anchorage is in the middle of the bay, in 4 or 4½ fathoms of water. At the head of the bay there is a village on a round, salient point, to the northward of which a river empties. The land around the bay is very high, and is intersected by two deep ravines extending into the interior.

Anchorage will be found in the middle of the bay, abreast of the village, in 5 or 6 fathoms of water.

Roche-à-Bateau bay.—A small river empties into the bay N. of the village.

Anchorage is in the northern part of the bay and to the westward of that part of the village.

Damassin bay lies NW. of Coteaux bay. A small river empties into the NE. part of it. From the scanty information we have regarding it, it seems to be clear and sheltered from the N. and E.

Port Piment is 1 mile NW. of Damassin bay. It is sheltered from NW. round by N. to SE. On the SE. side of the bay a river empties into the sea, and near it is a village on a high and prominent point which bounds the bay on the S.

The **anchorage** is with the town bearing S. 67° 30′ E., 1 mile off shore, in about 7 fathoms of water, which depth gradually diminishes toward the shore.

The bay of Three Rivers, so called from the three small streams which empty into it, is 2 miles in a northeasterly direction from Port Piment. It is entirely open to the southward, but with winds from the N. or E. it affords temporary anchorage; there are no dangers in it. At the head of the bay and back of the beach there is a village on a remarkable hill 150 feet high, the base of which is formed of red bluffs.

Salée Bay is immediately to the westward of the Three Rivers bay. It is quite small, surrounded by high land, and remarkable for two white bluffs, which form the points of entrance. A river of the same name empties into the bay, and on the shore is a small village.

Acul-à-Jean is a small bay. At the head of it, surrounded by high land, is a village. Like all these anchorages it is entirely open to the southward, but vessels may anchor 1 mile off shore in 7 or 8 fathoms of water.

Anglais bay is unsheltered and inconvenient. Temporary anchorage may be had in 6 or 7 fathoms of water SE. of some houses on the shore. Half a mile from these houses the river Anglais empties into the sea, but the surf is too heavy to obtain fresh water.

From the Tapion de Cahouane to Aigrettes point, 6 miles to the westward, the coast is low, with occasional pebbly beaches. Back of the shore the land rises rapidly, leaving between the sea and the hills a narrow plain cut up with lagoons.

All this part of the coast between the above-mentioned points is skirted by reefs and a white sand-bank to a distance varying from 400 yards to half a mile off shore. A portion of the reef between Point Aigrettes and Grande point, 4 miles to the eastward, is uncovered.

The reefs and sand banks off this part of the coast are easily perceived, but it should not be approached unless in case of necessity.

Point Aigrettes has a small round hill upon it. Its base is composed of white cliffs, and from a distance it appears like an island.

Tiburon bay.—The N. shore is bold, backed by high hills; at the head of the bay there is a small, three-cornered plain, with high land on two sides. The village of Tiburon is in the SE. angle of the bay, protected by a small battery, and the river of the same name empties into the sea N. of the village. The anchorage is not sheltered towards the W. or S. Small vessels can find shelter only from southerly winds N. of Burgos point and abreast of the village.

No difficulties present themselves in entering this bay, except those occasioned by the flaws and heavy squalls which come down off the high land. There is no danger to be avoided but the reef along the shore near Cape Tiburon and that off Point Burgos.

Supplies.—Water is easily obtained from the river, the mouth of which is marked by the five-gun battery which defends the shore. Wood and fresh provisions can also be procured.

Cape Tiburon.—Carcasses and Locos points from a distance seem to be one bold round point ending in Cape Tiburon. The three appearing as one are commonly called by the general name of Cape Tiburon, which name properly belongs only to a massive, lofty promontory about 700 feet high, rising abruptly from the shore and then ascending gradually, form, 1 mile inshore, a round-topped mountain, also called Tiburon; the western extremity of the extensive range is called La Hotte.

Carcasses bay.—Three brooks empty into the bay over a small beach, northward of which there is a hut on a little hill. The land around Carcasses bay is very high, like the rest of this part of the island. The bay is clear, but offers little shelter. Small vessels anchor in the middle of it in 5 or 5½ fathoms of water, bottom of mud and sand. Large vessels may anchor about 1¼ miles off either point in 11 or 12 fathoms.

Irois point is the western extreme of Santo Domingo, and, although not high, may be distinguished by a small hill on its extremity, which from a distance has the appearance of an island. The point is steep-to, and both it and the bay are clear of danger. The bay is 2 miles wide and half a mile deep. The village of Irois is on the NE. shore, on a small plain watered by the river of the same name. A little southward of the mouth of this river there is a cluster of black rocks, on a white sand-bank a short distance off shore; another brook or rivulet empties into the bay a little S. of these rocks.

Espagnol bay.—Its northern limit is Ibard point. Its shore is bordered by a white sand-bank or reef extending a cable's length off shore.

This bay is quite small and does not afford a desirable anchorage. Large vessels may anchor abreast it in 6 or 7 fathoms.

Pierre Joseph bay is to the northward of Ibard point. It is sheltered to the northward by the point and island of the same name. The point is low and sharp, and the islet is connected with a reef which skirts the entire shore of the bay as far as Point Ibard. The reef is steep-to. In the northern part of the bay there are several hidden dangers. The bay is surrounded by high land. At the foot of these hills and along the shore, where there is a sandy beach, are the scattered houses of the village of Pierre Joseph. To the southward of the village a river affording good water empties into the bay.

A small vessel anchoring in Pierre Joseph bay should bring the southern houses in the village to bear E. to avoid the above-mentioned dangers and anchor in 18 feet of water, with the islet bearing N. 11° 15' W.

Large vessels should anchor in 7 fathoms, with the islet bearing N. 56° 15' E. When the sky is clear the bottom can be distinctly seen and the dangers avoided.

Hospital bay is clear and anchorage may be had in the middle of the bay in 4 or 5 fathoms of water.

Cape Dame Marie is rather low, and on its extremity there is a small hill.

False cape, a short distance S. of Cape Dame Marie, is sometimes mistaken for it.

Dame Marie bay is between this point and Point Rousselin. It is entirely open to the westward. The bay is clear, and in entering it the only danger to be avoided is the reef which skirts the shore between Cape Dame Marie and False cape, at a distance of 300 yards.

-Rivière village is on the NE. shore of the bay and the village of Dame Marie on the SE. shore. Half-way between them is a white bluff called the Twelve Apostles. A convenient berth is with this bluff bearing S. 67° 30' E. in from 5 to 6 fathoms, half a mile to 1 mile off shore.

Seringue point, and bank is the NW. extreme of the long peninsula whose western shore we have been describing, and is a bold prominent headland. Between this and Cape Tiburon a sand-bank extends to the westward for 8 or 10 miles. The edge is abrupt, and the depth under 20 fathoms, decreasing toward the coast. The water is very clear, and the sandy bottom can be everywhere seen. Eastward of Point Seringue there is a little cove only fit for boats.

Abricots bay has a small stream emptying into it, and is separated from Clerc bay to the eastward by a large bluff promontory.

Point Jeremie is long and narrow, and makes out to the eastward, with a reef, which somewhat shelters the anchorage off the town from northerly winds.

Jeremie bay is small and open, and on its shore is the town of the same name. On the bank in front of the town the depth is from 3 to 6 fathoms, but with a strong NE. breeze the sea breaks and the anchorage is unsafe.

Larague reef extends off the point on which the sea breaks heavily with northerly winds.

The town contains about 5,000 inhabitants. Trade is carried on by five regular lines of steamers, principally by the Atlas line from New York. There is an American line (Diamond), from Boston.

The United States is represented by a consular agent.

Cayemites bay.—The entrance is between the eastern end of Cayemites island and Fantasque point, which will be recognized when nearly E. or W. of it by a low rocky point jutting out to the northward.

Mark.—Keeping Bec-à-Marsoin and Fantasque point open bearing N. 85° E. will clear the end of the reef.

Pesta.—Very little of the town is visible from the water; only two or three houses on the beach, and a few more on top of the hill.

Great Cayemites island is thickly wooded; about half a mile to the westward of it is Little Cayemites, with a channel 2 fathoms deep between.

There is also a passage with 1¼ to 2 fathoms water, running N. and S. for small vessels, westward of the Little Cayemites, over the white sand-bank between it and Grand reef. The latter is covered with about a foot of water, and on it are several rocks or small cays. To the southwestward of Grand reef there are two groups of cays covered with trees, which shelter the bay on the W. Near the coast there are various other cays and reefs.

Bec-à-Marsoin peninsula will be readily recognized by the deep bay back of it. From its eastern point the coast consists of perpendicular rocky cliffs, about 20 feet high, much worn and fissured by the action of the sea. A low table-land covered with dense foliage rises from the rocky cliffs, decreasing in height toward Point Fantasque. Back from the coast the main-land is mountainous.

Three miles and a half to the westward of Point Bec-à-Marsoin there is a shallow bay, at the bottom of which is a short sand-beach, the only landing place to the eastward of Point Fantasque. It affords no protection to vessels. There is a small fishing village near this sand-beach.

From this bay the coast is rocky, with occasional sand-patches until near Point Fantasque.

Baradaires bay, which is sheltered on its northern side by the peninsula of Bec-à-Marsoin, appears wide, but is obstructed by a reef extending from the southern shore. This reef extends from some small cays near Picolet point, in a northwesterly direction to within half a mile of Bec-à-Marsoin. It is steep-to and clear, with a channel for ships of the largest draught between it and the reef. A pilot is required, as the anchorage has many shoals.

Rochelois bank.—Between Gonave island and the coast is the Gonave channel, obstructed in its fairway by a dangerous rocky bank called the Rochelois. Some parts of the bank are uncovered, among others the Pirogues rocks, three of which cluster are always apparent; others only at low water.

Shoal.—A shoal has been reported 2 miles S. of the Pirogues. The bank is steep-to and the soundings on it are irregular, varying from 4 to 7 fathoms. To avoid this dangerous bank in the night vessels should keep the shore on either side close aboard, observing that the coast of Gonave island must not be approached nearer than 1 mile, while the coast of Hayti is perfectly clear and steep-to.

From Baradaires bay to Miragoane the coast is clear and steep-to, and affords no shelter. Three and a half miles E. of the entrance of Baradaires bay is the village of Petit Trou de Nippes. Thence the shore to the eastward is composed of perpendicular black cliffs as far as the village of Anse-à-Veau, and farther is the village of Petite Rivière, with the stream of that name emptying into the sea between them.

Miragoane bay.—The apparent width of the entrance is diminished by a reef which runs directly across from the western side, leaving a deep channel 1 mile wide between its end and the eastern point. The reef is dry in places, and on its western extremity is Black cay. The anchorage is in 10 to 12 fathoms, with the fort bearing about S. 33° 45' E. There is also a snug berth in the SW. part of the bay between two islets and the main-land, but it is very narrow. A spring of good water will be found in a cove 1¼ miles E. of Miragoane. In the cove there are 3½ and 4½ fathoms of water, but a bar of 12 feet runs across its entrance.

The United States is represented by a consular agent.

Petit Goave bay.—The town is on the eastern side of the bay, and just abreast of it there is a small sandy islet, 300 yards off shore, called Anglais, or Poules. Half a mile N. 67° 30' W. of it is a rocky bank with 2 fathoms of water on it. Between the Anglais islet and Carénage point the entrance of the bay is about 1 mile wide. It is sheltered from all but northerly winds; these are seldom strong, and Gonave island partially shelters the bay in this direction. Three small rivers empty into the bay, from any of which good water may be obtained.

The Atlas line of steamers call here twice a month.

The United States is represented by a consular agent.

Grand Goave bay is separated from the bay just described by a prominent rounded headland surmounted by a hill called Tapion du Petit Goave. It affords no shelter. The town is on the left bank of a small river emptying into the bay. A short distance to the eastward there is a wooded islet, with a 3-fathom channel 200 yards wide separating it from the main-land.

Coast.—Between Grand Goave bay and Leogane point, 8½ miles, the coast is low and wooded, and vessels may anchor off it in 7 or 8 fathoms of water.

Leogane is on the banks of the river of that name, 1 mile from the mouth. Anchorage in 9 or 10 fathoms of water will be found abreast the mouth of the river. This anchorage is entirely unsheltered. The bank of soundings is only half a mile wide, and steep-to. It should, therefore, be very carefully approached.

Gonave island lies immediately abreast of the deep bight called the Gulf of Port au Prince, and forms two channels leading toward the city of that name. At a distance from a NW. direction two round hills are seen. The highest, called the table, is in the SE. part of the island.

The W. coast is low and steep-to, there being 15 to 18 fathoms of water 200 yards off shore.

Gonave bank.—The SE. part of the island is connected with Hayti by a bank of coral, rocks, and mud, with varying depths of from 6 to 75 fathoms; the bank is steep-to.

Small vessels will find an anchorage under the W. end of Petite Gonave, which had better be entered from the southward. The only spot where vessels of large draught can anchor safely is in Park bay; its entrance, however, is so beset with dangerous rocky shoals, not easily seen, that it requires the assistance of a pilot.

Good water may be obtained about 5 miles eastward of the NW. point.

The **city of Port-au-Prince**, situated at the head of the bay of the same name, is the capital of Hayti, the western division of the island of Santo Domingo. It lies on the northern slope of a spur of the great mountain chain that runs through the island from E. to W. Its population is about 35,000, and it is a place of considerable commercial importance. It is regularly laid out, but most of the houses are of wood and the streets are unpaved. The town is nearly surrounded by marshes, and is very unclean and unhealthy, especially during the summer months. Behind the city is Fort Alexander, on elevated ground; 2 miles to the westward is Fort Bizothon, a low square building close to the shore. In the northern part of the harbor there is a small but well-sheltered basin, called the Inner harbor, large enough to hold a few vessels moored head and stern, and having a depth of 4 fathoms. On the northern side of this basin is a small cay called Fort islet, on which is a water battery.

There are other fortifications along shore all more or less in ruins.

Coal.—About 200 tons are kept on hand; poor quality; cost $16 per ton; $17.50 delivered alongside.

Water.—Supply is abundant, being carried to the town by pipes from springs in the mountains. Ships can send boats to the wharf at the custom-house.

The market is fair, fresh provisions being moderate in quality and price. Ship's stores are scarce and high-priced.

Yellow fever generally becomes epidemic during the summer months from April to August. There is a medical jury or board of health

There is no regular quarantine regulations, though the doctor of the port exercises a general supervision over vessels arriving at the port. The thermometer ranges from 75° to 91°. There are two French charity hospitals, which are conducted by the Sisters of Mercy.

Fort St. Blair is used as a saluting battery.

Imports are principally from the United States, being provisions, lumber, cotton goods, hardware.

Exports are coffee, logwood, cocoa, hides, wax, sugar, and mahogany.

Steamers.—Marquis de Campo line, Royal Mail line, Atlas line, French line, Imperial German Mail line, and Diamond line from Boston call here. There are four wharves here where vessels drawing 12 to 15 feet can load and discharge. No buoys can be relied upon.

Mail.—In time of peace there are regular mails to the principal places on the island.

The customs duties are very high.

Police duty is performed by the soldiers of the army.

Pilots can be had, but there is no necessity for them. There are no government regulations for them.

The authorities to visit are the President of the Republic and the United States minister resident, who is also consul-general. There is also a vice-consul-general.

Port charges.—Pilotage dues, 6 cents per ton; anchorage dues, 6 cents per ton; stage hire, $2 per day; wharf dues, $1 per ton; interpreter's fees, $4; water, $1 per cask; tonnage dues, vessels belonging to a nation having no treaty, $1.50 per ton.

In the northern part of the bay, as well as abreast of the town of Port au-Prince, there are numerous cays, rocks, and reefs, sheltering the anchorage on the N. and northwestern sides.

Pelican cays.—Some of these cays are barren and others wooded; the outside cluster have the general name of Pelican cays, and consist of five small, sandy, and mangrove cays. On their N. side they may be approached within half a mile. To the southward and SW. of these cays, and extending over a distance of 2 miles, are several rocks and dangerous reefs, among which are the Ambis rocks, four in number; and just above the water the Folleurs, Blanc, and Bellevue rocks, and the Bellevue bank.

Vessels coming from the NW. through St. Mark's channel may, after making St. Mark's point, steer to pass either between the Arcadius and the shore or between Gonave island and the Arcadius. The former leads more to windward, but for a stranger, at night, the latter is preferable. If the inside passage is taken the Arcadius should be passed at the distance of 1 mile and the course continued S. till the vessel is to the southward of the 3-fathom shoal, lying 2 miles from the main.

The channel for large vessels into Port-au-Prince harbor lies close along the southern shore, E. of Lamentin point.

In passing to the westward of the Arcadins, Princes peak, to the southward of the city, is a good mark; kept on a S. 50° 37' E. bearing it will lead clear of them and up to Lamentin point.

When Fort Alexander opens to the southward of Fort islet a vessel will be to the southward of the Pelican reefs, and may then haul to the eastward for the roads.

The sea breeze in the outside channel generally blows from WNW., commencing in settled weather about 11 a. m. and continuing till 7 p. m. The land-wind frequently comes off with a furious squall. These gusts come down frequently off the high land with great violence, and in hurricane months reach half-way across the channel between Santo Domingo, Cuba, and Jamaica. They frequently give but little warning, and the navigator should therefore be constantly on his guard.

In the harbor of Port au Prince the easterly breeze generally commences at day-break, and after 12 o'clock changes to the westward. This change takes place at 1 or 2 p. m., and is frequently accompanied by a heavy squall. In the spring and summer months it generally rains between 6 and 9 o'clock p. m. The direction of the land-wind varies with the trend of the coast.

Arcadins anchorage.—The best anchorage will be found in 11 or 12 fathoms water, with the smallest islet bearing S. 56° 15' W., distant about 1 mile. Vessels bound to Port au Prince would find this a good place to anchor for the night, if near it at sunset, with a land-wind. Under Montrou point small coasters find shelter in 5 fathoms of water from N. and northwesterly winds.

From Montrou point to St. Mark point the coast is low and bushy and steep-to all the way.

St. Mark point is a prominent round headland. To the eastward, 31 miles inland, is a mountain called the Devil's peak, forming an excellent landmark for the bay of St. Mark's.

Devil Point, the northern point of St. Mark bay, is a flat tableland covered with wood and ending in a steep, rocky cliff. The shores of the bay are very steep.

Caution.—A shoal extends about 200 yards from St. Mark point.

Morne à Vigie, situated eastward of the town, is a conspicuous flat-topped hill, when bearing E. leads to the anchorage.

The usual anchorage is in 15 fathoms, 300 or 400 yards from the shore and N. of the cemetery, which is white-washed. Vessels loading logwood and coffee moor with hawsers secured to anchors buried on the beach and remain in security at this anchorage at all seasons. An old fort stands on the Morne des Guespes, a hill on the N. side of the bay.

This port is considered one of the healthiest on the island. There is generally a land-breeze from 9 p. m. to 10 a. m., when the sea-breeze sets in.

Imports are provisions, lumber, furniture, dry goods.

Exports are coffee, logwood, mahogany, cotton, beeswax.

Pilotage, $15; bill of health, $2.50; landing ballast, $1 per ton; tonnage dues, $1.46 per ton, with reciprocity treaty; without treaty, $1.50 per ton; clearance, $2.

The same steamers call here as at Port au Prince.

The United States is represented by a commercial agent and vice-commercial agent.

Bay and river of Artibonde.—To the northward of Devil Point the coast is low, with high mountains inland. The bay of Artibonde, into which the river of the same name empties, is very small, and lies immediately N. of Devil point.

The entrance of this river is nearly dry at low water, and is seldom visited. Off Devil point the water is discolored by the river. At high water boats can proceed 5 or 6 miles above the mouth. During the rainy season a small steamer drawing 4 feet of water plies on the river for logwood.

Water may be obtained, but no wood.

Anchorage.—To anchor off Artibonde river, bring Devil point to bear S., distant about 3 miles, when a few houses will be seen close to the shore. These houses should be brought to bear S. 67° 30' E., and should be approached on that bearing within 2 miles, when a detached bank will be struck, with a depth of water from 6 to 20 fathoms. The lead must be kept carefully going, as within the bank there is no bottom till within half a mile of the shore, when suddenly a depth of 5 fathoms will be found. A vessel anchoring here must be ready to come to at a moment's notice.

Mark.—On the S. side of the entrance to the river there is a remarkable small cavern.

Point Salomon lies 3 miles N. of the Artibonde river, and forms the S. point of Grande Pierre bay, where, in case of necessity, temporary anchorage may be had close to the shore in 3 or 3½ fathoms of water.

Halle point.—From it a sand-bank, with a depth of one-half to 2¼ fathoms of water on it, extends more than 1 mile off shore, and is said to extend farther than is shown on the charts.

The shore from Gonaïves bay to Devil point must be approached with caution.

Verreur point is the northern end of a small island separated from the main-land by a channel only navigable for canoes at high water. The point is low and covered with bushes which extend to the water's edge. The fort that was situated on this point no longer exists.

Gonaïves bay.—The entrance is only obstructed by the sand-bank, which can in clear weather be seen and easily avoided. The entrance is not at first readily distinguished. The land N. of the bay is high, while to the southward a low, level plain extends as far as the river Artibonite.

Pierre head, on the N. side of the indentation which forms the bay, is a bold, rocky headland, above which is a hill of the same name.

The **town of Gonaïves** is near the shore on the E. side of the bay. The landing is abreast the middle of the town and just N. of a small battery. S. of the town are large salt-works, extending as far as Ligro point, bounding, to the eastward, Hospital bay, the western limit of which is Verreur point. These two points are low and covered with mangrove trees. The bank which lines the N. and E. shores of the bay of Gonaïves obstructs the entrance of Hospital bay, with several coral heads nearly awash, narrowing it from an apparent width of 1 mile to 7 00 yards. Approaching Gonaïves bay from the southward it is prudent to keep well off shore, outside of a line drawn from point St. Mark to Devil point. As soon as the perpendicular bluff of Mount Biénac, to the northward of the town, bears N. 56° 15′ E., this latter course will lead directly into the outer roads.

Caution.—A vessel working into Gonaïves bay should not stand farther to the southward than to keep the notch in the hill open to the northward of Mount Châtelain, or Châtenay, a large high mountain near Mount Biénac. In leaving the bay keep the notch open till St. Mark point opens out westward of Devil point, which, from this position, will appear like an island.

It will be prudent for a sailing-vessel to enter the bay with the sea-breeze and to wait for the land-breeze for leaving it.

The sea-breeze sets in from the NW. toward noon and continues till 10 p. m., when the land-breeze commences and blows about E. by S. till 6 a. m.

Population is about 8,000.

Exports are mahogany, lignum-vitæ, coffee, etc.

Port charges.—Pilotage, $5 in and out; health visit, $6; tonnage dues, $1 per ton for vessels whose nations have a reciprocity treaty; interpreter's fees, $4.

The United States is represented by a consular agent.

Between Pierre head and Corridon point an extensive bank of soundings makes off 4 or 5 miles, on which a vessel may anchor in 17 fathoms of water, with Pierre head bearing E. and Corridon point N. 39° 22′ W.

During the rainy season, from June to September, the weather in the evening on this part of the coast is very squally and uncertain, and vessels should therefore keep, if possible, 6 to 9 miles off.

Henne bay is open to the S. On its western side there is a mountain 1,700 feet high. Between the two points of entrance there are 24 fathoms of water; inside, the soundings are irregular.

It is not a good anchorage, but if obliged to anchor here the best place will be found on the eastern side of the bay, where the soundings are least irregular, in about 15 fathoms of water.

East of Henne point there is a remarkable white bluff.

Platform point is a white rocky bluff with a flat top. Three miles NW. of it there is a similar bluff called the Lower White Horses.

West of Platform point is the little village and bay of the same name, affording anchorage in from 2½ to 3¾ fathoms of water, abreast of the mouth of a small stream emptying into the bay.

Between Pearl point and Cape Locos, or Cape Fou, the coast is formed by bold cliffs, steep-to. There is a range of mountains 3 miles inland 2,000 feet high, under which vessels are frequently becalmed. In shore the current sets to the northward, but 6 miles off shore it generally sets to the W. and WSW.

Near the extremity of Cape Fou there is a rock resembling an islet, and a short distance to the southward a remarkable white cliff, called the Upper White Horses.

St. Nicolas mole.—Its northern side is formed by a low, flat peninsula, joined to the main-land by a narrow isthmus. From the flat surface of this peninsula the bay has received the name of St. Nicolas mole. In the outer part of the bay the water is so deep and the shore so bold that there is no safe anchorage. When seen from the offing the mountains back of the town of Le Môle present a burnt, brownish appearance. A conspicuous church stands a little to the southward of Fort St. George.

The bay is close and confined, however, and in the rainy season would probably be an unhealthy place. A sailing-vessel would have to work in to St. Nicolas anchorage. In doing so it will be well not to stand very near the southern shore as the sea-breeze generally blows fresh from NE. by N., and it being flawy she might miss stays.

If it is desired to enter the Carénage it will be best to wait till the sea-breeze lulls and then warp or tow in; in the winter this will not be till 8 p. m.

The land-wind generally blows moderately from the SE. till about 6 a. m. There is then a calm for about two hours, when the trade-wind sets in as a sea-breeze from NE. by E., backing to NE. by N. and blowing fresh till evening and sometimes as late as 10 or 11 p. m.

Water may be obtained at night from a brook used by washerwomen in the day-time, and emptying into the bay E. of Fort St. George.

No dependence can be placed upon procuring fresh provisions here.

The **current** about 6 miles off the NW. coast of Hayti generally sets to the NE., but within that distance it inclines towards the land and decreases in strength. As, however, the windward channel between Cuba and Santo Domingo is approached, it tends to the SW. and increases in strength.

The population is about 600.

No provisions can be obtained here.

There is a small stream of fresh-water which fails in the dry season.

The port is tolerably healthy and cool. There is no quarantine and no health-officer.

Salutes can be returned from Fort St. George.

There are no pilots, and there is no necessity for taking them.

The authority to visit is the general in command

From St. Nicolas mole to Juan Rabel bay the coast is bold, rocky, and steep-to, presenting no shelter, and is so inaccessible as to have received the name of the Iron coast.

Juan Rabel bay is a good and accessible anchorage. Salina point is low, bushy, and prominent; the shore in the neighborhood is diversified by bold rocky cliffs and sandy beaches, and the interior is mountainous and broken into ridges. A remarkable peak, resembling the ruins of a castle, rises from the bay about 2 miles inland.

The eastern shore is skirted by a reef, steep-to, with 8 fathoms clear to the edge. The best anchorage for large vessels will be found half a mile N., 22° 30′ W. of the town in 9 fathoms of water and half a mile from the reef, outside of a line drawn between the two points on the eastern shore; inside of this line the soundings diminish very rapidly and the bottom becomes foul.

Port à L'Ecu.—The entrance is narrowed by a reef which extends 400 yards from E. point. This is not an easy harbor for a sailing-vessel to work into with the usual winds. In entering, the E. point must be given a good berth on account of the above reef; then hauling close to the wind a good berth will be found in 7½ fathoms of water, sandy bottom, with a remarkable house on the southern shore, bearing S. 22° 30′ W.

Moustique bay is narrowed by a reef with 10 to 16 feet of water on it, stretching off from the latter point. The bottom is very uneven and strewn with rocks, making it necessary to pick out a clear place before anchoring. In the entrance there is a depth of 27 fathoms, irregularly diminishing towards the head of the bay, where a small stream empties.

On the western side of the bay there is a small islet, and SE. of it a small rock. The best anchorage is with this rock bearing about W. in 20 or 25 fathoms of water, near the middle of the bay. The bank is so steep that it is prudent to be certain that the vessel is on soundings before anchoring.

Between Moustique and Vigie points the coast should be avoided by a sailing-vessel unless she has a good working breeze.

River Salée bay is sheltered from easterly winds, and affords, in case of necessity, an anchorage with sandy bottom in 8 fathoms of water.

Port Paix is the northern extreme of the island, and immediately W. of it is the little bay of Port Paix, with Trois-Rivières point on its W. side. This little bay affords good anchorage, being protected to the northward by Tortuga island, and is opened only from NW. to W. The town, formerly protected by two small forts now in ruins, is on the southeastern shore of the bay. The land in the rear of the town is high, with a rather remarkable small conical hill sloping to the westward. From Pérez point N. of the town a reef is said to extend 600 yards.

Exports are coffee, logwood, cocoa, honey, hides.

Imports are provisions, lumber, dry goods.

The German line of steamers call here, also the Diamond line from Boston.

The United States is represented by a consular agent.

Directions.—To enter Port Paix a vessel should be under easy sail or steam, and having brought the village to bear S. 45° E., should steer for it, and anchor as soon as a less depth than 20 fathoms is reached, which will be about 300 yards off shore. In front of the town, about 100 yards from the beach, is a rock, which must be avoided by small vessels seeking an anchorage close in.

Tortuga channel.—The channel between the island of Tortuga and Santo Domingo is 4 miles wide in its narrowest part, and, as there is an easterly current generally setting through, it may be advantageously used by vessels bound to the eastward. In the day-time it is perfectly safe to beat through, as the reef can be seen, but it should not be attempted at night.

Currents.—There is an easterly set through this channel during a greater part of the year. On both sides of the channel, however, a contrary eddy may generally be found 1 mile off shore. They should not, therefore, be approached within that distance. A westerly current is only found here when southerly winds have been blowing for some days, which is rarely the case. If, however, a westerly current is experienced, vessels bound to the eastward should, instead of entering the channel, stand 15 or 20 miles to the northward. Winds are more variable in the channel than outside.

Tortuga island.—The center is moderately high, with low land at either end. The northern side is bold, steep, and inaccessible, while the southern shore is skirted by numerous reefs and shoals. The only good anchorage the island affords is situated on the S. coast 4½ miles from Point Portugal, the SE. point of the island.

Tierra Baja road is surrounded and sheltered by reefs stretching out from the coast, and is only fit for vessels drawing 14 or 16 feet of water, as the bottom is irregular, and the soundings vary from 3 to 6 fathoms.

To enter the anchorage, the village should be brought to bear N. 45° W., and should be approached on this course, which will lead between the reefs, which break and are easily distinguished by the eye. A good berth will be found in 6 fathoms of water, with sandy bottom, and with the village on the above bearing. At the entrance of this channel, called the eastern passage, there is a bank, with only 3¼ fathoms in mid-channel. The western passage has only 9 feet of water. Large vessels may anchor outside of the reefs, on the white ground, about 1 mile to leeward of the town.

Between Tierra Baja anchorage and Portugal point there are several small coves, affording temporary anchorage to small coasters.

There is also said to be anchorage under the W. end of the island.

Anchorage.—Between Grand point and Icague point are the following anchorages, only fit for small coasters: The bay and river of Cape Rouge, with 1¼ to 2¾ fathoms of water, well sheltered by the reefs; the bays of Great and Little Marigot, with 2¼ to 3¼ fathoms, and the bay of Petit

Rivière. These last anchorages are somewhat sheltered to the northward by Tortuga island, but hardly at all to the eastward.

From Cape Rouge to within a quarter of a mile of Icague point are a chain of reefs with a narrow channel between the reefs and the shore, having a depth of 1¼ to 2¼ fathoms of water. Through this reef are several cuts, but there appears to be none between the eastern end of the reef and Point Icague. Icague bay and the river Bas-de-Saint-Anne may be reached through the first cut to the westward (of Icague point), where there is anchorage for small vessels in 2¼ fathoms of water; bottom, sand and weeds.

Fond La Grange bay is easily distinguished by a chain of reefs 1½ miles off shore, which extends from the latter point to the westward nearly as far as Icague point. This bay affords good anchorage for vessels of the largest draught, and it is perfectly easy of access. To enter it, it is only necessary to keep the eastern point aboard.

The holding-ground is good, consisting of sand and mud. A vessel may anchor as convenient in the middle of the bay.

Salt River bay is only fit for coasters. Both the eastern and western points are skirted by a reef at a short distance from the shore.

Chouchou bay is open to the northward, but affords good temporary anchorage. To enter it under sail, stand close in round Marigot point, and be ready to anchor as soon as the ship loses her way, as it is almost always calm inside.

Point Marigot is eastward of Chouchou bay, and has a small round islet off it, which makes it a good landmark.

Acul bay is a well-sheltered inlet, narow and deep and of variable width. The water is deep enough for ships of the largest draught, and in some places the shores are steep-to.

There are three channels into the harbor: The eastern and middle channels between the reefs, at the mouth of the harbor, and the western or Limbé channel, safer and less intricate than the others, W. of the reefs and between them and the coast S. of Limbé island.

Limbé island is of circular shape and lies close to the shore off Marigot point, which is overlooked by a conical hill.

Anchorage.—To the southward of Limbé islet there is an anchorage for small vessels, sheltered to the northward by the islet of Limbé and by the reef called the Roche Pauvre, which extends to the eastward from Limbé point. This anchorage abreast of the village of Limbé is exposed to easterly winds, and is only fit for coasters drawing less than 1 fathom of water which anchor between the reefs off the coast and those surrounding the islet.

To enter the eastern channel from an offing of at least 3 miles, bring Rat islet to bear S. 19° 41′ W. and steer for it. From this distance, Marias and Belie points, described above, will be easily recognized. These two points in one will lead between the reefs in mid-channel with slight deviations to keep in a depth of 9 or 10 fathoms. On the edges of the banks on either side there are 4 fathoms.

After passing Rat island the channel widens, all the dangers are visible, and a vessel may, if desired, anchor outside the harbor in 13 to 16 fathoms, with the islet bearing N. 45° W.

Middle channel.—To enter by the middle channel into Acul bay it is necessary for a sailing vessel to have the wind well to the northward and steady, as she will have to haul up as high as SE., and there is no room to work. When at least 3 miles to the northward of Rat islet bring it to bear S. 11° 15′ E. and steer for it. When within 1½ miles of Rat islet it will be seen that this course leads just to leeward of some reefs to the northward of it; haul round these reefs, leaving Rat island and the reefs which surround it on the starboard hand. When Rat island bears N. 45° W. either anchor or stand farther into the harbor as before directed.

Caution.—The reefs in this channel can all be seen, but a vessel taking it must be prepared to anchor instantly should the wind die away or haul ahead. The holding-ground is good. Limbé channel is the widest and best. To enter it, bring Yeague point to bear S. or S. 11° 15′ W. and steer for it. As it is approached, the sea will be seen breaking on the eastern side of the entrance on Coq-Vieille cay or reef; steer midway between it and the point in 9 to 14 fathoms of water, so as to pass 600 or 800 yards from Gran Boucand point.

As the various charts of this locality differ, these instructions must be used with caution.

Little Port Francais is only accessible to coasters that can pick their way through the intricate mass of reefs and sand-banks which, commencing here, extend to the westward, obstructing the mouth of Acul bay.

Port Francais is a small bay which, though open to the N. and NW., affords good anchorage with ordinary winds.

Port St. Honoré, the eastern point of the bay, is skirted by a reef to the northward. To enter the bay, haul round this reef, leaving on the starboard hand two other small reefs nearly awash, off those reefs which skirt Baro point; then standing about a quarter of a mile to the southward, anchor in from 8 to 10 fathoms, with the fort bearing S.67° 30′ E.

The point on which the fort is situated projects so as to divide the bay into two smaller ones, of which the northern affords the best anchorage. In the middle of the southern one there is a small reef, and its shores also are foul.

Cape Haiti, formerly called Cape Francais and afterwards Cape Henri, is sheltered on the S. and W. sides by the coast, and to the E. and NE. by sand-banks and reefs. Although it is open to the northward, the anchorage is well sheltered in that direction by banks and shoals within the harbor, which is easy of access in the day-time. The approaches to the anchorages are not lighted, nor are the buoys on the shoals to be depended upon.

The town of Cape Haiti stands on a small plain on the W. side of the harbor, at the foot of a high range of mountains called Haut du Cap, which rises abruptly a short distance N. of the town. The Masonic temple is the highest and most conspicuous building in the town; its eastern gable has a portico and is painted gray. The cathedral, in the center of the town, is a large, conspicuous, square building, of a yellow color, with a dark sloping roof. The square tower and some other portions of the old cathedral are still standing. Lookout-house is on a hill N. of the town. It is surmounted by three signal masts and has the roof painted red and white. The custom-house is recognized by a house painted red standing next S. of it.

Reefs.—The reefs in the harbor can always be seen when it is smooth and the sun moderately high; if it is rough the sea breaks continuously on the weather side of all except La Trompeuse.

The population is about 10,000. The people are neat, cleanly, and the streets are dirty. The sanitary condition is fair, but in summer yellow fever generally becomes epidemic.

Fresh provisions can be had of fair quality and moderate in price; fruit is very cheap in season.

Coal can be had in small quantities; cost $13 to $14 per ton, transferred to ships in barges.

Water is abundant and of fair quality. It is brought to the town by pipes. Vessels can take water by boats from the wharf where there is a pipe. Merchant vessels pay $10 for the privilege of watering here.

There is a so-called military hospital, but the accommodations being poor, it is of no importance.

Imports are provisions, lumber, hardware, naval stores.

Exports are coffee, cocoa, honey, hides, logwood.

Steamers of Transatlantic (French), Imperial German Mail; Clyde line, from New York; Atlas line and Diamond line, from Boston, make regular trips; also the Royal Mail (English).

Mails are carried by steamers; also once a week by horseback to Port au Prince.

Port charges.—Pilotage in and out for vessels of 351 tons, $26; custom-house clerk, $1; interpreter's fees, $2; signaling vessel, $1; fort pass, $1; entering and clearing, $10; tonnage dues, $1.46 per ton; doctor's visit, $5; stowing cargo, 20 cents per ton.

Discharging and loading is done by lighters, which are expeditious and well constructed.

The authorities to visit are the general commanding the district and the commandant of the place.

The United States is represented by a consul and vice-consul.

The entrance to the harbor is formed by Point Picolet on the western and the reefs on the eastern side. On Point Picolet is a fort with white walls.

The shore to the southward of the town is very low. On it, a little more than 1 mile SE. of the town, is the village of Petite Anse. Between is a small hill covered with trees, having a ruined fort on it.

Shoals.—The principal shoal in the harbor, and the nearest to the entrance, is Le Grand Mouton. The sea generally breaks on its northern end.

In approaching the harbor of Cape Haiti from the eastward, a vessel should steer about S. 67° 30′ W., after passing the Monte Christo shoal, till the highest part of the mountains of Haut du Cap bear about S. 45° W. Then steer for them till the fort on Point Picolet is sighted. This fort should be brought to bear S. 22° 30′ W., and approached on this bearing. A pilot can generally be obtained off this point, and a stranger should take one. They should, however, be carefully watched and not implicitly trusted. In standing in, S. 22° 30′ W., for Point Picolet, by keeping the masts of the lookout station a little open to the right of Fort Picolet the detached bank of 19 feet on the E. side of the entrance is avoided; then as soon as Cape Hayti, the northern point of the promontory, bears W. a vessel will be abreast of the NW. point of the reef called the Coq Vieille, and may then haul to the southward.

In approaching Cape Haiti harbor from the westward, a vessel should keep at least 1½ or 2 miles off shore to avoid the coral reefs skirting the shore.

Le Grand Mouton shoal divides the approach to the anchorage into two channels, either of which may be used by vessels of the largest size. The clearing marks are of very little use to a stranger as they are not recognizable until well into the harbor.

The pillars of the ruined gateway between Forts St. Joseph and Picolet, open off Fort St. Joseph, lead to the eastward of the shoal stretching off shore in the western channel.

A wooden pier about a quarter of a mile long extends E. of the custom-house. There is a depth of 21 feet at the end of the pier at low water springs.

Boat landing is near the captain of the port's house, which is yellow, situated on the northern part of the town, near where the Tour d'Estaing formerly stood. The Haytien flag flies from this house.

Steamers may enter and leave this port at any time when the leading marks can be seen, but sailing vessels must enter with the sea-breeze and leave with the land-breeze, which blows during the evening and night from ESE. to SE. and dies away about 10 o'clock a. m. After an interval of calm the sea-breeze springs up about 11 o'clock a. m., blowing from NE. to ENE.

Throughout the twenty-four hours the winds off shore blow from the eastward, except when interrupted during the winter for a short time by N. and NW. winds. The former causes much sea in the harbor and outside and lessens or overpowers the land-breeze, so that until the sea goes down and a steady land-wind blows at night a sailing vessel's departure had better be delayed.

Currents.—After N. or NW. winds have been blowing for some days the current sets strongly to the eastward along this part of the coast.

Limonade bay is only used by coasters who find shelter under the reefs, passing through a deep cut running NW. and SE.

This part of the coast is skirted by the great reef which, commencing about 1 mile W. of Fort Dauphin harbor, sweeps to the northward toward Cape Haiti.

Fort Dauphin bay.—The harbor is an excellent one, being perfectly sheltered, commodious, and affording excellent holding-ground, with a depth of water sufficient for vessels of the largest size. The entrance is so narrow and crooked as to render it difficult for a sailing vessel, except with a commanding breeze. Shoals make off for a short distance from the points in the channel, making the turnings so that with a long vessel great care must be exercised. No directions can be given for the entrance except to keep in mid-channel, for which the eye will be the best guide. This narrow channel widens into a land-locked basin and free from shoals except to the eastward of Fort Dauphin. There is a small islet near the middle of the bay called Boyan, with a reef extending off its NE. side. A good berth will be found in 13 fathoms of water between Fort Dauphin, on a point N. of the town, and Boyau islet.

Manzanillo bay is a secure and accessible anchorage. The shores of the bay are low and covered with mangroves, the eastern shore forming the delta of Yaque river. On the S. shore is the mouth of the river Massacre, forming the northwestern boundary between the territories of Hayti and Santo Domingo.

There is no danger in Manzanillo bay; an excellent, well-sheltered anchorage will be found E. of Manzanillo point, about half a mile off shore in 7 fathoms, muddy bottom. The edge of the bank of soundings is very steep, and on the eastern side of the bay is only three-fourths of a mile off shore.

In approaching the Manzanillo bay from the eastward, the bank of Monte Cristi may be crossed with safety.

Monte Christi bay.—At the beginning of the present century the river Yaque emptied into a bay a short distance SW. of the village, but it now empties into Manzanillo bay, 10 miles farther to the southward.

If bound to Monte Christi from the eastward, steer from Cape Isabelle for Grange point, making allowance for the inset of the current, and round it less than 1 mile distant to avoid the inner Phaeton shoals.

In approaching the anchorage from the westward, Grange point should be brought to bear S. 67° 30′ E., and approached on that bearing, thus keeping to the southward of the Liverpool, Phaeton, and Monte Christi shoals.

In nearing the Seven islands it must be remembered that the current N. of them generally sets to the SE. On the bank the flood-tide runs to the SW. at the rate of half a mile an hour, and the ebb to the NE. at the same rate.

Point de la Grange is a bold headland, forming the eastern limit of Monte Christi bay. It is easily recognized by a remarkable hill, near the shore, having a flat summit, shaped somewhat like the roof of a barn.

A large marsh lies between Point de la Grange and the town of Monte Christi, and through it there is said to be a channel, connecting the bays of Monte Christi and Jicaquito, with a depth of 2 to 4 fathoms, and a rise of tide of 3 feet.

Monte Christi bank extends from Cape Isabelle to the westward as far as 12 miles NW. of Point de la Grange, then sweeping to the SW. for about 4 miles, it joins the shore again at Manzanillo point. It has never been thoroughly surveyed, and urgently needs examination. Within its limits are several islets, rocks, and shoals; until a more complete examination has been made, great caution must be used in passing over or near it. On this bank the water is discolored, the depth uneven, and the nature of the bottom very variable, being generally coral or coarse sand near the edge, and mud nearer the shore.

The Granja shoals or haut-fonds, are two small patches near the edge of the bank. The inner one is said to have 23 feet of water on it and from 12 to 25 fathoms all around. The outer one is said to have 6 fathoms on it. From this patch the two small cays, Fraile and Cabra, near Grange point, will be open of each other clear of the point, the westernmost islet bearing S. 28° W.

Till this vicinity can be thoroughly examined it will be prudent to keep Grange point on a S. 73° E. bearing, and not to approach Monte Christi from the northward.

Monte Christi shoal is composed of small pointed rocks on a white sand-bank, with as little as 2¾ fathoms on the heads and 4 to 7 fathoms between them.

The Seven Brothers are a group of small, low cays on the Monte Christi bank, to the westward of Grange point. Most of them are covered with mangrove trees, and numerous reefs and shoals lie between them. There are said to be passages between them; there is a navigable channel between the cays and the shore.

Anchorage will be found under the eastern islet, called Monte Chico, and also under the southern one, called Tororu. The latter lies near the edge of the bank.

Cabra or Monte Christi islet is partly covered with trees. A reef extends 400 yards to the N. and W. of this cay, on which the sea does not always break. In the passage between Cabra islet and the shore there are 1½ to 2 fathoms of water.

Cabra island has low bluffs at its N. and S. ends, is low in the middle, and will hardly be distinguished from the main-land by a vessel coming from the westward until close to.

Anchorage.—There is an excellent anchorage between Cabra island and a rocky cay or reef S. 11° 15′ W., three-fourths of a mile from it. There are no hidden dangers in this vicinity except a small shoal, with from 2½ to 4 fathoms over it, three-fourths of a mile to the westward of the anchorage.

This anchorage is completely protected from the trade-winds, which blow constantly during the day in summer time, and the water is very smooth.

In navigating off this part of the coast, when steering to the westward, if it is desired to pass to the northward of all the off-lying dangers just described, from a position 12 miles north of Cape Isabelle a course northward of W. should be steered to allow for the in-shore set of the current, and to give the Monte Christi bank a good berth.

When Grange point bears S., a vessel will be to the westward of the Grange shoals, and when Tercero cay, the most northerly of the Seven Brothers, and the third, counting from the eastward, bears S., she will be westward of Monte Christi shoal.

Jicaquito bay affords good anchorage in 4½ fathoms, and sheltered by a reef extending from Fregáta point, its eastern limit. The sea always breaks on this reef.

Tides rise 3 feet.

From Grange point to Cape Isabelle the coast is everywhere skirted by reefs extending 3 miles off shore; it is uninhabited, little known, and had better be avoided. There are, however, one or two anchorages available in case of emergency.

Rucia point.—The best, probably, is immediately W. of Rucia point, lying 7 miles W. of Isabelle bay. Vessels may anchor here in 12 fathoms of water, sheltered by Rucia point and the reef off it, as far round as NNW.

Arenas cay.—There is also said to be anchorage, with a depth of 5 or 6 fathoms of water, 3 miles westward of Rucia point and 1½ miles off shore. No definite instructions can, however, be given, and this dangerous vicinity had better be avoided.

Cape Isabelle appears like a low wooded island with some palm trees on its northern end. To the westward of the cape is Isabelle bay, open to the N. and NW., but affording good anchorage and easy of access. A good berth will be found with a bottom of mud and sand in 4½ fathoms of water, with the N. point bearing N. 45° E., about 1½ miles distant. Small vessels may anchor closer in shore, but the depths are irregular, with a reef and several sunken rocks in the way.

Fresh provisions, wood, and water may be procured here.

Port Caballos is a short distance to the eastward, and said to be a better and more sheltered anchorage than Port Plata, with, however, but 10 feet of water in the entrance.

Azufre, 6 miles W. of Algarroba point, is an anchorage near Port Caballos. E. of, and very near to, Cape Isabelle coasters of 10-feet draught find shelter under the reefs. A reef extends along the shore from Algarroba point to Port Plata. There is no anchorage along this part of the coast except for small vessels, which find shelter among the reefs.

Port Plata is the only port of entry in this part of the island. Its locality is easily recognized by a high isolated mountain called Isabelle de Torres, and having a conspicuous white spot on it. Westward of the mountain, at a distance of 4 or 5 miles, are some small conical hills. The harbor is semicircular in form, with a low, sandy beach, and affords good anchorage. On the eastern point there is a hill with a fort on it, near which, to the southward, is the town.

In the channel the soundings are regular, but between the points of entrance they diminish rapidly, and a vessel should therefore be prepared to anchor immediately under the eastern point, in about 5 fathoms of water. At one-fourth of a mile from the head of the harbor there are only 2 fathoms of water.

The engines and boilers of a steam-vessel lie close inside the breakers, on the NE. edge of the western reef, at the entrance to the port. A wooden pier extends a little beyond Fort rock, with 19 feet of water at the head of it.

The custom-house is situated close to the old pier, and a large square church, with the roof painted light red, is situated near the new pier.

The population is about 3,000.

Imports are provisions, lumber, petroleum, etc.

Exports are hides, honey, sugar, molasses, dye-woods.

It is the chief port of San Domingo on the N. side.

Steamers.—Atlas line, Royal Mail, Imperial German Mail, Diamond line of steamers from Boston make regular trips.

Port charges.—Tonnage dues, $1 per ton, gold; entry, 6 cents per ton; anchorage, 6 cents per ton; pilotage, 6 cents per ton; interpreter, $4; doctor's visit, $4.

The United States is represented by a consul and vice-consul.

Anchorage.—The holding-ground is good, but there is generally an uneasy swell, and vessels have to moor.

Current.—Outside the harbor the current generally sets to the westward, inclining toward the shore.

The sea-breeze in the winter sets in strong from ENE. about 9 a. m. and continues till sunset, when a light land-breeze comes off from about SE.

The harbor is exposed to the N., but winds from that quarter seldom blow.

Two small streams empty into the harbor, and in the rainy season large quantities of water flow from them. At that time the river of St. Mark, in the western part of the harbor, is the best watering place. In the dry season the eastern stream is the most convenient.

Between Port Plata and Point Cabaret there are three small ports, called Sosua, Bergantin, and Padrepino, but no instructions can be given for them, and they are rarely visited. The coast between these two points is very foul, and should not be approached nearer than 3 miles.

Port Santiago is seldom visited. It is about 1 mile wide at the entrance, formed by Cabaret point on the E. and Caleta point on the W. side. From the latter point a dangerous reef stretches off in a SE. direction toward Caleta point. Outside this reef, to the northward, is a sand-bank with 2½ fathoms of water on it, and also a rocky bank with 1¼ fathoms.

The passage W. of these dangers, and between them and the reef, is about 60 yards wide, with depths of 4½ to 5½ fathoms.

Vessels of 400 tons visit this port, anchoring in 4 to 5 fathoms of water within 300 yards of the shore. The holding-ground is not good Before entering it will be well to buoy the points of the reefs.

Point Macoris.—Between Point Macoris and La Roca are the small ports of Cabaret, Soufrière, Ananas, Grosse pointe, and Macoris. Port Soufriere affords anchorage for vessels of considerable size. The western channel is the better one of the two cuts through the reef which shelters the anchorage. The other so-called ports are only boat harbors.

The river Yasica empties into the sea 3½ miles SE. from Port Cabaret. There is absolutely no shelter here, and no vessel can anchor with safety. The mahogany cut in this vicinity is taken by land to Port Cabaret and shipped from there.

Coast.—Between Cape La Roca and Cape Viejo Frauces the coast is bold, steep, and thickly wooded; it should not be approached nearer than 3 miles on account of the off-lying reefs and shoals.

Cape Viejo Frances is steep and high, and can be seen from a distance of 30 miles. There is a high mountain lying 12 miles S. 33° 45' W., from it, visible 45 miles off. At the foot of the bluff of the cape there are some rocks and foul ground.

From Cape Viejo Frances to Matanzas, and then to the eastward to Cape Cabron, is an extensive bight called Escocesa bay.

The western coast affords no shelter and is uninhabited.

Port Matanzas, in the southwestern portion of the bay, is easily entered, but is only fit for small vessels. On the southern shore of the bay there are some small anchorages, where in fine weather coasters may load mahogany.

Grande Estero Colorado is a short distance E. of Port Matanzas, and formerly communicated with the bay of Samana. This channel is now entirely closed up.

The entrance to the Grande Estero affords anchorage, moderately well sheltered, with depths of from 5½ to 11 fathoms.

Port Jackson affords tolerable anchorage for vessels of moderate size, being somewhat sheltered by the cay and reef of the same name. The entrance is open to the NE., and is said to be clear of danger, except a shoal in mid-channel, easily seen, and having deep water on both sides. There are some large cays or rocks 4 miles E. of the entrance, and still farther to the eastward are some others. The entrance to the harbor is said to be abreast of a remarkable white rock.

The other ports in Escocesa bay are Moretes, the mouth of the Lateriana river, Pechem's point, Limon, l'Hermitano, San Juan, Escondido, Rincon, and Galeras.

Cape Cabron terminates in a perpendicular white cliff, higher than Cape Samana. S. 56° 15′ W. from Cape Cabron is a mountain called Mount Cabron, or el Pilon de Azucar.

Between Cape Cabron and Cape Samana to the southeastward the coast forms a deep bight, in which are several cays and reefs close to the shore. Between these two points the coast should not be approached nearer than 3 miles.

CHAPTER VIII.

MONA PASSAGE AND THE ISLAND OF PUERTO RICO.

The Mona passage.—The channel between the islands of Santo Domingo and Puerto Rico is clear of obstructions or dangers and is called the Mona passage, from the small island of that name lying midway between Cape Rojo and Saona island.

Mona island.—Its summit is nearly flat, with a few bushes and trees, and it may be seen from a distance of 18 miles. It is of volcanic formation; its N., E., and W. sides, consisting of high perpendicular bluffs, afford no landing-place. The surface of the island is composed of calcareous slate-colored rock, full of holes containing soil in which the trees and brush-wood grow.

There are numbers of wild goats and hogs on the island, and turtles during the season.

A ridge of rocks run off the SW. point, and a vessel should not come inside the depth of 8 fathoms of water, which will be found at the distance of one-quarter of a mile.

The eastern and northern parts of the island are said to be clear of danger, and steep-to. The NW. end terminates in a promontory, and its extremity rises to a lofty perpendicular rock, which when on a bearing N. 5° 37′ E., or S. 5° 37′ W., has the appearance of a sail, with Monito open westward of it. From this end, named Cape Barrionuevo, round by S. to the E. end, the island is bordered by a bank of white sand and rocks with 18 to 3½ fathoms water on it. It extends off 1½ miles between Capes Barrionuevo and Julia, also called Caigo ó no Caigo point (I fall, or I don't fall). It takes the latter name from an enormous rock on its summit which is very curiously balanced and threatens every moment to fall. Half a mile off, between Cape Julia and the E. end of the island, is the only anchorage for vessels of any size.

Point Arenas, or **Occidental**, divides this anchorage in two.

Santa Isabella bay is called by the fishermen Uvero bay. The bottom is of sand, but there are so many rocks that vessels are apt to lose their anchors. Vessels can stand in without risk to a depth of 6 to 8 fathoms and then anchor. The holding-ground, however, is bad, and a sea always sets in, so that a vessel must be ready to put to sea as soon as there is any sign of a hurricane from the W. or when the S. or SE. winds set in.

El Sardinero is the other, and undoubtedly the safer portion of the anchorage. It is only worthy of the name during the season of southerly winds. The sea in it is then smooth, as it is sheltered by Arenas point and the spit which makes out to the westward from the latter. The bottom throughout the anchorage is white sand, without specks, and the depth from 8 to 12 fathoms. Still it must be remembered that outside of the shoal and on the parallel of Cape Barrionuevo the bottom is rocky and the water very deep; hence it is necessary to stand well into the bight, where the bottom is white, without being alarmed at the rocky barrier at its head. In both Santa Isabella and Sardinero anchorages the beaches are so foul that a landing can only be effected with great risk. In Santa Isabella bay, however, there are several boat-channels through the reef or rocky heads, and in the center of the bay, SE. of the western point, there is a clear beach about 150 yards in length, where a landing may be effected under favorable circumstances by veering the boat in from a grapnel. The points forming this bay are shallow. These landings are well known to the fishermen, and with their assistance a boat may land, unless the sea is very heavy. During the season of the northers both of the above anchorages are untenable, as the wind from the Gulf and the current from the passage cause a tremendous sea.

Tides.—The flood sets N. 5° 37′ E. and the ebb S. 5° 37′ W. at the rate of half a mile an hour.

Monito island is circular, steep-to, and nearly inaccessible, its sides being formed of steep cliffs. The only place where landing can be effected, even with very smooth weather, is at a rock on the W. side of the islet. At all times great caution is necessary.

Desecheo, or **Zacheo**, is a small rocky islet covered with trees and has from a distance the appearance of a green mountain. The shores are steep-to, and present no hidden dangers. The vicinity affords no anchorage.

Currents.—Near the sides of the Mona passage there is generally a very perceptible current, frequently running to the N. and NW. with a velocity of 1 or 1½ miles an hour. In the middle of the passage the general direction of the current is with the wind to the SW. The tides also, in some parts of the passage, run with great force, especially to the southward of Cape Engaño, where, during the month of May, a velocity of 3¼ miles an hour has been experienced. The flood runs 9 hours to the SW., and the ebb to the NE. during 3 hours. Sometimes precisely the contrary duration occurs, and the tides have been known to run 6 hours in each direction. These irregularities necessitate great caution in navigating, and have doubtless been the cause of very many disasters.

The Mona passage is much frequented by vessels bound from ports in the United States to the Spanish Main and neighboring islands, and by those from Europe bound to Jamaica and ports on the southern coasts of Santo Domingo and Cuba. Especially is this the case in the winter, when the wind is apt to blow from the northward of E.

It has already been stated that this passage is free from danger; but great caution must be used in the vicinity of Saona island, which is low and foul, and a berth of at least 6 miles should be given it. Squalls are of frequent occurrence, especially in summer. They blow sometimes with hurricane force for a short time, and although they often rise rapidly, always give warning of their approach.

PUERTO RICO.

The island in 1509 was invaded by Spaniards from Santo Domingo, and has since that time been a Spanish colony.

A range of lofty mountains called Luquillo, covered with wood and intersected by numerous deep ravines, runs through the center of the island, beginning near the NE. point and terminating S. of Arecibo in a hill called the Silla de Caballo. The highest peak of this chain is visible in clear weather from a distance of 68 miles; it forms an excellent landmark. It is called El Yunque, or Anvil Peak. In the interior are extensive savannas, on which large herds of cattle are pastured, and along the coasts are tracts of level fertile land.

The principal ports of export are San Juan and Arecibo on the N. coast, Mayaguez and Aguadilla on the W., Ponce, Arroyo, Guayanilla, and Guanica on the S., and Humacao and Naguabo on the E. coast.

Exports are principally sugar, molasses, rum, tobacco, cotton, coffee, hides, and cattle.

Gold is found in small lumps and in dust in the streams flowing from the headland. Copper, iron, lead, and coal have also been found.

The population in 1880 was 666,000. Slavery was abolished in 1873.

Although the island is S. of the usual track of hurricanes it has been severely visited by them. The cyclones of 1782 and 1825 were especially destructive.

Customs regulations.—A decree was issued in 1877 making it compulsory that all goods be consigned to an established merchant; so that merchants only can clear a package through the custom-house, and not then unless it is consigned to them. The rules concerning manifests are very stringent, and are in accord with those of Cuba. Fines from $25 to $1,000 may be inflicted for breach of custom regulations, and entire confiscation of ship and cargo.

Coal when carried as sale cargo is exempt from tonnage or discharge duties; other articles on board, however small, will subject the whole cargo to duties.

A bill of health certified by Spanish consul will be required. Vessels failing to present a manifest in the required form will be fined $500.

Port charges.—Pilotage, $17 for taking a vessel in and out; $2 for each time moving a vessel. Interpreter, $4. Stamped paper, $3.75.

Tonnage dues, $1 per 1,000 kilograms of cargo, gross. Clearance, $1 to $8, according to value of cargo outwards. Wharfage: Vessels up to 200 tons, $4; above 250 tons, $4.50. Sanitary visit: Vessels of 200 tons, $10; 250 tons, $11; 300 tons, $12; 350 tons, $13; 400 tons, $14; above 450 tons, $16. Labor costs $1 per day. Ballast, 50 cents per ton discharging. $1 per day for guard while marking.

The coasts of the island are by no means well known, and urgently need to be resurveyed.

On the eastern coast of Puerto Rico there are nine small rivers emptying into the sea, and several ports frequented by small vessels to load with sugar and molasses. The instructions which can be given for this coast are so deficient that it would be by no means safe for a stranger to cruise here without a pilot, who may be obtained at San Juan, St. Thomas, or sometimes at Port Mula, on Vieques island.

Cordilleras.—A chain of islets and reefs, called the Cordilleras, extends from Cape San Juan (the NE. extremity of the island) for 11 miles. The eastern group of these islets is called the Barriles. They are steep-to, and between them and the Washer and Cactus cays there is a channel 2 miles wide and 10 fathoms deep.

Barriles passage.—With a SE. wind, a vessel bound northward may easily pass to the eastward of Puerto Rico and through this channel. It is also available for vessels bound from the N. to any of the ports on the E. or S. coasts.

Hermanos passage, the next channel through the reef, is between the Barriles and the Hermanos rocks. It is the third and western channel, and lies between St. John's head and the western end of the Cordilleras. It is three-quarters of a mile wide, and 9 to 10 fathoms in depth. The western extremity of the Cordilleras is composed of two groups of low rocks, the Icacos and the Cucarachas.

There is also a navigable passage between these two groups of rocks, and probably others at different points through the Cordilleras, but no trustworthy directions can be given for them.

Port Fajardo lies S. of Cape San Juan, the NE. extremity of the island. It is between Cueva point on the N. and Barrancas point on the S., and has a depth of from 16 to 23 feet.

On a point abreast of Obispo islet is a battery, and a few houses are scattered along the beach. The town of Fajardo is 1½ miles inland. Population, about 3,000.

Exports are sugar, molasses, logwood.

Imports are lumber, provisions, cooperage stock, machinery, hardware.

Pilots cruise off the NE. point. To signal for them, hoist national colors at foremast head. Pilotage (compulsory), $5 for vessel, without regard to size. For shifting berth, $2. Tonnage dues, $1 per each 1,000 kilograms of cargo. Harbor dues, $1.50 per day for ballast-guard. Health dues: Vessels from foreign ports up to 40 tons, $4; from 40 to

70 tons, $6; from 70 to 100 tons, $8; for every 50 tons up to 450 tons, $1 more; all above 450 tons, $16. Quarantine dues: If vessel is quarantined, $2 for each visit. Port warden's fees, $4. Interpreter's fees, $4. Discharging ballast, 75 cents per ton. Cost of labor, $1.50 per day. Dunnage wood, $4 per cord. Water, $1 per puncheon alongside. Vessel's stores, scarce and dear. Coal, $5 to $6 per ton alongside. Commissions on collecting freight, 2½ per cent.; on disbursements, 2½ per cent.; on procuring freight, 5 per cent.

The United States is represented by a consular agent.

This port is only a narrow canal, sheltered from easterly winds by three islets, called Obispo, Zancudo, and Ramos, and also by a reef between the two latter having 6 to 12 feet of water on it, where the sea breaks in some places. The northern and southern ends of this reef form, with the islets of Zancudo and Ramos, two narrow cuts, having 23 feet of water. The southern passage is the widest, but neither should be attempted except in case of emergency.

There are two entrances into Fajardo. Through the southern one a depth of 18 feet may be carried, and it is entirely clear. It lies between Point Barrancas and Ramos islet.

The northern entrance is between Point Cueva and Obispo islet, and has from 4 to 6 fathoms of water. Nearly in the middle of the passage is a coral-patch, with only 6 feet of water on it, which requires great care to avoid. Although narrow, this channel is the best to enter by.

In approaching Fajardo from the eastward through the channel between Culebra and Crab islands, the navigator may choose from three channels: 1st, between the Cordilleras reef and Palominos island; 2d, between this island and the Largo bank; and, 3d, between the Largo bank and the chain of islets and reefs extending to the eastward, called Piraguas and the Lavanderas.

Although the first-named channel is the narrowest, it seems the best, from the fact that all its dangers are apparent to the eye. With the wind from NE. it leads to windward of the port. The depth in this channel is from 8 to 12 fathoms; in the second from 7 to 11 fathoms, and in the third from 6 to 8 fathoms.

Middle channel.—To pass through this channel between Palominos and Largo bank, the track lies about 1 mile S. of Palominos island.

The **southern channel** is bounded on the N. by the Largo bank, and on the S. by the Piraguas and Lavanderas rocks and the Piñero islands, with a width of 2 miles. In using it, keep Soldier's point on Culebra island, bearing S. 87° 11′ E. until the center of Palominos island bears N. 16° 52′ E.; the Largo bank will have then been passed, and a course may be shaped towards Ramos island to enter Port Fajardo by the southern passage.

The **islet of Palominos** is of moderate height, and covered with trees. Its shores are foul to the distance of half a mile. Anchorage may be found about 1 mile off its western shore in 6 or 7 fathoms of water.

The **Largo bank** is narrow and steep-to. The sea generally breaks on it. As before stated, this bank forms the S. side of the middle channel of approach to Port Fajardo.

Between Largo bank and Ramos islet there is a clear channel with 7 fathoms of water in it. The least water on the bank is said to be 13 feet.

Great and Little Piñero islands are to the northward of Piñero point, the eastern extreme of Puerto Rico. Farther to the eastward, and forming a chain of dangers, are the Lavanderas rocks and the Piraguas. There are deep channels among these rocks and shoals, but without a pilot it would be prudent to pass to the eastward of them.

The Piñeros are two small islets, covered with wood and lying between Medio-Mundo point and Piñero point, which is also low and wooded. On the western side of Great Piñero is a reef which extends northerly to Medio-Mundo point, forming a bar on which there is only 13 feet of water. The channel between this islet and the main-land is only fit for boats.

Between the reef which extends from the shore between these two points on one side and the reef skirting Great Piñero island on the other there is a narrow bight where small vessels may anchor, but it is unsheltered to the SE. and S.

Little Piñero island is nearly joined to the S. end of Great Piñero by a reef, on which there are 13 feet of water. Near the eastern side of this islet there is a small detached rock, above water.

The **Lavanderas** are two small rocks on which the sea generally breaks. They are steep-to, with 5 fathoms of water close to them.

The **Piraguas** are two small rocky islets, 1 mile apart; they may be seen at a considerable distance, are steep-to, and have a clear passage between them, with not less than 5 fathoms of water.

The **Chinchorros** are two dangerous shoals. The northern shoal is small and has 13 feet of water on it, with 5 fathoms all around. The southern shoal is three-quarters of a mile long and half a mile across, with only 5 feet of water on it; it is also steep-to. On both these shoals the sea generally breaks.

A vessel may pass between these dangers or between the northern shoal and the Piraguas. A more prudent course would be, however, S. of all of them. Soldier's point, kept on a bearing of N. 70° 18' E., will lead clear of all dangers in the channel between the SE. end of Puerto Rico and Vieques or Crab island. A short distance to the southward of Piñero point are the Cabras islets, two small flat cays, covered with brush-wood, with foul ground surrounding them.

Bahia Honda.—Puerca point is low and sharp and forms the E. side of the entrance. The W. side terminates in a bold headland, crowned by a little hill, near which is a dry rock on the reef. These points are

1 mile apart, but the reef which skirts the interior of the bay extends off from them so far that the entrance is reduced to about one-fourth of a mile in breadth.

This reef, as well as some patches with 13 feet of water on them, are easily seen.

To enter Bahia Honda, Puerca point should be brought to bear about N. 14° W., when this course will lead up toward the entrance of the harbor. In entering, the eye from aloft will be the best guide for avoiding the reefs and shoal-patches, and for picking out a clear spot for anchoring.

The anchorage has from 5 to 8 fathoms of water, but as it is open to the southward and is quite limited in extent, a large vessel had better lie outside in from 6 to 8 fathoms.

Algodon bay.—From the western point of Bahia Honda to Point Lima the coast forms a large bay, in the middle of which is the islet of Algodon, moderately high, and near the coast. In this bay, which is sheltered from SW. by N. round to NE., the depth of water varies from 16 to 13 feet near the shore. Three small streams empty into it.

Just outside of a line drawn from Point Lima to Point Algodon, the NE. point of the bay, are three shoals.

Algodon bank lies with its eastern part S. of the western part of Algodon point, a large round headland presenting, as seen from the S., a face nearly half a mile long. The channel between the bank and the point is 400 yards wide, with from $3\frac{1}{2}$ to $4\frac{1}{2}$ fathoms of water in it. In entering by this channel, haul close round Algodon point and anchor in 16 feet of water.

The **Piedras bank** is separated from the Algodon bank by a narrow channel. The position of this bank is doubtful, but it is about 1,000 yards from Algodon islet, between the bearings of S. 50° E. and S. 70° E.

Lima bank is a rocky ledge nearly awash, the sea generally breaking upon it. It is about 600 yards in diameter. About $1\frac{1}{2}$ miles from Algodon islet there is said to be a sunken rock.

There is a good channel between the Lima and Piedras banks, in which the least depth of water is 10 feet. To pass through it, bring Lima point to bear W. or S. 78° 45′ W., and steer for it until the S. point of Algodon islet bears N. 22° 30′ W.

Haul up then for this island and anchor in 16 feet of water, with the island bearing N. 33° 45′ E., 1,000 yards distant. The anchorage is exposed to easterly winds, and the holding-ground is not good; moreover, as the position of the foregoing dangers can not be accurately given, the neighborhood must be approached with great caution.

The **Port of Naguabo** lies between Point Lima and Santiago islet. One and a-half miles west of Point Lima the river Naguabo empties. On its western bank is the little village of Ucaris, off which in the month of the river there is anchorage for a few coasters, with the wind from

SW. round by N. to E. Large quantities of cattle are exported from here to the other islands. The town of Naguabo lies 2 miles inland

Tonnage dues, $1 per ton; anchorage, $4; interpreter and doctor, $12; pilot and port captain, $16. These dues are for a vessel of 280 tons.

The United States is represented by a consular agent.

Customs regulations. (See page 211.)

Santiago islet is small and of moderate height. From it a reef extends in a SE. direction to the distance of 1 mile. Its northern shore is perfectly clear. Candeleros point may be known by the little hill upon it, and between the point and the islet is Puerto Humacao.

Candeleros point is bordered by a reef extending off a short distance. About 1 mile N. of the mouth of the river Humacao, which empties into the bay, are two small islets called the Morrillos.

No trustworthy directions can be given for the anchorage.

The town of Humacao is 2½ miles inland, on the river of the same name.

Pilot, in and out and entry, $36; interpreter and stamps, $12; anchorage and port captain, $26.50. Customs regulations. (See page 211.) These dues are for a vessel of 280 tons.

In approaching either Naguabo or Humacao, the best route is S. of Crab island.

Icacos bay, S. of Humacao, lies between Candeleros point and Icacos point. Near the latter is a small rocky cay of the same name.

Port Yabucoa is about 2 miles inland on a branch of the river Guallanes, which empties into the northern part of Yabucoa bay.

From Cape Mala Pascua the S. coast of Puerto Rico tends almost in an E. and W. direction. From a distance it appears high and bold, but on a nearer approach the shore is seen to be low and covered with mangroves. The coast line as shown on existing charts can not wholly be relied upon, consequently the coast should not be approached within a distance of 6 or 7 miles without great caution.

Guayama reef.—Its outside edge is at an average distance of 3½ miles from the shore. It is divided into three parts, the eastern being named Media Luna, the middle Algarroba, and the western Ola-Grande.

Vessels sailing along this part of the coast are cautioned to keep well outside of this reef.

From Corcho point, 1 mile SW. of Cape Mala Pascua, the coast curves to the northward and westward, then to the southward, forming a bay into which the Guardawaya river empties. Point Viento forms the western limit of this bay and the eastern limit of the bay of Patillas, the western limit of the latter bay being Point Figuera. No accurate information can be given with regard to these bays, but they are believed to be more or less obstructed by reefs.

Port Patillas is situated about 3 miles inland, on the left bank of the Chiquito river.

Arroyo is a small bay immediately westward of point Figuera. It

ARROYO—SALINAS DE COAMO. 217

can be easily recognized by the village of Arroyo, lying 3 or 4 miles inland and visible 12 or 15 miles. There is a white church on a little hill above the village, having on its western end a square tower and a cupola on the eastern end.

The **anchorage** may also be recognized by the custom-house, a large yellow building. To enter the port, bring the custom-house to bear N. 11° 15′ W. and steer in on this course to avoid a bank, with 3½ fathoms of water on it, lying 3 miles S. of the bay. This bank is a spit running off from the eastern reef, and will be cleared by keeping the middle of the village of Arroyo bearing N. 22° 30′ E.

A good berth is three-fourths of a mile off shore, with the custom-house bearing N. This anchorage is not at all well sheltered, and a constant SE. swell is felt, and vessels anchor with port anchor with a spring in the cable, or run a kedge to keep head to the swell.

Port charges.—Vessels calling in ballast pay captain of the port pilotage, $10; health visit, according to tonnage, $10 to $15; interpreter, $4; stamped paper, if the vessel takes cargo, $10; custom-house fees, $4; tonnage dues, $1 per 1,000 kilograms.

The United States is represented by a consular agent.

About 1 mile to the westward of Port Guayama a narrow peninsula runs to the W. for 3 miles, which, with a couple of islands lying off its western end, forms Port Jobos or Boca de Infierno. No trustworthy information is attainable with regard to this port. Several small streams from the hills inland lose themselves in the swamp at the head of the bay, none of them emptying directly into the sea.

Port Salinas de Coamo is well sheltered by reefs. The entrance may be easily distinguished by several cays lying near Point Arenas and a guard-house about 4 miles to the northward of the western cay. The channel lies between this western cay and a reef 1¼ miles W. of it, on which the sea always breaks.

Coming from the eastward, after bringing Cape Mala Pascua to bear N., distant 4 miles, the course for the entrance will be S. 84° 22′ W., which will carry a vessel outside all the cays lying along shore.

Steer boldly in between the outer or westernmost of the cays lying off Point Arenas and the reef 1¼ miles to the westward, passing the cay at a distance of 200 yards. Stand in toward the guard-house and anchor with it bearing N. 5° 37′ E., about 1 mile distant, in 4 or 5 fathoms of water.

Discolored water extends for some distance to the southward of the cays. Three miles off shore the depth is 10 fathoms, decreasing to 7 fathoms as the coast is approached.

Nina shoal.—Within the harbor is a rocky shoal, with 16½ feet on it, with 22 feet all around.

In leaving this harbor a vessel should, if bound to the westward, stand to the southward until Muertos island bears to the northward of W. before keeping away.

Port Aguirre is at the head of the bay, between Arenas and Colchones points. No exact information can be given for this port or for the large bay in which it lies.

Coamo bay.—Its shore is skirted by reefs throughout its length. The river Coamo empties into the bay. Near the bay are several small cays, and 2 miles to the southward are the Berberia cays, with dangerous banks near them.

The reef continues to the westward around Point Coamo as far as Puerto Pastillo. Boca Chica is a small trading-place, and the approach to it is said to be clear of dangers. Soundings should be carefully attended to.

Port Jacagua is situated at the mouth of the small river of the same name, 1½ miles W. of Boca Chica. To the westward of the mouth of the river are two small cays, called the Frios. This port is said to be easy of access, but we can give no exact directions. As the soundings diminish regularly from 6½ to 3½ fathoms in approaching the shore here, the lead will be a good guide.

Muertos or **Dead Chest island** lies off the S. coast of Puerto Rico and nearly midway between the SW. and SE. points of the island. The southern part of the island is high and rocky, sloping toward the N., and from a distance looks like a separate island. The island is nearly connected to the S. coast of Puerto Rico by a reef extending from its NE. point, on which the sea generally breaks heavily. This reef seems to skirt the E. and S. sides of the island. In the latter direction it extends half a mile off shore. At about 200 yards distance from the SW. end of the island there is a small flat rock, called the Hammock, with a dry reef between them. The Hammock should not be rounded nearer than 1½ miles.

Water can be obtained on Dead Chest island by digging wells a little above high-water mark. Turtles are plenty in the proper season, and the neighboring banks abound with fish.

The western side of the island is clear, and affords good anchorage in from 7 to 12 fathoms of water.

The **Berberia cays** are often submerged and are dangerous to approach on the W. and S. sides; but to the northward of the larger there is good anchorage in 4½ to 7 fathoms, mud bottom. In their neighborhood are several dangerous shoals very imperfectly known. With the island bearing W., distant 3 or 4 miles, the depth is 6 fathoms.

Great caution must be observed by the navigator in this vicinity.

The **bay of Ponce** is nearly 3 miles across between Cucharros, the western, and Carenero the eastern point; the port is in the NE. corner of the bay, and on its shore is the village of Port Ponce, containing 1,500 inhabitants. The custom-house, a long, white, two-storied building, with flat roof and flag staff, is the most prominent object in the village, and is very conspicuous from seaward. The shores are low and bounded by mangrove and cocoa-nut trees, but 2 or 3 miles westward of Cucharros point the land rises and becomes hilly. Ratones island is low and covered with brush-wood; its surrounding reef, which nearly dries at low water, stretches off southeastward for 600 yards. Arenas cay is small and bushy.

Cardones island is low, covered with brush-wood, and in its center is a wooden house.

Cayito reef is a dangerous coral bank which seldom breaks. There are 9 feet on its eastern edge, and probably shoaler water will be found; a white chimney open eastward of the negro huts, near the cocoa nut grove on the N. side of the bay, bearing N., clears the E. side of the bank. There is a 7-fathom channel between Cardones island and Cayito reef, but it should not be taken without a pilot. The Gatas, four small, low cays off Carenero, appear as a continuation of that point; its projecting reef, upon which the sea breaks, is steep-to. At the extremity of the reef off Peñoncillo point northward of Carenero, are two small rocks which uncover 4 feet at low water. Cabrillon point lies about three-fourths of a mile eastward of Carenero point; two small islets or cays lie off it.

Vessels approaching Port Ponce should not come within 5 miles of the land until the light-house bears N. 67° 30′ E., which should then be steered for, passing westward of Tasmanian shoal. When abreast of Cardones islet, alter course to N. 11° 15′ E. for anchorage. The fore and main masts of a steamer wrecked on Tasmanian shoal show two-thirds above the water.

Port Ponce, the second in size, third in commercial importance in the island, and numbering 17,000 inhabitants, lies 3 miles N. 67° 30′ E. of the port.

The law holds the masters of vessels responsible and liable to fines for any false declaration in contents, quantity, weight, or measure.

The supply of coal and wood is uncertain. Water is scarce and bad.

Imports are provisions, lumber, petroleum, iron, cooperage, dry-goods.

Exports are sugar, molasses, tobacco, hides, cattle, coffee, oranges, cotton.

The city has a public hospital and is lighted with gas. It is connected with Jamaica by a telegraph cable, and also has telegraphic communication with the principal places on the island. Vessel's stores, being mostly imported, are high.

Port charges.—Tonnage dues, $1 on each 1,000 kilograms of cargo; health dues on vessels of 100 tons, $8, and $1 for each 50 tons in excess up to 450; $16 for all over 400 tons; pilotage in and out, $10; tug-boat charged by agreement; wharfage, for each lighter load of cargo, $1; sand, per lighter, $5; interpreter and duplicate manifest, $12; stamp paper, entrance and clearance, $10; fort pass, $2; hospital fee, $4; taking in stone ballast, per ton, $1.50; sand ballast, per ton,

$1; ballast guard, $1; hose hire for filling molasses casks, per puncheon, 6½ cents; water delivered alongside, per puncheon, $1; labor, per day, $2; stevedore, per hogshead, 20 cents; coal, from $7 to $12 per ton. Cargo is handled by lighters. Vessels with clean bills of health are quarantined for twenty-four hours; vessels from infected ports, from eight to forty days.

Harbor rules.—No vessel is allowed to change her anchorage without permit from harbor-master; fine for doing so equals double pilotage. All vessels from foreign ports are obliged to wait the sanitary and revenue visit. Vessels in quarantine will fly a quarantine flag. All boats must come alongside the wharf in front of the custom-house. No vessel can ballast or unballast without permission from the harbor-master. Mineral coal is considered as ballast. No vessel can leave after sunset or before sunrise. Colored men as passengers or crew can not land.

The United States is represented by a consular agent.

Shoal and **uneven soundings** exist southward of the bay for some distance from the shore, probably on irregular banks extending from Ratones island on the westward, and from Muertos island on the eastward, leaving a deep channel between them into the port, eastward of Cardones island.

Port Matainsa is a small bay open to the southward. The river Peñuelas empties into it. Ratones island serves as a mark to the entrance to this port. From Port Matainsa the coast trends SW. to Guayanilla point, between which and Majagua point is the bay of Guayanilla. Near the former point are several small islands. The latter point is skirted by a reef.

Guayanilla bay is semicircular in form and open to the southward. Guayanilla river empties into the bay.

Port Guanica is one of the best harbors on the S. coast of the island, and the first one coming E. from Cape Rojo.

The shore of the bay on both sides of the entrance is skirted by a reef. Outside of the reef there is a rocky patch with 12 feet of water on it.

In approaching Port Guanica from the eastward, bring Meseta point well on with the eastern pap of the Cerro Gordo, keeping the latter open to the westward from the former, a mark easily recognized. Steer in on this bearing, which will carry a vessel a safe distance from the rocky ledge above mentioned.

In coming from the westward, Point Brea may be passed at the distance of 200 yards. Then steer for Point Meseta until the middle of the entrance bears N., when stand boldly in and anchor, as convenient, in from 3½ to 4 fathoms of water. The deepest water is on the western side.

The depths in this port are shoaling on account of the alluvium carried down by rains. A mud-bank with a few scattered rocks, extending from the N. shore almost to the center of the port, has only 2 feet of water.

As before stated, a chain of reefs extends from Point Brea to Cape Rojo. This reef has three passages.

Terremoto passage.—In the neighborhood of Salinas bay, between Carcovado point and Terremoto cay (the largest of the outer cays), is Terremoto passage, where the soundings are 4½ to 7 fathoms, and by which coasting vessels enter Salinas bay.

Faluch or **Middle passage** is near Cabras or Mateo island, and has 9¾ fathoms of water. The eastern edge is marked by a small mangrove cay, from which a reef extends to the NW. Faluch passage, the best of the three, leads to the port of Guijano, which is formed by the coast and an inner line of reefs, and has a depth of 7 to 9 fathoms. The port is spacious, deep, and sheltered from all seas.

Indio passage, the western one, is about 4 miles W. of the middle passage. It is abreast of Pitajaya. It is about 400 yards broad and has 7 fathoms of water inside. Anchorage, sheltered from the sea, is found under the lee of the reefs.

Cape Rojo, the SW. point of Puerto Rico, is a bold bluff sloping down from a hill with two peaks. Seen from the E. or W. it has the appearance of two small islands close to high land. When seen from the southward two remarkable bluffs are seen to the eastward of it.

A bank of white sand and coral, on which there are large quantities of fish, extends 8 or 9 miles from the cape, with from 6 to 15 fathoms of water on it. The edge of the bank is steep-to, and the bottom may be seen in 12 or 13 fathoms.

Port of **Cabo Rojo** is an almost circular basin. The entrance is narrow and tortuous and has only 9 feet of water; in the center of the basin there is not more than 16 feet of water. The inhabitants in the vicinity subsist chiefly on fish. Boats leave here during the season for the turtle fisheries of Mona island.

Boqueron bay may be entered by two channels, having not less than 4 fathoms of water, which lead into a spacious and sheltered anchorage.

This bay appears to be the line of separation as regards the climate and productions of Puerto Rico. On the N. side, where there is an abundant rain-fall, the country is fertile, covered with trees and rich pasture lands, where cattle feed. To the S., toward Point Melones, there is a chain of arid mountains, without trees or pasture; an uninterrupted drought does not permit the growth of vegetation on this side.

Port Real is a nearly circular basin. In the entrance there are 18 and in the middle of the harbor there are 16 feet of water. The channel is very narrow and lies on the southern side of the entrance. From the N. point an extensive reef runs out, which, after skirting Fanduco cay, ends just to the northward of Varas point.

Caution.—The approaches to the southern part of the W. coast of Puerto Rico are rendered dangerous from the want of definite knowledge as to the positions of the various off-lying rocks and shoals.

From Port Real the coast trends to the northward, very irregularly, to Point Guanajivo, forming several quite large bays, none of which, however, can be reached on account of the reefs and shoals which extend off shore along this part of the coast.

Mayaguez bay affords good anchorage for vessels of moderate size.

Algarrobo point may be known by a house with a red roof, built upon high piles on the hill just above the point. S. 45° W., half a mile from Algarrobo point, lies the bank of that name, which at the outer part is nearly dry and steep to. At about a third of a mile southward of Puntilla, at the head of the bay, is the entrance of the river Mayaguez, in which small coasters lay up for the hurricane season, and before it is the best anchorage, sheltered from the northward round by E. to SW., and good holding-ground. The channel between Rodriguez bank and Guanajivo point has 13 feet least water and is used only by coasters.

Guadeloupe reef.—In 1876 the French mail steamer *Guadeloupe* ran aground while entering Mayaguez bay. The following bearings were taken while the vessel was aground: Jiguero point, N. 20° W.; Desecheo island, N. 60° W. No information has been received as to the vessel's draught, or as to the depth of water on the bank.

Tourmaline reef.—Westward of Mayaguez, an extensive reef having as little as 4 fathoms of water over it, and possibly less, was recently passed over by H. M. S. *Tourmaline*. From the reef the peak of Cerro Montuoso bore E.; Desecheo island N. 30° W. The bottom is apparently of coral, with remarkable white stripes extending N. and S. across it. The bottom was visible in 12 fathoms.

A good mark for entering Mayaguez bay through the channel between Allart bank and Inner Las Manchas is Cerro Montuoso peak in line with the northern and higher hummock of a wooded, saddle-shaped hill bearing S. 78° 45′ E.

For a steamer, or for a sailing-vessel with a fair wind, the best course will be found by bringing Montuoso peak over the custom-house, bearing S. 73° E.

The custom-house is near the water's edge, and is the most southerly of four large houses with flat roofs, lying close together. The church on with Montuoso peak also leads over the bar of the Mayaguez river, in 12 feet of water. If the buoys are in place a vessel has only to steer in midway between them.

In beating in, a vessel may stand toward La Mancha de Tierra until the custom-house and church are one; but to the southward, towards the Allart shoal, she must tack before the peak of Montuoso comes in line with the church, until within the two shoals. When the land to the southward of Guanajivo point is shut in with that point bearing S. a vessel will be eastward of the outer banks. In coming from the northward, the channel may be taken between Las Manchas and the Algarrobo reef. In this case take care not to haul in round Algarrobo point until the peak of Montuoso opens S. of the chimney of Vigo's sugar-house, which is white, and a conspicuous object near the shore N. of the Puntilla battery.

With a large vessel it is advisable to take a pilot.

The **tide** rises and falls in Mayaguez bay from 2 to 3 feet, but no exact determination of the time of high and low water has been made. The periods are said to be irregular.

There is said to be good anchorage to the westward of the Mayaguez banks, but in the absence of trustworthy information of the neighborhood it should be approached with caution.

Population is 8,000.

Exports are sugar, molasses, coffee, cocoa.

Imports are provisions, vegetables, lumber, dry goods.

The town is clean, orderly, and well kept. Generally but one family lives in a house. Yellow fever is sometimes epidemic. The temperature in summer ranges from 75° to 90°.

Quarantine is not very strict; there is a health-officer.

Provisions are nearly all imported from the United States and are expensive.

Water can be had, both spring and rain water; cost, $2.50 per ship no matter what quantity is taken; ship's boats must be used.

The Atlas line makes monthly trips, and the Ramon de Herrera line (Spanish) three times a month.

There is telegraphic communication with the principal ports of the island.

The authority to visit is the military commandant.

There are two hospitals: one private which has six beds for foreign seamen at a cost of 50 cents per day; also a military hospital for the use of the soldiers.

Port charges.—Pilot and harbor-master's fees, $10. Interpreter, $4. Tonnage dues, $1 per 1,000 kilograms of cargo. Health visit: vessels of 150 tons, $9; and on each 50 tons in excess of 150, $1 additional. Custom-house fees, in and out, and stamped paper, $17.50. Discharging ballast: sand, 50 cents per ton; stone, free; ballast guard, $2 per day. Discharging general cargo, $10 per load of 40 tons.

The United States is represented by a commercial agent and vice-commercial agent.

The dangers off the SW. coast, so far as known, and their approximate positions, are as follows:

Negro rock is small, and the sea nearly always breaks on it.

Media Luna shoal is said to be a reef two-thirds of a mile long and about 400 yards wide. The sea sometimes breaks upon it. From its N. end, Guanajivo point is said to bear N. 62° E. and Jiguero point N. 5° 37' E.; half a mile E. of it are said to be three rocks on which the sea breaks constantly, but the existence of both shoal and rocks is very doubtful.

Las Coronas are sand-banks, half a mile in extent and just awash, on which the sea generally breaks.

Guaniquilla shoal is not marked on the Spanish chart, but is said to lie 2 miles W. of Guaniquilla point. It is a rocky ledge, 400 yards in extent, with 16 feet of water on it.

The **Gallardo bank** is also a rocky ledge, which lies nearly W. from Melones point. It is 600 yards in extent, and has 16 feet of water on it.

Mount Atalaya is the highest and northernmost of two peaks at the western extreme of the chain of mountains which runs from E. to W. in the NW. part of the island. It has a noticeable appearance, and forms an excellent landmark.

Anasco bay lies between Cadena point on the N. and Algarrobo point to the southeastward.

The river Anasco empties into the bay and has caused a shallow bar to form extending half a mile off shore.

Anchorage.—Outside this bar there is good anchorage with ordinary winds for vessels of any size.

Cadena point should not be approached within the distance of a mile. The shore of the bay may be approached within half a mile.

Rincon bay is between Jiguero point on the N. and Cadena point on the S. The bottom is foul and affords no good anchorage.

Pelegrino reef is a reef with 10 feet of water over it, and on which four vessels have been lost. It lies about 1 mile off the W. coast, midway between Cadena and Jiguero point.

Aguadilla bay.—On the northern shore of this bay is the town of San Carlos de Aguadilla, on the banks of the river from which it takes its name.

Toward the southern part of the bay is the village of San Francisco.

The town of San Carlos is an excellent place to obtain water and all kinds of provisions.

Vessels of any size may anchor here with ordinary wind, but during the winter months a heavy swell rolls into the bay. The only dangers are the reef off Penas Blancas and the sand-bars at the mouths of the small streams, which extend off about 400 yards.

A narrow bank of soundings about one-fourth of a mile wide and very steep to skirts the shore. In anchoring be careful not to do so too near the edge of the bank, as a vessel is liable to drag off. In the winter time it would be prudent to be prepared to go to sea at once upon any indication of a shift of wind to the N. or NW.

A good berth will be found with the church in the town of San Carlos bearing S. $84° 22'$ E. and the N. point of the bay N. $11° 15'$ W. in 18 fathoms, about half a mile from the shore. In approaching Aguadilla bay from the southward, care must be taken to keep Jiguero point to the eastward of N. $11° 15'$ E. to avoid the foul ground which extends as far to the southward as the SW. point of the island.

The population of the district is about 12,500. The Herrera line of steamers call here, also the Atlas line.

The United States is represented by a consular agent.

Penas Blancas, to the northward of San Carlos, is covered with reefs. A reef stretches off from it a distance of a mile. From Penas Blancas to Bruquen point the coast is low and sandy.

Bruquen point may be given a berth of a mile, where the depth will be from 20 to 25 fathoms. From Bruquen point a rocky bluff begins extending to the NE. as far as Point Pena Ahujercada.

The coast trends almost directly E. from Point Ahujercada to San Juan head. Toward the eastern end it is mountainous, and rugged and broken throughout its extent. There are several small towns along this coast, and a number of rivers, draining the northern water-shed of the island, flow into the sea.

Point Arecito.—The harbor is formed by a small bay sheltered to the northward by reefs. In the winter season it is only safe for small craft that can get inside the reef.

Large vessels must anchor outside and be prepared to slip and go to sea at once if the wind threatens to blow from N. or W. In the months of April, May, June, and July vessels of moderate draught may anchor close in to the reef. The anchorage is generally rough and uncomfortable.

The town stands on the western side of the bay and is protected by a circular fort to the eastward of it; and about 1 mile to the windward of the town, a tower and signal-post will be seen on a steep hill. Near the center of the reef is the cut or channel for small vessels; and at the E. end, between it and the cliff, there is a passage for boats.

There is a rivulet of excellent water, deep enough to admit launches, at the NE. end of the bay, near the town of Arecibo.

Population is 8,000.

Port charges.—For a vessel of 226 tons, with ballast in and cargo out, the expenses were $408.

The United States is represented by a consular agent.

Tortuguero is a small town on the shore, about 20 miles W. of Puerto San Juan. No safe directions can be given for this part of the coast, but it should not be approached nearer than 3 miles.

Port San Juan.—About 30 miles W. of San Juan head is the harbor and city of San Juan. The city is well laid out and is one of the healthiest cities in the West Indies. It is situated on Morro island, which forms the N. side of the harbor, and is separated from the main-land by a narrow creek, called the channel of San Antonio.

The city is almost hidden from seaward by the high land on the northern shore.

The population is about 20,000. The sanitary condition of the city is good. The streets are clean and the people orderly.

Coal can be had in any quantity. The amount usually on hand is about 3,000 tons, and costs $9 per ton. It is transferred to the ship by lighters, which hold about 10 tons each.

Provisions can be had; beef is quite poor; vegetables are good and quite cheap.

Water.—Either spring or rain water can be had at a cost of 1 cent per gallon. There are two water-boats.

Quarantine is strict and well maintained. There is a quarantine station on an island. A health officer boards all vessels.

There are three hospitals: one military, which is for use of the soldiers, and two private, which are small and cost $2 per day. For subscribers, only $1 per day.

Steamers of the Lopez line from Havana to Liverpool, three times a month; to Bremen, three times a month; Barcelona, four times a month; and the Atlas line.

Telegraph.—There is cable communication with St. Thomas; also have a telegraph line connecting the principal places on the island.

Customs duties are high; nearly everything is taxed.

Pilots are efficient, but are not necessary for a steamer. Pilotage is $17 in and out, and $4 for moving a ship in the harbor.

The authorities to visit are the captain-general and Brigadier de Monica, the commodore of the station.

Exports.—Sugar, molasses, coffee, tobacco.

The United States is represented by a consul and vice-consul.

The E. and S. sides of the harbor are low, swampy, and covered with mangrove trees.

The W. side of the entrance is formed by the Cabras and Cabritas islets and the reefs which connect them with the shore. On the southernmost islet, called Canuelo, which is the nearest to Puerto Rico and nearly a quarter of a mile from the largest islet, there is a fort which commands the entrance. Between the Morro and the Cabras the channel into the port is barred, and with strong northerly winds it breaks and becomes dangerous, although there is a depth of from $4\frac{1}{2}$ to $5\frac{1}{4}$ fathoms.

Off Morro island, at the eastern point of entrance, the ground is foul for about 200 yards, the eastern side of the channel being marked by a conical bell-buoy moored in 17 feet of water on the edge of the bank called St. Helena shoal. The western side of the channel has also been marked by buoys, but they can not be depended upon.

St. Augustine shoal also makes out from Morro island to about 200 yards from the shore, nearly abreast of San Juan gate. Its edge is marked by a red barrel-buoy.

Vessels of large draught, or those intending to make but a short stay, will find the most convenient anchorage between the St. Augustine and Tablazo shoals, abreast of St. John's gate.

To the eastward of the Puntilla sand-spit is the inner harbor, a deep bight, sheltered from all winds. The inner channel is marked on each side by posts, with small white tin flags on them denoting the depth of water; in standing in, those marked with black figures are to be left on the port hand, those in red figures on the starboard hand.

The inner has, it is stated by various authorities, filled up considerably of late years, and there is probably less water there than is marked on the charts.

There is a line of buoys for mooring and warping extending the length of the harbor.

For a steamer, and with the buoys and beacons, as just described, in place, the entrance to San Juan presents no difficulties. It must be remembered, however, that with fresh northerly winds the sea frequently breaks on the bar at the entrance, and good headway must be kept in order that the vessel may mind her helm readily.

After passing Culebra island from the eastward Cape San Juan will be easily recognized by the light-house upon its summit. Between San Juan and Luquillo the coast line is high, the mountain range appearing to reach to the sea. About 4 miles SW. of the light-house is a prominent conical peak, seen from the northward.

Los Embarcaderos point will not be noticeable until well to the westward of it, when it will be seen projecting, low and covered with trees.

From Luquillo to the Loisa river the coast is low, with a range of hillocks 2 or 3 miles inland; back of Loisa is a hill, which, seen from the eastward, looks like an island. Between the Herrero and Loisa rivers and between Vacia Telegas and Maldonado points are white sandy beaches.

Vacia Telegas point is formed by two low bluffs, covered with trees. Maldonado point has the appearance from the eastward of an island.

The **Morro of San Juan** will now come in sight, and will be easily recognized. There are two towers upon it, and the light is shown from the northeastern one. When within 5 miles of the entrance Cabras island will open out; upon it are several buildings, and off the eastern end of it is the wreck of a steamer. Care must be taken not to confound this wreck with the buoy off St. Helena shoal, which, from a distance, might easily be done.

San Juan harbor.—The course now will be parallel to the coast, keeping about 3 miles off, until Fort Canuelo, a small yellow building to the southward of Cabras island, bears S. 45° W., when head for it until Morro light bears S. 56° 15′ E., when steer S. 11° 15′ E., which will lead over the bar, between the reefs, into the outer harbor.

There is a red barrel-buoy on the edge of St. Helena shoal, but, owing to the swell on the bar, it may not come in sight until quite close to.

By following the above directions, however, the harbor may be entered even if the buoy is not seen until close aboard.

There is another red barrel-buoy off San Juan gate, and, if not desirous of going into the inner harbor, it will be best to anchor before coming abreast of it, with Fort Cannelo bearing N. 87° 11′ W. and Morro light N. 22° 30′ E.

Inner harbor.—The channel to the inner harbor is marked by three red barrel-buoys on the port hand and two small conical light-red buoys on the starboard hand. From the outer harbor the passage to the inner harbor will look puzzling to a stranger, as more than this number of buoys will be visible.

To enter the inner harbor, steer to pass the red barrel buoy off San Juan gate at 100 yards distance, and then between the red barrel-buoy off the Barrio de la Puntilla and the two conical light-red buoys on Tablazo shoal, keeping well over to the port hand. When abreast the inner conical buoy, the barrel-buoy off the end of Puntilla shoal will not fail to be recognized, and it must be passed close to on the port hand, and two small red conical buoys on Punta Largo shoal, off the city, brought immediately on the starboard bow, to avoid going on that shoal.

There is one red mooring-buoy off the city for the use of the Spanish man-of-war generally kept there, and an anchorage may be had either above or below this buoy.

Buoys.—There are no beacons on Punta Largo, Yufri, and Anegado shoals, but red conical buoys instead.

South of Yufri shoal are two mooring-buoys; these, together with the buoys on Yufri and Anegado shoals, are seen from the outer harbor and tend to confuse a stranger; but by following the above directions the passage to the inner harbor is not difficult.

In the inner harbor, though the full force of the sea-breeze is felt, the water is quite foul, owing to the number of sewers emptying into it; it is also limited in space, and, as a vessel rides to the wind, it will be better to get under way about 6 or 7 o'clock in the morning, at the time when the land-breeze from the SW. dies away, when the vessel will be pointed fair for standing out.

Coast.—To the westward of San Juan the coast-line is low, with a remarkable line of hummocks a few miles back.

The entrance to the harbor presents fewer difficulties approaching from the westward, as the light-house may be steered for on a SE. bearing until the buoy off St. Helena shoal is discovered, when the course in will be as described above.

Caution.—The western side of the entrance to San Juan is unmarked, save by the wreck of the steamer mentioned above, off the eastern end of Cabras island, and there are no beacons or wooden posts.

If any of the buoys are out of place the chart will be the best guide. Pilots are always in readiness to board vessels off the entrance. Vessels entering the harbor under sail should have a hawser and boat ready, and should be prepared to reduce sail as quickly as possible.

In the outer harbor ships should moor with an open hawse to the NW. In the inner harbor anchors should be laid out N. and S.

GENERAL DIRECTIONS.

Between San Juan and the cape of San Juan there appears to be no shelter whatever.

This part of the coast is very little known. It is bordered by a reef within which are many cays and rocks, and on which the sea breaks with great violence. It should not, therefore, be approached nearer than 4 miles.

A small sunken rock, with 14 feet of water on it and 5 fathoms close to, is said to lie 20 miles E. of Port San Juan and 3 miles off shore.

General directions.—The sea on the E. coast of Puerto Rico is generally smooth, so that vessels may lie comfortably in the anchorages. On leaving them, time will be saved by passing out through the Barriles or Hermanos passage instead of running round the W. end of Puerto Rico and out through the Mona passage. Being off the SE. coast of Puerto Rico and near the entrance to the channel formed by it and Arenas banks, when standing toward the Lima bank, the W. point of Bahia Honda should not be brought eastward of N. 28° E. When approaching the N. end of the Arenas reef, in standing to the southward do not open out Cape Mala Pascua off Naranjo point. When El Yunque or Anvil peak is shut in with the hill on the W. point of Bahia Honda a vessel will be to the eastward of the Arenas reef, and the southern boards may be prolonged.

Do not, however, bring Cape Mala Pascua to the westward of S. 65° W., which will avoid the Musquito, Corona, and Caballo Blanco banks, which lie off the N. shore of Vieques, in the neighborhood of Port Mula, and on which the sea does not always break. In standing to the northward, go no farther than to bring West mountain, St. Thomas, in one with Soldier point, Culebra, N. 73° E. until to windward of the South Chinchorro bank, which lies with the S. point of Palominos in one with the westernmost Piraguas. When the latter is in one with Zancudo islet, N. 50° 30' W., a vessel will be to the eastward of the Chinchorros and eastward of the narrowest and most dangerous part of this channel, and may then work to windward without fear.

When sufficiently far to the eastward, a vessel may pass out through the channel between the Barriles and Hermanos islets; or between Icacos, Cucaracha (the westernmost of the Cordillera), and San Juan head, according as the wind may be to the northward or southward of E. The last being the westernmost, she may proceed through it as soon as she has rounded the eastern Piraguas, which, however, must be given a wide berth.

With the wind from the NE. a vessel may beat through in a day and a half, and from the SE. may run through in half a day.

With a pilot it may be accomplished in much less time, as follows:

Having cleared the N. extreme of Arenas bank, steer to the northward, so as to pass between the western Lavanderas and the Little Piñero, or between the Lavanderas, on which the sea always breaks.

Steer E. or W. of the Largo bank, and thence W. of Palominos, and through the channel by San Juan head; but to do this the wind should be to the southward of E. In passing between the Little Piñero and the western Lavanderas, bring the outer extremity of San Juan head on a N. 16° 50' W. bearing, which course will lead to the westward of Largo bank and close up to the head. In taking this route the position assigned to the doubtful Descubridor bank, said to be S. 1¼ miles from the western Lavandera and about the same distance from Little Piñero, should be carefully avoided.

These directions, however imperfect, will serve to point out the most prominent dangers, and at the same time warn strangers not to get entangled among them without the assistance of a pilot.

The **tides** on the eastern coast of Puerto Rico run with great strength to the NE. 7 hours, and to the SE. 5 hours.

CHAPTER IX.

THE VIRGIN ISLANDS.

The line of demarcation between the English and Danish islands runs from the N. between Little Tobago and Haus-Lollik; from thence to the ESE. midway in the channel between Thatch island, Tortola, and St. John, round the E. end of the latter, and from thence to the S. through the Flanagan passage.

The majority of the islets which lie off the larger islands are barren and of no value.

The only islands of any commercial importance are Virgin Gorda, Tortola, St. John, St. Thomas, and Santa Cruz.

The island of Anegada only merits description on account of the reefs which surround it, where many vessels have been wrecked.

On making the Virgin islands from the northward, Virgin Gorda will be seen on the extreme left, rising in a clear, well-defined peak. Anegada being only 30 feet above the sea, will not be seen more than 5 or 6 miles from an elevation of 10 feet. Next to Virgin Gorda, Tortola will appear the most conspicuous; Sage mountain, the highest in the island, does not rise into a peak from this direction, but appears flattened and elongated. Immediately to the right or to the westward of it will be seen the rugged pointed peaks of Jost Van Dyke, and behind them the irregular small peaks rising from the table-land of St. John, and varying in elevation from 800 to 1,270 feet.

If on or near the meridian of 64° 50′ W., and about 20 miles to the northward of the islands, a separation will be observed between St. John and St. Thomas, as the small cays which lie off and between them will not be above the horizon, while Virgin Gorda, Tortola, Jost Van Dyke, and St. John will seem to form one large island, the prominent peaks on each being alone distinguishable.

The island of St. Thomas may be recognized by having a large saddle on its center, formed by Signal hill and West mountain, and the island is less rugged in outline than the others. The saddle is equally conspicuous from the southward. Culebra, from the above meridian, will be only just in sight. Its hills are more rounded than the others and much less elevated. From hence also, in clear weather, El Yunque or Anvil peak, on the Sierra Luquillo, at the E. end of Puerto Rico, may be seen.

Tides.

Tides.—The phenomena of the tides among the Virgin islands, although of the highest importance to navigators, are extremely difficult of explanation. The following rule is given by the fishermen, and, in general, it may be safely adopted: From the moon's rising until her meridian passage, the flood runs to the southeastward, or to windward; and from thence to her setting the ebb runs to the northwestward, or to leeward, and *vice versa* with the lower transit; hence there is a six-hours' stream each way. This rule, however, is greatly interfered with in different localities, as will be seen hereafter, and by the force and direction of the wind.

It is observed that the southern tide predominates during the summer months, from the middle of June to the middle of August, and two tides have been then known to follow in succession, particularly if the wind has been westerly; and on such occasions the perpendicular rise was increased by 2 feet. Near the commencement of this remarkable change the stream is observed to set for eight or ten days continually to the southward with a force seldom surpassed, and is called by the fishermen St. John's tide, from its occurring near the day of that saint. For the remainder of the above period, the ebb or northerly stream will run only for about one or two hours.

During the months of September, November, March, and April the northern tide prevails, and with considerable force, being assisted by the current. At this period also the highest water is generally in the morning, and there is only a half-tide in the evening; the reverse takes place during the summer months. The establishment for high water at full and change appears to be about $9^h\ 0^m$, but it is liable to great uncertainty, for sometimes it is as early as $7^h\ 0^m$. The rise and fall at springs is from 1 to $1\frac{1}{2}$ feet; but in the months of April and May the mean level of the sea is observed to be a foot lower than at other periods, which agrees with the observations of Dr. Fahlberg. The duration of the stream (as before stated) is six hours each way, and to which the stranger must pay strict attention, leaving the time of high water as a thing altogether of minor importance.

As already observed, the northern stream is called the flood, and that coming from the southward the ebb; strictly, however, this may be an error, although not of much consequence, for the change of set takes place at about half-tide on the shore, and, the rise and fall being so small, it is difficult to say to which set the term "flood" should be applied.

It happens, however, that the commencement of the flood-stream takes place at full and change, at about $6^h\ 0^m$, and as it runs for six hours and then changes to the ebb, by remembering this establishment for the first beginning of the flood, the turn of tide can of course be calculated for any intermediate day during the lunation.

As $6^h\ 0^m$ happens to be nearly the time of the moon's rising at full and change, we have the fisherman's rule explained.

Soundings.—The Virgin islands lie on the southern edge of an extensive bank of soundings. NW. of Anegada, the bank is said to be extending, on account of the loose sand and strong current. The northern and southern portions of the bank differ very much in their character as well as their extent.

Anegada or **Drowned island** is covered with brush-wood. Until the establishment of the light-house on Sombrero island numerous vessels were wrecked on this island and the dangerous reefs which surround it. Now the land-fall sought by vessels from the northward is Sombrero light-house, from which an accurate departure can be taken, making the Anegada channel, once so famous for its dangers, perfectly safe with ordinary care and attention.

The island is skirted by a very dangerous reef, running close in shore on the northern and western sides. From the eastern end of the island a broken reef trends off, on which most of the wrecks alluded to have occurred.

Currents.—After SE. or southerly winds, which blow at times throughout the year, but are most frequent in May or June, a NW. current of sometimes a mile an hour runs along the reefs. For this reason especially vessels bound from the northward through the Anegada passage should not fail to sight, by night or day, Sombrero light-house.

Caution.—The edge of soundings is so near the reef that the lead is not a trustworthy warning of the approach to danger, and therefore a sailing-vessel bound to the southward and having a head-wind in this channel should not approach these reefs nearer than 10 miles, but should work to the southward in the eastern part of the channel till past all danger.

The **rollers**, or **ground-swell**, frequently occur from October to May, and continue sometimes three or four days. In general they set in after a prevalence of light E. or SE. winds. Between Tortola and Guano islands they have been seen to top and break in 9 fathoms, and on the SW. side of Anegada, in $4\frac{1}{2}$ fathoms, anchors are sometimes lifted; it is consequently dangerous for sailing-vessels to come too near any part of the northern shores of the Virgin islands, for they get up suddenly, and during their continuance the wind is too light to keep a vessel under command. They appear to have great influence on the bottom in loosening the sand and in discoloring the water for some miles to the northward of the islands, as far as the edge of the bank. In some places near the W. end of Anegada, where the bottom is composed of very fine sand, the formation of the banks is frequently changed.

Anchorage.—There is good temporary anchorage off the W. end of the island in from 5 to 6 fathoms water, at about a mile distant. It will not be prudent, however, to remain here any time during the period of the rollers, which frequently occur from October to May; but it will be better during this season to anchor well under the S. side of the island if intending to remain the night.

The best anchorage will be found in 6 fathoms, with the W. end bearing N. 20° W., the cocoa-nut trees at the settlement at Pearl point N. 34° E., and the E. point N. 70° E. Great care, however, must be taken not to haul up too suddenly after rounding the W. end and not to come within the depth of 5 fathoms. Great attention must be paid to the lead after passing within the 10-fathom line.

The bank to the westward of the meridian of Anegada is composed chiefly of fine sand, and in light weather vessels may anchor on it in safety with a kedge or stream, taking care, however, to avoid the rocky banks already described.

Virgin Gorda, the easternmost of the Virgin islands, is easily distinguished by its rising gradually to a peak 1,370 feet high. It is sometimes called Peniston, or Spanish Town. The inhabitants are few in number, and are principally employed in raising fruit and vegetables and burning charcoal for the markets of St. Thomas and Santa Cruz.

The outline of the island is exceedingly irregular.

The center portion is occupied by the immense hill, the summit of which, named Virgin peak, has been already described. From thence the E. end of the island is a narrow strip of land composed of irregular rugged hills, terminating at Pajaros point in a remarkable pinnacle rock. The southern portion is more regular in outline, and nearly separated from the center by a small isthmus.

The most remarkable feature of Virgin Gorda is on its western side, between Colison point and the S. end of the island. The eastern side of this peninsula has been broken up by some violent action of nature into immense granite blocks, which lie scattered about on the shore.

The cays and islets to the southward as far as Round rock are also composed of the same kind of rock, and the largest (which lies nearly half a mile from the S. end of the island), from its having the appearance of a town in ruins, is named Fallen Jerusalem.

Many of these blocks are 60 to 70 feet square; some are merely confined in their places by the weight of others leaning on them; and many, with deep rents and fissures in their sides, appear ready to fall by the slightest shock. In one or two places the sea finds its way through the crevices and forms beautiful natural baths. It is also a curious circumstance that similar granite blocks are found scattered about on Beef island, on the opposite side of Sir Francis Drake channel, and nowhere else.

Anchorage.—There are two excellent anchorages on the western side of Virgin Gorda. The water is smooth at both anchorages, except at the season of rollers, and the holding-ground good, and they can easily be reached from either N. or S.

Tow rock.—The islets are all steep-to, and the passages between them clear, except that between Scrub island and the Dog islands, in which lies the Tow rock with 15 feet of water on it. The best direction to give for clearing it is to keep either Dog island or Scrub island close aboard, as they are steep-to.

Virgin Gorda sound.—The anchorage to the northward of the island is called Gorda sound, and is an excellent and capacious harbor. It is sheltered from all winds and from the rollers.

Prickly Pear island.—The entrance lies between Prickly Pear island on the E. and Musquito island on the W. side, but is much narrowed by the Cactus and Colquhoun reefs making off from the islands on either side toward mid-channel.

The **mark** for entering would not be easily recognized by a stranger, and a better way would be to anchor a boat on the point of the eastern reef as a buoy.

Anchorage.—A good berth is on a line from Gnat point to the S. end of Prickly Pear island, and half-way between them, in from 10 to 12 fathoms of water.

Tides.—The tides at the entrance of the sound, between the reefs, seldom run more than half a knot, and the flood-tide sets to the eastward at the rate of 1 and 1½ knots. Between Pajaros and Horseshoe reef it seldom runs more than a knot, but its duration varies.

Necker island.—On its N. side it is bold and steep-to; from the eastern, southern, and western sides reefs stretch out, that to the southward having a clear channel one-fourth of a mile wide between it and the reefs from the islands farther S.

Eustatia island is small. Its N. side is foul to the distance of 200 yards, and from it a broken reef stretches to Pajaros point. Inside the reef there is a snug anchorage for small vessels, reached through a narrow cut in the reef half a mile E. of the island.

The **Invisibles** are two small rocks and do not always break.

The **Great, George** and **West dogs** are three rocky islets, steep-to, from 150 to 270 feet high.

The **Seal Dogs** form a cluster of smaller islets. The northernmost islet is only 6 feet high, the others 74 and 100.

Scrub island, four hundred and fifty feet high, is the easternmost of the numerous small islets and rocks which lie close off the E. end of Tortola, and which are only separated from each other by small intricate cuts.

Among these islands, which do not need any further description, are Guano island, Great and Little Camanoe islands, Beef island, Buck island, and Marina cay. Most of these are high, averaging from 500 to 650 feet, except Marina cay, which is low.

On the charts an anchorage is marked W. of Guano island, but during the season of rollers it is unsafe, as they break here in 8 or 9 fathoms.

Between the S. end of Virgin Gorda and the E. end of St. John's is a range of very remarkable small, rugged, and most irregularly shaped islets and rocks, the shores of which rise abruptly from the sea to the height of from 350 to 550 feet. Between most of them are deep and navigable passages leading into Sir Francis Drake channel, simple and easy of access in the day-time. In the smaller ones, however, a little precaution is necessary in a sailing-vessel to guard against the eddy tides and flaws of wind when coming under the lee of the larger islands.

Round rock is S. of Fallen Jerusalem cay, 220 feet high. Between them lie the Blinders and other barren rocks, and the ground is rocky and foul in the cuts between them.

Ginger island, SW. of Round rock is irregularly shaped. Between these two islands is Round Rock passage, the best channel for vessels coming from the eastward, as the small islands to windward are too small to obstruct the regular breeze, and the channel is easily recognized by the remarkable appearance of Fallen Jerusalem, a mile to the northward of it.

Both sides of the channel are bold and steep-to, and there is no danger whatever in it.

Between Ginger island and Cooper island to the westward the channel is three-quarters of a mile wide.

Carval rock is in the southern part of this channel. It is 110 feet high, bold and steep-to, and may be left on either hand.

Ginger island is so high that a sailing-vessel is very likely to be becalmed under its lee. For a steamer, or for a sailing-vessel with a SE. breeze, this passage is as good as Round Rock channel.

Cooper rocks are in the northern part of this channel and just to the eastward of Cooper island. The channel between, though deep, is too narrow to be used by a sailing-vessel.

Salt island.—Off its NE. point is a rock awash, between which and Cooper island is a narrow channel, less than a quarter of a mile wide, and should not be attempted by a sailing-vessel.

Dead Chest island is a small islet 200 feet high, and a little more than one-half a mile from it is Blonde rock, with 12 feet of water on it. Between this danger and Salt island is, however, a clear channel nearly a mile wide. To be sure of avoiding it, keep Salt island close aboard.

Peter island forms an elbow. The eastern part is 540 feet high, the northern part is 440 feet high. The channel between it and Norman island, to the westward, is crooked and seldom used.

Great harbor is a snug little bight on the N. side of Peter island, and may be entered without the slightest difficulty at any time. The water is deep close up to the shore, and it has excellent holding ground. The harbor is open to the NW., but Tortola protects it in that direction and makes it quite smooth.

Little harbor, a short distance to leeward of Great harbor, is of much the same character, but more confined and more open. There is no water on Peter island. Both this island and Salt island are inhabited by fishermen.

Norman island is crooked, high, and 440 feet high in its western part. On the western side is a good anchorage in from 7 to 11 fathoms in a small inlet called the Bight. The shores on each side are steep-to, and the only danger to be avoided is Ringdove rock. The mark to clear it is Treasure point, in line with the summit of the western hill. There is a narrow but deep channel between Ringdove rock and the northern point of the entrance.

Although the bight is open to the westward, it is sheltered in that direction by the island of St. John.

Privateer bay.—There is good anchorage in this bay, just S. of Treasure point, with the regular trade-wind.

Flanagan or Norman pass.—This passage is the most difficult to enter from the southeastward, on account of the Santa Monica rock, which lies right in the way. This rock is very small, with only 10 feet of water on it. Fort Charlotte, on Tortola, in one with the highest of the Indian rocks, N. 2° 49′ E., leads to the eastward of it, and Bellevue, the highest hill on the E. end of Tortola, in one with Indian rocks, N. 16° 52′ E., leads to the westward.

The Indians are four remarkable small pinnacle rocks, 50 feet high, close together, at about 200 yards westward of a small islet 180 feet high named Pelican island.

When approaching Flanagan passage from the eastward the best way will be to haul close round the W. side of Norman island, which may be done without fear at the distance of about 300 yards.

In beating up or running down along the shore, by keeping Cooper and Ginger island just open of Peter island, a vessel will pass half a mile to the southward of the Sta. Monica rock.

Sir Francis Drake channel lies between the islands we have just been describing on the S., and Tortola on the islands E. of it on the N. It is clear of dangers except in the vicinity of Road harbor, in the island of Tortola, where there are several shallow banks. In the other parts of the channel a vessel may anchor anywhere to the eastward of a line drawn from Buck island to Dead Chest island.

With strong N. and NE. winds there is good anchorage on the SW. side of Beef island.

Tortola island is of a very irregular outline and is very mountainous. In 1885 the inhabitants numbered about 5,300, including a few persons on Beef, Guano, Camanoe, and Thatch islands.

Road harbor is on the SE. side of Tortola, and the only port of entry in the British portion of the Virgin islands. Being completely exposed to the SE., it may be more properly described as a bay surrounded by an amphitheater of lofty hills, the spurs of which reach the edge of the shore, Mount Sage overlooking it on the W. and Mount Bellevue on the E.

Vessels of large draught should not attempt to enter without a pilot.

Road Town, the seat of government, stands on the western shore of the harbor, and immediately above it a spur of the main ridge where Fort Charlotte formerly stood, but no part of it is now seen.

The flag-staff formerly used as a leading mark for entering, is now placed in the center of the town, near the custom-house.

On the eastern side, immediately opposite, and scattered along the shore is the village of Kingston.

The Anchorage is so confined by the numerous shoals at its entrance and within it, especially on the lee or western side, that it is only adapted for vessels of moderate draught; and it is very inconvenient, from the heavy swell which prevails in the winter season.

Under the lee of the reef at Fort Burt point, on the western side of the entrance to the harbor, there is a small well-sheltered vein of deep water, which affords a good careening place for coasters of about 9 or 10 feet draught.

Denmark, Scotch and Lark banks.—There are from 2 to $6\frac{1}{2}$ fathoms water on the Denmark banks, the eastern extreme of which lies nearly midway between Hog and Slaney points, the outer extremes of the harbor.

Wickham and Little Wickham cays are low, covered with mangrove-bushes, and show well against the cultivated ground behind them; there are several large cocoa-nut trees on the SE. part of Wickham cay.

Having entered the harbor under easy sail, when Fort Burt point bears S. 78° 45′ W. the vessel will be just within the shoals, and may then round to an anchor in 10 fathoms, with Shirley point bearing about N. 45° E., distant 400 yards, in from 7 to 13 fathoms water, very uneven bottom.

Handy vessels of light draught, or steamers, having brought Fort Burt point on the above bearing, may haul up about N. 22° 30′ W. and proceed in so far as to bring the cocoa-nut trees on the SE. end of Wickham cay to bear N. 78° 45′ W., taking care to anchor eastward of the line of the outer part of Slaney point, touching the right extreme of Flanagan island. They will here have room to weigh and avoid the harbor-spit, which stretches out from the westward into nearly the middle of the anchorage.

Sea cow bay may be used as a temporary anchorage for small vessels.

Sopers hole is a deep, snug bight between Frenchmans cay and Little Thatch island on the S. and the western point of Tortola on the N. side, and sheltered from westerly winds by Great Thatch island. In the middle of the anchorage there are 12 fathoms, gradually decreasing to 6 fathoms close to shore.

Sopers hole may be approached either by the passage between Little Thatch island or by that between the former and Frenchman's cay. The W. point of Tortola must not be approached nearer than 200 yards, on account of off-lying rock which extend to that distance in each case.

Thatch island cut is the passage between Thatch island and Tortola, and must not be attempted by a sailing vessel from the northward except with a flood-tide, as the eddies and stream are very strong.

Great Thatch island.—Its eastern point, forming the western side of Thatch Island cut, is bold and steep-to.

Tides.—In the channel between St. John and Tortola the flood-tide runs to the eastward and the ebb-tide to the westward, with a velocity of from 3 to 4 knots.

Vessels should be prepared to meet the gusts and baffling winds which rush down through the valleys of Tortola.

Cane Garden bay is the only anchorage on the N. side of Tortola, where small vessels may find a temporary shelter. Across the entrance there is a bar with 12 feet of water. Inside of this bar there are 3 and 4 fathoms, within a reef which runs out from the S. side of the bay. The small village of Cane Garden extends along the shore at the bottom of the bay.

St. John island is of irregular breadth. Ram head forms the S. point of the island; the western portion is composed of irregular hills and peaks. The spurs from the heights terminate abruptly at all the projecting points, and, with the exception of a small spot at Coral bay, nothing is seen but hill and dale.

Coral or Crawl bay.—The shore is divided into three smaller bays, and these are cut up into into several small coves and creeks.

The westernmost of these three bays is called Coral harbor, the middle one Hurricane hole, and the eastern one Round bay.

There is no town or village in Coral bay, but at Coral harbor the Moravian missionaries have a little establishment called Carolina, from which place bridle-paths lead to all parts of the island.

Large vessels seldom visit this bay, and the produce of the neighboring country is carried by coasters to St. Thomas and Santa Cruz.

About half-way between Ram head and Moors point is Buck islet, 84 feet high. There is a channel on both sides of it.

Eagle shoal.—In using the channel to the westward, care must be taken to avoid this shoal.

The shoal consists of two patches of coral, about 40 yards each in diameter. The easternmost has only 4 feet, and the westernmost 12 feet of water upon it. They are steep-to, with from 6 or 7 fathoms all around them.

Hurricane hole.—Of the three anchorages in Coral bay this, being partly sheltered from SE. winds, is the best and safest. A good berth is in 11 fathoms of water with Turner's point bearing S. 50° 37' E. and Harbor point S. 78° 45' W.

In Round bay the best anchorage is in 13 fathoms of water, with Moors point bearing S. 61° 52' E., 600 yards. As a temporary anchorage with the usual trade-winds this is a good berth, but with a SE. wind it is very rough.

In Coral harbor there is a less depth of water than in the two other anchorages of Coral bay, and it is only fit for a temporary berth for a small steamer.

The **tides** set across the mouth of Coral bay; the flood to the SW. and the ebb to the NE. at the rate of three-fourths of a mile an hour. There is no tidal stream within the bay, and the rise and fall of springs rarely exceeds 1 foot.

Great Lameshur bay affords shelter for small vessels in 9 fathoms of water just under Cabrite point.

Reef bay is easily distinguished by a remarkable white cliff, 135 feet high.

There is no shelter except for boats.

Fish bay, westward of Reef bay, is only 200 yards wide between the reefs at its entrance, but nearly 800 yards deep; within the bay the soundings gradually decrease from 4 fathoms to the shore.

Rendezvous bay, to the westward of Dittless point, is quite free of danger, but open to the southward.

Great Cruz bay, at the SW. end of St. John, affords good shelter for drogers. From between the two bluffs at its entrance the water gradually decreases from 4 to 3 fathoms, and then suddenly to 2 fathoms.

Little Cruz bay is a small cove at the western extremity of St. John, but only fit for coasters. There is a village on the shore, and a white building called the fort. An excellent road leads thence to the upper parts of the island and Coral bay.

Anchorage.—To the westward of Little Cruz bay there is anchorage in 11 fathoms water, over sand and mud, with the fort bearing S. 73° E, the center of the Two Brothers in one with the W. point of Grass cay; and the dry rocks off the E. side of Meeren cay in one with the Dog rock.

Directions.—A vessel may approach this anchorage by the passage between Meeren cay and St. John, but it can not be recommended to sailing-vessels on account of the baffling winds under the high land. The best mark to run through it from the southward is the Carval rock, off the E. end of Congo cay, and the western hummock on the W. end of Jost Van Dyke in one, bearing N. 11° 15′ E.

Caution.—The reef off Turner bay and the dry rocks off Meeren cay are bold and steep-to; but care must be taken to guard against being set out of the course by the strong tide that runs at the rate of 2 knots between the islands and the main, the flood to the southward, the ebb to the northward. The best way, however, will be to pass to leeward of Meeren cay, and to stand on until the vessel can fetch the anchorage.

Johnson reef.—At 1¼ miles northward of Little Cruz bay, and one-fourth of a mile from Hogsnest point, is the largest of the three Durloe cays, 68 feet high; the other two cays, 45 and 18 feet high, are about 300 and 400 yards NE. and NW. of it. Nearly midway between these cays and Whistling cay, 250 feet high, is Johnson reef. It is one-fourth of a mile in length, lies half a mile from the shore, and always breaks.

There are 3½ fathoms water 200 yards N. of it, 3 fathoms at about the same distance E. and W. of it, and between it and the shore irregular soundings, varying from 1½ to 10 fathoms.

Francis bay, formed by Mary point, and somewhat protected as far round as NW. by Whistling cay, and affords good anchorage in 9 fathoms water, sand. Between Whistling cay and the shore southward of it is a bank 800 yards in length and 250 in breadth, fronting the bay, with 3¾ to 4½ fathoms water on it. The cut between Whistling cay and the main is clear, but not easily navigated on account of the baffling winds from the high land forming Mary point.

Leinster bay is separated from Francis bay by a narrow neck of land, and the shore is here fringed with a coral ledge awash, easily seen from the deck.

There are several other small bays on the northern side of St. Johns, where small vessels may find temporary shelter, but, being exposed to the rollers, they are not safe for the night.

St. Thomas island.—The island is mountainous, and in its general aspect much resembles St. John. A chain of mountains runs along the middle of the island, with spurs branching to the N. and S., and terminating abruptly at the sea-shore. The two principal eminences are Signal hill, nearly in the middle of the island, 1,500 feet high, and West mountain, 1,550 feet high. The island is surrounded by small isles and rocks, which are almost universally steep-to, with very few hidden dangers.

St. Thomas harbor, on the S. side of the island, is excellently protected from all ordinary winds, and is perfectly easy of access. The town called Charlotte Amalia owes its commercial importance to its being a free port, and also to its being headquarters in the West Indies for numerous steam-ship lines. It is also the seat of government of the Danish West Indies. During the last few years it has suffered very severely from hurricanes and earthquakes. St. Thomas is gradually losing the commercial importance and prosperity it once enjoyed. Yellow fever is said to be here and may be taken aboard of a vessel in the coal.

The population of the island is about 16,000; of Charlotte Amalia, about 14,000. The city has been visited by yellow fever, and vessels have carried it away with them. It is lighted by gas.

Provisions of all kinds can be obtained at an advance of 25 per cent. over those of New York.

Water can be had in any quantity; costs 1 cent per gallon.

Coal.—The usual supply is about 7,500 tons and costs from $7 to $9.50 per ton. Vessels coal alongside the dock. If the coal is brought off in lighters 50 cents per ton is charged; stowing, 10 cents per ton.

Dock.—There is one floating dock; length, 230 feet; length of yard, 283 feet; inside breadth, 72 feet; greatest draught, 21 feet; capacity, 3,000 tons; crane lifts 40 tons.

Repairs may be made to steamers at the shops of the Royal Mail Steam Packet Company. Sailing vessels may be repaired here, there being many ship carpenters, sail-makers, and riggers.

Hospitals.—There is one general, one marine, one for the poor, and a lazaretto. The charges are very high. The sanitary condition of the place is good, the streets being clean and well kept.

Pilots are not necessary; the charge is about $3 for 18 feet, not compulsory.

Port charges.—Light dues, ½ cent per ton. Anchorage, $2.50 for a ship; $1.25 for a brig; 60 cents for a schooner. Tonnage in or out of the harbor, $15 for a vessel of 500 tons and $20 for a vessel of 1,000 tons. Health officer from infected ports only, night service, double fees, $3 to $5. Doctor's visit, $1.50 for each visit or $3 per head if entire crew is contracted for. Pratique, $3 to $7. Laborers, $1.25 per day without meals, $1 with meals. Stone ballast, 75 cents per ton. Spanish bills of health and manifest to Porto Rico and Cuba in ballast, $17. Bill of health for St. Domingo, $7; for Venezuela, $6 to $8. Fort pass, $2.50. Each vessel on arrival will receive a copy of harbor regulations free.

Telegraph.—There are three cables, and there is telegraphic communication with all parts of the world.

Steamers.—There are several lines to Europe and ports in the West Indies, also to the United States.

The authority to visit is the governor.

The United States is represented by a consul and vice-consul.

In approaching the harbor of St. Thomas from the eastward, two small islands to the southward will be observed.

Frenchman's cap, the most southerly of these, is a small islet, and is perfectly steep-to.

Buck island, the other, is larger than Frenchman's cap. On the S. and E. sides it is steep-to; on the N. side there are 5 fathoms of water at the distance of 100 yards, and off the W. end a ledge of rocks runs to the same distance.

Packet rock, at the distance of a mile and a tenth N. of the central part of Buck island and a little more than half a mile from the shore of St. Thomas, is a small coral shoal, with only 5 feet of water on it. The sea does not always break on it, and it is steep-to, and can only be seen at a short distance.

There is a clear channel between it and St. Thomas.

To avoid it coming from the eastward do not pass to the northward of a line drawn from Ram head through the S. extreme of Dog island till you are to the westward of Buck island.

The Triangles are from 1 to 4 feet above low water and about one third of a mile from the shore. S. of these three rocks, about 200 yards, there is a small detached rock about 35 yards in diameter and having 17 feet of water upon it.

The houses on the summit of the middle hill of the town well open westward of Muhlenfels point clears both these dangers.

Point knoll.—Off Muhlenfels point at a distance of 150 yards is a small coral head with 3 fathoms of water on it, called Point knoll.

Scorpion rock.—In the entrance to the harbor and about half-way between Cowell point and Muhlenfels point lies the Scorpion rock, about 27 yards long, 10 yards wide, and having 20 feet of water on it at the lowest spring tides. At 50 yards distance on each side of the rock there are from 28 to 30 feet.

Rupert rock, being kept whitewashed, is easily distinguished by night or day. At its base are some large bowlders which extend westerly 50 yards, and are just covered with water.

On the westernmost of the rocks is an iron beacon with a diamond-shaped head painted white. Between Rupert rocks and the nearest point there are only 15 feet of water.

The **anchorage** for vessels in quarantine lies between Rupert rock and Rhode bank, having from 5 to $3\frac{1}{2}$ fathoms.

Frederik knoll.—On the W. side of the entrance the shore is steep-to except directly off Frederik point at the narrowest part of the entrance, where there are two rocky heads with 16 to 17 feet of water on them from 75 to 100 yards from the battery. These are the only dangers on the W. side of the channel.

Care must, however, be taken to observe the port regulation, which forbids a vessel anchoring in front of the fort so as to mask it or prevent it from taking a range of the whole entrance of the harbor. The sterns of vessels anchoring to the eastward must consequently not be more westerly than to bring the flag-staff of the fort to bear N. 22° 30′ W., and the bows of vessels anchoring on the western side of the harbor not more easterly than to bring it N. 11° 15′ E. Merchant vessels discharging cargo lie off the town to the westward of the fort; those ready for sea, preparatory for sailing, warp into Long bay, to the eastward of it.

At night there is no difficulty in entering St. Thomas harbor, but in this case it will be better to pass outside Buck island, between it and Frenchman's cap, and having brought the light to bear N.—to avoid the Triangles and the 17-foot rock S. of them—stand boldly in toward the entrance. The Rupert rock, being whitewashed, will soon show itself.

Pilots.—Although the entrance to St. Thomas harbor presents no difficulties, the assistance of a government pilot, one of whom always comes alongside to offer his services, is frequently useful to point out a convenient berth.

Anchorage will be found anywhere in Gregerie channel clear of the shoals. The safest and most convenient spots are in the elbow and SW. arm, for a vessel will there be more sheltered.

In passing through Gregerie channel with a long vessel it must be remembered that the turn in the channel is quite short, and it would therefore be well to mark Gregerie bank with a boat.

Great Krum bay is a small inlet running up between two lofty hills at the western side of the entrance to the SW. arm of Gregerie channel. This bay is used as a convenient spot for breaking up vessels.

Mosquito bay is close to the westward of Great Krum bay, about half a mile wide between Mosquito and Red points, half a mile deep, and open to the southward. Off the latter point a narrow rocky ledge extends along a quarter of a mile to the S. 11° 15′ W., and on its extreme end is a small coral head, called Red Point shoal, with only 2 feet water on it, and steep-to. Within the bay the depth from 5 fathoms gradually decreases toward the shore, but with this dangerous ledge under the lee it is only safe for drogers.

Porpoise rocks are three small rocks, just out of water, and connected by a shallow ledge. They are steep-to, and lie W. about two-thirds of a mile from the SW. end of Water island, with a deep and clear channel between.

Water Island anchorage.—There is excellent anchorage under the W. side of Water island for vessels of the largest draught. If intending to anchor here, run in about midway between the Porpoise rocks and the island, and come to in 9 fathoms of water, as soon as the town of St. Thomas is seen coming open to the northward of the island; or with the S. extreme of the island S. 33° 45′ E., and the N. end of Drif Bay beach N. 78° 45′ E.

Southwest road, between Perseverance bay and Flat cays, is a good temporary anchorage with the wind as far to the southward as ESE. The approaches to it are free of danger, except Red Point shoal. This shoal lies a long quarter of a mile off Red point, and to avoid it keep Flag Hill peak (on the E. side of the harbor of St. Thomas) open to the southward of Mosquito point, until the S. points of Flat and Turtle Dove cays are in one S. 50° 37′ W., when haul up and anchor as most convenient. Mosquito point and Flag Hill peak in one N. 81° 34′ E. leads 100 yards southward of the Red Point shoal in 9 fathoms of water.

Tides.—In shore there is scarcely any stream, but between Flat cays and Saba island the flood during the springs runs to the ESE. at the rate of about a knot, and the ebb in the opposite direction with the same velocity.

On the N. side of the island of St. Thomas there are no good anchorages. Directly across the island from St. Thomas harbor is a deep bight called Great North Side bay, the eastern side of which is formed by a long tongue of land extending to the NW. from the main island.

The bay is open to the NW., and therefore liable to rollers. A temporary anchorage may be found under the weather-shore.

The only danger in approaching is the Ornen rock, lying half a mile N. 61° 52′ W. from the extreme point of the tongue of land just mentioned.

St. James bay is at the eastern end of St. Thomas, and between it and Great St. James island. It is well sheltered, except to the SW., and affords a good and secure anchorage except during the hurricane season. To enter it, pass the rocks called the Stragglers, off the S. end of Great St. James island, at a distance of 100 yards, and anchor with the S. extreme of these rocks bearing about S. 28° E., distant 700 yards, and Fish cay in the eastern part of the bay, bearing N. 73° E.

Cow and Calf rocks are W. of the Stragglers, between which and the nearest point of St. Thomas Island there is a channel having irregular soundings of from 5 to 9 fathoms. In passing through this channel the fort in Little Cruz bay (St. John)—which being whitewashed and standing alone is easily distinguished—should not be opened to the northward of Great St. James; the fort in one with the NW. point of that island will bear N. 61° 52′ E.

Anchorage.—There is an excellent anchorage in the space between the islands of St. Thomas and St. John, quite sheltered from all winds except southerly ones, which only blow during the hurricane months.

This space is called the Sound, and is secured against rollers, but the tides are very strong.

The Two Brothers are two small barren rocks, 20 feet high, lying in the middle of the sound. A ledge runs off gradually from their N. side, deepening to 5 fathoms at the distance of 250 yards; they may be approached on their S. side to the distance of 100 yards.

To enter the Sound from the southward the channel lies between St. John and Dog islands, at the E. end of St. Thomas.

South Channel to the Sound.—The Two Brothers may be passed on either side, but care must be taken not to pass to the eastward of a line drawn from the W. end of Grass cay to the S. end of Meeren cay, in order to keep clear of the reef off Turner bay.

There are three channels by which a vessel may enter the sound from the N., called the Windward, Middle, and Leeward channels. The approaches to the northern channels between the islands to the northward of Tortola, St. John, and St. Thomas present no serious difficulty. The eastern passage between Tortola and Jost Van Dyke is especially clear and safe. It is only necessary to keep in mid-channel, where the least water is 9 fathoms.

Jost Van Dyke island is lofty and rugged, bold and steep-to, and toward the E. end it rises to the height of 1,060 feet. On the S. side are two small bays called Great and Little harbors; they are only fit anchorages for coasters.

Little Jost Van Dyke island is separated from the E. end of the greater island by a shallow ledge 200 yards wide. Close to its E. end is a small islet named Green cay. S. of the cay there is a small dry rock, and shallow water for nearly one-quarter of a mile.

Sandy cay.—Its E. end is 66 feet high, but to the westward it terminates in a low sand-spit, and both ends are foul to the distance of 200 yards. The channel between it and Jost Van Dyke is half a mile wide, but the Jost Van Dyke shore, which is steep-to, must be kept aboard.

Great Tobago.—A small rock awash and steep-to lies about 100 yards from the N. point. The S. side of the island is fringed with coral to a short distance, but all elsewhere the shore is bold, close home to the cliffs.

Watson rock is a remarkable small, barren, perpendicular rock, steep-to, and terminates in a peak 90 feet high.

Mercurias rock.—The channel between Jost Van Dyke and Great Tobago is clear of dangers with this exception, having 7 feet of water on it.

The rock is small and steep-to, and can be easily avoided by keeping the Jost Van Dyke shore aboard.

Little Tobago is nearly half a mile in length, one-quarter of a mile in breadth, and 280 feet high. There is a safe and clear channel between these islands, but as nothing would be gained it will be better to pass through either of the others; should it be necessary, however, to take it, keep a little to windward or eastward of Little Tobago, taking the bearing of Watson rock to avoid the King rock.

King rock is small, bold, and steep-to, and between it and Great Tobago the depth is 6 and 7 fathoms.

Hans-Lollik is a high rocky islet.

Little Hans-Lollik is a smaller and lower islet 400 yards to the northward. The two are connected by a coral ledge nearly dry. Still farther to the N., at a distance of 200 yards, is a third and smaller islet with a sunken rock close off its N. side.

The W. sides of these islets are steep-to, but to the southward is the Hans-Lollik rock, 700 yards from the S. point of Hans-Lollik. This rock is about 200 yards in diameter, is awash, and can be seen from a ship's deck about 1 mile.

To the southward of the chain of islets just described are the northern entrances into the sound.

Durloe cays are three small islets near the NW. point of St. Johns and are easily distinguished. The most southerly and largest of these cays is 60 feet high. They are clear and steep-to.

Blunder rocks, off the E. end of Lovango cay, are awash and extend about 400 yards from the cay.

Congo cay is a short distance N. of Lovango cay, and has two remarkable rocks off its eastern point, of which the easternmost, about 400 yards distant, is called the Carval rock, and marks the western side of the entrance to the windward channel.

Tides.—In this channel the ebb runs NE. by N., the flood SW., at the rate of 2 miles an hour. The channel may be used by the largest vessels as long as a speed of 4 knots can be depended upon, the current at times reaching $2\frac{1}{2}$ miles an hour. Should the wind die out, a vessel may anchor, observing that under 10 fathoms the bottom is rocky and not good holding-ground.

The dangers in this channel are all apparent, but, with the ebb-tide running against the wind, there is a tide rip which looks like broken water, and is apt to alarm a stranger.

Between the Durloe cays and between them and the island of St. Johns there are deep and clear passages, but it is better to pass to the westward of the Durloe cays. Between Lovango and Mingo cays there is a 3-fathom passage, but, as it is narrow and the tides strong, it is only fit for boats.

In Middle channel the flood sets to the southward about 2 knots, and takes a SE. direction inside. The ebb runs in the opposite direction with the same strength.

Leeward passage is entirely clear of danger. The flood sets through to the eastward at the rate of from 2 to 2¼ knots, and the ebb with the same velocity in the opposite direction.

Shark islet.—If the channel between Hans-Lollik and the Ornen rock is taken, keep the W. point of Thatch cay in one with Shark islet, S. 56° 15′ E., until clear of the Hans-Lollik rock. Shark islet is small, rocky, 40 feet high, and lies near the shore at the E. end of St. Thomas.

Current hole and passge.—Between Current Hole point, at the E. end of the island of St. Thomas and Great St. James island, is Current hole and passage. In the center of the passage is the Current rock, between which and St. Thomas there are only 9 feet of water, but E. of this rock there is a narrow channel about 100 yards wide and 200 yards long. The tides rush through here with great violence, the flood running to the southward with a velocity of 3 knots, and the ebb with equal force to the northward.

This channel is only fit to be used by small steamers or by handy sailing vessels with a commanding breeze.

St. James channel.—A depth of 20 feet may be carried through the cut between Great and Little St. James, passing on either side of the Welk rock, which lies on the E. side of the islands. The channel is on the Great St. James side, but so circuitous as to be by no means safe. The eye will be the best guide for it.

The opening between Dog island and Little St. James is barred across with only 3 fathoms of water, and having also a 9-foot rock in mid-channel.

Neither of the last three channels should be attempted by a sailing vessel except in a case of emergency and with a commanding breeze.

Brass islands are two small islets close off the N. side of St. Thomas, and about 3 miles westward of Hans-Lollik; the Inner Brass is 260 feet and the Outer Brass 430 feet high. Between the inner islet and St. Thomas there is a 5-fathom channel, 400 yards wide; and between the two islets there is one of 7 fathoms, 600 yards wide, but they are only safe for coasters.

Tides.—The flood sets between them to the SW. at the rate of about a knot, but the ebb is scarcely perceptible.

Anchorage.—Under the Inner Brass there is secure and well-sheltered anchorage for coasters in 6 or 7 fathoms water, at about half a mile off shore, with the N. end of the islet N. 11° 15′ E.

Lizard rock is a small, rugged islet, 15 feet high, bold and steep-to on all sides; it lies westward of the Inner Brass island.

West and **Salt cays** are only separated from the W. end of St. Thomas by a small boat channel. They are each about half a mile long, and lie close together; Salt cay, the outer one, is 250 feet high, bold and steep-to.

Dutchman's cap, to the northward of Salt cay, is a remarkable small, rocky islet, rising abruptly from the sea to a peak 270 feet high, with deep water close around. At about 100 yards from its SW. side there is a small rock 3 feet out of water. Between it and Salt cay the soundings are from 14 to 18 fathoms.

Cockroach island is a small rocky islet of irregular shape, with a flattish summit, and bold perpendicular cliffs, 155 feet high. It is nearly of the same size as Dutchman's cap. The passage between is quite free of danger.

Cricket rock is the most northern islet of the group in this direction. It is 45 feet high, bold and steep-to, and there is a clear channel between the two islets.

Savana island is uninhabited, but used for breeding goats. On its W. side it is steep-to, having 16 fathoms 100 yards from the rocks. Some detached dry rocks extend nearly 100 yards from its S. point, with 15 fathoms close to their outer edge; there are also some straggling rocks 8 or 10 feet high, bold and steep-to, extending about a quarter of a mile off its eastern side. Close to its N. point is a small sunken rock.

Turkey cay, in the middle of Savana Island passage, is a small narrow islet, 80 feet high, and surrounded by deep water, except at the S. end, where there are 3 fathoms at a short distance.

Salt Water Money rock is about one-half a mile to the SE. of the cay, is 10 feet high, bold and steep-to, with a clear channel between.

About half-way between the N. end of Savana island and the W. end of Salt cay there is a small coral patch with only 5 fathoms of water on it.

Everywhere else in the passage the depths are from 13 to 16 fathoms.

Tides.—In the Savana passage the tides run at the rate of 3 knots; the ebb to the NW. and the flood to the SE. West of Savana island their direction is the same, but with a velocity of only 2 miles an hour.

Sail rock, so called from its great resemblance to a vessel under sail, rises precipitously from the sea to the height of 125 feet. It is about 100 yards in diameter, quite barren, with a light-grayish appearance, from its being the residence of birds at certain seasons.

Santa Cruz or **St. Croix island.**—The eastern end terminates in a bluff point, with a conical hill a short distance W. of it. The western part of the island is more elevated.

North coast.—From Ham's bluff, formed of remarkable steep cliffs, to Baron's bluff the shore is steep-to and the bank of soundings does not extend more than half a mile off shore.

Between Baron's bluff and Salt River point, but nearer the latter, is a narrow cut in a reef leading to a deep inlet called Salt river, in which, however, there is only shelter for boats. Salt River point is rather low, and forms the N. extreme of Santa Cruz and the NW. point of the bight of Christiansted.

Four hundred yards N. of the point lies the White Horse, a dangerous rock which generally breaks, and between it and the shore there is a boat channel carrying a depth of 2 fathoms.

Christiansted harbor is well protected on the N. by reefs almost dry. The harbor is small and only fit for a few vessels drawing not more than 17 feet.

In approaching the harbor from the N. or NE., after passing Buck island, haul in toward Green cay, a small islet with two hillocks on it 1½ miles eastward of the fort. In standing toward the Scotch bank take care to keep Baron's bluff open of Salt River point. Having neared it Fort Louisa Augusta will be seen at the NE. end of the town, when it should be brought in line with the first hill to the eastward of a large notch or saddle formed by two hills. Steer in on this line very carefully and it will lead to the entrance of the channel and outer buoys which lie about 400 yards within it.

Vessels drawing only 10 feet may lie alongside the jetty of the town.

Eastern channel.—There is a channel over the inner part of the Scotch bank with the depth of 12 feet in the center, which may be used by vessels of light draught. The chart will be the best guide.

Richmond House is a large building with a red roof, standing in grounds of a park-like appearance on the sloping land near the sea.

For a sailing vessel, although easy of access at almost all periods, it is difficult to get out of the inner harbor, and in the months of January and February, when the wind hangs to the northward of E., a vessel may meet with considerable detention. With the usual trade-wind she must warp up to the entrance; buoys are conveniently placed for that purpose. Toward daylight it is generally calm, when a vessel may be able to tow out, assisted sometimes by a light land air from the SE. which will enable her to obtain an offing clear of the shoals before meeting the regular breeze.

Pilots are prompt to answer a signal made for them from any vessel needing their services. Their station is on Protestant cay, close off the town.

The population is about 8,000. The streets are clean and the sanitary condition is excellent.

Provisions of all kinds can be obtained at a cost of from one-quarter to one-half more than in the United States.

Water can be had at a cost of ½ a cent per gallon. It is river water collected in tanks and brought to the pier by pipes, from which boats can take it on board.

Coal can be had in small quantities; cost, about $9 per ton.

Telegraph.—There is telegraphic communication with St. Thomas, also a telegraph and telephone to Frederichsted.

There are no steamers, but the mail leaves for St. Thomas twice a week.

Hospitals.—There is one which is well conducted by two Danish doctors and has accommodation for 230 patients; cost, from $2.50 to $3 per day; one for the insane, one for ulcerated patients. Private patients have separate apartments.

Port charges.—Anchorage, dues, $15; mooring, $4; bill of health and health officer, $5 to $10; pilotage, $1 per foot draught.

Exports.—Rum, sugar, molasses.

Imports.—Provisions, machinery, cooperage, stock.

The duties on exports are 5 per cent. on sugar, 3 per cent. on rum and molasses.

The United States is represented by a consular agent.

The governor, by law, now resides six months of the year at St. Thomas and six months at this place.

The town of Christiansted is easily made out, but Fort Louisa Augusta, the front mark of the range leading to the entrance buoys, has, at a distance, no appearance of a fort, and is not easily distinguished.

Protestant cay can easily be mistaken for the fort, especially as a flag is kept flying from a staff on the cay and none on the fort. The range should be used with caution and only for the purpose of finding the entrance buoys.

When expecting vessels of more than usual size the pilots place a small wooden buoy on the inner (SW.) point of the Scotch bank.

Changes of channel.—After a heavy northerly swell has continued for several days, the western extremity of the Scotch bank will change its location. This is particularly noticeable at the SW. point. The Welcome bank is gradually extending into the harbor, but has not advanced, as yet, enough to cause any change of importance.

There is no great difficulty or danger in entering the harbor provided the wind is not strong nor the sea heavy. Vessels drawing over 12 feet and over 200 feet long, especially if they do not turn quickly, should take a pilot, for the first visit at least. The harbor being small, the buoys numerous, of the same color and in close proximity to each other, make the first entrance confusing to a stranger. All vessels should be prepared to anchor with a stream anchor by the stern, and should have ready warping lines on each bow, with boats to run them to the buoys. There are two turns in the channel over 90°, and the radius of the curve is not greater than 600 feet, while the radical changes of course occur within 400 yards length of each other. Going out less difficulty will be experienced, as the prevailing wind, the NE. trade, assists the turning. The harbor is said to be filling up slowly.

Buck island, 340 feet high, is 1 mile in length, and rises on the southern edge of a dangerous coral bank, which extends westward about three-quarters of a mile and sweeps round 1 mile N. of the island. There are also several shallow patches as far eastward as 1¼ miles.

The island lies directly in the route to the harbor, and should therefore be carefully approached. For this purpose Hams bluff must be kept well open of Barons bluff; these bluffs in one will lead 400 yards outside the reef, in 4 fathoms water. The channel between the W. end of the reef and the NE. end of Scotch bank is 1½ miles wide. To the westward it leads to the eastern channel into Christiansted harbor, and to the eastward toward Buck Island anchorage.

Anchorage.—There is a good anchorage, in 4 fathoms, to the SW. of Buck island, and it is generally chosen by vessels of war. The usual way of approaching it is from the northward, round the W. end of the reef. The latter may be passed by the eye, or by bringing the dwelling-house of Green cay estate (on a mound near the shore) in a line with Sight mill bearing S. 14° W. The mill stands on the center ridge of hills—which is here lower than elsewhere—and has neither head nor vanes. In running in upon this mark, however, the vessel will cross over 27 or 28 feet water, and then deepen to 7 fathoms SW. of the island. Soon after passing within the edge of the bank, she may haul up for the anchorage, and anchor when the E. point of Buck island comes open of the sandy point on its S. side.

Buck Island channel.—From Green cay the shore of Santa Cruz is skirted by a reef all the way to the E. end. Within it there is snug anchorage for small craft which find their way through a small cut N. of Coakley Bay mill, and warp up. With good local knowledge a vessel may enter Buck Island channel from the SE. by running in between the island and the reef skirting Santa Cruz, keeping the N. extreme of Green cay in line with Mount Eagle S. 84° 22′ W. The latter from this direction will appear the left of two hills, apparently very nearly of the same height; the northern one is Salt River mound, rising near the shore 2 miles farther eastward. The least water will be 6½ fathoms, the depth generally being 10 fathoms; but great care must be taken to keep the leading mark on until the vessel is abreast of Buck island, when she may haul to the northward.

Lang bank.—An extensive bank of soundings, stretches off from Santa Cruz, curving round Buck Island reef on the N. and W., and passing at about a third of a mile N. of the Scotch bank at about 1¼ miles from the shore. On its extreme edge there is one of those remarkable wall-sided narrow coral ledges, which, commencing about 3 miles N. 78° 45″ E. of Buck Island reef, sweeps round in a convex form outward at the extreme E. end, and terminates 2 miles from the E. end of Santa Cruz; the northern part has a depth of from 6 to 10 fathoms on it; the southern portion has from 8 to 10 fathoms on it, and in the space between there are from 12 to 17 fathoms.

The shoalest part of the northern ledge bears N. 73° E. from Buck island, and N. 50° 37′ E. from the E. end of Santa Cruz, and in heavy weather it breaks and becomes dangerous; it is therefore advisable, under such circumstances, if coming from the southward, not to approach the E. end within 12 miles, and not to bear up before Buck island bears N. 67° 30′ W.

The S. coast of the island is bordered by a dangerous, broken, coral reef, which extends from the E. end to nearly abreast of Long point, $3\frac{1}{4}$ miles from the SW. point of the island, where it terminates in the SW. shoal, which has only 1 fathom water on it, with Long point bearing N. 30° 15′ W., distant nearly $1\frac{1}{4}$ miles. The most dangerous part is from the latter point to Signal hill, 8 miles to the eastward, where it runs along shore more than $1\frac{1}{2}$ miles off. It generally breaks, and, as several shallow patches exist outside, it should be cautiously approached. There are several cuts through the reef, capable of admitting small coasters into tolerable anchorage within. One of the best is off the entrance of Krausse lagoon. At Great Pond bay there is a narrow cut leading into safe anchorage for vessels of 10 feet draught.

Frederichsted.—The W. end of Santa Cruz forms a bay, and near the center of its shores is the town of Frederichsted. In front of it there is good anchorage in from 6 to 7 fathoms water with the fort bearing S. 78° 45′ E., and the SW. point S. 16° 52′ W. The edge of the bank is not more than half a mile from the shore, consequently in the hurricane season the anchorage is unsafe. Should the wind blow from the westward, as it sometimes does during the fall and winter months, a heavy swell rolls in, making the anchorage uncomfortable and landing difficult.

Shallow water extends a quarter of a mile from the N. point of the bay, and nearly a mile southward of SW. point, the SW. extreme of the island. In rounding the latter point carefully with the lead in not less than 6 or 7 fathoms water at the distance of a mile, a vessel should not haul in until the N. point bears N. 11° 15′ E. The edge of the bank lies nearly 3 miles SW. of SW. point, and terminates abruptly; within it is a narrow coral ledge of 7 to 9 fathoms.

There are three small wharves near the custom-house at either of which landing is easy.

The population is about 2,500. The town is clean and well kept. The temperature is from 80° to 90° F.

Provisions can be obtained at a cost of 30 to 50 per cent. more than in the United States.

Water can be had from the export wharf at a cost of half a cent per gallon. The water is collected in cisterns and then pumped.

Coal.—A small amount of coal can be had at a cost of $9 per ton.

Hospitals.—There are two in one building, a civil and a military hospital. The cost is from $2.50 to $3 per day. Quarantine is maintained. The quarantine flag is green.

Telegraph.—There is communication with Christiansted both by telegraph and telephone.

The port charges are the same as for Christiansted.

The United States is represented by a consular agent.

Winds.—There is no regular land-breeze at Santa Cruz, but when the trade-wind is light during the day it generally falls calm during the night. Northers, with the accompanying heavy groundswell, do not appear to reach this island.

Tides.—No perceptible tidal stream has been observed at Santa Cruz, but a rise and fall takes place of from 4 to 8 inches, according to the strength of the wind, which will sometimes raise it to 18 inches. Between this island and St. Thomas a slight easterly current has been observed.

Passage islands.—The islands and cays lying between the Virgin passage and the E. end of Puerto Rico are called the Passage islands. They belong to Spain and are dependencies of Puerto Rico.

CULEBRA ISLAND.

It is sometimes called Carlit and Serpent island; is of a very irregular outline. It is uninhabited, of moderate elevation, broken and rugged, thickly wooded, with scarcely a level spot on the surface, and near the center rises to the height of 650 feet. The northern shore is bold and steep-to.

On all other sides there are small islets and reefs which shelter good anchorages, and at the E. end there are two excellent harbors.

Northeast cay is oval-shaped, 340 feet high, and thickly wooded.

Bird cay is 300 yards N. of the E. end; it is a remarkable small rocky islet, 60 feet high; and at about a mile to the NE. of this end are the Shark and Whale rocks, two small rocky islets 16 and 10 feet high; SE. 800 yards from these, are the Palada cays, two small rocky islets, 80 and 84 feet high, and steep-to.

Culebrita island is 260 feet high and thickly wooded. A lighthouse stands on the summit of the island, a tower on a square brick building.

Anchorage.—Excellent anchorage will be found within the cays and islands just described, but the best is toward their southern end under the lee of the reef, in front of Great harbor, called the Sound, a clear space 1½ miles in length and half a mile in breadth.

The best anchorage in the Sound is with the extreme W. end of Davy cay touching the E. end of Bird cay N. 16° 52′ W., and the SE. end of Culebrita S. 67° 30′ W., in 10 or 12 fathoms water, sand. Here a vessel will be in a good position for weighing, and will be protected by the reef to the southward, which, although broken and scattered, is sufficiently compact to break the sea.

Middle ground.—In the approach to the Sound the space between Culebrita and the main island is somewhat obstructed by a shoal on which the depth varies from 2 to 5 fathoms; the shallowest part lies about 500 yards from the nearest part of Culebrita.

Lee channel.—In approaching the Sound from the northward this channel between Northeast cay and Culebra is the clearest and best for a steamer, but unless the wind is as far to the northward as NNE., it had better not be attempted by a sailing-vessel, except with the aid of a pilot and on the flood tide.

In proceeding through the Lee channel, keep midway between Northeast cay and the S. shore, until nearly abreast of Duck point, when the Culebra side should be kept aboard, to avoid the Middle ground. The bottom is distinctly seen when in less depth than 10 fathoms, and the shoal ground may be avoided by the eye.

The Weather channel lies between Northeast cay and Culebrita. To enter this channel there are three passages. The southern of these, between Palada cays and Culebrita, is the most direct.

To use it, run between Palada cays and Culebrita for the eastern end of Northeast cay, being careful not to approach nearer than within one-fourth of a mile of Palada cays; bring the western extreme of Davy cay to touch the extreme of the remarkable bluff at the E. end of Culebra. Keep them in one until the southern sandy beach of Northeast cay comes on with the N. end of Scrub cay, a small rocky islet, near the N. side of Culebra; then bear away S. 56° 15′ W. and steer for the Dolphin head, a remarkable hill at the E. end of Culebra. When Sandy point of Culebrita opens out clear of Pond point, haul up gradually for the bluff and anchor as most convenient. If going above the Middle ground, keep the Culebra shore rather aboard.

By marking the extreme of the shoal extending SE. from Northeast cay with a boat, vessels of the largest size may enter by this channel without difficulty.

The second or middle passage is between Palada cays on the one side and the Shark and Whale rocks on the other. The western and safest passage is between the latter rocks and Northeast cay. From the latter cay a reef extends to the SE. for one-fourth of a mile, and from Davy cay a shallow ledge runs off nearly 400 yards, leaving between them the Weather channel, about 300 yards in breadth, and the least depth 23 feet.

To take the western passage, steer boldly down toward Northeast cay, and having passed the rocks at the distance of rather more than 200 yards, run through on the same marks given for the southern passage.

Tides.—It is necessary to observe that the flood sets in from the N., between Northeast cay and the Palada cays, at the rate of 1½ knots, and the ebb runs out with equal force in the opposite direction.

There is also a passage into the Sound from the southward. Sailing-vessels will seldom have a fair wind into the sound by this channel, but for a steamer it is safe and easy.

In the South channel the tides run at the rate of 2 knots, the flood to the SW. by S., and the ebb NE. by N.

On the eastern coast of Culebra are three bays communicating with South channel. These are Mangrove harbor, Mosquito bay, and Great harbor.

Mangrove harbor is small but well sheltered. Its entrance lies between Bluff point on the N. and Water and Battle cays on the S. The entrance is about 300 yards wide with a depth of 7 to 8 fathoms, decreasing inside to 5 fathoms, with a bottom of sand and mud. The head of the bay is shallow. In entering the harbor, having rounded Bluff point, steer in midway between the reefs, which are bold and can be seen distinctly, and anchor as convenient. It may not be easy to get out under sail, as the channel trends NW. and SE.

The Basin.—On the S. side of Mangrove harbor there is a bight about 600 yards long and 200 yards wide, and having a depth of 4 fathoms of water. It is separated from the harbor by a bar with 14 feet of water on it, and is a secure place for a small vessel to anchor.

Mosquito bay lies close to the entrance of Great harbor, between Harbor and Breeze points. It is a good temporary anchorage, but, being partially open to the southward, a heavy swell frequently sets in from that quarter.

Great harbor is one of the best and safest harbors in the West Indies. Directly opposite the mouth of the harbor are four coral shoals, for which no good leading marks can be given.

These shoals can be seen from aloft, and, to a steamer, are not formidable, as she has only to steer along the reef between Soldier point and the entrance at a distance of 300 yards, and, having passed the shoals, haul in for the entrance to the harbor.

For a sailing-vessel the best channel is between the Grouper and Shrimp shoals. The navigation is, however, too intricate for a stranger without the assistance of a pilot.

The Grampus shoals are a group of small isolated coral heads, with from 3 to 4 fathoms of water on them, rising from a bank with 10 fathoms of water on it, and extending to a distance of 4 miles to SE. of Culebra.

There is a passage between these shoals and the reef which extends to the S. from Culebrita, but no safe directions can be given for it. Large vessels had better pass to the southward of these shoals.

Southwest cay.—From its center a wooded peak rises 500 feet. All along the eastern side, at 200 yards distance, there is a coral reef, and the Culebra shore is also foul at half this distance.

The channel between the N. point of Southwest cay and Stream point, on the Culebra shore, is 700 yards wide, with a shoal in the center on which the least water is 26 feet, with 6 and 7 fathoms of water all around it. The tides sweep through this channel with a velocity of 3 knots; the flood to the S. and the ebb to the northward.

There is good anchorage, with the prevailing winds, between Southwest cay and Culebra. A good berth will be found, in 13 fathoms of water, with Scorpion point, which runs out low and terminates in a small pinnacle, bearing S. 78° 45′ E., distant 700 yards.

In fact there is good anchorage anywhere on the lee side of Culebra.

In Seine bay, just to the eastward of Scorpion point, there is a good beach and excellent fishing with the seine.

Snug bay, the next cove to the eastward, is a good boat harbor.

The channels between the NW. point of Culebra and the cays and rocks to the westward are clear and easy to navigate, as all the dangers are apparent to the eye.

Pilot Rock channel.—All that is to be done in taking this channel is to avoid the reef, seen running off 300 yards from the point, and steep-to.

Pilot rock is barren, 30 feet high, bold, and steep-to.

Twin pass is formed by the Pilot Rock and the Twins; the latter are two small barren rocky islets, about 20 feet high, lying close to each other about three-quarters of a mile westward of the Pilot. At a quarter of a mile SE. from the Twins is a rock awash, named High Breaker, and steep-to. The best channel is between it and the Pilot, as there is generally a leading wind through either way.

Fungy Bowt is a remarkable barren round whitish rock, 145 feet high, with rugged perpendicular sides. The channel is clear and safe, but be careful of a small head 200 yards westward of the Twins, and on which the depth is only 1 fathom.

Washer passage is between Fungy Bowt and the Washer, a small rock only 2 feet out of water, lying N. 33° 45′ W. two-thirds of a mile from Fungy Bowt. This channel is bold and clear, with a depth of 14 and 15 fathoms in it. A vessel may also pass to the westward of the Washer, which is bold and steep-to.

After passing to the southward of Fungy Bowt another chain of small islets will be observed lying to the WNW. of Southwest cay.

The three islets nearest Southwest cay are the Sisters, all nearly of the same size, about 35 feet in height, and not more than a quarter of a mile apart. The two western appear in one when bearing S. 11° 15′ E., consequently when on that line the three islets appear as only two. The eastern one is 700 yards from the NW. point of Southwest cay, with a clear channel between.

Cross cay is narrow, its central part projects to the NE. nearly one-fourth of a mile, thus forming three legs; it is 130 feet high, and covered with long grass and bushes. At about midway in the channel between it and the Sisters is the Black rock, a small islet 15 feet high.

Cactus cay is 95 feet high. At its S. end there is a remarkable pillar-shaped rock, 75 feet high.

The channels between the cays of which we have just spoken are all clear and free of hidden dangers; all the rocks are steep-to. For sailing-vessels, however, the best passages are to the westward of the Sister cays, for under the high land of southwest cay the wind is apt to be variable.

Tides.—In all of these channels the flood-tide runs to the southward at the rate of about 1 mile an hour, and the ebb in the contrary direction at the same rate. The rise and fall seldom exceed a foot, and, as is the case near the islands of St. Thomas and St. Johns, the mean level of the sea is about a foot lower in April and May than during the remainder of the year.

The flood coming in from the northward sweeps round the bluff and over the reef to the SW. of Culebrita at the rate of about 2 knots at the springs; it there slackens its pace, and meeting the stream setting down on the western side of Culebra, it then trends to the southward toward the E. end of Vieques, or Crab island.

The ebb sets over the Culebrita reef, taking the lee and weather channels out of the sound in a reverse direction, and much at the same rate.

On the W. side of Culebra the stream of flood, having reached southwest cay, runs to the SSE. toward the E. end of Vieques.

The channels lying between Cactus cay and the Washer on the E. and the coast of Porto Rico on the W. have not been accurately surveyed.

Crab island.—A ridge of small hills runs nearly its whole length along the middle of the island, and rises to a moderate height, named Mount Pirata, at Vaca point, the SW. extremity of the island. Between it and Culebra the soundings are regular and the depth from 12 to 16 fathoms. The E. end of the island is low, bold, and steep-to, and on the S. side the edge of soundings runs along at the distance of about 1½ miles.

The S. coast of the island is indented by several small bays and is free from danger.

Danes bay, the first of any consequence, is about 2 miles from the E. end. Nearly abreast the bay, about one-quarter of a mile from the points, are two small islets, which may be passed on either side.

To the westward of Danes bay there are several anchorages for small vessels: Grand port, Man-of-war cay, Tapoon creek, Port Ferro harbor, and Mosquito bay. At the entrance of Port Ferro there are 10 feet of water, increasing to 17 feet inside.

Sound or **Settlement bay**, is to the W. of these small harbors and is defended by a small fort. In front of it are two small islets called Soldier and Water cays; the latter, which is the outermost, lies

1018—No. 85——17

nearly a mile westward of the SE. point of the bay, and about half a mile from the shore. On the W. side, within a quarter of a mile of it, there is anchorage in 4 or 5 fathoms water.

Toward the SW. point the bottom is rocky and the soundings irregular.

Port Mula is a small bight nearly in the center of the N. coast of the island. At the mouth of a small creek on the S. side of the bight is a village of about 1,000 inhabitants, which is the residence of the governor, a subordinate of the governor of Puerto Rico. A short distance back of the village is a hill called Mount Soldier.

Anchorage.—Small vessels may anchor in 3 fathoms of water, with the center of the village bearing S. 45° E. and the N. point of the bay N. 67° 30′ E.

In fine weather larger vessels may anchor outside in 5 fathoms, with the N. point of the bay bearing SE. about half a mile distant.

Mula shoals.—There are three dangerous shoals lying northwesterly from Port Mula, about 1½ miles from the shore, called the Caballo Blanco, Corona, and the Mosquito shoals. All three of these shoals are awash, or nearly so.

The **Caballo Blanco** bears N. 50° 37′ W., 1½ miles from the N. point of Point Mula; the Corona is S. 47° 30′ W., 1½ miles from the Caballo Blanco, and the Mosquito half a mile S. 67° 30′ W. from the Corona.

Directions.—In approaching Port Mula from the eastward, after getting abreast of Point Caballo Colorado, the northern extreme of the island, the coast should be skirted at the distance of half a mile till arriving at Point Mula, which should be rounded at a distance of 600 yards, when a convenient anchorage may be picked out, with the village bearing S. 45° E. This course will lead between the Caballo Blanco and the coast of the island.

Caballo Colorado point is rocky and steep-to. Half-way between this point and Diavolo point, 4 miles to the eastward, there is close in shore a small rock called Rouge or Red rock. E. of this rock the coast is clear, but to the westward it is skirted by a reef.

Cockroach rock is half a mile N. of Diavolo point and is a dangerous coral head, nearly awash.

CHAPTER X.

THE WINDWARD ISLANDS, SOMBRERO TO BARBADOES, INCLUSIVE.

SOMBRERO ISLAND.

The island is a sterile rock. Phosphate of lime for fertilizing purposes is shipped from here, the deposit being worked by a company. The island belongs to Great Britain.

The prevailing winds are from NNE. to S. by E.; westerly winds seldom blow home.

Before the light was established many vessels in attempting to pass through this entrance to the Caribbean sea were lost by being set to the westward on to the reefs surrounding Anegada. Now, however, this channel may be navigated with perfect safety.

The islands of Anguilla, St. Martin, and St. Bartholomew (commonly called St. Barts), with Dog island and other islets adjacent, may be considered as a separate group. They rise from an extensive bank of irregular shape, extending, as shown on the chart, in some places 25 to 27 miles outside of the islands. On this bank the bottom consists principally of shells, gray and white sand, with a little coral and crust. This last substance appears to be peculiar to the Caribbean sea. It seems to be a very small, thin, flat, marine plant of somewhat circular outline, with corrugated edges, and, being incrusted with hard lime, has somewhat the appearance of a white, flat stone.

ANGUILLA ISLAND.

Anguilla belongs to the English, and is attached to the government of Antigua. The chief magistrate resides at the little village at Crocus bay, on the western side of the island.

Population, 2,500; of whom 100 are white and the remainder colored or black.

Cattle, ponies, and garden stock are raised. Phosphate of lime and salt are exported; the trade in these articles is increasing of late years.

Near the center of the island the land is about 213 feet high, but there are no remarkable hills. The SW. end is only 30 feet high.

The southern shore as far to the westward as Rendezvous bay is fringed by a coral reef from 200 to 400 yards off shore. The reef is dry in many places, but has several cuts through it which will admit boats of large size into good shelter.

Rendezvous bay, on the southern shore, affords good shelter to small vessels. In entering the bay give a berth to the reef, which extends a quarter of a mile off Shaddick point, the eastern limit of the bay. It can be seen from aloft. From Blowing point, about a mile eastward of Shaddick point, there is a road leading to the two anchorages, Road and Crocus bay on the western coast.

Blowing rock is a small rocky islet, about 6 feet above the level of the sea. It is bold and steep-to outside, but within it there is only a channel for boats.

The Dowling shoal.—Small vessels leaving Road bay may run through it, but in beating up from the westward it is better to keep outside of the shoal. Fork mountain, in St. Martin, in line with Mead point bearing S. 22° 30′ E., leads nearly half a mile westward of the shoal.

Dowling rock.—On the northern edge of the shoal there is a small rocky islet, 4 feet above the sea, and steep-to on the NW., but foul to the distance of a quarter of a mile to the NE. At nearly half a mile S. 67° 30′ E. of the islet, on the eastern edge of the shoal, is a small low sandy cay, called Sandy island, covered with brush-wood to the height of 6 feet. There is no safe channel between, and to the S. and SE. it is foul for more than a third of a mile.

Road bay is a small bight about three-quarters of a mile deep, affording good anchorage for small vessels. On the narrow ridge of sand at the head of the bay there is a small village, and back of it an extensive salt-pond. There is no danger in the bay. The bluff point to the northward is steep-to, and a vessel may anchor as convenient.

Crocus bay is formed by perpendicular white wooded cliffs. The bay is limited to the northward by Flat Cap point, so called from its terminating in a small flat-topped rock.

The principal settlement is in the SE. corner of the bay, and the houses are scattered about the valley and adjacent hills. The custom-house, with its flag-staff, stands on the S. side of the bay, on the summit of a hill 213 feet high, the loftiest in the island. The best landing-place is a little to the northward of the road leading up the valley, but there is always a heavy surf on the beach.

Supplies.—Fresh provisions and fire-wood may be obtained at Crocus bay, but no water. Yams are abundant and of excellent quality.

The United States is represented by a consular agent.

Anchorage.—A good berth will be found with Flat Cap point bearing N. 22° 30′ E. and the custom-house S. 50° 37′ E. in 7 fathoms water, sandy bottom, and excellent holding-ground. The bay is open to the westward, but winds seldom blow from that quarter. Heavy rollers, however, frequently set in with violence, making the anchorage rough and landing difficult.

Directions.—A stranger bound to either Crocus or Road bay had better run to leeward of Dog island and beat up. If from the E. or

SE., run through the clear bold channel between Anguilla and St. Martin, haul round Anguilla, and act in the same way. There will be no difficulty in doing this; there is seldom any current; the water is smooth, and if overtaken by night good anchorage will be found anywhere under the S. side of the cays and reefs NW. of Crocus bay, taking care, however, to avoid the Dowling shoal. Vessels when leaving the bays and bound to windward, with the assistance of a pilot, may take the northern channel.

Current.—A strong weather or easterly current will sometimes be found in Crocus bay, to which a vessel will swing even in fresh winds, but there is no perceptible tide.

Scrub island (called by Spanish navigators Anguillita) is separated from Anguilla by a narrow channel of deep water about a quarter of a mile wide; but it should not be navigated, as its western side is skirted by a reef nearly dry to the distance of 200 yards, upon which a vessel may be forced by the sudden flaws which come off the lee side of all these islands.

It is covered with brush-wood and stunted trees, which, at the W. end, are about 50 feet above the level of the sea. The E. end is low, and from it extends a narrow strip of low rocks, to the distance of half a mile. They are 8 or 10 feet high, steep-to, and in general the sea breaks violently over them, but in approaching them from the NE. they are hidden under the high part of the island and are exceedingly dangerous, for the soundings are so deep, the depths being 27 fathoms within half a mile of them, that the lead will scarcely give warning.

Near the center of the N. shore of Scrub island there is a little hill of white sandstone, which, when the sun shines on it, is very conspicuous. There is a tolerable landing on the beach at the NW. end of the island and good shooting.

Little Scrub island is equally conspicuous from the contrast in color, it being a barren precipitous black rock 40 feet high, bold and steep-to.

Dog island is covered with brush-wood and grass, affording pasturage to an excellent breed of horses and sheep, which are tended by two or three of the inhabitants of Anguilla; there is consequently water on the island.

Bay rock is a remarkable small black rock; nearly abreast of it, just within the bluff rocky point which forms the S. extreme of the island, is the landing-place.

East cay is covered with brush-wood and is steep-to on its N. side.

West cay in the day-time may be passed within one-quarter of a mile without fear, but at night it should be approached very guardedly, for the soundings are so deep alongside that the lead will be of little use; within a mile of the cay the depth is from 17 to 20 fathoms.

Dog Island channel.—Between Prickly Pear cays and Dog island there is a clear channel 2½ miles wide, with a depth in it of from 9 to 10 fathoms to within half a mile of the western Prickly Pear, when the soundings become so irregular that in strong winds, especially when accompanied by rollers, the sea tops and frequently breaks. It will, therefore, be always better to pass to the westward of Dog island, except with a free wind and smooth sea.

Seal reef commences a short distance eastward of the Flirt rocks and continues in an unbroken line for about 5 miles to the eastward, its eastern point forming one side of the northern entrance into Crocus bay. On the N. side it is bold, steep-to, and dangerous of approach at night nearer than 4 miles. On the S. side there are numerous detached shoals and coral heads, extending three-quarters of a mile from the reef.

North Wager is a small, black, square rock, about 3 feet high. In beating up to Crocus bay it serves as a guide when approaching the reef, and a vessel should not stand within or to the northward of it.

To the southward of the North Wager, from Prickly Pear cays to Crocus bay, there is excellent anchorage in 9 or 10 fathoms water, over sandy bottom, and out of the influence of the rollers.

Anguilla and the small islands and cays just described are so low that when approaching them from the northward at night it is extremely difficult to estimate correctly the distance from them on account of their being backed by the high land of St. Martin. From this cause vessels have frequently gone ashore on the N. side of Anguilla.

By proper attention to the lead, however, this danger may be easily avoided.

Tides.—At all the islands of this group, viz, St. Bartholomew, St. Martin, Anguilla, and Dog island, there is a rise and fall of from 1 to 2 feet, but the periods are so irregular that the exact time of high water can not be correctly defined. The following observations, made by Dr. Fahlberg, a resident of these islands for a long period, are valuable, and no doubt give the best information on the subject:

"About St. Bartholomew the flood at full and change runs SE., and it is then generally high water at 10.30 p. m., while the sun is farthest to the N. of the equator, but comes about two hours sooner in the succeeding months, until the sun gets farthest to the S., when it is high water at 10.30 a. m., and it runs afterward in the same proportion back again. The winds, which are of long continuance, sometimes make a trifling difference. The sea is always lowest at the time when the sun is farthest to the N., and the contrary."

During the surveys of these islands, which were conducted during the winter season, between the months of November and March, by Capt. E. Barnett, R. N., neither tidal stream nor current were detected, except on one or two occasions, when at anchor in Crocus bay, on the N. side of Anguilla, a strong easterly or weather set was observed; and on one occasion to the eastward of St. Bartholomew, after a long period of strong trade-wind, a westerly set ran for a short time 1 mile an hour; but in general no difficulty was found in beating up from one island to the other.

St. Martin island.—The island is very irregular in outline, the shores being deeply indented by numerous bays and creeks, some of which afford good anchorage. The NW. part belongs to the French, and is attached to the government of Guadeloupe, and the remainder to the Dutch.

The W. end of the island terminates in a dangerous, low, sandy point. The NE. end is high and bold; and being separated from the main ridge by a deep, broad valley, when seen at a distance from the WNW. or ESE. it has the appearance of a separate island. The SE. end is formed by a high bluff, faced by a perpendicular white cliff, from which it receives the name of Blanche or White point.

Grande bay is the most frequented anchorage in the Dutch part of the island. At the head of the bay, on a low, sandy ridge, is the town of Philipsburg, the seat of government, and back of it an extensive salt-pond, affording large quantities of salt.

The town contains about 3,000 inhabitants.

The exports are sugar and rum.

Port charges.

	Tonnage.	Harbor master.	Wharfage.	Light dues.	Certificate of measurement.
	Per ton.			*Per ton.*	
Vessels under 100 tons	$0.08	$2.60	$1.00	$0.01½	$2.00
Vessels from 100 to 150 tons	.10	3.60	1.60	.01½	2.00
Vessels over 150 tons	.10	3.60	2.00	.01½	2.00

The United States is represented by a consul and vice-consul.

Pelican point is low and rocky, and from it a reef with from 2 to 4 fathoms of water on it extends half a mile to the southward; 300 yards NW. of the point are the Pelican rocks, 3 or 4 feet above the sea.

Simpson bay.—From Pelican point a low sandy shore sweeps round to the westward, forming Simpson bay, with indifferent anchorage in the center of it, midway between the points, in 4½ fathoms of water. At the E. end of the bay there is generally a boat channel into the lagoon, but it is not always open. Thence to the W. end of the island the shore is low and bounded by sandy beaches, separated by low rocky and sandy cliffs.

Terre-Basse point is the western extremity of St. Martin. In rounding it in the night-time great care must be exercised, as the spit is so steep-to the lead will give little or no warning of its proximity. In the day-time the shoal may be seen from aloft. If the weather is so cloudy as to make it difficult to see the shoal, keep Fourche island (lying 2½ miles NW. of St. Bartholomew) open to the southward of St. Martin till Terre-Basse point bears to the southward of E.

After rounding this point, in proceeding toward Marigot bay, do not come within the depth of 7 fathoms, as this part of the shore is fringed with reefs and sand-banks to the distance of 1 mile from the shore.

Marigot bay affords good shelter from the usual trade-winds, but is open to the NW. and is exposed to the rollers which sometimes break half a mile off shore, sending a heavy surf into the beach.

The **town of Marigot** is situated at the head of the bay and is the seat of government for the French portion of the island.

Landing is inconvenient at all times, and sometimes attended with risk, especially at night, on account of the numerous sunken rocks which skirt the shore; the best spot is at the extreme E. end of the beach, at the foot of the Fort hill. Having effected a landing, the boat had better lie off at a grapnel to the eastward of Round hill, which cuts the beach in two nearly in the center, and is very remarkable; the shore of the bay is skirted by a flat coral ledge.

Crole rock is the most remarkable object on this part of the coast; it is a small, barren, black, rocky islet, with a rounded summit, rising on its N. side 120 feet perpendicularly from the sea.

Grand Case bay is a deep sandy bay to the southward of Crole rock and is a secure anchorage for drogers. In entering it, they are guided by the eye. From the head of this bay an extensive low valley, in which there are several cultivated salt-ponds, runs across to Orient bay, on the opposite side of the island.

Orient bay is about 1 mile deep, and vessels sometimes visit it with the assistance of a pilot, but, being exposed to the full force of the trade-wind and heavy sea, it is only secure for drogers or small fore-and-aft vessels, which find shelter at both ends of it.

Oyster pond is a well-sheltered creek, furnishing sheltered anchorage with a depth of 10 feet for small vessels. The entrance channel is so narrow and crooked that the assistance of a pilot is necessary to enter it.

Caution.—The sea is generally so heavy on the eastern side of St. Martin that the shore should not be approached by large vessels within the adjacent islets except in case of necessity.

Tintamarre island (called also Hat or Flat island) is a small uninhabited island lying 2 miles eastward of the N. point of St. Martin.

The N. side is formed by a bold rocky cliff, topped with trees, which toward the E. end rises almost perpendicular from the sea to the height of 90 feet, and when seen from the eastward is very remarkable; its S. and W. sides are low and sandy. It is bordered on all sides but the W. by a coral reef, which extends a quarter of a mile from the N. shore, and half a mile from the S., and terminates at that distance at the SW. point of the island. There is tolerable landing in the sandy bay at the W. end, and a small vessel will find temporary anchorage at about half a mile from this part of the shore in 8 or 9 fathoms of water.

The **channel** between Tintamarre and Pinels Island reef is obstructed by the Spaniard rock, a small, dangerous coral head just beneath the surface. In moderate weather it does not show itself, but with a fresh breeze the sea breaks heavily on it.

Vessels running or beating through the channel between St. Martin and Anguilla have only to be careful when approaching this danger not to shut in the Crole rock.

The channel between St. Martin and St. Bartholomew is free from hidden danger, but is not safe to navigate during the night, as many of the small, rocky islets are quite low, and being steep-to the lead gives no warning of their vicinity.

The **Great Grouper** is a barren islet 150 feet high, much resembling in appearance Mollibeday rock and the Sugar-loaf, off Gustaf harbor.

A **coral ledge**, partly above water, extends 200 yards off its S. side, leaving a narrow, deep channel between it and the Little Groupers.

The **Little Groupers** form a cluster of small, black rocks, the southernmost lying half a mile from the Great Grouper.

The southern and northern rocks are 15 feet above the water, but the middle ones are much lower. They are steep-to all around.

Fourche island.—From this island rise five small, conical hills, two of them, the highest and westernmost, 350 feet high. At a distance these two hills, and nearer all five of the hills, appear as separate islets.

Both at the eastern and the western end of the island there is a small, dry rock, connected with the shore by a ledge. About 200 yards westward of the S. point there is another rock just above water.

Anchorage.—Vessels may anchor in from 6 to 8 fathoms of water with the prevailing winds to the SW. of Fourche island.

Boulanger rock is a small, barren, rugged, rocky islet about 50 feet high, rising abruptly from the sea on all sides. About 400 yards eastward of it will be seen a rock, nearly of the same height which, from its resemblance to a vessel under sail, is called the Sail rock. They are bold and steep-to, and can not be mistaken.

ST. BARTHOLOMEW ISLAND.

This island (frequently called St. Bart's) is a French possession, being ceded by Sweden to France in 1878, with a population of about 2,300.

The exports are unimportant, the commerce depending chiefly upon the port being free. Products are sugar, tobacco, cotton, and cacao.

The island is of irregular shape, the coast-line being indented with numerous small bays, separated by rocky headlands. The hills are, compared with the high land of other islands, only moderate in height. Near the E. end are three hills, of about the same height, so placed with regard to each other that when seen from a distance on the bearings SSW., W. by S., NW. by W., and their opposites only two of them can be seen.

The **Sugar-loaf**, lying off the western side of St. Bartholomew, is a remarkable, small, barren, rocky islet having the exact form its name imports when seen from any direction, and, although similar in appearance to the Grouper rock, its position and greater elevation readily point it out. It is an excellent guide to strangers for finding the entrance of Gustaf harbor, which from a distance is not easily made out. It is high, bold, and steep-to, except on the N. side, whence a narrow ledge of dry and sunken rocks extends 400 yards in that direction; at its extremity there are two small rocks about 4 feet out of the water, bold and steep-to outside.

Gustaf or **Gustavia** is the seat of government, and a free port.

Imports are breadstuffs, lumber, and general merchandise.

Exports are rum, molasses, and fruits.

Port charges, including port captain's fees, do not exceed $5 for a vessel of 500 tons.

The only portion of it, however, that can be called a harbor is the inner part, or little arm of the sea, named the Carenage, on the shores of which the town is built; but it will only admit vessels of 5 or 6 feet draught. The outer harbor or bay is a commodious and safe anchorage, with the prevailing winds, for a few vessels drawing not over 17 feet; but, being exposed to the S. and W., it is not secure in the hurricane season. Vessels of larger draught will find temporary anchorage under the SW. side of the island, between the Syndare islets and the W. end.

Caution.—The winds in these channels to the anchorage are apt to be so baffling and variable that sailing vessels had better avail themselves of the services of a pilot, who can always be procured.

Colombier bay, at the NW. end of the island, affords shelter and tolerable anchorage.

Fregatte and **Goat Islands** are of considerable elevation, clothed with grass and low brush-wood, and readily distinguished. The latter is separated from the NW. end of St. Bartholomew by a clear channel one-quarter of a mile wide, but the sea is generally so heavy that it should not be attempted except in a case of necessity.

Toc Vers is a small, pointed, rocky islet. When seen from the E. or W. its N. point resembles a lofty pillar standing close by the side of the perpendicular cliff, which is about 120 feet high and very remarkable. It is steep-to on its N. and E. sides.

The population is 2,002.

SABA.

The **products** are poultry and vegetables, which are exported to the neighboring islands. The islanders speak English, and are excellent ship-builders, their small craft being celebrated throughout the Windward islands.

Landing is generally difficult and sometimes dangerous, from the heavy surf which breaks upon the shore.

The landing most used is not quite one-half a mile eastward of Ladder point, on the S. side of the island, and is called the Southside landing. It is a small rocky cove, from which a pathway leads through a deep ravine up to the village.

Ladder landing is about three-fourths of a mile northward of Ladder point, on the W. side of the island. It is so called from the pathway which leads from it being cut out of the precipice.

The principal boat-building spot is on the W. side of the island, near the NW. point. Landing may be effected here with moderate trade-winds.

Wood and water are difficult to obtain.

The **anchorages** off Saba are neither commodious nor particularly safe, as the 100-fathom line runs within 600 yards of the E. side and only half a mile off on the western side.

Small sailing vessels or steamers may anchor temporarily off the Southside landing. Another anchorage, where the bank of soundings is somewhat wider, is on the western side of the island, between Ladder landing and Torrens point. Here a vessel may anchor in 12 or 15 fathoms, sandy bottom, about 400 yards off shore, with the outer part of Torrens point, the NW. extremity of the island, bearing N. 22° 30′ E.

Caution.—Sailing-vessels should not attempt to anchor at Saba except in case of necessity, as the wind under the high land is almost invariably baffling and flawy.

Saba bank.—The northern edge affords good fishing, but the barracouta caught here, as well as between the islands of Saba and St. Eustatius, are often found to be poisonous.

ST. EUSTATIUS ISLANDS.

St. Eustatius, generally called Statia by the inhabitants, belonging to the Dutch, is a lofty volcanic island; its summit, like that of Saba, is generally hidden by clouds. The island, when seen from the NE. or SW., at a distance appears like two distinct islands. On the northern parts are rugged hills; the southern portion is occupied by the volcanic mountain, on the southern side of which is a bold white cliff called the White Wall. The island has been a Dutch colony, with but little interruption, since the year 1600. The lieutenant-governor, who has Saba also under his control, is subordinate to the government of St. Martin.

The population is 3,500.

Products.—Formerly it was a place of some importance, but its trade now is insignificant. Yams are the principal articles of export, with some sugar, molasses, and rum.

Orange town, the only town on the island, is on the western shore, partly on the beach and partly on the cliff above it, 130 feet high. The two parts, called the lower and upper town, are connected by a road cut in the face of the cliff. Fort Orange stands on a cliff in front of the town.

The only safe landing-place is on the beach abreast of the town, and here the surf is frequently so heavy that the boat must be veered in with a long line from a grapnel.

In approaching the anchorage, the only danger to be avoided is a rock, nearly awash, at the SW. end of the island, between the White Wall and the town.

The **wind** hardly ever varies to the northward of NE., or to the southward of E.

Coast.—The northern part of St. Eustatius is bold, and may be rounded at the distance of 200 yards; but breakers extend from the SE. side, and in coming from either quarter it will be better to keep half a mile from the shore, to avoid the baffling winds under the high land.

This island, with St. Christopher and Nevis, may be considered as a separate cluster, as they rise from a bank of soundings separated from the adjacent islands by channels of a greater depth than 200 fathoms.

ST. CHRISTOPHER OR ST. KITTS ISLAND.

This island, frequently called St. Kitts, is an English colony, and with the islands of Nevis and Anguilla forms the presidency of St. Christopher and Nevis.

The **government** consists of a governor, a president, an executive council, and a legislative council. The seat of government is at Basse Terre.

Its population is about 30,000.

Climate, for a tropical one, is healthy.

The island is of volcanic origin. It appears at a short distance as two islands, and farther off the irregular hills at the SE. end will appear as several detached islets.

Basse-Terre anchorage.—The best anchorage is off the center of the town in 8 or 9 fathoms water, with the flag-staff of the old fort at the W. end of the bay bearing N. 78° 45' W. No directions are necessary, for there is no danger whatever.

The city is clean and healthy; the sickly season being from September to November.

Provisions can be had, but they are from 30 to 50 per cent. more than in New York.

Water can be obtained at a cost of 6 cents per gallon. It is brought off in casks.

Coal can be had in very small quantities at a cost from $9 to $10.25 per ton.

Hospital.—There is only one, but there is a branch one at Sandy Point. The staff is well organized and efficient.

Telegraph.—The island is in communication with the United States and Europe.

Salutes can be returned by the battery on shore.

Steamers from the United States and Europe call here. There is also communication with the other West India islands. The authority to call upon is the president of the island.

Exports are sugar, molasses, rum.

Imports are grain, petroleum, lumber, etc.

Port charges.—Tonnage dues, over 40 tons, every time of entry, 31 cents per ton. Custom-house officer, $4. Ballast, 72 cents per ton. Stowage of cargo, 25 cents per hogshead. Cargoes are put alongside free; inward cargo is landed by the vessel.

The United States is represented by a commercial agent and vice-commercial agent.

Old road lies about 5 miles westward of Basse-Terre, and a little eastward of the town there is a temporary anchorage in 9 or 10 fathoms water, stony ground, at 200 yards from the shore, abreast a river of excellent water.

There is also a similar anchorage a little northward of the small fort, at the foot of Brimstone hill, with the flag-staff on the hill bearing N. 84° 22' E. and the church N. 5° 37' E.; a convenient spot for steamers to land troops or supplies.

Caution.—Neither of these anchorages is, however, fit for a sailing vessel, as the wind under the high land is very baffling. In passing to leeward of the island sailing vessels should keep at least 3 miles off shore to avoid being becalmed or exposed to the very violent gusts which frequently rush down without warning through the ravines.

In rounding the NW. end of St. Christopher in the night-time a good berth must be given to Belltete or Sandy point, as it is very low and is foul for half a mile off shore.

Deep bay.—The N. end of the island has a reef about 1¼ miles long protecting the anchorage. The outer edge of the reef lies three-quarters of a mile off shore, with shallow water a short distance outside of it. Deep bay affords good anchorage for coasters.

The channel between St. Christopher and the island of Nevis is called the Narrows. From the westward, against the trade-winds, it can only be used safely by handy coasting vessels, as no leading marks can be given for beating, and the off-lying shoals are numerous.

There are also channels for coasters between these shoals and the shores of the islands, but no good leading marks can be given for them.

There is excellent anchorage in the Narrows, with good holding-ground in 6 fathoms of water, with the Cow rocks bearing N. 56° 15' E., Scotch bonnet head N. 14° 04' E., and Horseshoe point N. 56° 15' W.

NEVIS ISLAND.

The island is an English colony and is attached to the presidency of St. Christopher. The formation is volcanic; the highest peak is generally hidden by clouds, but several other elevations on the island are visible, and are useful landmarks.

On the S. side of the island Saddle hill may be readily made out from its features, except from the ESE. and WNW. when the hummocks are in one; the hill, however, from these points is equally conspicuous. On the E. side of the island are two remarkable wooded peaks, standing on a fork of the mountain.

On the NW. side Hurricane hill is easily known, being large and massive, and terminating in a peak, and having at its base a small detached rounded hill, which forms a prominent bluff at the extreme NW. end of the island, called Windy hill. With the exception of this point and the base of Saddle hill the shores are low, and rise gradually to the interior, the plains and slopes being highly cultivated.

Charlestown, the capital of the island, has in front of it an excellent anchorage with the prevailing winds, although an open roadstead.

Except on the W. side, between Fort Charles and Cades bay the shore is fringed with a coral reef, and should not be approached within three-quarters of a mile, or the depth of 10 fathoms.

In approaching the anchorage off Charlestown from the southward the lead must be hove quickly, as the 10-fathom line is less than 1 mile off shore and steep-to.

In the daytime, having rounded the S. end of Nevis, if the island of St. Eustatius can be seen, keep it open of Brimstone hill on St. Christopher. This mark will lead clear of the reef on the western side.

When Booby island comes open of the N. side of Nevis steer for it. This mark will lead just outside the ledge off Fort Charles, and to an anchorage at about half a mile off shore, in 5 fathoms water, abreast the flag-staff in the town.

It is supposed that the shoal water off Fort Charles (in ruins) extends out much farther than the chart shows, as 5 fathoms have been attained 1 mile from the shore, the center of the town bearing N. 78° 45′ E.

Neither coaling nor provisioning facilities exist at Charlestown.

The United States is represented by a consular agent.

Vessels of large draught approaching the anchorage off Charlestown from the NW. must avoid the Monkey shoals, which are the only dangers on this side of Nevis. The discolored water over them can be seen at some distance from aloft.

Rodonda is a small rocky island. It is inhabited. Phosphate is exported; labor can be supplied if required; fresh water and provisions in small quantities can be obtained; wild goats are plentiful on the northern end of the island. The prevailing winds are from the ESE.

MONTSERRAT ISLAND.

This island, discovered by Columbus during his second voyage, was named by him from its resemblance to the mountain of the same name near Barcelona, which is rugged, uneven, and exhibits many lofty peaks, as its name in the Spanish language implies. The first settlement on the island was formed by the English in 1632, and is now a presidency forming part of the colony of the Leeward islands.

Government is similar to that of St. Christopher.

Population is about 10,000.

Its products are sugar and lime-juice.

The island is of volcanic origin, and its lofty heights, clothed with wood to their summits, may, when unclouded, be seen at a distance of about 45 miles; the highest is Soufriere hill. Its shores are bold, steep, and free of danger. Its E. and NW. sides are precipitous, but the SE. and W. sides slope gradually to the sea, and are highly cultivated.

Water.—Many springs of excellent water flow into the sea; but from the surf watering is attended with difficulty.

Anchorage.—The anchorage ground off Bransby point is extensive, the depths moderate and the holding-ground good.

The anchorage off the town of Plymouth is not good, owing to the great depth of water, but the anchorage given on the chart is very good.

The best anchorage is about three-fourths of a mile from Plymouth wharf.

Plymouth.—The town is well built, and is the cleanest in the small islands. The streets are paved; there is an excellent market place, with plentiful supplies for one ship at least, the mutton and potatoes being excellent. There is a very good wharf, and landing is as easy as at Basse-Terre, St. Kitts, or Nevis. With westerly winds, rollers prevail. Montserrat is as good a port of call as any in the West Indies.

The United States is represented by a consular agent.

During the hurricane months a vessel should put to sea immediately on the approach of bad weather.

When the mail steamer is expected, a fixed light is shown from a staff on the beach in front of the town of Plymouth.

Off the N. and S. points the western stream runs at times 2 knots, the eastern being weak; along its other shore it runs about half a knot.

BARBUDA ISLAND.

The island contains about 1,000 inhabitants.

It is attached to the presidency of Antigua.

It is only partially cultivated, but quantities of cattle, horses, sheep, and deer are raised, as well as corn, tobacco, and sugar.

The N., S., and W. sides of the island are low, sandy, and scantily wooded, with nothing remarkable on them except on the S. side, where about 2 miles from the SW. point there is an old martello tower, in a ruinous state, near the beach, and a little to the eastward of it a remarkable clump of trees, which are useful objects in approaching this side.

From Spanish point, the N. side of which is a white cliff 35 feet high, the eastern shore of the island begins to rise, and about midway, over a space of 2 miles, it is composed of perpendicular cliffs 200 feet in height, and is the highest part of the island. On this side a dry broken coral ledge skirts the shore at the distance of about half a mile, upon which the sea breaks with great violence, and it is so steep that there is no bottom with 90 fathoms $1\frac{1}{2}$ miles outside it.

At the NW. end of the island the ledge is composed of detached coral heads, which do not break. Here, however, the soundings give warning of approach, and a vessel in the night-time, when passing the W. side of the island, should not come within the depth of 10 fathoms.

The W. side of Barbuda is formed by a low, narrow sand-ridge, scantily wooded, at the back of which is an extensive lagoon, carrying from 5 to 12 feet of water. The entrance to it lies a short distance to the eastward of Billy point, at the NW. end of the island, but it is obstructed by a bar of mud.

The bank on this side extends for a considerable distance to the westward. This coast is foul in places for 2 miles off shore; vessels should not approach within the depth of 6 fathoms without caution.

The S. side of Barbuda is by far the most dangerous, and must be approached with extreme caution, for the lead is of little use; indeed, in the night-time it should be avoided, if possible, altogether.

This island is connected with Antigua by a bank varying in depth from 7 to 30 fathoms.

No good water can be procured at Barbuda. The inhabitants use rain-water. Fresh provisions and wood can, however, be readily procured, and at moderate prices.

There is excellent anchorage on the S. side of the island to the westward, and under the lee of the shoals which shelter it with the wind as far to the southward as SE. The best position for communicating with the island will be found at about half a mile from the shore, with the River fort bearing N. 11° 15′ E., and Palmetto point N. 61° 50′ W., in $5\frac{1}{2}$ fathoms. Be careful, however, when standing in, not to bring the fort to the northward of N. 11° 15′ E. until quite certain that the vessel is to the northward of the shoals.

Both this and the anchorage on the W. side of the island are exposed to rollers; but as they take the vessel in the stern, she is eased of the strain on her cable, and rides far more comfortably than if at most of the anchorages about Antigua. At this period, however, landing is attended with great difficulty and risk, for should the boat be thrown ashore broadside on the next wave would inevitably destroy her. From a short distance to the westward of the River fort as far as the SE. end of the island the beach is skirted by small coral heads, with deep water between, through which the way must be picked to the landing. The clearest spot will be found abreast the fort.

Navigators undertaking to pass between Barbuda and Antigua in the night-time should be very sure of their latitude, as the soundings are so irregular that it would be difficult to tell from them which way to steer.

ANTIGUA ISLAND.

The island was discovered by Columbus on his second voyage in 1493, and was named by him for the church of Santa Maria de la Antigua, in Seville.

It was first settled by the English in 1632, and, with the exception of a short interval from 1666 to 1668, has ever since been an English colony.

Population in 1881, 34,964.

The government consists of the governor, an executive council, and a legislative council.

The island is of moderate elevation compared with the lofty islands to the southward, so that the heights are but seldom obscured by clouds.

The shores are deeply indented, particularly on the NE. side, where there are many bays and creeks navigable for small vessels.

This end of the island is low, but it rises gradually in height toward its SW. end, where the hills become very irregular and so remarkable as to serve the purpose of guides through the dangerous reefs and shoals which surround almost the whole island. The only clear space is on the S. side between Willoughby bay and Old Road where it is bold and steep-to. Elsewhere it should be approached with great caution and with the lead continually going.

Bank of soundings.—Antigua lies in the middle of the southern edge of an extensive bank of coral and sand, which extends a little northward of Barbuda, on its NE. edge.

Green island forms the E. end of Antigua, the eastern extreme of which terminates in a bold, rocky headland, called Man-of-war point, which is steep-to, and may be rounded at the distance of 1 mile. The sea generally rolls in so heavily that it should not be approached within this distance, and great caution should be observed when closing with Green island either from the northward or southward.

Willoughby bay is capable of affording safe anchorage to large vessels, but is so difficult and dangerous of access that it is seldom visited, the produce of this part of the country being sent by drogers to St. Johns. The head of the bay is low and sandy, and its entrance is protected by a coral ledge, dry in many parts, through which there are two cuts; that to the NE. named Horseshoe channel; the other is nearly 200 yards wide, but so crooked and intricate that no good marks can be given for its safe navigation.

The **anchorage** in this bay is only free to steamers, and they will require the assistance of an experienced pilot. The bay is exposed to the full force of the sea, which makes it even dangerous to approach in strong winds.

Shirley heights is a remarkable, bold, rocky promontory rising almost perpendicularly from the sea to the height of 545 feet. On the flat summit will be seen the barracks and other buildings formerly occupied by the garrison; and at the western edge of the precipice, a little more elevated, the two signal posts of Fort Shirley, which overlooks the entrance to English harbor. Between Willoughby bay and the heights are two small inlets, Mamora bay and Indian creek, which afford safe anchorage to drogers.

English harbor, being entirely occupied by the government as a naval arsenal, is mostly visited by vessels of war, and is perfectly sheltered from all winds and sea. Water may be obtained with facility by hauling the vessel to the wharf, where it is conveyed on board through pipes. The harbor is very confined in space, and its turnings are so sharp that vessels of great length must warp in.

Vessels of 17 feet draught may moor alongside the northern wharf of the dock-yard, with a bower anchor to the eastward; or, if wanting coal, alongside the eastern wharf, with an anchor to the southward, securing with her own hawsers or chains. There are 22 feet water close off this wharf. At times the tide ranges 3 feet, but it is very irregular.

There are no stores in the dock-yard except coal.

Supplies are scarce and dear.

A sailing-vessel should not attempt to enter the harbor with the wind to the eastward of N., but should anchor outside and prepare to tow or warp in.

There are no hidden dangers, and for a steamer or sailing-vessel undertaking to enter without a pilot it is only necessary to keep in mid-channel. Long steamers will find it difficult to make the short turn round Barclay point, and it will be more convenient for them to anchor in Freeman bay, where moorings are laid down.

The wind generally moderates toward evening, and the land breeze in the early morning will enable a sailing vessel to leave the harbor without much difficulty.

Falmouth harbor affords excellent anchorage for a few vessels of large draught; it is, however, never made use of, except by drogers. A sailing-vessel of large draught would have to warp through against the prevailing wind.

The heads of the inner part of Falmouth and English harbors are only separated from each other by a narrow, low, sandy ridge, about 200 yards across.

Standing in for Falmouth harbor from the eastward, having passed Shirley heights, the entrance immediately shows itself, and a vessel may then steer boldly toward the center of the opening, until the E. end of the fort on Blake islet comes in one with a remarkable house on the western slope of Monk hill, bearing N. 8° 26′ W. This mark will lead through the entrance, and having passed the Bishop shoal, which always shows itself, haul up and anchor as most convenient, according to the vessel's draught.

Westward of Falmouth harbor is the loftiest part of Antigua, in many places the rugged irregular hills rising abruptly from the shore, particularly between that harbor and Old Road bluff. In the immediate vicinity of the harbor are two conspicuous elevations, which are frequently of great value to vessels navigating the N. side of the island. The first is Monk hill, on the N. side of the harbor, readily distinguished by the fort and signal-staff which crowns its summit, the SE. side overlooking a rocky precipice 695 feet above the level of the sea.

The other, on the NW. side of the harbor, nearly 1¼ miles westward of Monk hill, is a much larger conical hill, thickly wooded, and rises to the height of 1,058 feet. When seen from the NE. and SW. its summit appears to terminate in a peak; but from the NW. and N. and points opposite it forms two peaks, and is consequently sometimes named the Saddle hill. It is also called Falmouth peak, which seems a preferable name, as there is another hill called the Saddle.

In clear weather both Monk hill and Falmouth peak may be seen from Barbuda, 45 miles distant. The hills farther westward are higher, but with the exception of Baggy peak, slightly elevated above the adjoining hills, are not particularly remarkable.

Cade reef.—Its southern or outer edge is wall-sided, and consequently very dangerous to approach during the night, as the lead will give no warning, and, being under high land, no estimated distance can be depended upon. In the day-time it may generally be seen, and will be avoided by keeping the governor's house on Dow hill just open of Old Road bluff.

Middle reef, an inner danger, is within the barrier; lying nearly half a mile from the shore and running also parallel to it.

Anchorage.—Between it and the land there is excellent anchorage off Cade bay, where there is a good watering place. The eastern or Goat Head channel leading into it has not less than 25 feet water and is easy of access, but too narrow to work out of; a vessel will therefore have to run out through the western passage, which is barred by a flat, rocky ledge, on which there is not more than 21 feet of water.

Vessels running for the anchorage in Cade bay, or with a view to take the inner route to St. Johns between the reefs and the shore, should haul close round Old Road bluff in toward Morris Old mill, passing Curtain bluff, which forms the eastern side of Morris bay, within one-quarter of a mile. When abreast of the mill, if the weather be clear overhead, discolored water will be seen off the end of the reef and the edge of the ledge which runs off Goat head, and this will enable the mariner to direct his course in mid-channel, which is nearly one-quarter of a mile wide.

No leading mark can be given, and the directions therefore are not sufficiently trustworthy to guide a stranger without the assistance of an experienced pilot.

Heights on the west coast.—The Saddle and Flat top are the most eastern, and are at once distinguished by their names. Leonards, Pearns, and Mosquito hills are conical, with peaked summits thickly wooded. The two former are nearly of the same elevation, the latter much lower. Mount Thomas or Round hill rises on the N. side of Five Island harbor, and makes as a large, rounded, woody hill from all directions except the NNW., when it appears more peaked. Three-quarters of a mile to the westward of it there is a narrow table ridge of moderate elevation, terminating near its E. end in a small peak, named Table hill, which may be seen at a long distance, and is a valuable landmark.

Reed point lies at the foot of a wooded hill of moderate height, separated from the shore by a narrow neck of low, swampy land.

All this part of the coast of Antigua is extremely dangerous to approach, as it is fronted by a coral ledge. The ledge is studded with rocky heads, having as little as 9 feet of water on them; and three-quarters of a mile off Fry's bay there is one which is nearly awash.

There is, however, a good channel within the shoals for vessels of 14-feet draught, provided the trade-wind is not too far to the northward and they have the aid of a pilot.

The Five islands are readily distinguished when seen from the northward or southward; but from the westward, being backed by high land, they are not easily made out, except the largest, which is 50 feet above the sea. There are in fact but four islets, for the NE. part of the highest, which is called the fifth, from its appearing disconnected at a certain distance, is attached to its western end by a low rocky ledge. They are all, with the exception of the largest, low, small, rugged, rocky, and scantily clothed with brush-wood. The channel, with 15 feet of water, lies between the highest and the one eastward of it.

Five Island harbor, although exposed to the rollers, is a secure anchorage, with the prevailing winds, for vessels of 16-feet draught. In the inner part of the harbor is a remarkable small round islet, called Maiden island, with precipitous rocky sides, crowned with small trees, the tops of which are 90 feet above the sea.

The anchorage is obstructed by Cook shoal, a small rocky head with 9 feet of water on it, in the center of the harbor, with Sandy island in one with Pelican point.

St. Johns harbor, at the head of which is situated the city of St. Johns, the capital of the island, is the chief commercial port in Antigua, from whence is finally shipped almost all the produce of the island, which is brought by drogers from the outports. The city lies on the side of a gentle acclivity, which at the upper part is about 80 feet above the sea, and contains about 18,000 inhabitants. From the offing its locality is at once pointed out by the cathedral, a large, massive, white structure, with two lofty towers, the vanes of which are 163 feet above the sea.

The only other remarkable object is a kirk, a much smaller white building, with a sloping roof and a small bell-turret at its W. end.

The harbor is secure against all winds except hurricanes, but confined, and not at all convenient, for vessels of only 12-feet draught cannot come within three-fourths of a mile of the wharves, and those drawing over 14 feet are obliged to load in St. Johns road. It is also exposed to rollers, which frequently break over the jetties and inflict serious damage.

Rat islet is small, rugged, steep, and rocky; on its summit is a large building and lofty signal-staff, which are conspicuous objects; the wall surrounding the building is 137 feet above the sea. The islet is connected to the shore by a well-built causeway, with a carriage road to the foot of the hill.

The NW. point of the harbor terminates in a small rocky bluff 37 feet high, on which is Fort James, and the breadth across the entrance is half a mile. A little without the entrance a flat of sand runs along the whole front of the harbor, on which the greatest depth at low water is 15½ feet, which is near the southern shore, and the channel is not 100 yards wide.

Provisions of all kinds can be obtained.

Water costs 50 cents per puncheon.

Coal can be obtained in small quantities at a cost of $9.60 per ton delivered and stowed.

There are facilities for making slight repairs.

Hospital.—There is one, to which is united the insane asylum and the poor-house. It has an efficient staff.

The city has a public library and many other charitable societies.

Telegraph.—The island is in telegraphic communication with the United States and Europe.

Steamers call here from Europe, the United States, and the other West India islands.

Imports are provisions and general merchandise.

Exports are sugar, cotton, tobacco, rum.

Port charges.—Pilotage, inwards, under 6 feet, $4.80; 8 feet, $5.76; 9 feet, $7.20; 10 feet, $8.64; every foot beyond, $1.50 per foot. Tonnage dues, 6 cents per ton every time of entry. Ballast, sand, 60 cents; stone, 90 cents per ton. Labor, 60 to 75 cents per day. Harbor fees, from 120 to 150 tons, $3.84; 150 to 200 tons, $4.80; 200 to 250 tons, $5.76; 300 tons and upwards, $7.68.

The authority to call on is the governor.

The United States is represented by a consul and vice consul.

There are three principal channels which may be used to enter the road and harbor of St. Johns, the NW., W., and SW. or Sandy Island channel. The west channel is, however, but seldom used, except by vessels leaving the harbor.

Pilots.—Vessels bound in from windward, having made the E. side of Antigua, generally pass round the N. end and receive their pilot, who is always on the lookout, in the office near Parham. The shore, however, should not be approached within at least 3 miles, as it is everywhere foul and exceedingly dangerous to strangers.

Boon point is the extreme northern end of the island. The shore turns abruptly to the eastward and forms a bight, which terminates about 2 miles distant at Hodge point. This part of the shore is low, rocky, and skirted by sunken shoals, and there is only one spot, nearly three-fourths of a mile westward of Hodge point and named Port Royal bay, where boats can effect a landing with safety. The hill just within this point becomes a useful object in the navigation of this extremely dangerous neighborhood.

From Hodge point the coast takes a SE. direction for 2½ miles to Fort Byham, Judge Bay point being intermediate. On the former there is a flag-staff. The shore is low and foul. From the fort the shore becomes deeply indented, and forms two deep bights, the southern of which is Parham harbor.

Parham harbor is capable of admitting vessels drawing 13 feet, but the channels to it are so narrow and intricate that the few vessels which load here receive their cargoes in the North sound, or Roads. The town of Parham stands in the SE. corner of the bight, under a wooded hill 165 feet high, on the W. side of which is the church, a conspicuous object from the offing. It was at one period the seat of government, and is still of some importance, being the place of transit for the greater part of the commerce of this end of Antigua.

The eastern side of the harbor is protected by a long, irregular, low, swampy neck of land, about three-fourths of a mile in length, which terminates at North Sound point in a small hill 60 feet high. From the E. side of the neck numerous small islets, rocks, and reefs sweep all round to the NW., inclosing a large basin of water, completely sheltered, called the North sound.

Great Bird island is the most remarkable of the islets which inclose North sound, and a valuable object to the pilots. It is of irregular form, its W. side very low, but its E. side is a narrow strip of black barren rock 600 yards long, rising perpendicularly from the sea to the height of 110 feet, and may be seen from a long distance, the N. end particularly, as it forms a bold headland. The NE point of the dangerous reef and coral ledge extends all along the N. side of Antigua as far as the Diamond bank.

Four Fathom bank is composed of small detached rocky heads, having a depth of 4½ and 4¾ fathoms, and on which there is generally a heavy sea. In beating up to the eastward, do not attempt to pass to the southward of these banks before the hill at the E. end of Green island bears S. 5° 37′ E.

Long island protects the N. side of North sound and the E. side of Parham sound. It is very irregular in shape. The shores are low, but on its SW. end there are some trees 40 feet high.

Parham sound is capable of receiving a few vessels of large draught, it is well sheltered, has good holding-ground, and not exposed to the action of rollers. It may be approached from several points between NE. and NW. through narrow openings in the Kettle Bottom shoals. The leading marks for them are given on the chart, but they are far too dangerous for a stranger to navigate, and it is only a well-experienced pilot that can attempt to make use of them.

Vessels leaving Parham sound for St. Johns will find it to their advantage to pass within the shoals through Boon channel, which is quite straight and clear.

Guana and Belfast bays are well sheltered by the islets and numerous reefs to the eastward, and of sufficient depth for vessels of large draught; but the channels are far too intricate for them to navigate, particularly as the prevailing winds, which are here accompanied by a heavy short sea, make even a near approach to this part of Antigua very hazardous. They are frequented by drogers, which are sometimes exposed to accidents and long delays, as they can not beat out, except under favorable circumstances. There is a boat communication between the bays and North sound through the narrows at the W. end of Guana island.

Nonsuch bay is so completely protected by reefs, nearly dry, as to be a secure harbor, with a depth of from 5 to 8 fathoms, but it is equally difficult to navigate as those just described, and quite closed against sailing vessels of large draught.

Tides.—There is a rise and fall of tide at the island of Antigua, sometimes amounting to 2 feet, but generally less, and so uncertain in its periods as to be of little use to navigation. No regular tidal stream can be detected.

The **current** is equally variable in its movements, and the oldest pilots can give no certain accounts of either its strength or direction. During the period of the survey of these islands, between November and May, little or no current was met with between Antigua and Barbuda, although that is the period when the trade-wind blows strongest. In June it has been found running strong to the westward, on the S. side of Antigua, when at the same time there was little or none on the N. side, and an eddy stream close inshore.

GUADELOUPE ISLAND.

The island was discovered by Columbus during his second voyage in 1493. It was colonized by the French in 1635, and with but slight interruption has remained ever since in their possession.

The island is separated by the river Salée into two parts, the western, or Guadeloupe proper, called Basse-Terre, and the eastern, called Grande Terre. The whole territory is under a governor appointed by the French Government, and with the dependencies of Marie-Galante, the Saintes, Petite Terre, and Desirade has a population of 178,000 inhabitants.

The north part of the island of St. Martin is also under the control of the government of Guadeloupe.

Although only separated by a shallow arm of the sea, the eastern and western portions of the island differ very materially in appearance and in their geological character.

The western portion is of volcanic origin; the soil is clayey, and the surface rugged and uneven. A chain of lofty wooded mountains traverse this part of the island from NNW. to SSE. The most northern peak of this chain is called Sainte-Rose; the most southern, Trou-aux-Chiens. Near the southern end is the Soufrière, an active volcano, and near the middle are two conical peaks called the Mamelles. The last eruption of Soufrière took place in 1799.

On the western side of the mountains the declivities are steep, with rapid torrents rushing down to the sea, but on the eastern slope the descent is more gradual.

There are among the mountains numerous mineral springs of various descriptions.

Grande Terre, the eastern division of the island, is almost a level plain, having a limestone formation, with two ranges of small hills—one on the northern shore, 300 feet high, called the heights of Bertrand, and another farther south and running nearly parallel with the southern shore, called the hills of Ste. Anne. These hills are about 375 feet high, and are separated by deep gorges, having at the bottom sluggish and sometimes stagnant streams, which gradually filter into the sea through the sand-bars at their mouths.

The principal productions of the island are sugar and manioc, but all kinds of tropical fruits and vegetables are raised, and large quantities of sugar, coffee, cocoa, rum, molasses, annatto, cotton, dye-woods, etc., are exported. The importations consist principally of rice, salt fish, wines, machinery, hardware, cotton, silk, and worsted goods.

Mails.—Guadeloupe has mail communication with the other West India islands and with Europe and America at least four times a month, while almost daily communication takes place between the different towns of the island and its dependencies.

Telegraph.—By means of the telegraph cable landed at Basse-Terre and joined to numerous land lines, the ports of the island are in constant communication with the United States and Europe.

Climate.—Except during the rainy season, the climate of Guadeloupe varies very slightly as regards either barometric pressure, temperature, or winds. The barometer rises regularly every day till about half-past 9 a. m., then falling till half-past 4 p. m., rises again till 10 o'clock in the evening, when it again falls till half-past 4 in the morning, oscillating during each twenty-four hours between $29^{in}.99$ and $30^{in}.07$. The mean daily height also varies during the year, being lowest in October, increasing till March or April, then remaining nearly stationary till July, when the maximum height is attained, after which the mean daily pressure gradually decreases during the rainy season. The abnormal variations of the barometer are almost always accompanied by hurricanes, which take place during the rainy season, between

July and November. When observed at other times of the year they indicate atmospheric disturbances taking place at a distance too great to be otherwise felt in this island.

The mean temperature of Guadeloupe is about 79° Fahrenheit throughout the island, except at Basse-Terre, where it is 80°. Its minimum is reached between January and March, ranging from 70° early in the morning to 84° at noon, while during the rainy season the least temperature is about 77°, rising in the middle of the day to 88°, sometimes, but very rarely, attaining a height of 95°.

The average amount of moisture in the air of Guadeloupe is very great. If complete saturation to the point of precipitation be considered as unity, the usual amount of moisture may be represented as from 0.64 to 0.73.

Heavy rains are most frequent from the middle of July to the middle of October, being then attended by violent thunder-squalls.

Showers fall occasionally at all times of the year, but are less frequent on the weather side of the island than to leeward.

At Point-à-Pitre the annual rain-fall is nearly 40 inches; at Basse-Terre, nearly 60.

Winds.—The winds blow almost constantly from the eastward. The following table, showing the direction of the wind during one year, has been derived from the observations during three years:

	Direction of the wind.										
	North.	NNE.	NE.	ENE.	East.	ESE.	SE.	SSE.	South.	Calm.	Light westerly airs.
Number of days during the year....................	8½	5½	68½	40	136½	26½	40½	3	2½	30½	5

During the months of December, January, February, and March the wind has the most northing, somewhat heavy but short squalls from N. and NE., attended with copious showers, being not infrequent about the end of the year.

In February the wind blows freshly from the E. during the day, with fine weather, the breeze decreasing every evening and rising again about 8 or 9 o'clock in the morning.

In May the winds become comparatively regular between ESE. and SE., continuing until November, when they gradually draw round to the northward. The commencement of the rainy season, about the end of May or beginning of June, is marked by thick weather, with a heavy swell along the coasts. Generally, however, with the exception of squalls and occasional hurricanes, calms and light variable winds prevail during the rainy season. Calms also occur sometimes during March and April. The summit of the Soufrière mountain is generally visible shortly after sunrise for a quarter or a half an hour, when it becomes hidden. If during the day it is again uncovered it is an indication of calms and fine weather.

When the breeze is fresh on the weather side of the island it also blows strongly to leeward, but when it is light to windward it is very apt to be calm on the lee side of the island, or else a light westerly wind is experienced, modifying very agreeably the excessive heat frequently felt.

At Basse-Terre rollers are experienced during the rainy season, while at port Moule they are only felt toward the end of the year.

Earthquakes are frequent at Guadeloupe; the most violent on record was in February, 1843, when the town of Point-à-Pitre was destroyed.

Chateaux point, the eastern extreme of Guadeloupe, is a bluff, rocky point, of quite remarkable appearance, having off its northern side two sharp-peaked, rocky islets. The point is clear of danger, and may be passed close to.

Port St. François is only a reef-harbor, about 200 yards in diameter and with a depth of 13 feet. With a SE. wind a heavy sea sets in here.

There are two sugar-factories in the neighborhood, but no stores can be procured, and vessels must be entered and cleared at the custom-house of Point-à-Pitre.

The position of the harbor may be known by the houses of the town, partly in ruins.

During the season of NE. winds vessels may anchor to the southward of port St. François, half a mile off shore, in 6 fathoms of water, with a bottom of sand and broken shells.

Sainte Anne anchorage is fit for vessels drawing not more than 13 feet. The harbor, though small, is well sheltered and not difficult to enter. The best channel, called the Grande pass, is on the eastern side of the reefs which protect the mouth of the harbor. At the western end of the village the gaol will be perceived, having a square tower in in the middle, surmounted by a pointed roof, and inland a little way are the gray ruins of the Plaisance mill, which must not be confounded with another ruined mill close to the beach.

The bay of Point-à-Pitre, or Petit Cul-de-sac Marin, is formed by the coasts of Grande-Terre and Basse-Terre.

An outer barrier of reefs and shoals extends in a NE. direction from the mouth of the river Goyave, with depths of over 100 fathoms just outside. Within this outer line of shoals, and separated from them by an outer road or anchorage, are numerous other reefs and islets.

Caution.—In approaching the entrance to Point-à-Pitre all these shoals may be avoided by keeping the Saintes islands open of the island of Guadeloupe.

Gozier island is a pilot station, not only for Point-à-Pitre, but for all the ports and anchorages on the E. and S. sides of the island.

Grande bay is a slight indentation in the land just outside the entrance to Point-à-Pitre. The western limit of the bay is a bold headland, on which is a fortification called Fleur d'Epée. There is good temporary anchorage here in 4½ fathoms, with the fort N. 33° 45′ E. and Gozier light-house S. 73° 07′ E. Vessels loading in any of the neighboring sugar ports anchor here while effecting their clearance at the custom-house of Point à-Pitre.

Bacchus point, one of the most important landmarks in approaching Point-à-Pitre, lies on the western side of the bay. It is a triangular bluff surmounted by two hillocks, and is marked by horizontal shelves all along the face of the bluff.

Cochons island is in the northern part of the bay, and forms the western side of the channel leading to Point-à-Pitre; it is easily distinguished by the fort and flag-staff on its eastern end. It is low and wooded, steep-to on the southern side, and on the eastern side has a coral reef awash at low water, and running off 300 yards.

Point-à-Pitre harbor, near the entrance of the river Salée, is approached through a somewhat crooked channel. It is formed by Cochons island and the neighboring islands on the W., and by the cays and reefs extending from the shore on the E.

The beacons on the W. side of the harbor mark shoals of small extent having passages between them.

A spit extends westward from off the northern wharf, having at its extreme a bank of 6 feet.

The town of Point-à-Pitre, on the NE. side of the harbor, is one of the most important commercial places in the Windward islands. It is a clean, well-kept, thriving place of 18,000 inhabitants. It was settled in 1763, and was in 1843 destroyed by an earthquake.

The harbor is perfectly secure even in hurricanes. On the eastern side is an extensive sugar-factory called the Usine d'Arbousier, the numerous chimneys of which form excellent landmarks for approaching the port.

Provisions of all kinds can be obtained at reasonable rates.

Water can be obtained by sending ship's boats to the pipe at the wharf. It is poor in quality. All merchant ships pay 6 cents per ton as a water rate, whether they take water or not.

Coal.—There is a very small quantity to be bought; cost from 30 to 35 francs per ton. The sugar factories import from 30,000 to 40,000 tons a year, but it is for their own use only.

Hospitals.—There is one military hospital in charge of a naval surgeon; capacity of about 120 patients and is kept very clean. Sailors from foreign vessels are admitted for about $1 per day.

There is also a civil hospital, capacity about 200 patients, charge 1 franc 75 centimes. The sanitary condition is very good, the city being clean. Malaria and dysentery are common.

Salutes can be fired from Cochons island.

Telegraph.—A land line connects the city with Basse-Terre and from there is a cable connecting the island with Europe and the United States.

Steamers.—The French line and Royal Mail line steamers call at this place.

Repairs can be made here to small vessels, but no extensive repairs can be made.

Imports.—Provisions and manufactured goods.

Exports.—Sugar, molasses, dye and cabinet woods.

Authorities to visit, the mayor, captain of the port.

Pilots are efficient and trustworthy.

Port charges.—The general council of Guadeloupe have enacted a law exempting the vessels of all nationalities from all port charges, including pilotage in and out. This law applies to all the ports in the island of Guadeloupe.

The United States is represented by a consul and vice consul.

Vessels approaching Guadeloupe from windward should endeavor to make the island of Desirade, keeping on the parallel of 16° 20′. On making this island, which can be seen at a distance of 30 miles, the course lies between Chateaux point and Petite-Terre, and then along the coast of Grande-Terre, keeping at least 1 mile off shore on account of the 17 feet bank. When abreast of Gozier island, haul to the northward to take a pilot if intending to go inside.

With a vessel drawing 20 feet or more, and being to the SW. of Gozier island, bring Jarry mill, now in ruins and not easily picked up, the west side of the harbor, to bear N. 45° W. It will then be just open to the eastward of the east point of Cochons island, and open to the southward of the only outer buoy; this line will lead up to the outer anchorage or to the entrance buoy.

Vessels coming from the W. and S. will usually have to tack before they can fetch the entrance. In approaching the entrance of Point-à-Pitre, they should not stand so far to the westward as to shut in the Saintes islands with Capesterre point.

On nearing the entrance by keeping to windward of a line drawn from the Usine d'Arbousier through Manroux Island light-house, S. 11° 15′ E., the outer shoals will be avoided.

If Desirade Island should be made during the night, the navigator should keep in sight the light on Petite-Terre, visible 15 miles in clear weather, and guided by it there will be no difficulty in coasting along the S. side of Grande-Terre, keeping in from 11 to 14 fathoms of water until Gozier Island light is made. Care should be taken to keep clear of the coral reefs on the W. side of the bay by keeping this light bearing to the northward of N. 45° E. till daylight. Although the buoys are lighted, strangers should not attempt to enter at night.

Vessels generally go to sea with the land-breeze at early daylight, usually taking a tow-boat at the cost of 10 cents a ton.

Bound to Europe or the United States they generally pass to leeward of Guadeloupe. Some navigators prefer to go to windward of Grande-Terre, beating through the channel N. of Marie Galante and passing between Chateaux point and the island of Desirade.

Petit-Bourg is frequented by small vessels and may be reached after passing within the line of outer shoals, by passing close to the southward of Fregate de Haut island and of Hache island, half a mile farther W., and keeping on the same course half a mile farther, when good anchorage in 20 feet will be found 300 yards off shore.

Goyave anchorage.—Local knowledge is necessary to take a ship in and out.

Sainte-Marie is an important port of export for sugar. Its locality is easily distinguished by three red bluffs just N. of the town.

It is an excellent anchorage for vessels not drawing over 15 feet, but the approaches are intricate, and the assistance of a pilot is necessary.

The **district of Capesterre**, lying S. of Sainte-Marie, was formerly the richest and most highly cultivated part of Guadeloupe. Rising high above it is Madelaine mountain, with numerous torrents rushing down its abrupt slopes.

Off Capesterre point the soundings are very irregular, and a berth of one mile at least should be given to the coast.

Basse-Terre.—The anchorage is a perfectly open roadstead, with very deep water at a short distance from shore. With the wind from S. or W. the anchorage is very unsafe, and vessels should at once go to sea, but during the season of strong trades, although a somewhat heavy swell almost always sets in, the anchorage is safe. Even during this season heavy rollers sometimes cut off all communication with the shore for a time.

Vessels approaching the anchorage from the southward should haul close round the S. point of the island, keeping always prepared for the violent puffs of wind which rush down from the mountain, and, keeping the shore close aboard, should haul up for the anchorage inside the mooring buoy of the steamers, and anchor off the town, as most convenient, in from 16 to 22 fathoms, 300 to 400 yards from the shore.

The town of Basse-Terre is the seat of government of the island, and has a population of about 9,000.

Telegraph.—There is frequent mail communication with other islands, and the West India and Panama Telegraph Company have an office there.

Water can be easily obtained from a pipe emptying near the center of the town.

A fine hospital has recently been built for foreigners at the foot of Camp Jacob.

West coast.—Along this coast is found anchorage for small vessels in numerous coves and small bays generally, with a village of the same name on the shore of the bay.

Winds and currents.—On the western coast of Guadeloupe there is a land breeze almost every night, extending about 2 miles off shore, and exceedingly useful to vessels bound either N. or S.

Outside of this limit light variable breezes and calms lasting several days are sometimes experienced, so that vessels which do not approach the land close enough to benefit from the land breeze would do well to keep 20 or 25 miles off shore to avoid these calms.

A strong SE. current, depending on the strength of the NE. tradewind, is frequently felt off the west coast of Guadeloupe. Tides are very little felt.

On the north coast the land forms a deep bay called Grand Cul-de-sac Marin. To the eastward it is limited by Gris-Gris point, with the islands abreast of it, and its western limit is point Allègre, also with off-lying islets.

From Kahouanne islet a bank with numerous islets and reefs upon it stretches off to the eastward at distances of from 1 to 3 miles off shore and extending nearly to the coast of Grande-Terre.

The sea inside of it is of course nearly always smooth, but the passages between the numerous reefs and shoals can only be navigated with the aid of a pilot. The islets and cays on the outer reef are used as landmarks for coasters beating along the N. shore and also for entering the channel leading to the various harbors in the bay.

The pilots who are familiar with the intricate channels of Cul-de-sac Marin are almost all fishermen and, like those of the Bahama bank, endeavor in navigating these channels to have the sun behind them, and are guided to great degree by the color of the water in avoiding dangerous shoals.

Passes through the reef.—There are several passes through the outside reef, of which the principal are Grande-Coulée and Passe à Caret.

Rose bay is sheltered on the N. by a reef, through which are two small openings; the western opening leads to the small bay of Ramée; the Grande-Coulée channel lies N. of it. On this part of the shore a long, low, narrow, level plain lies at the foot of the great mountain range.

Mahault bay.—There is excellent anchorage in the outer part in 7 or 8 fathoms of water, and farther in, off the town in from $3\frac{1}{4}$ to $4\frac{1}{2}$ fathoms. The best pass to enter is the Caret, about 4 miles N. 22° 30′ W. of the bay, and Fajou isle on the E. side of this opening bears N. from it.

Port Louis is an open roadstead. The anchorage is tolerably well sheltered from June to October, although a NNW. swell is felt; at other times, however, it is quite exposed.

It is easily recognized by the high chimney of the usine, or sugar-factory, 1 mile E. of the town.

The population is about 4,100. Provisions are scarce and dear and rain-water only can be obtained. Vessels come here to load sugar, but must enter and clear at the custom-house at Point-à-Pitre.

Anchorage.—The best anchorage will be found directly abreast of the town in 8 fathoms of water, about one-fourth of a mile off shore.

This part of the coast is foul to the distance of nearly one-fourth of a mile, and the bank of soundings only extends about two thirds of a mile off shore. Five feet of water will be found at the end of the wharf.

Grande-Vigie point is quite remarkable, being formed by a sharp rocky point, something like a ship's cutwater, and surmounted by a flat table-land.

Port Moule is a very small harbor, but is tolerably well sheltered. The coral bank which extends along the coast protects the port and is here about one-third of a mile wide, with two narrow openings.

Pilots.—The harbor can only be entered with the aid of a pilot, who is ready to board ships on their appearance if the bar is passable.

Vessels are moored head and stern in about 4 fathoms of water to anchors on the reefs, but as they lie across the swell it is a very uneasy berth. When rollers set in the moorings are sometimes carried away and the vessels lost on the reefs. The current of the river which empties into the harbor is sometimes strong enough to set vessels ashore.

La Moule is quite an important place, there being nearly 10,000 inhabitants and five large sugar factories.

Mails.—There is daily mail communication with Point-à-Pitre.

Vessels discharge coal here and load sugar. Provisions and water of good quality are difficult to obtain.

The position of the town is easily distinguished by the high chimney of the Duchassing factory, SW. of the town, by flags hoisted on the approach of vessels and by the battery on the western point of the bay.

The following signals are shown from the flag-staff when vessels are seen approaching:

A *red flag* signifies that the bar is not passable and the vessel should haul off.

A *white flag with a red square* signifies that the pilot will lead the way in ahead of the ship.

A *white flag with red diagonal* signifies that the vessel can enter the harbor.

There are two passes through the coral reef which shelters the port. The northern opening, called Grande pass, lies between the Barrel of Beef on the E. and Mouton de Haut on the W., the latter reef being dry at low water.

The **island of Desirade** lies 4 miles eastward of Guadeloupe, of which it is a dependency, is 6 miles long, from 1 mile to 1¼ wide, and about 900 feet high. The population is about 1,600. The climate is very dry, little rain falling.

Cotton is cultivated, but most of the inhabitants are fishermen.

Water is only to be obtained from a deep ravine on the NE. side of the island.

Grande-Anse is the principal town of Desirade. Small vessels can pass through a cut in the reef and find sheltered anchorage inside, and in fine weather larger vessels may anchor outside in 5 fathoms of water with the church bearing N.; but the soundings are irregular.

Mahault bay, near the eastern end of the island, is a similar small reef-harbor for coasters. The government has established here a leper hospital.

The eastern point of the island should be given a good berth on account of the Mouton rock, lying 600 yds. off it, and generally breaking.

The channel between Desirade and Chateaux point is frequently used by vessels bound to the northward. The Desirade shore should be kept aboard.

Currents.—After strong easterly winds there is a westerly current of 2 knots and upward off Colibris point.

Petite Terre is the name given to the low, sandy islets separated by a narrow cut, and lying SE. from Chateaux point. The northeastern islet is called Terre d'en Haut; the southwestern one Terre d'en Bas. They are mostly covered with vegetation, and have a narrow sand beach along the water's edge. The inhabitants are mostly fishermen.

As all the shores are foul and rocky to the distance of from one-fourth to half a mile, the island should not be approached in passing nearer than 2 miles, at which distance there is a depth of from 13 to 20 fathoms of water.

Sans nom, or Banc des Vaisseaux, is a bank of coral and sand, and when the sun is shining can be easily distinguished by the color of the water.

Marie Galante island is a dependency of Guadeloupe, and is situated in the channel between Dominica and Guadeloupe. Population about 15,000.

The general appearance of the island is flat and low, the soil in many places marshy, and the climate unhealthy. The weather side of the island is not generally cultivated; on the lee side are several sugar plantations.

The western side is generally steep-to and clear of danger, so that vessels may anchor almost anywhere within 1 mile of the land. Inside of this distance the soundings generally decrease from 8 fathoms toward the shore, but outside of this line the depths increase rapidly. The southern and eastern shores are dangerous, being skirted by a reef to the distance of from 2 to 3 miles.

Grand-bourg, at the SW. extremity of the island, is the principal town, and has a population of about 6,500. The harbor is formed by low cays, only uncovered at low water, and is very small, with a depth of from 10 to 15 feet. The channel between the cays leading to it has 16 feet of water, and is 600 feet wide. Large vessels anchor outside the reef in about 8 fathoms of water, with the church-tower in line with the end of the breakers, bearing N. 45° E. The bank of soundings is quite narrow, and three-fourths of a mile outside of the reef there are 28 fathoms of water.

St. Louis bay is the best anchorage for large vessels. The holding-ground is good, and there is anchorage half a mile off the village in 4 fathoms of water. The bay is full of excellent fish, and by hauling a seine large quantities may be easily taken.

Vieux Fort is a small village of little importance. Abreast of it is a small islet of the same name, with a 15-foot channel between the islet and the main-land.

Anchorage in 5 fathoms of water will be found half a mile off shore, with this islet bearing N. 45° E. at the same distance.

A shoal, with from 3 to 5 fathoms of water, extends half a mile northward of this islet, with a 5-fathom patch lying three-quarters of a mile from the islet N. 11° 15′ W.

Capesterre has a small reef-harbor, where coasters load the sugar brought from the plantations of the E. and NE. parts of the island.

Les Saintes, so called from their having been discovered on All Saints Day, form a group of islands attached to the government of Guadeloupe, and lie in the channel between Guadeloupe and Dominica, from both of which they are separated by clear and deep channels.

Terre d'en Haut, or St. Peter, the largest and easternmost of the group, is separated from Terre d'en Bas, the westernmost, by a channel navigable for vessels of any size. There is but little vegetation on the island. The inhabitants are skillful fishermen and boatmen.

The climate of these islands is exceedingly healthy; fevers are said never to occur.

Water is scarce, people generally depending on rain-water, and the fall of rain being less than in the neighboring island. Fresh provisions can generally be obtained.

Terre d'en Haut is of a very irregular shape. Mount Chameau, at the SW. end, has a tower on it, the summit of which is 1,037 feet above the sea. On one of the northern hills is Fort Napoleon, used as a military prison, and the NW. end of the island ends in a steep promontory called the Sugar-loaf.

The town and principal anchorage are on the W. side of the island, in a bay abreast of Cabrit islet.

The shore of Terre d'en Haut is generally clear of danger; there is, however, a hundred yards N. 33° 45′ E. from Point Portail (at the foot of the hill surmounted by Fort Napoleon), a rock with 12 feet of water on it, which breaks when the sea is at all rough. All round Terre d'en Haut are small bays and coves, in most of which landing is practicable.

There is temporary anchorage in 10 fathoms of water between Boisjoli point and Redonde islet, off the southern point of the island; but the best anchorage is off the town, a good harbor, with a depth of from 9 to 14 fathoms, and well sheltered to the westward by Cabrit island.

For vessels not wishing to enter this harbor, good anchorage may be found between the Sugar-loaf and the SW. side of Cabrit islet, in 11 fathoms of water, with a bottom of sand and coral.

Cabrit or St. George islet, serves as a quarantine station. There is also a penitentiary on it. Vessels in quarantine anchor here, abreast of the cove, with the S. point of the islet bearing about S. 67° 30′ E., in 11 fathoms of water, with a bottom of sand and shells.

Sugar-loaf passage lies between the southern point of Cabrit island and Red head, both of which points are steep-to and clear of danger; but the channel is obstructed by a coral shoal 100 yards in diameter, on which there are only 7 feet of water. A white buoy is moored on the SE. extremity of this shoal. The water does not generally break on this shoal, but the discolored water indicates its position. Sugar-loaf channel is convenient for leaving Bourg anchorage.

Saint Paul's island, or Terre d'en Bas. The sides are not deeply indented, and are free of danger 200 yards from shore. The summit of the island is somewhat rounded.

Anchorage may be found on the W. side of the island, and on the E. side are two small coves.

St. John's or **Grand islet** is the largest and highest of the islets S. of St. Paul's.

Off the W. end of St. John's islet are rocky islets called the Sow, or Coche, and the Augustins, but the channels between, though deep in places, are foul and only fit for boats.

The **Southwest channel** is clear of danger, with the exception of a reef which extends about 400 yards off the W. end of Augustins islet. The southern extreme of Cabrit islet in line with Boisjoli point, bearing N. 42° 11′ E., leads through in mid-channel.

Great Cay channel, between St. John's islet and Redonde, is clear of danger, but a berth should be given to the 10-foot patch W. of Redonde.

Aves islet is so called from the multitudes of sea-birds of various kinds which frequent it. The island is about 10 feet above the level of the sea. It is of coral formation, and is skirted by a reef on the NW., N., and S. sides. On the W. side there is anchorage and a landing-place. The islet appears to rise from a bank of soundings of consider-able extent, which has not been minutely examined, but which seems to be irregular in depth. Fishermen from St. Eustatius and other neighboring islands visit the island in March and April to gather sea-birds' eggs, which are taken to St. Thomas and sold in large quantities. No fresh-water is to be found.

Landing is sometimes impracticable on account of rollers.

The islet may be seen at a distance of 8 miles during the day, but at night not farther than 2 miles.

Anchorage will be found with the middle of the islet bearing N. 45° E., with a bottom of sand and rock. Care should be taken to anchor on a sandy spot, which may be easily picked out by the eye. The fishermen who resort to Aves islet state that the anchorage in-shore or within half a mile of the landing-place is not good, and that when a groundswell sets in the water breaks heavily. Occasionally, though not frequently, it is impossible to leave the islet for several days together during a ground swell, which sometimes causes a detention of three weeks.

The sea-birds usually visit the islet about the beginning of March and the egg season ends at the same time as the fishing season.

There are no trees on the islet, and the vegetation is very scanty; the grass, however, is about 6 inches high. There is no appearance of guano now, but it is said that a vessel took some away about sixteen or eighteen years ago.

During the fishing season a schooner makes three voyages between Aves, St. Thomas, Saba, and St. Eustatius islands.

DOMINICA ISLAND.

The island has been in possession of Great Britain since 1783. It is of volcanic origin, with lofty rugged mountains running through the center of the island from N. to S. Mount Soufrière, near the southern end of the island, has several openings, around which sulphur in large quantities can be obtained. In the Roseau valley there are several boiling springs, the principal one being 4 miles from the sea, and near the Wotten Waven estate.

About 6 miles NE. of Roseau, and more than half way across the island, on top of a high mountain and surrounded by others more lofty, is a lake of fresh water covering several acres. The valleys are fertile and watered by numerous streams, which abound with excellent fish, and there is an abundance of game in the island. The dry season (February and March) only lasts for about six weeks; in the remaining part of the year much rain falls. The highest mountains are only seen on an average twice a month.

The greatest rain-fall is in August and September, and during these months hurricanes and thunder storms are frequent and violent. The minimum temperature is 75°, maximum 90°; the latter is experienced for fully three months in the year. The annual rain-fall at Roseau is about 80 inches; in other parts of the island it is even more.

Climate.—The southern part of the island is healthy, mild fevers alone prevailing, as in other healthy parts of the West Indies. Prince Rupert bay and the northeastern part are considered unhealthy.

The principal articles of export are rum, sugar, molasses, coffee, etc. The population is about 27,000.

Government.—Dominica belongs to the general establishment of the Leeward islands.

The local government is vested in a president, aided by an executive council of seven members, and a legislative assembly of fourteen members.

There are several good roadsteads on the western side of the island, the principal of which is Roseau, where is situated Charlottetown, the capital of the island.

Caution.—Vessels sailing under the lee of Dominica should be on their guard against the heavy squalls which come off the high land and through the deep valleys, blowing with great force during the strong trades. Off Soufrière bay and the Layou valley are the two most dangerous places. When the trades are light calms are frequent.

Le Cachacrou or **Scott head**, the SW. point of Dominica, a small promontory connected with the island by a narrow neck, is a conspicuous object, and when seen from the N. or S., clear of the land, appears as an island. It should not be approached to within a distance of half a mile.

Soufrière bay can not be recommended as an anchorage, as it is very steep-to, small drogers having to make fast to the shore as well as anchor.

Point Michelle.—On the point is a well-built Roman Catholic church, with a large conspicuous cross S. of it. Off this point, with the church S. of E. and 300 yards off shore, a vessel may anchor in from 5 to 8 fathoms. Care must be taken to let go the anchor smartly, as the water deepens so suddenly that drifting a few hundred feet will change the depth from 10 to 20 or 30 fathoms.

Roseau.—The town stands on one of the few sloping points found on the coast of Dominica, and immediately S. of the Roseau river. The table-land of Mount Bruce, dotted over with old military buildings, overlooks the town. Fort Young and the conspicuous square-built court-house are slightly higher than the other buildings in the S. part of Roseau. The spire of the Roman Catholic cathedral is the most conspicuous object, and is distinctly seen when approaching from the N. or S.

Telegraph.—The telegraph cables connecting the island with Guadeloupe and Martinique are landed in Woodbridge bay, a short distance N. of Roseau river.

The best anchorage is off the Goodwill plantation.

Tides.—To leeward of the island no dependence can be placed on the turn of the tide. For several days the set may be N. or S. with the direction of the coast, the strength in some places being two knots an hour; and within a distance of 10 miles, the set may be quite in opposite directions. On the windward side the flood and ebb are regular; off Point à Peine the flood runs with a velocity of 1.5 miles per hour. Off the NE. part of the island the flood attains a velocity of 2 miles per hour; but the ebb, only half a mile an hour, is hardly perceptible.

Supplies.—The market at Roseau is generally well supplied. Beef can be obtained at 6d. per pound, pork at the same price, and mutton at 9d. per pound. The island vegetables, of great variety, are excellent and cheap, and fruit is plentiful. Vessels lying here water from the river.

Woodbridge bay is 1¼ miles wide, and lies between Roseau on the S. and the high land of Mount Daniel on the N. A conspicuous row of palms, running in an easterly direction and leading up from the Goodwill estate, which is in the southern part of the bay, is an excellent guide. The table-lands at the back of the bay, intersected by ravines, are much lower than Mounts Bruce and Daniel. Off the N. point of the bay rocks extend for 200 yards, and, on a coast so steep and free from dangers, show out conspicuously.

Anchorage can be obtained in from 8 to 12 fathoms, 300 yards from the beach, with the Goodwill chimney just open to the southward of the conspicuous row of palms bearing S. 73° 07′ E., and Scott head touching the shingly point of Roseau river.

Water may be obtained from a river in Woodbridge bay, but, the beach being rough and stony, it is attended with much inconvenience.

Layou river is the largest in the island, and when seen from the westward the entrance may be easily distinguished by the lowness of the land. The source of the river lies near the foot of the Couronne hill, which is comparatively low when seen with Diablotin to the N. and Trois Pitons to the S.

Good anchorage for drogers can be obtained N. or S. of the entrance to the river, 400 yards from the shore, the depths being 8 and 10 fathoms. The northern anchorage is most frequented by small craft shipping wood or sugar. In a SW. by S. direction from the entrance of the river, the water is very deep, and at anchoring distance off shore there are 40 fathoms. Wood in large quantities is shipped from this river.

Grand Savanna is the largest sloping piece of land on the western side of the island. This land is generally extremely parched in appearance, with little or no cultivation.

Anchorage.—The western point of Grand Savanna brought to bear N. 67° 30′ E., distant about 600 yards, and in from 10 to 20 fathoms, rock and sand, is the best anchorage ground. Closer in shore there are several patches of mushroom rocks, which a vessel's cable is likely to foul and be difficult to recover.

Wood and water.—A small river immediately N. of the Grand Savanna is favorable for watering, and wood can be obtained at $2.75 per cord.

Barber's Block is a conspicuous hill 5 miles to the northward of Grand Savanna. When seen from the N. or S. it is, as its name denotes, like a barber's block, the facial part being the summit and shoulders of the hill. From a westerly view it makes like a sharp cone.

Prince Rupert bluff is a steep bluff surmounted by two remarkable hills, known as the East and West Cabris. To vessels coming from northward or southward they appear as islands, but they are joined to the shore by a neck of low swampy ground. This prominent peninsula forms the N. side of Prince Rupert bay.

Prince Rupert bay is the best anchorage in Dominica. In the NE. part of the bay and facing the beach is the small and dilapidated town of Portsmouth. The Roman Catholic church, with its tall spire, stands a few hundred feet from the shore. The Methodist chapel, a white building, is half a mile inland and on the foot of a long, low spur. Morne au Diable stands to the NE. of the bay, the spurs from its summit meeting those from mount Diablotin, at the back of the bay, in a neck about 600 feet high.

This bay is the best and most convenient place for obtaining wood and water. Wood is brought alongside at from 10 to 12 shillings per cord. The Indian river, which is S. of the Roman Catholic church, is a good place to water from. A market is held in the town on Saturday and is generally well supplied.

If bound to this bay from the eastward, it will be better to pass to windward of the island and round its N. end to avoid the risk of being becalmed under the high lands.

Douglas bay.—Small vessels visit this place for fire-wood.

La Soye point.—A small anchorage of 4 fathoms is formed by the point and reef stretching to the NW., but it is very confined, scarcely allowing a small schooner room to swing at her anchorage; vessels are steadied by hawsers made fast to the shore. A pier is built inside the point and landing is easy. The bays to the westward of Crumpton point afford good landing for about 4 miles, when again the coast to Point Jaquet assumes a rugged character.

Coast.—The character of Dominica in the NE. quarter presents a distinct contrast when compared with any other portion. The land rises from the sea less abruptly, the soundings off the coast showing a continuation of this gradual slope, 100 fathoms being found $3\frac{1}{2}$ miles off shore.

St. David bay.—On its S. side is a small rocky islet, which, with an adjacent promontory, affords shelter for drogers. With a northerly wind a heavy sea sets in, making it difficult for vessels to put to sea. The anchorage is only safe with the wind S. of ENE. In the valley is the well-cultivated estate Castle Bruce; all its produce is shipped in drogers, which anchor under the rocky islet.

Grand bay is the principal and safest anchorage on the windward side of the island. The largest and best-cultivated estate near the bay is Geneva, with a water-mill half a mile from the beach. Grand bay terminates in a comparatively low point called Carib. Under this point and close in shore small vessels may anchor in from 5 to 10 fathoms and find shelter during the greatest strength of the trades, when the wind is N. and E. When the trade becomes slack and inclined to veer round to the SE., the anchorage is not safe.

Morne Fous is a remarkable conical cliff. When viewed with the higher land as a background the steep cliff, which falls almost perpendicular to the sea, has a most striking appearance, and when seen clear of the land it appears as a cone. The eastern extreme of this cliff is known as Point des Fous.

MARTINIQUE ISLAND.

The island was settled in 1635 by the French, to whom it now belongs. Its area is about 380 square miles, one-third of the surface consisting of plains, the rest being mountainous. The mountains are very high and irregular, the island being easily recognizable from a distance by the peculiar shape of three of the peaks, which rise above the rest and visible at a distance of 45 miles. The most northerly of these mountains is Mount Pelée. From a distance its summit appears of a rounded form.

The Pitons du Carbet form a group of rugged, conical peaks, with very steeply sloping sides, but their tops are generally hidden in the clouds. At the southeastern extremity of the island the most prominent peak is Vauclin mountain, shaped like a flattened cone, and lying at the eastern extremity of a range of mountains which divides into two branches, one joining the heights which overlook the bays of Fort de France on the N. and Grand Anse du Diamant on the S. These mountains, with many others in the island, show evidences of being extinct volcanoes.

Emptying into the sea from the sides of the mountain ranges are no less than 75 streams, of which only 2 are navigable. There are also 4 mineral springs. The mountains in the center of the island are covered with impenetrable forests.

The soil is generally formed of pumice, mixed with decayed vegetable matter; in the southern part being more fertile than the northern, where the land is barren and rocky.

The population of the island is about 165,000.

The products of the island are sugar, molasses, rum, coffee, cotton, cocoa, cassia, dye-woods, and annatto.

Government is administered by a governor and a privy council aided by a colonial council.

Within the last few years extensive central factories for the manufacture of sugar and rum have been established at various places on the shores of the island. The system pursued, of purchasing sugar-cane from the planters and manufacturing the products in large quantities with every appliance of modern skill and science, has been of very great benefit.

Climate.—The year is divided in Martinique into two periods of unequal length—the wet season from July to October, and the dry season lasting the rest of the year. The dry season only merits its name in comparison with the other, as a very considerable amount of rain falls during its continuance, and, although the showers do not last very long, they are copious and frequent.

The weather during the rainy season is much more variable and the rains heavier than during the so-called dry season.

The amount of moisture in the air is very great. The average range of the barometer is from $30^{in}.0$ to $30^{in}.12$, but on the approach of a hurricane it has been known to descend as low as $29^{in}.53$.

At a height of $6\frac{1}{2}$ feet above the level of the sea the maximum temperature in the shade has been found to be 95° F. and the minimum 68° F., while the mean yearly temperature is 78°.8 F.

During the dry season the winds are generally between E. and NE., without varying much either in direction or force; but during the rainy season they are far less regular, varying from ENE. to W., passing by the S. This is not only the most unhealthy season of the year, but also that of hurricanes, which frequently occur between July and October, and are often accompanied by more or less violent shocks of earthquake and heavy rollers. Hardly a year passes, in fact, without earthquake shocks at Martinique.

The Pearl rock may be passed on either side. Sailing ships, however, had better keep a little farther off shore, to avoid the calms under the high land, and the same vigilance must be exercised here that is required to leeward of all these islands, to guard against the squalls which rush down through the valleys.

St. Pierre bay lies between Point La Mare on the N. and Point Carbet on the S., the shore between them being low and sandy.

St. Pierre.—The roadstead is entirely open to the westward; and from July to November, when the trade-winds are interrupted and hurricanes and rollers occur, it is by no means a safe anchorage.

On the shore is the town of St. Pierre, the chief commercial port of the island, and having a population of 38,000.

Anchorage.—The best anchorage for men-of-war is a little to the southward of St. Marthe point, about 400 yards off shore, in 20 fathoms of water. The bank of soundings extends a little farther off shore here than abreast of the town, is less steep, and is called the Plateau du Carbet.

On the edge of the bank there is a buoy, outside of which there is no good anchorage.

The anchorage for merchant vessels extends from Ste. Marthe point northward to the river Pères, the northern boundary of the city. French vessels occupy the space S. of Place Bertin, those under other flags being moored farther to the northward.

In approaching the anchorage of St. Pierre, although the vessel may seem to be very close in shore, the anchor should never be let go till the lead shows that the anchorage has been reached.

The **currents** in the offing from St. Pierre road generally set to the southward.

Water of excellent quality can be procured. Casks can be filled in the boats by iron pipes leading from the fountain near the landing-place.

Telegraph.—The West India and Panama Telegraph Company have an office here, the submarine cable connecting the island with Dominica and St. Lucia.

Steamers.—Two lines ply regularly between New York and Martinique.

Provisions and ship's stores can be had here of excellent quality.

The sanitary condition is very good. The prevalent diseases are malaria and dysentery. Yellow fever becomes epidemic about once in eight or nine years, but never endemic.

Hospitals.—There are two hospitals. The military has a capacity for two hundred patients, costs 11 francs per day; the civil hospital is in charge of Sisters of Charity, costs 4 francs a day.

Salutes can be returned from Ste. Marthe battery.

The authorities to be visited are the mayor and the captain of the port.

Port charges.—Tonnage dues are abolished for all ports except Fort de France. Pilotage, 30 tons and less, 12 francs; 31 to 60 tons, 18 francs; 61 to 100 tons, 43 francs; 101 to 150 tons, 65 francs; 151 to 200 tons, 82 francs; 201 to 250 tons, 100 francs; 301 to 350 tons, 135 francs; above 351 tons, 153 francs. Light dues, 20 francs per vessel. Bill of health, from 6 to 15 francs. Buoy tax, 5 francs per vessel. Water tax, 10 centimes per ton. Interpreter's fees, from 10 to 100 francs. Stone ballast, 3 francs per ton.

Vessels trying the market can come in and stay three days, paying only 11 francs, including pilotage.

The United States is represented by a consul and vice-consul.

Fort Royal bay.—The shore is deeply indented and irregular in outline, narrowing the bay very considerably to the eastward of the town. The various anchorages in the bay are well sheltered from all winds.

Fort de France, the capital of the island, lies on the N. side of the bay. It is built on a low plain bounded on the W. by the river Madame, and is the headquarters for the French naval forces in the West Indies. The governor of the island resides here.

The **anchorage** for men-of-war lies off the town and is protected by Fort St. Louis, built on a narrow peninsula, rising abruptly from the sea and separating the anchorage called Flamands roads from the Carénage.

This anchorage is entirely open to the westward. During the hurricane season men-of-war are secured in Trois Islets anchorage, on the S. side of the bay.

Caution.—Vessels coming to the anchorage from the southward in thick weather should be careful not to mistake the electric light for the one on Fort St. Louis.

The approach to the anchorage in Flamands roads presents no difficulties whatever. Should it be necessary to go farther in a pilot should be taken. To anchor at night bring the light on Fort St. Louis to bear N. 73° 07′ E. and steer for it. Anchor on that line when Negro Point light bears N. 67° 30′ W. The channel leading to the cove E. of Fort St. Louis, called the Carénage, is buoyed, and the largest ships can haul alongside of the wharves there for repairs and coal.

Dock.—An excellent dry-dock has been completed, belonging to the French Government, capable of receiving vessels 360 feet long, 82 feet beam(outside of paddle-boxes), and drawing 26 feet. The dock charges are 3½ francs (67.2 cents) per ton for the first day, and 90 centimes (17.3 cents) for each succeeding day.

To the eastward of the Carénage and nearly 2 miles farther up the bay is an inlet forming a secure anchorage called the Cohé du Lamentin. S. of it on the S. side of the bay is another secure anchorage. This part of the bay is nearly cut off from the western portion by coral banks extending from both northern and southern shores of the bay, and the assistance of a pilot is necessary to conduct a vessel through the intricate channels leading to these anchorages.

There is but little tidal current in Fort Royal bay.

All sorts of supplies, provisions, coal, and naval stores can be obtained with ease at Fort de France.

Water is supplied from government water-boats.

Mail steamers ply regularly.

At several places on the shores of Fort Royal bay central sugar factories, or *usines*, have been established.

With the assistance of a pilot the approach to these factories is not difficult for vessels intending to load there.

Grand and Petite Anse d'Arlet and Petite Anse du Diamant bays.—The two former are separated by a bold promontory called Bourgos point. All three of these coves have sandy beaches and afford good temporary anchorage one-quarter of a mile off shore in from 7 to 10 fathoms of water. There are no hidden dangers and the shore is perfectly bold as far as the E. side of Diamond hill.

Anchorages on south side of Martinique.—Eastward of Diamond hill are the following anchorages for small vessels: Grande Anse du Diamant, Anse du Marigot, Anse du Ceron, and Anse des Trois Rivieres. At the latter place a central sugar factory has been established. Pilote river has also an anchorage off its mouth. In entering, pass eastward of Ste. Luce cay, which is surrounded by reefs. In approaching the anchorage of Grande Anse du Diamant the Olbian reef must be avoided, lying half a mile from the shore on the E. side of the bay, and having 6 feet of water on it.

Cul de Sac Marin between the shoals is so narrow that large vessels can not work in under sail. The water is so clear that the shoals and rocks can be easily seen and avoided. The entrance is obstructed by the Singe bank, having only 3 feet of water on it, and forming two channels at the entrance. The southeastern channel is the best. The eastern point of the entrance is flat and marshy, and is called Marin point. The best anchorage will be found with this point bearing S. 45° W. and the Piton Crève-Cœur, a hill 663 feet high on the eastern side of the bay, S. 73° E. In this berth a vessel will have 12 fathoms of water and good holding-ground. The anchorage nearer the town is only fit for coasters. At the head of the bay, near the village of Marin, a central sugar factory has been established.

Saline point, the southern extremity of Martinique, is very low.

Cabrit islet is also low, and foul ground extends for half a mile S. 45° W. of the islet. The shore should not be approached in this neighborhood nearer than three-fourths of a mile.

The eastern shore of Martinique, as far N. as the peninsula of Caravelle, is bordered by coral banks and reefs which extend off shore to a distance of $2\frac{1}{4}$ miles. There are several passages through these reefs leading to harbors and anchorages inside.

Vauclin point is the extremity of a spur of the mountain of that name.

Mark.—The point terminates in a steep hill, which is the mark for entering the Vauclin pass.

Brigot pass is the next opening, but it is too intricate to attempt without a pilot.

Pinsonelle cay is a dry, flat, rocky ledge between the Mitan and Pinsonelle channel. On the southern end of this cay the United States and Brazil mail-steamer *Mississippi* was lost in May, 1869. Her boilers are still visible there.

Caution.—The establishment of central sugar factories, or *usines*, at various points on the E. coast of Martinique and of neighboring ports of entry for the exportation of their productions renders it necessary to caution ship-masters as to chartering their vessels to load at those ports, unless they have some previous knowledge of the locality.

Such factories have been established at Simon, François, Galion, and Ste. Marie. All these ports can be reached without much difficulty, but they are difficult to get away from, owing to the strong NE. wind blowing directly on to this coast and the heavy sea.

No trustworthy descriptions of these ports and the approaches can be given. Generally the outlines of the reefs and shoals can be seen, especially when the sun is not ahead. Except for those having local knowledge the assistance of a pilot is almost indispensable.

Currents.—The currents on this coast are uncertain, and are to a great extent governed by the wind. After a SE. wind they sometimes set to the NW. more than 3 miles an hour, and in approaching the channel between Martinique and St. Lucia from the eastward this must be borne in mind. The loss of the numerous vessels was probably due to this cause, and many others have narrowly escaped going ashore on the reefs.

The two principal passages through these outer reefs are the Caracoli channel, close to the point of the same name, and the Mitan channel, 7 miles farther S. and midway between the Mitan cay and Thiery isle, 2½ miles S. of it.

Mitan cay is small and low.

Thiery isle is the easternmost of a small cluster lying 1½ miles off shore. Its summit is rounded, covered with bushes, and about 100 feet high.

Caracoli channel is the easiest of access and therefore the best of all the channels leading to the anchorages and bays inside the reefs.

Caracoli point is a bare, steep, rocky headland 95 feet high. The land slopes from the heights above down to the point, off which a coral reef extends about 200 yards. The N. end of the bank is 1 mile S., 22° 30′ E. of the point; nearly midway between, however, is a small 5½-fathom patch which causes a heavy roller, and should be avoided by keeping Caracoli point close aboard.

Caravelle peninsula, of which Caracoli point is the SE. extremity, is of very irregular breadth, varying from half a mile to 2 miles. The narrow isthmus which connects the peninsula with the main-land is only half a mile wide and separates the two bays of Trinité and Galion. Farther to the eastward the land is higher, gradually rising to the summit of Mount Tartane, which is surmounted by a semaphore 623 feet above the level of the sea.

The Caravelle rock affords an excellent landmark for vessels approaching this part of the island. It is steep-to, quite barren, and its peaked summit has been completely whitened by birds. From a distance it looks like a vessel under sail. The channel between the Caravelle peninsula and this rock is deep and free from danger.

Galion bay.—The W. coast is deeply indented, forming several smal coves fringed with coral reefs, making landing difficult with a heavy sea. Galion river empties into the bay a short distance to the SW. of the remarkable conical, wooded island of the same name. On the bank of the river, about half a mile from the mouth, is a central sugar factory, the products of which are shipped from this port. This anchorage, although not difficult to approach, is difficult to leave. Vessels approaching the anchorage should pass close to Caracoli point, and, giving the coast a berth of one-third of a mile, should haul close round Brunet point, where the coast suddenly trends to the northward, and should anchor with the latter point bearing about S. 45° E. one-fourth of a mile distant.

Pilots.—It is said that pilots can not always be depended upon, as they frequently do not present themselves till the vessel is close to the anchorage and no longer needs their assistance.

In beating out, great care must be taken to avoid the numerous shoals which abound in this neighborhood, and for which the chart will be the best guide. With the wind at NE. or even ENE. vessels leaving Galion bay are recommended to go to sea through the channel S. of Mitan cay.

The assistance of a pilot is necessary.

Robert harbor is quite large and well sheltered by the reefs lying abreast of the entrance. The soundings diminish gradually from 11 or 12 fathoms at the entrance to 4½ fathoms near the reefs which line the shore. The coast-line of the bay is much indented, forming numerous coves, which afford excellent shelter for small craft.

Anchorage.—A mile and three-fourths to the westward of Grotte rock is the islet of Petit Martinique, to the westward of which is the best anchorage for large vessels. Here smooth water and good holding-ground will be found with from 5 to 6 fathoms of water. Abreast of the town from 13 to 16 feet of water will be found.

The town of Robert lies on the NW. shore of the bay. It contains about 6,500 inhabitants, and moderate quantities of provisions may be obtained.

After a ship is inside of Caracoli point the entrance to Robert harbor is very easy, as the reefs on each side of the entrance are visible and are steep-to. To leave the harbor is more difficult for the reasons already stated.

Vessels should not haul to the southward, to round the reefs to the eastward of Chardon islet, till the semaphore on mount Tartane can be seen outside of Ramville islet. When this line is passed vessels may keep away to the southward so as to pass half a mile S. of Mitan cay, when they will be clear of all danger. The semaphore on mount Tartane kept on with Mitan cay will clear all the reefs on the SE. coast of Martinique.

François anchorage is 8 miles to the southward of Caracoli point, where a central sugar factory has been established. The town lies at the head of a small bay about three-fourths of a mile long, and the anchorage is well sheltered and has excellent holding-ground. It is, however, so surrounded by reefs and shoals, and the channels are so narrow, that the assistance of a pilot is indispensable.

The anchorages of Frégate, Simon, Sans-Souci, and Vauclin are small coves, where small vessels may, with the assistance of a pilot, find good anchorage. At Simon there is a central sugar factory. As the water is everywhere very clear the shoals are easily seen, particularly in good weather and when the sun is astern.

Trinité bay affords a safe anchorage during ordinary winds, and, next to St. Pierre and Fort Royal, is the most important commercial port, having a population of over 7,000. The bay is somewhat sheltered to the northward by a shallow, rocky bank, on which there are several dangerous shoals. The irregular depths on the bank raise so rough a sea, that large vessels from the northward had better pass between the western end of the bank and the shore than try to cross it.

The northern side of Caravelle peninsula forms the eastern shore of

Trinité bay. It is composed of low, reddish cliffs and sandy bays, skirted at a distance of 200 to 600 yards by a coral reef, on which the sea generally breaks.

St. Aubin isle is an excellent landmark in approaching Trinité bay. This isle is high and steep, with a round, bushy summit. Its north side is steep-to and clear of danger, but to the ESE. it is foul for one-fourth of a mile, and its south side is joined to the shore by a coral reef nearly dry in places.

Loup-Ministre has 6 to 9 feet of water on it, and as the sea breaks heavily nearly all times, it forms a useful guide to the entrance of the bay.

Between this reef and Caravelle peninsula there are many other reefs, which make the passage to the eastward of the reef dangerous.

Loup de Ste. Marie.—The western end of the bank on which the Loup-Ministre lies terminates about 1½ miles north of St. Aubin isle, but rather less than 1 mile farther N. 67° 30′ W. is the Loup Ste. Marie, with 5¼ fathoms of water on it. With strong NE. winds the sea breaks heavily.

There is a clear channel between this shoal and the west end of the Loup-Ministre bank, as well as between it and Ste. Marie islet, in front of the village of the same name, and joined to the main-land by a sandy bank.

The **Beau Sejour mill** (situated on the isthmus connecting Caravelle peninsula with the main-land), kept open a little to the eastward of St. Aubin isle, carries a vessel to windward of the Loup de Ste. Marie; kept open to the westward it leads to leeward of the same danger.

There are good outer anchorages in 8½ fathoms of water, or if desirable a berth farther in may be reached, keeping clear of the shoals on either side, which are easily seen.

With the wind from E. or SE. a vessel must beat in, and in order to avoid Loup-Ministre bank, should it not break, St. Aubin isle should not be brought to the southward of S. 11° 15′ E. till it is within 1 mile of the vessel.

With the prevailing winds it is usually difficult to leave the bay. In beating, out the eastern reefs, which are visible, should be kept aboard until the reef stretching off 400 yards from Fort point can be cleared. After this is done the edges of the channel are plainly marked by the breakers. Care must be taken to keep clear of the Mitan bank.

Ste. Marie anchorage.—Immediately to the westward of Ste. Marie islet is the mouth of the river of the same name. A central sugar factory has been established near the mouth of the river, but the anchorage off it is very much exposed and is unsafe.

The locality is marked by the chimneys of the *usine*. Vessels lie in from 5 to 8 fathoms of water about half a mile off shore.

From Sugar Loaf point to Maconba point, the coast is bold, steep-to, and affords no anchorage. It consists of small, sandy bays, separated from each other by bold, rocky bluffs, and is exposed to the full force of the wind and sea.

ST. LUCIA ISLAND.

The island was first settled by the French in 1635, and after various changes came into the possession of the English in 1803, and has ever since remained in their hands. The traces of French occupation are still apparent, a large portion of the population speaking that language.

The government is conducted by an administrator, who is subordinate to the governor-in-chief of the Windward Islands, aided by an executive and a legislative council.

It is mountainous and broken throughout, excepting a small plain at the SE. end. The volcanic peaks rise to a great height; the highest one, called the Soufrière, at the SW. end of the island, can be seen at a distance of 55 miles. The vapor which issues from its crater may be seen from a considerable distance. Near the base of this mountain are two conical, rocky peaks, called the Pitons or Sugar-loaves. They lie N. and S. of each other, 1½ miles apart, the southern one forming the SW. point of the island.

The island is covered with valuable timber for building and cabinet purposes as well as dye woods. The low lands are covered with swamps and marshes, making the island very unhealthy. Venomous snakes and insects abound.

The exports are cocoa, coffee, molasses, rum, sugar, and a small quantity of cotton.

The shores of St. Lucia have not been thoroughly surveyed, and no good description can be given of its eastern shore, which, however does not appear to have any secure anchorage. It is said to be free of danger, with the exception of the Champiguy bank, lying about 1 mile off shore and 3 miles to the southward of the NE. part of the island. This part of the island is only visited by the drogers which collect the produce and bring it to the harbors on the E. side for export.

The French cruiser *La Flore* in 1885 obtained soundings of from 10 to 17 fathoms for several miles in the St. Lucia channel between latitude 14° 3′ N. and 14° 14′ N., and between longitude 60° 33′ W. and 60° 45′ W.

The NW. point of the island is called Gros-Cáp point.

Gros or **Pigeon Island** is high, bold, steep-to, and surmounted by a fortification called Fort Rodney. It lies about half a mile from the shore, with a channel for small coasters between. In the channel are two large rocks called the Burgaux.

Gros Islet bay is to the southward of Pigeon islet, the southern limit of which is Fourreur or Barrel of Beef islet, which is small, low, and rocky, about one-fourth of a mile off shore. The bay affords excellent anchorage. There is no danger in approaching it, and either point may be rounded at 200 yards distance. Care should be taken not to go farther in, as at one-fourth of a mile from the shore there are only 2 fathoms of water.

There is a village on the eastern shore and a watering place on the S. side of the bay.

Brelotte point is the southern point of Gros Islet bay; between it and Port Castries, to the southward, is a bight called Anse du Choc, affording anchorage in 6 or 8 fathoms of water, to the westward of a small islet lying in the center of the bay, not far off shore.

Brelotte shoal.—In this bight there is a rocky shoal nearly 1 mile long and 400 yards wide, lying parallel to and half a mile off shore.

To avoid it keep the W. side of Pigeon islet open of Brelotte point. This is the only danger on the western side of St. Lucia.

Port Castries is an excellent harbor. At the head of the inlet is the town of Castries, the capital of the island, having a population of 5,000.

It is a coaling station for the steamers of the Royal Mail Company, and is the most convenient place for coaling in the Windward islands. There is a clear passage to the coaling wharf, with 27 feet of water alongside of it.

Harbor improvements.—The new quay is nearly completed and the face dredged to a depth of 27 feet. The cove at east end of the town has been faced with a sea-wall and the inclosed part filled in for wharfage space. The channel SW. of the town has been dredged to a depth of 27 feet to enable vessels to get alongside the wharf. The shoal at the west face of the wharf is to be dredged to a depth of 27 feet on its northwestern half and the remainder to a depth of 18 feet. The shoal marked by a perch to the northward of the wharf will be dredged to a depth of 27 feet as far as necessary to make a passage 600 feet wide between the wharf and the shoal.

Coal of good quality is plentiful at $7 to $8 per ton, there being generally a stock of several thousand tons of Scotch and Welsh coal on hand, but no anthracite coal is to be had. It is intended that vessels shall be coaled at the rate of 55 tons an hour.

Provisions can be procured at an advance of about 25 per cent. on New York prices, and ice can now be purchased.

Water is not good, because the washerwomen foul the streams, and the surface drainage is into them also. There are no regular water boats, but there are two small steam lighters, though the island trade keeps them so constantly employed that they can rarely be secured.

Signal station and **wharves.**—The signal station is no longer on Point Vigie but on Morne Fortunee, near the government house. There is a fine line of wharves, with 27 feet at low water alongside of them, so that vessels load and unload directly into the warehouses.

Steamers.—There is regular mail communication with New York and Europe by steamers.

Telegraph.—There is telegraphic communication with the United States and South America.

Hospitals.—The island is divided into six hospital districts, each having a hospital. There is also a lunatic asylum and a hospital for lepers. The hospital at Castries will accommodate about 150 patients. All vessels pay a hospital tax, which entitles them to use the hospital.

Salutes can be returned.

The authority to visit is the administrator.

Port charges.—Pilotage, $1 per foot; tonnage dues, 50 cents per ton; harbor-master's dues, 60 cents per ton; clearance, $1.

Imports consist of general merchandise.

Exports are mahogany, dye-woods, coffee, sugar, rum.

The United States is represented by a consular agent.

Directions.—When bound to Port Castries from the northward, which is the best route, having passed Gros islet, the entrance may be easily recognized by the high, bold bluff, having on its summit a small fort and signal-tower, but the narrow entrance will not be seen until nearly abreast it. This point, named Vigie, is steep-to, therefore haul sharp round it within 100 yards, and anchor as close under the N. shore as can be conveniently done for weighing.

Coming from the southward, the position of the port is as readily pointed out by the barracks on the Morne and the government house in a clump of trees just below the barracks. Tapion rock is low, with a small fort and light-house on it. A shoal extends for nearly 450 yards N. 67° 30' W. from the rock, having 4 fathoms at its outer extreme, and 16 feet at the distance of 200 yards. The NW. point of St. Lucia open of a dark bluff point S. of it leads westward of this shoal in 7 fathoms of water, and the battery within Tapion rock well open clears to the northward.

Winds.—In general, during the middle of the day, the wind rushes down the port with great violence; every preparation should therefore be made to give a good scope of cable in bringing up, to prevent dragging, and it will, perhaps, be found more safe and convenient not to commence warping in until the breeze slackens, which is usually the case from toward evening to about 10 o'clock the following morning.

In warping, be careful to keep in mid-channel, for shallow, rocky flats extend off most of the points; but the water is here so clear that, with the sun unclouded, they are readily seen and avoided.

Grand Cul-de-sac bay.—A pier has been constructed for convenience of loading lighters.

Good **anchorage** is afforded for the vessels which load here. The river Cul-de-sac empties into the NE. side of the bay.

Marigot harbor is a remarkable little inlet leading into two deep basins, capable of holding two or three large vessels and several small ones, with perfectly sheltered anchorage. This vicinity, however, is **exceedingly unhealthy.**

Roseau bay is small, and its banks are steep-to, there being a depth of 15 fathoms within 200 yards of the beach.

The coast between Roseau bay and Soufrière bay, 10 miles to the southward, is bold, and in places rises vertically from the sea.

La Raye bay is between the last-named bays, on the shore of which is a small village of the same name. There are 10 fathoms of water in La Raye bay 100 yards from the beach.

Soufrière bay.—The shore all around, however, is so bold that there are 30 fathoms water at less than 200 yards from the beach, and 3 fathoms only 10 yards from it; it therefore possesses no convenient anchorage; still it is visited by merchant-vessels, which load here, moored stern on to the shore.

The town of Soufrière is next in importance to Castries, and contains 2,286 inhabitants.

Directions.—In entering Soufrière bay the wind must be guarded against, as it rushes off from the valleys with such force as to endanger the spars; therefore, before entering, sail should be reduced, and if the breeze outside is strong, a reef taken in. When beating in, the wind will be found more steady on the S. side than on the N.

Caution.—Having approached to within a short distance of the town a strong hawser should be sent to the shore and made fast to one of the trees on the beach in front of it, and another hawser coiled in a boat ready to leave the ship and bend on, if required. The moment the end of the hawser is on board all sail must be quickly furled, for should it part it would be useless to drop the anchor, as it would immediately drag into deep water.

It will be necessary to hang the vessel by the stern by a stream-chain from either quarter, and drop a bower-anchor on the edge of the bank, in case the wind should veer to the westward; this, however, never takes place except in the hurricane months, and at all other times the sea is as smooth as in a mill-pond.

About half-way between Great Piton and Moulacique points, the SW. and SE. extremities of the island, is the bay of Ballenbouche, off which a reef, which does not always break, extends out upward of 1 mile, leaving between it and the shore a boat channel in moderate weather. In running down or beating up, the reef will be avoided by keeping the Great Piton just open of the land to the eastward of it; the water shoals rapidly on nearing the reef, but the lead is a safe guide either by day or by night.

River Dorée is a short distance to the westward of Ballenbouche, off which there is anchorage in 5 or 6 fathoms water, good holding-ground, sand, but at nearly half a mile from the shore, with the Little Piton open eastward of the Great Piton, bearing about N. 11° 15′ W., and Dorée church N. 50° 37′ E., but it is exposed to the prevailing trade-winds. In the dry season the river is scarcely seen from seaward, being then narrowed at the mouth to a few yards, but during rains it rushes down with force and overflows the banks. The landing here is not good. A little farther on there is also anchoring-ground in 7 fathoms off the village of Choiseul, about one-fourth mile from the shore, abreast the church that stands on the beach.

Water and **wood** may be obtained at Choiseul in case of need, and vessels bound to windward, being unable to stem the current, will find the above anchorages convenient stopping-places.

Vieux, or **Old Fort bay,** lies between the Moulacique peninsula at the SE. point of the island and Caret islet, NW. from it. With the usual trade-winds this capacious bay affords excellent anchorage and shelter. There is no danger whatever. On the NE. side of the bay, about 50 yards from the shore and nearly abreast the mouth of the river, is a small rocky ledge, steep-to, and nearly awash.

Good **anchorage** within one-quarter of a mile of the shore will be found in 5 fathoms of water, with the village church bearing N. 33° 45′ E. and Moulacique point S. 11° 15′ E., or farther out in 12 fathoms, with the church on the same bearing and the western point of the island N. 56° 15′ W.

Turtle, fish of various kinds, and fruit may be had in abundance.

The **current** around St. Lucia runs generally with great strength to the WNW. and NW., more particularly in the passage between it and St. Vincent. Within 2 or 3 miles of its S. and W. sides, however, there is often a strong eddy which will assist a vessel in beating to windward. The native fishermen say there are periodical changes in the currents that observe great regularity, and of which they avail themselves to catch fish, always going out when the current sets to windward.

ST. VINCENT ISLAND.

The island has been in the possession of the English since 1783. A lofty range of mountains running N. and S. occupies the center of the island, Mount Soufrière, in the NW. end of the island, rising to a height of 3,700 feet. This mountain is volcanic, and may be seen at a distance of 55 miles. On its NW. side it rises abruptly, but on its NE. side it gradually slopes to an extensive plain.

The shores are almost everywhere bold and rocky, with, however, several sandy bays where coasters load produce for Kingstown, the capital of the island and place of export.

The climate is said to be healthier than that of any of the other West India islands.

The principal exports are sugar, rum, molasses, cocoa, arrowroot, and a mineral cement called *pozzuolana*, made from volcanic ashes.

The government is vested in a governor, with an executive and a legislative council.

Kingstown bay and **anchorage** on the SW. side of St. Vincent, is the principal anchorage, on the shore of which is the town of the same name, the capital of the island, which lies along the shore of the bay and is backed by the mountains.

Good **anchorage** will be found with the church bearing from N. to N. 5° 37' E. in from 10 to 20 fathoms within one-fourth of a mile of the shore.

A good scope of chain must be veered, as the wind frequently comes off the shore in heavy gusts.

Population is about 12,000. The city is very clean and healthy.

Supplies can be obtained at reasonable rates. Water is brought to the city in iron pipes; vessels water at the wharf—cost 1 cent per gallon.

Coal.—There is only about 100 tons on hand. Cost from $10 to $12 per ton. Coal in boats containing only 2 tons.

There are several hospitals. The Colonial hospital accommodates about 300 patients. Patients pay $5 on entering, which is the only charge. There is a quarantine and a lepers' hospital.

Telegraph.—There is telegraphic communication with the other West India islands and thence to the United States and Europe.

Steamers.—There are several regular lines. Mails leave for the United States about every ten days.

Salutes can be returned.

The authority to visit is the governor.

Port charges.—Tonnage dues, 44 cents per ton. Ballast, 3 cents per ton. Pilotage, three-masted vessel, $4; two-masted vessel, $2.50. Harbor dues same as pilotage.

The United States is represented by a consular agent.

Young and **Duvernette islets** are on the S. side of the island. The latter is the outer and smaller of the two, is conical in shape, 204 feet high, and surmounted by an old fort.

These islets are bordered on the E. and S. sides by a rocky bank extending off 200 yards.

There is a narrow 5-fathom channel between these islets and the mainland.

Calliaqua or **Tyrrel bay**, immediately E. of these two islets, is a secure anchorage, but is now only frequented by coasters. Between this bay and Young island a reef runs 400 yards off shore to the southward.

Boccamaw bay is noted for the stream of excellent water which flows into it. It lies NNW. and SSE., with a depth of 26 fathoms across, within 100 yards of the shore; a vessel may anchor at that distance off shore, a little to the northward of the river, in 17 fathoms of water.

Princes or **Barrawally bay.**—Its N. side is formed by some remarkable rocks, called the Bottle and Glass, which are clear of danger, and have a boat channel within them.

Anchorage.—If coming from the northward, haul close round these rocks and anchor in 20 fathoms of water, sandy bottom, with the rocks bearing NW. and the barracks N. 61° 52' E. The bottom on the N. side of the bay is foul. The wind is so variable and unsteady under the high land that if intending to remain any time it will be better to warp in, and drop a second anchor to the eastward in about 12 fathoms. If coming from the southward, the shore may be kept aboard equally close, and the vessel may probably shoot far enough in to drop the inner anchor first. The water being deep so close in, the anchorage is only fit for small vessels.

Water may be obtained from a stream at the head of the bay.

From the Bottle and Glass rocks to a bluff called Cumberland point, the NW. extreme of St. Vincent, it is all along bold, and a vessel may stand in to half a mile from the shore. Between are several small bays.

Chateau Belair, the largest, affords anchorage at about 400 yards off its eastern shore in 13 or 14 fathoms of water, with the N. point of the bay bearing N. 2° 48' E., the W. point S. 78° 45' W., and the town S. 16° 52' W.

In the middle of the bay there is no bottom with 50 fathoms, nor on the W. side with 30 fathoms, at 100 yards from the shore. The landing is not good, and with northerly winds a heavy surf rolls in on the beach.

THE GRENADINES.

The Grenadines form a chain of about 100 islands, cays, and rocks, 60 miles long N. and S., lying between St. Vincent and Grenada.

They, with the adjacent islands, were settled by the French about 1650. They are now in the possession of the English Government.

The islands are of moderate height, none exceeding 1,100 feet, and have no off-lying dangers. They may be safely approached either in the day-time or by moonlight, and have several channels between them.

Bequia island, the northernmost as well as the largest of the Grenadines, is of irregular breadth, its coast-line forming several bays.

Its population is about 900, all of whom are utterly lazy and apathetic. The island is attached to the government of St. Vincent.

Admiralty bay, on the western side of the island, affords good anchorage, though open to the SW. The wind, however, rarely blows from that direction; but if such an unusual event should occur the sea would be broken by the banks which project from the shores of the bay.

Water and supplies can not be easily obtained here, or of good quality.

Friendship bay is a circular indentation, on the SE. side of Bequia island, affording anchorage and shelter to vessels of 10 feet draught. It is formed by St. Elair point on the E. and the cay of the same name on the W. the cay being joined by a reef to Bequia. The channel is midway between the cay and point. This place is frequented by American whaling schooners.

Quatre isle is 400 feet high, with projecting points on the E. and SE. sides, forming little bays.

Pigeon islet, 220 feet high, lies one-third of a mile off its W. end. To the westward of these islets and cays is an open space of moderately smooth water, affording safe anchorage except in the hurricane season. There are four channels formed by these islets and cays which might be used in case of emergency. As a general rule keep in mid-channel, except between Quatre island and Petit Nevis, where keep nearer Quatre to avoid a shoal off the SW. end of Petit Nevis, on which the sea generally breaks.

Battowia island, bold, steep-to, and 686 feet high, is the easternmost of the Grenadine islets. Close to its N. end is the Bullet, a conical rock 318 feet high, having a breaker about 300 yards NW. of it.

Baliceaux island.—Off its western side is a 5-fathom bank, on the edge of which a vessel may anchor, but the water is not smooth. Close to, on the NW. side, there are two shallow patches, and an uncovered reef on the SW. side.

Mustique island.—The E. side of the island is skirted by a reef, and off it is Rabbit islet, with the Brooks rock 60 feet high, and other rocks; but as there is no anchorage here a vessel should avoid this side of the island.

Grand bay is an indentation on the western side of the island and affords temporary anchorage. To approach it a vessel should pass W. and northward of the Montezuma shoal, and enter between it and the N. point of the bay, or make short tacks in the S. part of the bay.

Montezuma shoal is extremely dangerous, as when the water is smooth it does not break, and can not be seen until too late to avoid it. A vessel may also anchor N. of the shoal off Cheltenham, in the NW. part of the island.

The **Savan islets** form a group of small islets and rocks extending over the space of 1 mile. The largest islet is about 600 yards long, 200 yards wide, 133 feet high, and being covered with grass has a bright green appearance when seen in the sun.

Savan rock is remarkable from having whitish sides and somewhat the appearance of the Sail rock, which lies 11 miles farther to the southward, but from its being the southernmost of the group it can not be mistaken for the isolated Sail rock. These islets and rocks are more or less skirted by reefs, and rise from a bank having from 4 to 10 fathoms water on it. Temporary anchorage will be found for small vessels NW. of the largest islet, but there is always a swell. The channel between this group and Petit Cannouan is $3\frac{1}{2}$ miles in breadth and clear of danger.

Cannouan island is very irregular in outline; an indentation on its western side, called Charlestown bay, affords anchorage in 17 fathoms of water.

The next group to the southward of Cannouan island consists of Mayero island, the Catholic islet and rocks, and Tobago cays and reefs.

Mayero island is the largest. It contains about 260 inhabitants, who live by fishing and raising a few vegetables.

Directions.—In passing through the channel between Cannouan and the Mayero group, a vessel should pass to the northward of the Channel rock, 8 feet high, and in mid-channel, to avoid a shoal awash.

Good **anchorage** in 6 or 7 fathoms water may be had on a bank extending about three-fourths of a mile westward from Mayero island. The best and most roomy berth for leaving, with any wind, is near the edge of the bank with the middle of the island bearing N. 67° 30′ E., but as the trade-wind is almost always between NE. and SE., a vessel may anchor much closer in, out of the swell, taking care, however, to avoid a 3-foot shoal at 300 yards off the middle point of the island. The NW. point of Cannouan island well open of the NW. point of Mayero, leads to the westward of the shoal; the two points in line lead on it.

In working for this anchorage keep on the parallel of Mayero, and do not open the channel between it and Union island unless the tide is setting to the northward.

On the E. side of Mayero island is a secure anchorage for small vessels, in from 6 to 9 fathoms water, under cover of the extensive reefs which surround this side of the island. The passage in is from the southward between the reefs on the E. and those skirting the shore of the island.

Tobago cays are four small islets. Three of them are nearly in line N. and S., the two northernmost being the largest, and the middle one 150 feet high. The fourth islet is E. of the middle one. They are within a semicircular reef, just awash, named the Horseshoe, the extremes of which are nearly 2½ miles N. and S. of each other. There are two small sand-banks, about 2 feet above water, rising from the reefs at about one-third of a mile SW. and SE. of the islets. The space between these cays and Mayero island is also filled with reefs, with narrow channels between them.

Good **anchorage** for small vessels in smooth water will be found under the lee of the cays, and between them and the Horseshoe reef, the latter forming a perfect breakwater. The route to the anchorage is from the northward, between Baline reef, at the NW. end of the Horseshoe, and Mayero island, keeping nearer the latter to avoid a rock, with 6 feet water on it, lying S. 22° 30′ W. 500 yards from the Baline reef. Small vessels may pass between Baline reef and the NW. end of the Horseshoe. A vessel may leave the anchorage by the channels to the southward, but a sailing-vessel can not well get to it by them.

World's End reef is the most eastern danger belonging to the group of the Tobago cays and reefs. It is dangerous for sailing-vessels to be near in light winds, as the current sets strong over it. It has probably received its name from the fishermen having a long pull to reach it from the cays.

Egg reef is close to the westward of World's End, separated by a narrow passage. Sandy cay is westward of the latter, with a tree on it encompassed by a reef above water, with channels on either side of it. The cay is 6 feet high and the tree 20 feet. These channels are narrow, deep, and may be taken in case of necessity. There is anchorage sheltered from the N. under the lee of Egg reef. Vessels should, however, avoid the vicinity of the whole of these reefs eastward of Tobago cays, as the tides are strong.

Union island lies S. 45° W. of Mayero islands, and is the southernmost of those islands attached to the government of St. Vincent. The population in 1861 was 477. It is more or less skirted by reefs which connect to it Frigate islet, distant about two-thirds of a mile on the S. and Red islet, 140 feet high, close to it on the E. About one-third of a mile from its north side is a small sand cay.

Chatham bay, on the W. side, affords fair anchorage for large vessels in 17 fathoms water, sand; but care should be taken not to go far into the bay, as there is a small shoal with 6 feet water on it at about one-fourth of a mile from the shore, and a little inside the depth of 10 fathoms. Small vessels may anchor farther in on the N. side of the bay. There are no dangers in entering the bay, which should be from the northward on the port tack. Give the NW. point of the island a berth of about 300 yards and pass close to a remarkable small islet, 52 feet high, at the N. point of the bay, and when abreast it, with good way on, shorten sail and the vessel will shoot into the anchorage. Temporary anchorage may be had to the SW. of Frigate islet in 8 fathoms water, if wishing to communicate with the villages on the SE. side of the island. Small vessels may go close to Frigate islet into 2 or 3 fathoms.

Clifton cove, at the E. end of the island, is a secure smooth anchorage for small vessels, close to the NE. of a large house. The channel into it is close to the reef which protects the anchorage.

Supplies.—In Chatham bay fish can be procured with the seine in great abundance. Fire-wood is plentiful, but no water. The inhabitants are entirely dependent on what is collected in tanks during the rainy season.

Prune island is nearly surrounded by reefs, and on the N. side they extend off nearly half a mile. The navigable channel between the NW. end of the reefs and those extending from Union island is more than one-quarter of a mile wide, with from 4 to 16 fathoms water. The route through from the northward is in mid-channel, but to the westward of the shoal, nearly awash, which lies W. of the SW. end of Prune island.

Carriacou island is the largest of the Grenadines. Population, 5,000. Products: Cotton, live-stock, and ground provisions.

The eastern and southern sides are more or less bordered by reefs above water, which protect shallow anchorages inside them. The western side of the island is clearer and the water deeper, and there are two good anchorages for large vessels. Wood is plentiful, but water is scarcely to be had, as there are no streams, and the inhabitants depend on rain for their supply.

Tyrrel bay, called also Southwest or Great Carénage bay, at the W. end of the island, is an indentation formed by two points, one projecting to the NW. and the other to the SW. The inner part of the bay is circular and more than half a mile in diameter.

Anchorage.—Large vessels may anchor in the northern and outer part of the bay, in from 15 to 5 fathoms water, sandy bottom, at about 400 yards from the shore; small vessels anchor in the inner part in from 5 to 2 fathoms. A reef extends to the northward from the S. side of the bay for nearly 400 yards, and a shoal with 1½ fathoms water on it lies in the northern part, both within the line of anchorage for large vessels. Small vessels can pass between and above them almost up to the beach.

In the northern part of this bay, inside the low land, is a lagoon nearly half a mile in length, with from 4 to 26 feet of water in it. The entrance to it, called the Carénage, is through a lane of deep water northward of the 1½-fathom shoal in the N. part of the bay.

The W. point of Carriacou is foul for nearly 200 yards; two-thirds of a mile off this point are the Sister Rocks, 73 feet high, with a shoal extending S. 67° 30′ E. for nearly 100 yards.

From Cistern point, projecting a little northward from the W. point of the island, the shore curves to the eastward and northward, forming Hillsborough bay, on the shore of which stands the little village of that name, and off it is the principal anchorage in Carriacou.

A bank, with 5 to 7 fathoms of water on it lies 1 mile N. 45° W. of the N. part of the island, where vessels may anchor if necessary.

The N. point of Carriacou is clear, and may be passed at a distance of 400 yards. For Hillsborough bay a vessel may pass close to Jack-a-Dan on its W. side, and anchor in 14 fathoms of water, sand and coral, with the isle bearing N. 11° 15′ W., distant 600 yards, and Sandy isle on with the Sister rocks. If necessary a vessel may anchor farther to the eastward, but not in less than 7 fathoms, as from this depth the water suddenly shoals to 2 fathoms, and the wind sometimes comes from the NW., causing a swell. Small vessels can go in almost to the beach. Landing is exceedingly good, except when interrupted by the NW. swell. Anchorage for large ships may also be taken in 17 fathoms, with Jack-a-Dan bearing S. 45° E., distant 1 mile.

Watering and **Grand bays**, on the E. side of Carriacou, are protected by reefs, which are uncovered and skirt the whole of this side of the island at from one-third to a mile distant. The northern is called Limlair or Watering bay, the southern, Grand bay, off two estates of the same name, and they afford anchorage for small vessels of 9-feet draught. There are three channels for entering, but that between the reefs at the N. end northward of the dry sand-bank is the safest. The two southern channels, although deep breaks in the reef, are difficult to enter without local knowledge.

Little Martinique.—Off the SW. side are the islets Little Tobago and Fota, the former 200 and the latter 80 feet high.

The channel between the Carriacou coast reefs and the islet of Little Tobago is 1,400 yards wide; in using it from the SE., keep one-third the breadth of the channel from the edge of the reef, and when Fota opens off the NW. part of Little Tobago a vessel will be to the westward of the 1½ fathoms rock. Between the rock and the reef there are from 6 to 10 fathoms water, but the tides in this channel are very strong, and it is not recommended. Fota channel, or that between Little Tobago and Fota, although narrow, is better than the former. A small reef above water extends rather more than 50 yards N. from Little Tobago.

Between Fota and Little Martinique is a passage carrying 3½ fathoms water, but it is not so good as the Fota channel.

Caution.—As the tide sets fully 3 knots through the above channels, it is necessary in working through from the NW. that the tide should be setting to the SE.; and in standing to the southward do not approach too near the Carriacou reefs, as the sea runs heavily on them.

Anchorage.—At about half a mile off the NW. side of Little Martinique, protected by Little St. Vincent, the sand-banks, and reef surrounding these islands, there is most excellent anchorage in from 8 to 12 fathoms water, taking care to avoid the 2-fathom shoals three-fourths of a mile from the W. sand-bank.

Large and **Frigate islets** are the largest of a number of islets and rocks, which, with Saline, White, Mushroom, Rose, and the Bonaparte, form a group at the S. end of Carriacou island. Between the Bonaparte rocks there is a narrow channel 9 fathoms deep, but a rock almost dry lies a little to the northward of the fairway, which renders it unfit to pass through. In the channel between Large islet and the Bonaparte rocks, southward of it, is a shoal stretching to the northward from the latter, and one with 3 fathoms water on it at half a mile to the NW. of the rocks, and nearly the same distance SW. of the W. end of Large islet. The current runs with great strength, which renders it dangerous to use this channel, or to approach the rocks on the eastern side, unless in cases of extreme necessity. A rock 1 foot out of water lies 250 yards westward of Large islet.

Frigate channel is narrow but clear of danger, and may be used by passing to the southward of the Rose rock, 32 feet high. There is also a channel carrying 5 fathoms water between the Rose and Frigate islands.

Saline channels.—The channel between Frigate and Saline islets is 1,400 yards wide, carries 18 fathoms water, and may be used from E. to W. by any sized ship. A rock 1 foot above water lies N. 45° W. 400 yards from the NW. point of Frigate islet. There is also a narrow channel with 6 fathoms water in it northward of Saline island, between it and Cassada rocks (20 feet high) and White islet. Also a channel 8 to 10 fathoms deep on the N. side of Cassada rocks and White islet and the reef adjoining them. In using this latter channel pass about half a mile westward of White islet and southward of the Mushroom islet. The latter may be passed close to on the S. side.

There is a narrow passage to the northward between the Mushroom islet and Little Mushroom, but rocks above water lie off the SW. point of Carriacou, at the distance of 300 yards.

Caution.—The above channels can be taken only from E. to W. with the usual trade-winds, except by steamers. Small vessels having local knowledge, with the assistance of the tide, may work through them.

Anchorage, with the usual trade-wind, for small vessels in convenient depths will be found under the lee of De Caille islet; in the S. and NW. bays of Ronde islet; and on the W. side of Les Tantes.

Tides and currents.—The strength, duration, and general direction of the tides among the Grenadines are very much influenced by local causes; but generally in the course of twenty-four hours there are two tides each way. It is generally high water at full and change at 3^h, the tide seldom rising and falling as much as 1 foot. The flood or tide setting to the westward is aided and accelerated by the westerly equatorial current, and in proportion as this takes place the ebb stream to the eastward is retarded or overcome.

The direction of the tides is governed to a great extent by the inclination of the trade-winds, which, although they do not vary much from E., still greatly affect the tide.

The flood-tide is of longer duration usually than the ebb, and in mid-channel will sometimes, aided by the current, run all day, while close to the islands the ebb-tide may be found running to the eastward.

When the ebb-tide runs against a strong trade-wind, a heavy, confused sea is raised.

The average strength of the tides in the channels is about 2 knots, and in some places 3 knots an hour. Sometimes, however, aided by the current, the flood-tide rushes through the passages at the rate of 4 knots.

GRENADA ISLAND.

This island was first settled by the French in 1650, and has been since 1783 an English colony. Population, 42,000.

The land is of volcanic origin, and is traversed by a chain of mountains of irregular height. The island has the reputation of being a healthier residence than most of the other West India islands.

Products are cocoa, spices, and sugar.

Government of Grenada and Carriacou is vested in a governor-in-chief, an executive council, and a legislative council.

The island is surrounded by reefs and banks, which make off from the points, limiting the harbors, thus making the pilotage almost everywhere quite intricate, and necessitating great caution when approaching the shores.

Winds.—The trade-wind blows almost without interruption from between NE. and SE., sometimes very fresh indeed; but hurricanes are of very rare occurrence.

Tides and currents.—The general set of the current is to the westward, and in approaching its shores this current must be carefully allowed for.

Off the bank to the southward the current generally sets 2 knots an hour to the westward. On the bank it is checked by the ebb-tide, which sets round the SW. point of the island and along the S. shore, but which is only felt for two or three hours, while the current and flood-tide run for eight or nine hours to the westward. Off Grand Bacolet, on the SE. side of the island, where the ebb scarcely reaches, the current united to the flood-stream runs down strong for six hours and weak for two hours, while the ebb-tide overcomes the current only for four hours.

During the wet season, from June to the fall of the year, the ebb is often entirely overcome by the current, probably caused by the water discharged from the South American rivers. Therefore a sailing-vessel from Saint George to Grenville bay should go round the N. end of the island, as it is scarcely possible to work past Grand Bacolet bay. Scarcely any tide or current is felt under the lee of Grenada, and, if any, it is quite uncertain, except close along shore, where it is also weak. The water in the southern harbors is unaffected by the tide.

In approaching Grenada from the NE. the best channel is that between De Caille islet on the N. and the London Bridge rocks on the S.

London Bridge rocks.—These rocks form a small cluster, one of them being 75 feet high, with a hole through it, and having two smaller ones near it. There is a rock just uncovered lying 400 yards S. 45° W. of it.

Another channel of approach lies between the London Bridge rocks and *Levera* island, lying close off the NE. point of Grenada and 343 feet high. In taking this channel steer midway between Levera and London bridge, where a depth of 17 fathoms will be carried. After passing through either of these channels, if bound to St. George, follow the western shore of the island at half a mile distance, there being no danger to apprehend till arriving abreast of the entrance to St. George harbor.

Between David point, the northern extremity of the island, and St. George harbor, the following bays abreast of the villages of the same name afford temporary anchorage for coasters, viz:

Du Quesne, Cray-fish, St. Marks, or Grand Pauvre, Goyave, or Charlottetown, Halifax, and Grand Mal Bays.—There is also anchorage on the 5-fathom bank 2 miles N. of Grand Mal bay. All these bays are exposed to the northward and westward and are very subject to strong gusts off the land.

St. George, the principal town in the island, stands on a point of land ranging from 115 to 180 feet high, which forms the harbor called the Carénage, in a bay of the same name. The bank off the town is intersected by veins of deep water. It affords, however, excellent anchoring-ground, but it is necessary to guard against the inconvenience of anchoring in the deep-water holes.

A groundswell sets in here from the month of November to March, sometimes causing a swell in the Carénage. The groundswell takes place in the same months throughout all the islands. The locality of the harbor or Carénage may be easily known by the extensive fortified heights immediately above it, which reach 750 feet above the sea.

On its SE. side is a large indentation with shallow water, the southern part of which, separated from the northern by a point of land, is somewhat circular. Although small, the harbor is secure, and is entered by vessels of the largest draught, through a deep channel carrying from 23 to 11 fathoms water to the anchorage. The harbor-master acts as pilot. The usual anchorage for vessels of war is in the bay.

St. George is healthy and recommended as a good port in which to give liberty.

Sailing-vessels from the southward whose draught will admit of crossing the Annas shoal should make a tack into Grand Anse bay, to take advantage of the flaws of wind which occasionally come from the SE., and which enable them to lay well up for the Carénage.

Anchor when 200 yards off the coal-wharf, or in the middle of the Carénage. If intending to make any stay, it will be requisite to moor open hawse to the SW., as there is but little room to swing at single anchor. In leaving the harbor, it will be necessary to place the vessel's head in the right direction before starting, and in a vessel of 26 feet draught the elbows of the channel should be buoyed.

Vessels of large draught and men-of-war generally anchor outside of Fort George point. A good berth will be found one-half mile off shore in 7 fathoms of water, sandy bottom, with Fort George flag-staff bearing S. 84° 22′ E., and Boismorice point N. 5° 37′ W.

Coal and supplies.—Facilities for coaling are poor. There is not a sufficient stock of coal in store to supply a ship, and the 60 or 70 tons on hand in St. George's is of the quality known as blacksmith's coal, and unfit for steaming purposes. Water can be had in any quantity at the watering place at the quay, but vessels must use their own boats to bring it on board, as there are no water lighters. Water, if taken, is paid for according to the tonnage. Provisions to a limited extent can be procured at an advance on New York prices. Fruit is plentiful, but exorbitant prices are charged for it. Ice is brought in small sailing-vessels from Trinidad, but the supply is by no means certain.

Telegraph.—St. George is connected by the submarine cable of the West Indies and Panama Telegraph Company with St. Vincent on the N. and Trinidad on the S.

The authority to visit is the lieutenant-governor.

There is one general hospital, also one for the insane. These are apparently well conducted.

Steamers leave for the United States about every two weeks.

Pilotage is not compulsory.

Harbor dues, 36 cents per ton.

Two miles SW. of the entrance to St. George harbor is Long or Goat point, to the northward of which is an indentation in the coast called Grand Anse bay.

Long Point shoal is 900 yards W. of Long point, having only 2 feet of water on it, and on which the sea generally breaks. In approaching St. George harbor from the southward, the eastern extremity of Fort George point kept on with the government house, a large red brick building on the first ridge, bearing N. 56° 15′ E., will lead clear of the shoal. There is a narrow channel between Long point and the shoal, but it should only be used in case of necessity.

Anchorage.—There is good anchorage in 5 or 6 fathoms of water on the bank extending to the SW. from Long Point shoal, at rather more than a mile to the NE. of Saline point, and a long half-mile from the shore. This anchorage is the resort of the American whaling-vessels in bad weather, or for the purpose of boiling oil during the season from February to May. There is a hole 10 to 13 fathoms deep nearer the shore, about three-fourths of a mile in extent.

Saline point, so called from a salt-pond near it, is bold, perpendicular, and 100 feet high. It should not be approached in a large ship nearer than 1 mile, to avoid the Seringapatam shoal and the bank joining Saline point and Glover island.

Prickly bay is easy of access, and affords good temporary anchorage for vessels of 18 feet draught. There is a shoal with $1\frac{1}{2}$ fathoms water on it at about a quarter of a mile from the head of the bay, not distinctly seen. To the westward are True Blue and Hardy bays, which may be used by vessels of 15 feet draught.

Mount Hardman bay, between Prickly point on the W. and Mount Hardman point on the E., affords good anchorage in 4 or 5 fathoms of water, but the channel is crooked. With smooth water the reefs on the sides of the channel can be seen, and the eye will then be the best guide.

Clarkes Court bay.—The entrance is formed by Caliveney and Hog islands, and the shoals and reefs extending from them. It is larger than Port Egmont, capable of holding a large number of vessels, and would present no difficulty in entering under steam were the shallows buoyed. The anchoring ground is about a mile in length and 600 yards wide, in 7 and 8 fathoms water, muddy bottom. The passage is through a narrow vein of deep water, between the banks on either side with 2 to 4 fathoms on them. Here vessels may lie quite secure even in a hurricane.

Directions.—Being to the eastward of Caliveney island, approach it with caution, and bring the two eastern points of Hog island in line bearing N. 29° 30′ W., taking care not to go leeward of this mark. When the S. extreme of Caliveny island is in line with Fort Jeudy point, haul up midway between the reefs, or close with the weather shore, and anchor in the bay where convenient, avoiding the shoal before mentioned.

There is good anchorage for small vessels between Hog island and the main in 4 fathoms of water; the channel is narrow, but may be taken in fine weather.

Port Egmont is an inlet carrying 8 fathoms water to the upper part, where there is a narrow passage to an inner harbor, landlocked, 4 and 5½ fathoms deep, with 21 feet water at the entrance, and where vessels may lie hidden from seaward. At the head of this harbor the French landed 3,000 troops in the year 1779.

There is secure anchorage for small vessels on the W. side of Adam islet, S. of Egmont point, which forms the W. side of entrance to the port, but it is difficult for a sailing vessel to get to sea, the course out being SE.

Caliveney harbor.—The entrance will be known by Westerhall point, trending to the eastward, with three hills upon it, and light-colored cliffs on the SE. side. The course in is N. 45° W., between the shallows on either side.

Bacaye harbor affords good anchorage for small vessels.

St. Davids harbor affords anchorage for small vessels. To enter it, steer midway between St. Davids point on the E. and the reef extending off Middle point on the western side. St. Davids point is square, bluff, and foul for a short distance. Anchor with Middle point bearing W. in 5½ fathoms of water.

Coast.—From St. David's point to Grenville bay the E. coast of Grenada is indented with numerous small bays, only frequented by coasters for the collection of produce. The bays are all more or less open to wind and sea.

Grenville bay is very much obstructed by reefs, which, however, afford shelter to the anchorage. The bay is entirely open to the eastward. The inner anchorage can only be approached by vessels drawing less than 12 feet. Vessels lie in the outer anchorage also, under the shelter of a reef, until lightened to that draught. There are no good marks for entering; the assistance of a pilot is therefore necessary.

The village of Grenville, on the shore of the bay, is the second place in importance in the island.

Caution.—In coming in from seaward toward Grenville bay it will be necessary to guard against being set to leeward by the current. Here it runs so strong to the SW. that a sailing vessel missing the bay will have to go round the island and again come in from the NE. The stream, striking Grenada on its eastern face, turns along shore both to the NW. and SW.

The coast from Grenville bay to Bedford point is an open sandy shore, exposed to the whole force of the wind and sea. On the shallows off the shore the sea breaks everywhere inside of the 5-fathom line.

Sandy and Green islands.—Anchorages under their lee are safe and accessible, but, as the lee tide sets strong round Bedford point, and the trade-wind tends to increase it, there would be considerable delay in loading vessels at either of these anchorages. Sandy island is surrounded by a reef which extends southward about one-fourth of a mile. The S. side of Green island is also foul 200 yards off.

Irvin's bay is the principal anchorage on the N. side of Grenada, where about one-half of the annual crop of the island is shipped. Vessels generally moor on a 7-fathom bank extending from the shore with open hawse to the NE. It is recommended to drop the outer anchor with the S. end of the island of Levera in line with the N. extreme of Grenada, and to place the starboard or inshore anchor to the southeastward, with about 70 fathoms of cable on the outer and 30 fathoms on the inner anchor. The ship will then be about 800 yards from the shore. This anchorage is exposed, and the wind occasionally blows hard from NNE. It is not, however, dangerous in the spring of the year, the holding-ground being good. Drogers and small vessels may take shelter in Levera bay, under the lee of the island of the same name.

Barbados island.—This island was taken possession of by the English in 1605, in whose hands it has since remained.

Notwithstanding its small extent, Barbados presents considerable variety of surface, as valley, hill, table-land, etc. A deep valley, running almost E. from Bridgetown, divides the island into two parts, of which the northern is by much the larger. The general appearance of the island is low and level.

From the W. coast the land rises in successive distinct terraces, interrupted by numerous and deep ravines, to the central ridge; from which, and principally from mount Hillaby, hills of a conical form range in a NE. direction toward the sea; this high land is called Scotland; the hills are rugged and worn by the heavy rains and torrents which pour down their sides. Between the E. and S. points the ground is nearly level, sloping gently to the sea cliffs, while from the E. to the N. point the outline is broken and irregular. In clear weather the highest hills may be seen at a distance of about 40 miles.

The N., W., and S. parts of the island consist of rocks of coralline limestone, with beds of calcareous marl, containing numerous recent shells of various species; the E. is composed of strata of siliceous sandstone, intermixed with ferruginous matter, calcareous sandstone passing into siliceous limestone, different kinds of clay, selenite, earthy marls, frequently containing minute fragments of pumice, strata of volcanic ashes, seams of bitumen, and springs of petroleum. The island has the appearance of a well-kept garden.

The rivers are small except during the rainy season, when they are much increased; the average yearly rain-fall amounts to 58 inches, and the greatest known occurred in October, 1867, when 6 inches fell in four hours. There are several chalybeate springs, containing chiefly iron, carbonic acid, and fixed alkali, in different proportions. Barbados is considered to be one of the healthiest islands in the West Indies, and the climate, though warm, is very salubrious. In the forenoon, the mean temperature during the year is about 80°, and in the afternoon, 82°; the minimum being 75°, and the maximum 87°.

The island is divided into 11 parishes or districts. The population in 1881 was 171,860. The chief staple articles produced in Barbados are sugar, arrowroot, aloes, and cotton.

The government is vested in a governor, who is also governor-in-chief of St. Vincent, Grenada, Tobago, and St. Lucia, an executive council, a legislative council, and a house of assembly. Bridgetown on the SW. side of the island is the seat of government. Barbados is in the International Postal Union.

Northeast coast—From Kitridge point, the E. end of Barbados, the coast, forming a slight indentation, trends about NW. to the N. point, and is formed of rocky cliffs varying from 50 to 800 feet in height, intersected by sandy bays and beaches, which are skirted by a coral reef, always breaking, and which encircles almost the whole island; in this space the reef extends from about a quarter to a half mile from the shore. Conset bay affords shelter for boats, but is difficult of access.

The E. end of the island is about 50 or 60 feet high, and continues flat for about 2 miles inland, when it becomes more elevated. Moncrieffe Hill signal-post is 3 miles W. of the E. point, and stands 521 feet above the level of the sea. At 3 or 4 miles to the NW. the island begins to rise in rugged hills abruptly from the shore, and at 8 miles from the N. end and about midway between the eastern and western sides of the island is Mount Hillaby, the highest peak of the island. The high ridge terminates at Pico Teneriffe, about 4 miles from the N. point of the island, a remarkable hill 269 feet high, which at a distance appears almost detached from the shore.

The **coast** from Pico Teneriffe is composed entirely of low rugged cliffs from 40 to 60 feet in height, and sweeps round the N. end of the island, in a semicircle, to Harrison point on the opposite shore, and between these two points the island is about 4½ miles broad. For the first mile from the N. point inland the ground is level and open, and thence commences to rise gradually to the southward. The reef in this space borders the shore at the distance of about a half mile.

West coast.—From Harrison point to Pelican island the shore is generally low, but a short distance inland it begins to rise in successive distinct terraces, interrupted by ravines toward the central ridge. These terraces may be traced all the way from Bridgetown to near Harrison point, where they terminate in a bold bluff. The shore is slightly indented with sand beaches, the points being fringed by coral reefs, which off Harrison point extend nearly half a mile, and are dangerous.

Speights Town is the most considerable place next to Bridgetown; off it there is anchorage, but the roadstead is not frequented, as it is found more convenient to ship the produce in drogers, or small craft and convey it to the vessels in Carlisle bay.

Holetown, a small village about 4 miles farther to the southward, has also anchorage off it, and the roadstead is used for the same purpose as that of Speights Town.

Pelican shoals.—They are nearly dry, with 5 fathoms water about 200 yards outside them. There are also detached coral patches about 1,200 yards off Spring Garden point, the shoalest of which has 4 fathoms water on it.

Pelican island is a small, low, rocky islet, with a quarantine building, painted black, on it, lying about 300 yards from the shore, within the reef, and with it forms the N. end of Carlisle bay.

Carlisle bay, the principal anchorage, along the shores of which is situated Bridgetown, the capital of Barbados, is an indentation of about half a mile and formed between Pelican island and Needham point.

Bridgetown, the capital, is situated mainly N. of a rivulet in Carlisle bay, but it extends along the shores of the bay for nearly 2 miles. Though irregularly built, it contains several handsome houses and a large square, adorned with a good statue of Nelson. It has a cathedral, which is spacious and plain, its tower scarcely rising above the roof, for fear of hurricanes, for which reason also the churches are without steeples. Besides the churches there are several chapels and 100 schools. A college or grammar school, founded by General Codrington, formerly governor, is pleasantly situated on the eastern side of the island. The town is abundantly supplied with excellent water, led in from Newcastle on the E. coast and an effective system of hydrants is maintained.

Bridgetown has an extensive commerce with the neighboring islands, large amounts of merchandise imported from the United States and Europe being reshipped here for consumption in Tobago, Grenada, St. Lucia, and St. Vincent. Numerous vessels also seeking employment call here for charters and are engaged to load at other islands.

The population is about 19,000.

Supplies.—Coal and provisions can be purchased. Water is delivered on board from tanks at a cost of 72 cents per 100 gallons.

Steamers.—Several lines of steamers from Europe and the United States call regularly.

Telegraph.—The island is in telegraphic communication with the United States, Europe, and the other West India islands.

Hospitals.—There is a general hospital, with accommodations for about 250 patients; a quarantine and a hospital for the insane. The military hospital is only for the use of the garrison. All are well kept.

Pilots are unnecessary; everything is handled by lighters, and labor is cheap.

Boat landing.—It is near the lower bridge over the Constitution River. For official visits the wharf near the adjutant-general's office is used.

Imports are lumber, provisions, petroleum, coal, and general merchandise.

Exports are sugar, molasses, rum, tar.

The authorities to visit are the governor, officer commanding the troops.

Port charges.—Tonnage dues, 54 cents per ton; bond fee, $3; harbor master's pass, $3; harbor police fee, vessels not exceeding 100 tons, $4 each; 100 tons up to 300 tons, $1 extra; over 300 tons, $6.

The United States is represented by a consul and vice-consul.

Oistin bay.—There is anchorage for small vessels in from 5 to 10 fathoms water; clear ground will be found in about 6 fathoms with Christ church N. 11° 15′ E., and Kendal point S. 61° 52′ E. In hauling up for this anchorage take care to give a good berth to the south point. The whole of this shore is flat and low, but at a short distance inland the ground rises somewhat in terraces, and half a mile northward of Christ church attains the height of 180 feet.

From South point the coast trends about NE. to Kitridge point, curving outward a little about midway. The shore is flat, and composed chiefly of bold rocky cliffs from 50 to 60 feet high; in some places, however, the cliffs have been undermined by the sea and fallen in huge masses on the beach beneath. This is the most dangerous part of the island, coral reefs extending almost continuously at from 400 to 600 yards off shore, having 1 to 4 feet water on them, and generally breaking heavily for the whole distance. There is a boat channel inside these shoals.

Cobbler reef extends from abreast New Fall cliff to Kitridge point, with two gaps in the reef, one having 2½ fathoms of water, the other 1¾. Inside of this reef there is 3 and 4 fathoms smooth water. Abreast of Palmetto bay the reef has from 2 to 8 feet of water on it, and the sea breaks heavily even in the finest weather. Eastward of the Cobbler reef, and nearly 1½ miles from the coast, a remarkable coral ridge, with from 7 to 10 fathoms on it, curves and extends to the SW. at nearly a uniform distance off shore till abreast the south point. Between this and the inner reefs there are from 12 to 26 fathoms. To seaward of these reefs the water quickly deepens to the 100-fathom line, which will be found about 2 miles off shore. At spring-tides there are overfalls off the Cobbler and South Point reefs.

Directions.—In approaching Barbadoes from the eastward the latitude of 13° N., which is that of south point, should be attained at a considerable distance to the eastward of the island.

In these latitudes, where the atmosphere is in general so clear and favorable (except in the rainy season), this may be readily accomplished by observing at day-dawn and evening twilight the meridian altitudes of stars N. and S. for latitude, and of others E. and W. for longitude.

If South Point light has been made from the SE. care should be taken not to approach the shore within 3 miles until it bears NE., when a course may be shaped for Needham point.

When approaching Barbadoes from the northward keep if possible well to the eastward of the island in order to pass to windward of it, and having rounded the Cobbler reef at the distance of 3 miles, the coast may be skirted about 2 miles off shore. Should it be sighted in the night from the NE., the light on Ragged point will be the guide, remembering that to clear the Cobbler reef it must not be brought to bear northward of N. 67° 30′ W. till the South Point light is seen.

Should vessels coming from this direction get to leeward and be obliged to pass W. of the island, a berth of about 2 miles should be given to the reef off the NW. point, and the shore must be approached carefully. Soundings extend some short distance outside the reefs, 20 fathoms being found at about half a mile; a depth of not less than 10 fathoms will clear them. Approaching Carlisle bay from the northward, do not haul round Pelican island until the clock tower is in one with the gateway bearing S. 56° 15′ E.

Making Barbadoes from the eastward toward night-fall, it should be borne in mind that the first land seen will be that near Moncrieffe, about 540 feet high, and not the south point of the island, which is more than 300 feet lower (the upper ridge falling abruptly to the lower land), so that vessels steering a careful course to pass the supposed south point at a safe distance have, from this mistake and the increased current on nearing the land, frequently run into danger; the light on Ragged point will now be the guide, as previously stated, for avoiding the Cobbler reef, where the 100-fathom line is only two thirds of a mile off shore.

At night, vessels bound to Carlisle bay from the southward should give the light on South point a berth of at least 2 or 3 miles, and after passing it may haul up about N. 73° W. for the bay, when the red light on Needham point will soon be seen. Keep the lead going in nearing the point, and on hauling up into the bay when the white light is seen, bear in mind that the rocky spit from Needham point is steep-to, the anchoring ground is full of holes, and frequently crowded with vessels.

In approaching the bay from the northward, when the light is seen bring it to bear eastward of S. 50° 37′ E., to clear the shoals off Pelican island.

Currents.—When beating up to Barbadoes from the westward endeavor to keep directly under its lee in order to avoid the current, which generally sets strong to the westward. Sometimes, however, the current varies its direction to NW., and even as far as N., particularly between the island and Tobago, and its rate is chiefly governed by the strength of the wind; in the rainy season it is sometimes scarcely perceptible.

Winds and weather.—January is generally dry at Barbadoes; the breeze sets in early, and it is altogether one of the finest and most healthy months of the year. February partakes of the same character. March and April are the driest months. May is also dry in the early part, but rain sets in toward the end. In June the breeze is light, the clouds are heavy, and thunder and lightning set in with frequent showers. July is most oppressive, the regular trade-wind is interrupted, and breezes frequently prevail from SW. and W.; rain descends in torrents. August and September are very similar, with calms and light airs from the southward. October, toward the middle, becomes drier, and the refreshing trade-winds sets in after thunder-storms. November is still rainy, the winds variable, and not unfrequently from the SW. December has almost daily slight showers, but the month is generally cool, and the trade-wind steady.

ADDENDA.

Havana.—The following regulations for entering the port of Havana at night were published by the captain of the port, December 31, 1887:

Vessels will stop at about 2 miles from the entrance, which can be easily distinguished by the lights on the wharves in the interior of the port. In this situation the vessel will light a signal rocket, and steamers carrying the mail may fire a gun as a demand for a pilot. A similar signal will be made from the office of the captain of the port to announce the departure of the pilot, after which the vessel will proceed slowly in the direction of the port in order to allow the pilot to reach her half way.

The signal from the vessel repeated three times, at intervals of 10 minutes, remaining unanswered from the shore, will mean that there is some danger or obstacle to the entrance of the vessel at that time.

Port Antonio.—Information has been received that the governor of Jamaica has fixed the following rate of fees to be paid as light dues after March 1, 1888, by vessels entering or calling at the harbor of Port Antonio, Jamaica:

Steamers, 1 penny per registered ton, not payable oftener than once in any three months.

Sailing vessels of any tonnage, not being droghers, 16 shillings on each clearance.

Drogers, 2 shillings, not payable oftener than once in any three months.

The above fees shall be paid by all vessels except government vessels and pleasure yachts.

Puerto Juanita.—The harbor of Puerto Juanita is about 20 miles east of the port of Monte Christi. A reef stretching east to west along the entire coast-line, at about 2 to 2½ miles from shore, is pierced at this place by two natural openings, one at the eastern end of the port and the other at the opposite or western end, each opening affording a passage through the reef. Within the reef there is a spacious and tranquil harbor with deep and safe anchorage everywhere. Vessels of from 10 to 12 feet draught may safely approach to within a very short distance from shore. The eastern entrance to the harbor consists of a wide and deep channel, the soundings varying from 8 to 14 fathoms throughout, excepting in mid-channel, at about the center of the passage, where a small sand bank exists at a depth of from 2 to 2½ fathoms with deep water on either side.

Fresh water is unobtainable at this port, but vessels proceeding there can obtain a supply at Monte Christi.

Guadeloupe.—Sainte Anne.—Vessels approaching Sainte Anne, Guadeloupe, intending to make the anchorage should bring Grande Passe buoy (*red*) in line with the east side of the jail and hold this alignment (N. 31° W.) through the pass to the anchorage. The buoy is placed just to the westward of the 5-fathom shoal spot at entrance to the Grande Passe.

At the anchorage the holding ground is very bad. With the wind from SE. a heavy swell sets in. Several vessels in getting under way have gone ashore on the reef to the leeward. Mariners are cautioned accordingly.

INDEX.

A.

	Page.		Page.
Abaco anchorage	35	Alcatraces cays	111
—— cay	23	—— reefs	111
—— custom-house	21	Alcatraz cay	90
—— island	13, 24, 26	Alejandro bay	176
—— light	24, 33	Alert bank	167
Abacou point	185	—— rock	167
Abraham's bay	49	Alexander, fort	193
—— hill	50	Alfred road	59
Abricot's bay	188	—— sound	58, 59
Acculs	178	Algarroba point	205
Acklin island	48, 50	—— reef	216
Acostas hill	99	Algarrobo bank	222
Acul-à-Jeau bay	186	—— point	222
Acul bay	199	Algodon bank	215
—— —— middle channel	200	—— bay	215
Adam islet	319	—— islet	215
Adderly cay	43	—— point	215
Admiralty bay	309	Algodonal point	98
Agabama point	86	Allart bank	222
—— river	86	Allègre point	226
Aguacate, port	124	Allen cays	43
Agua bay	183	Alligator hole	139
Aguada bay	161, 162	—— point	140
Agua de la Estancia	174	—— Pond bay	140
Agua del Rey	170	—— reef	10, 140
Agua Dulce	169	—— —— light-house	11, 12, 66
Aguadilla anchorage	224	Altars Bluffs	74
—— bay	224	Altares point	25
Aguadores river	74	Alta Vela islet	173
Aguila point	168	Alto de Asi	116
Aguilas bay	179	Alto de Juan Danue	117
Aguirre, port	218	Ambia rocks	192
Agujero Azul bay	178	Anamuya river	165
—— Chico	172, 177	Ananas, port	207
—— river	177	Anasco bay	224
Aigrettes point	186, 187	—— river	224
Alacranes cay	101	—— —— anchorage	224
—— pass	101	Anderson cay	29
Albatross bank	127	Andres bay	170

INDEX.

	Page.
Andros island	30
Anegada channel	233
—— island	7, 233, 234
—— —— anchorage	233
—— —— caution	233
—— —— currents	233
—— —— reef	233
—— —— rollers	233, 234
Anegado shoal	228
Angeles castle	69
Anglais bay	186
—— islet	190
—— river	186
Anguilla cay	65
—— island	259
—— —— coast	259
—— —— products	259
Anguille cay	182
Anguillita island	261
Annas bay	300
—— cay	101
—— shoal	317
Annatto bay	149
—— —— directions	149
—— river	151
Anse-à-Veau	190
Anse des Trois Rivières anchorage	208
Anse du Ceron anchorage	298
Anse du Choc bight	304
Anse du Marigot anchorage	208
Antigua	272–279
—— government	273
—— population	273
—— tides	279
Antonio knoll	96
—— point	143
Antonio port	150, 328
Anvil peak	69, 211
Apostles battery	134
—— shoal	104
Aquin bay	181
—— cay	181, 182
Arbalatos point	102
Arcadins anchorage	193
—— cays	192
Arecibo	225
—— consular agent	225
—— population	225
—— port charges	225
Arecito anchorage	225
—— point	225
Arena Gorda	165
Arenas cay	101, 121, 161, 205, 219
—— point	171, 209, 210, 217
Argus bank	18

	Page.
Arroyo anchorage	217
—— bay	216
—— consular agent	217
—— port charges	217
Arroyos anchorage	98, 99
Artibonde bay	194
—— river	194
—— —— anchorage	194
Atalaya mount	224
Athol island	32, 34
—— —— anchorage	35
Atwood's cay	47
Augustina islets	290
Aux Cayes	183
—— consular agent	184
—— east channel	184
—— inner anchorage	184
—— population	184
—— port charges	184
—— provisions	184
—— south channel	184
—— steamers	184
—— trade	184
Avalo point	98
Avarena point	175, 177
Aves islet	290
—— anchorage	290
—— landing	290, 291
—— water	290
Azua	176
—— bay	175, 176
—— consular agent	176
Azufre	205

B.

	Page.
Babaro bay	165
Bacanagua river	107
Bacaye harbor	319
Bacchus point	283
Bacuranao river	107
Baburuco hill	174
Baga point	126
Baggy peak	275
Bahama bank	44, 67
—— currents	6
—— islands, general description	21, 25
—— —— winds	22, 23
—— —— tides	22, 23
—— —— currents	22, 23
—— passage	6
Bahia de Cadiz cay	110, 111
—— —— supplies	111
Bahia Honda	96, 101, 102, 214, 215
—— —— harbor	101, 102

	Page.
Bainet bay	181
Baitiqueri	72
—— river	72
Baja	99
Baja Nuevo	108
Bajas	99
Bajo Grande	122, 123
—— Nuevo	155
Balamina channel	79, 80
Balaudra point	160, 162
Bulandras cays	79
—— channel	78, 79
—— head	162
Baliceaux island	310
Baline reef	311
Ballast ground	141
Ballenatos, los	117
Ballenbonche bay	306
Bamboo cay	29
—— point	40
Banes port	120, 174
—— river	104
Bani port	174
Bank blink	23
Banner reef	154
Banta river	104
Barabona	177
—— harbor	177
Baracoa	124
—— anvil	124
—— authorities	125
—— consular agent	125
—— population	125
—— steamers	125
—— supplies	125
—— telegraph	125
—— winds	125
Baradaires bay	189, 190
Barbadoes island, description, currents	320, 323, 324, 325
Barbara hill	144
Barbers Block hill	293
Barbuda island	271
—— —— anchorage	272
—— —— coast	271, 272
—— —— provisions	272
Barcas channel	78
Barclay point	274
Barco Perdido shoals	160
Barcos channel	78, 97
Bare Bush cays	137, 138
—— reefs	139
Baria, port	119
Barnett's harbor	27
Baro point	200

	Page.
Baron's bluff	249, 251
Barracks reef	141
Barracoa river	104
Barracouta river	164
Barrancas point	212, 213
Barrawally bay	308
Barrel of Beef	207
—— —— islet	303
Barriles passage	212
Barronuevo cape	209, 210
Bas de Saint Anne river	199
Basse Terre	268, 285
—— —— anchorage	268, 269, 285
—— —— coal and provisions	268
—— —— commercial agent	268
—— —— port charges	268
—— —— salutes	268
—— —— telegraph	268, 285
Batabano road	91, 93
Battery point	184
Battle cay	255
Battowia island	310
Bayabibe	168
Bayamo port	78
Bay point	123, 124
—— port	124
—— rock	261
Beata island	171, 177, 178
—— point	175, 178
Bean Séjour mill	302
Beacon shoal	133
Bec à Marsoin point	189
Bedford point	320
Beef island	234, 235
—— —— anchorage	237
Belfast bay	279
Belle point	199
Belle Roche point	180
Bellevue bank	192
—— peak	237
—— rock	192
Bemini custom-house	21
Bequia island	309
Berbina cays	218
Bergautin cay	82
—— port	206
Bermuda islands	54
—— —— general directions	18, 19
—— —— climate	14
—— —— coal	15
—— —— government	14
—— —— hurricanes	15
—— —— pilots	15
—— —— provisions	15
—— —— signal stations	15

	Page.		Page.
Bermuda islands, trade	14	Boccamaw bay	308
Berracos bay	100	Bodden town	156
—— cays	100, 101	Boeuf bay	179
—— point	74	Boiler channel	16
Berry islands	28	Boisjoli point	289, 290
Bertrand heights	240	Boismorice point	317
Beverland house	147	Boma port	125
Biénne, Mount	195	Bonaparte islet	15
Bight, the	237	Bonita point	182
—— settlement	45	Bonito cay	92
Billy point	272	Booby cay	45, 143
Bird cay	45, 253	—— island	270
—— point	45	—— —— ledge	36
—— rock	48, 50, 63	—— rocks	41
—— rock light-house	63	Boon point	277
Bishop shoal	274	Boqueron bay	221
Black river	141	Bottle and Glass rock	308, 309
—— —— anchorage	141	—— —— —— anchorage	308
—— —— port	141	Boulanger rock	265
—— rock point	62, 256	Bourg anchorage	290
—— spring point	140	Bourgos point	298
Blackwoods bush cay	30	Boyan islet	203
Blake islet	274	Boyet point	182, 184
Blanc rock	192	Bracos channel	80
Blanche point	203	Bransby point	271
Blanco cay	87, 91, 101	Brass island	247
—— Zarza cay	85	—— —— anchorage	248
Blewfield's bay	142	—— —— tides	247
—— —— anchorage	142	Brazaletta hill	137–139
—— —— water	142	Brea point	220
Blinders rocks	236	Breeze point	255
Blonde rocks	236	Brelotte point	304
Blossom bank	143	—— shoal	304
—— channel	31	Bridge point	39
Bloody bay	157	Bridgetown, description	320–323
Blower rock	153	Brigot pass	299
Blowing point	260	Brimstone hill	260
—— rock	260	Broa bay	92
Blue mountains	129, 130	Brooks rock	310
Bluff cay	43, 44	Brothers rocks	26, 61, 64
—— point	225	Brown shoal	61
Blunder rocks	246	Brune bank	140
Boca Chica	218	Brunet point	208
—— —— cay	113	Bruquen point	225
—— —— point	178	Buba cay	109
—— Grande	81, 82, 84	Buck island	35, 242, 249, 251
—— Guajaba	117	—— —— anchorage	251
—— de Alcatraces	111	—— —— channel	251
—— —— Caballones	84	—— —— reef	251
—— —— Caravola	115–117	—— —— islet	239
—— —— Caravelos	115, 117	Buckner reef	144
—— —— —— Inflerno	217	Buena Esperanza	78, 79
—— —— —— Lanzanillo	112	—— —— bank	80
—— —— —— Marvillas	111	—— Vista bank	98
Bocadde reef	111	—— —— cay	98, 99

INDEX.

	Page.
Buena Vista mount	113
—— —— pass	95
—— —— river	95
Buff bay	149
—— —— anchorage	149
Bull point	145
—— shoals	8
Bullet rock	310
Bullock harbor	20
Buren rock	124
Burgado port	168
Burgado cay	82, 84
Burgados bay	178
Burgeaux rocks	303
Burgos point	185, 187
Burnt ship point	141
Bush cay	44, 94
—— reef	135
Busu mountain	174
Byham, Fort	278

C.

	Page.
Caballo Bahia anchorage	167
—— —— supplies	167
—— Blanco shoal	258
—— Colorado point	258
Caballones bay	88
—— cay	82
—— channel	81
Caballas hills	95
Caballos port	205
Cabanas	102
—— harbor	102
Cabañas point	122
Caburet point	206, 207
—— port	207
Cabeza de Toro	165
Cabezote Barlovento islet	165
—— Sotavento	165
Cabonico port	121
Cabo Rojo port	221
Cabra cay	204
—— anchorage	204
Cabras islands	226
—— islet	214, 221
Cabrestante bank	101
Cabrietta point	139
Cabrillon point	219
Cubrit island	299
—— islet	289, 290
Cabrita island	148, 149
Cabritas island	226
Cabrito point	240
Cabron cape	204

	Page.
Cabron cape mount	208
Cochacron promontory	282
Cacimba point	77, 78
Cactus cay	212, 257
—— reef	215
Cade bay	275
—— reef	275
Cadena point	224
Cades bay	270
Caibarien	110–115
—— exports	115
—— imports	114
—— pilotage	113, 114
—— water	115
Caicos bank	53
—— group	51
—— islands	53, 57
Caigo á no Caigo point	209
Caimanera point	78
Caiman cay	115
Caimito	92
Cajon point	96, 97, 101
Calapatch Mehagan reef	94
Caldera	175
—— bay	174
—— —— caution	175
—— —— tides	175
—— —— water	175
—— point	174, 175
Caleta, La, anchorage	70
—— bay	170
—— beach	70
—— point	70, 72, 207
—— ravine	69
Caletilla ravine	69
Caleton port	168
California bank	137
Caliveney harbor	319
—— island	318, 319
Camacho landing	109
Camaricoa river	109
Camel's hump	148
Cana anchorage	99
Canandaigua bank	160
Cananova port	121
Canasi river	107
Candelaria mount	119
Candeleros point	216
Cañete bay	123
Caney point	85, 86
Cane Garden bay	239
Canimar river	103
Cannouan island	310
Canones point	120
Cantilla cay	94

	Page.
Canto river	28
Cannelo islands	226
Caoba bay	71
Cape Bajo	74
Cape Canaveral	8, 12
—— anchorage	8
—— Comete	51
—— Corrientes	95
—— Cruz	64, 75, 76, 77, 78, 80, 81
—— —— reef	77
—— Engaño	7
—— Florida	10
—— Haiti anchorage	201
—— —— reef	201
—— —— coal	201
—— —— consul	201
—— —— harbor	202
—— —— winds	202
—— —— port charges	201
—— —— provisions	201
—— —— steamer	201
—— —— town, trade	200, 201
—— —— water	201
Cape Maysi	64
—— Ronge bay	198
—— river	198
—— San Antonio	95, 96, 106
Capesterre	289
—— point	284, 285
Capitan river	164
Caracoles anchorage	175
—— river	175
Caracoli channel	300
—— point	300, 301
Caragan point	122
Carahattas town	112
Caravela Chica point	97
Caravela, Boca de	117
Caravelle peninsula	299-302
—— rock	300
Carcasses bay	187
—— point	187
Carcovado point	221
Cardenas	110
—— anchorage	109
—— bay	109
—— coal	110
—— consular agent	110
—— pilots	110
—— steamers	110
—— supplies, trade	110
Cardones island	219
Careening cay	138
Carénage	297, 298
—— bay	313, 317

	Page.
Carénage point	190
Carenero cay	80, 112, 113, 161, 162
—— coal	161
—— point	102, 218, 219
—— reef	113
Carib point	294
Caribbean sea	2, 7, 51
Carlisle bay	139, 322
Carlit island	253
Carmichael point	59
Carolina port	239
Carriacou island	312-314
Carval rock	236, 240, 246
Carysfort reef light-house	11, 12
Casa river	94
Casas hills	95
Cascajal reef	88
Cascajo bank	94
Casco de Sau Vicente	119
Cusigua cays	107
Casilda harbor	86, 88
—— point	86
Cassada rocks	315
Castillo point	162
Castle island	48, 50, 60
—— rock	27
—— Bruce estate	294
Castries town	304
—— —— authorities, salutes	305
—— —— coal	304
—— —— directions	305
—— —— harbor improvements	304
—— —— hospital	305
—— —— port charges	305
—— —— signal station	304
—— —— steamers, mail	304
—— —— telegraph	305
—— —— water	304
—— —— wharves	304
—— —— winds	305
Cat cays	27
—— island	45
Catalina bay	174
—— island	168
—— —— anchorage	169
—— —— point	174
Catalinita island	166, 167
Catholic islets and rocks	310, 311
Catuano pass	167
Caucedo point	170
Cay Breton	83
—— Grande	82
—— Piedras	67
Cayemites bay	189
—— island	189

INDEX.

	Page.
Cayes bay	183, 185
—— —— tides	185
—— —— winds	185
Cayito reef	219
Cayman bank	157
—— Brac caution	157
—— —— island	157
Cayo Blanco	87, 91
—— de Carenas	89, 90, 91
—— Grande	122
—— Moa anchorage	121
—— —— port	121
Cayos de Moa	121
Cay Sal bank	66
Cazones bay	91, 92
—— gulf	92, 93
Cebollas port	121
Cerro Gordo mountain	174, 220
—— Montuso peak	222
Chalupa cay	109
Champigny bank	303
Chameau mount	289
Channel cay	42
—— rock	23, 24
Chardon islet	301, 307
Charles fort	270
—— —— anchorage	270
Charlestown	270
—— bay	310
Charlotte Amalia	241
—— —— coal	241
—— —— consul	242
—— —— dock	241
—— —— hospitals	242
—— —— pilots	242
—— —— population	241
—— —— port charges	242
—— —— provisions	241
—— —— steamers	242
Charlotte fort	237
Charlottetown	292, 316
Chateau Belair	309
Chateaudin road	183, 184
—— —— anchorage	184
Chateaux point	289
Châtelain mount	195
Châtenay mount	105
Chatham bay	312
—— —— supplies	312
Cheerio sound	23
Cheltenham	310
Chico cay	162, 163
—— shoals	162
Chinchilline cay	111
Chinchorro shoals	214

	Page.
Choiseul village	307
—— —— anchorage	307
—— —— water and wood	307
Chorrero harbor	104
Chouchou bay	199
Christ church	34
Christal, Sierras del	120, 121
Christiansted harbor	249
—— —— east channel	249
—— —— coal	250
—— —— consular agent	250
—— —— directions	250
—— —— hospital	250
—— —— pilots	249, 250
—— —— population	249, 250
—— —— port charges	250
—— —— provisions	249, 250
—— —— trade	250
Christo cay	111
Club cays	30
Ciego point	86
Cienfuegos	89
—— coal	89
—— harbor	89, 91
—— mails	90
—— pilots	90
—— population	89
—— port charges	90
—— provisions	90
—— steamers	90
—— telegraph	90
—— water	90
Cinco Bolas cays	83
Ciudado reef	60
Cirioles point	89
Cistern cay	29
—— point	313
Clara bay	161
Clarence harbor	41
—— settlement	41
Clarion shoal	60
Clarkes Court bay	318
—— —— —— directions	319
Clifton bluff	31, 35
—— cove	312
Clyde line steamers	54
Coakley Bay mill	251
Coamo bay	218
—— point	218
—— river	218
Cobbler reef	323
Cobos cay	113, 115
Cobre mountain	69, 74
Cochons island	283, 284
Coche islet	290

INDEX.

	Page.
Cochinos	63
—— bay	91
Cochrane anchorage	34, 36
Cockburn harbor anchorage	52
—— —— buoys	52
—— —— pilot	52
Cockroach island	248
—— rock	258
Coco cay	113, 115, 117
Cocoa point	162
Coq-Vieille reef	200, 202
Coiba cay	80
Cojimar river	107
Colibris point	258
Cobé du Lamentin inlet anchorage	208
Colison point	234
Colombier bay	206
Colorado point	77
Colorados point	79, 90
—— reefs	96, 97, 101, 106
Colquhoun reef	235
Columbus point	45
Conception island	45, 50
Confites cay	115, 116
—— —— anchorage	116
Congo cay	240, 246
—— —— tides	246
Conset bay	321
Cook shoal	276
Cooper island	236
—— rocks	236
Coral bay	239, 240
—— —— tides	240
—— harbor	239
Corcho point	216
Cordilleras	212
Coronas banks	224
Corozos point	163
Corridon point	195
Corrora shoal	258
Cortis lagoon	93
Coteaux bay	186
Cotton cay	55
Cotton Field point	46
Cotuy town	164
Conch cay	42
—— cut	43
—— reef	12, 43
—— rock	35
Couronne hill	213
Cove cay	52
Cow and Bull rocks	39
Cow and Calf rocks	245
—— Bay point	131, 133
Cowell cay	246

	Page.
Crab island	214, 257
Crawl bay	239
Cray fish bay	316
Creek point	49
—— pond	134
Cricket rock	248
Cristobal point	91
Crocus bay	259, 260
—— —— anchorage	260
—— —— consular agent	260
—— —— current	261
—— —— direction	260
—— —— supplies	260
Crole rock	264
Crooked island	48, 49
—— —— anchorage	49
—— —— group	48
—— —— passage	50, 60, 63
Cross cay	256
Cruces anchorage	117
Cuarto Reales channel	80, 81
Cuba	1, 50, 67
—— climate	68
—— currents	95
—— earthquakes	68
—— fevers	68
—— hurricanes	68
—— population	68
—— temporary anchorage	96
—— winds	1
Cubagan river	89
Cucarachas rock	212
Cucharros point	218
Cudjoe hill	138, 139
Cueva de Jauco	69
—— fort	124
—— point	212, 213
Cuevita point	166
—— —— tides	166
Cul de Sac Marin	208
Culebra island	213, 253
—— —— tides	254, 257
Culebrita island	253
—— —— anchorage	253
Cumayazo river	169
Cumberland point	309
Cunard line steamers	54
Cupid cay	40
Current islands	37, 38
——, Jamaica, north coast	152
——, passage and hole	247
——, Pedro bank	155
—— rock	247
Currents, Cape Maysi to Baracoa	126
——, general remarks on	6

INDEX.

	Page.
Curtain bluff	275
Cutlass point	140

D.

	Page.
Damassin bay	186
Dame Marie bay	188
—— cape	188
Darvill spit	62, 63
David point	316
Davy cay	253
Dead Chest island	218, 236
De Caille islet anchorage	315, 316
Deep bay	269
Delaport bay	32
Denmark bank	218
Derrumbadero	186
Desecheo island	210, 222
Desirade island	284, 287
—— —— water	287
—— —— currents	288
Devil peak	193
—— point	193, 194
Diablo bay	185
—— mount	160
Diablotin mount	293, 294
Diamante de Afuera shoal	75
Diamond bank	278
—— hill	208
—— island	181, 183
—— point	64, 67, 183, 184
—— rock	184
Diana bank	50
—— cay	109
Diavalo point	258
Diego cay	101
—— Perez cay	91, 92
Difuntos point	101, 102
Dios cays	101
Dittless point	240
Doce Leguas cays	80, 81, 84
Doctor reef	141
Dog channel	261
—— island	261
—— islands	234, 247
—— rock	240
—— rocks	43, 66
Dollar harbor	27
Dolphin head	94, 143, 254
Dominica island	291, 292
—— —— caution	292
—— —— climate	291
—— —— coast	294
—— —— government	291
—— —— supplies	292

	Page.
Dominica tides	292
Don Juan Tomas cay	102
Dorée river	306
Double-head Shot cays	65, 66
Douglas bay	294
—— channel	36, 40
—— road	34
Dow hill	275
Dowling rock	260
—— shoal	260
Drick bay	186
Drowned island	233
—— —— currents	233
Drunkenman's cay	135, 136
Dry harbor	147
—— —— anchorage	147
—— —— directions	147
—— —— provisions	147
—— Shingle bank	94
Dry Tortugas	7, 9, 67
—— anchorage	11
Duaba point	124
Duck point	254
Dunbar shoals	55
Dunmore point	40
Du Quesne bay	316
Dutchman's cap	248
Durloe cays	240, 246
Duvernette isle	308

E.

	Page.
Eagle mount	251
—— shoal	239
Earthquakes	7
East Cabris hill	293
—— Caicos island	51, 54
—— cay	54, 57, 183, 184, 261
Eastern channel	80
East Guano cay	93
—— harbor	39
—— Middle ground	132
—— —— shoal	135
—— reef	183
Edgecombe mount	111
Edward shoal	160
Egg Island reef	33, 38
—— reef	311, 312
Egmont point	319
—— port	319
Elbow bank	29
—— cay	13, 23
—— light	66, 67
—— reef	24
—— cay	24
Eleuthera	33

1018—No. 85——22

	Page.		Page.
Eleuthera custom-house	21	Falnch passage	221
—— island	39, 40, 45	Fanduco cay	221
Elies harbor	16	Fantasque point	189
Embarcadero del Mangle	86	Ferdinando de Xagua	89
Embarcaderos point	227	Feret bay	183
Endymion rock	56	Ferro harbor	257
Engaño cape	164, 165	Figuera point	216
English bay	181	Fincastle, fort	33
—— harbor	274	Finley cay	40
—— —— coal	274	Fisga point	93
—— —— directions	274	Fisherman bay	131
—— —— supplies	274	—— point	9
Enllabado cay	99	Fish bay	240
Escocesa bay	207	—— cay	245
Escondida	208	—— cays	29, 48
—— point	161	Five-fathoms hole	17
——, port	73, 176	—— —— anchorage	18
—— —— anchorage	176	—— island harbor	276
—— —— directions	176	Flag point	147
—— river	107	—— Hill peak	244
Espada point	165, 166	Flamand bay	182, 183
Espagnol bay	187	Flamand's roads	297, 298
Estancia Colorado	171	Flamenco cay	92
Estudios bank	170	Flanagan island	236
—— —— anchorage	170	—— pass	237
Etron du Porc	184	Flat Cap point	260
Eustatia island	233	—— cay	47, 244
Exuma custom-house	21	—— island	264
—— harbor	42	—— Top peak	275
—— island	61	Fleming channel	35, 40
—— sound	40	Fleur d' Epée, fort	283
F.		Flirt rocks	262
Fabrica cay	92	Florida cays	8
Fajardo, port	212	—— channel	65
—— —— consular agent	213	—— reefs	11, 13
—— —— directions	213	—— strait	7, 8, 13, 106
—— —— middle channel	213	—— stream	25
—— —— pilots	212	Flowery rocks	10
—— —— population	212	Folleurs rock	192
—— —— port charges	212	Folly point	150
—— —— southern channel	213	Fond la Grange bay	199
—— —— trade	212	Fork mountain	260
Fajou isle	286	Formigas bank	127
Falcones cays	111	Fort Alexander	193
Fallen Jerusalem cay	234, 236	—— anchorage	52
Falmouth	115	—— Barbara	182
—— harbor	145, 274	—— Bizothon	191
—— consular agent	146	—— Burt point	238
—— current	146	—— cay	52
—— directions	146, 274	—— Charles	135, 136
—— quarantine	146	—— Charlotte	33
—— supplies	146	—— Dauphin bay	203
—— peak	275	—— de France	297
False cape	166, 178, 188	—— —— bay	295
—— Diamond rock	181	—— —— anchorage	297

INDEX.

	Page.
Fort de France dock	295
—— water	294
—— Fincastle	33
—— George flagstaff	317
—— —— point	317, 318
—— Henrietta	5*
—— islet	191, 193
—— Jefferson	10, 11
—— Jendy point	311
—— Montagne	31
—— Rodney	303
—— Royal	301
—— —— bay	297
—— St. Catherine	17
—— —— George	17
—— —— Louis	297
—— Victoria	17
—— Young	293
Fortune island	49, 50
Fota islet	311
Fou cape	136
Fourche island	263, 265
—— anchorage	265
Four-fathom bank	274
Fourreur islet	304
Fowey rock light	12
Fraile cay	201
—— rock	178
—— currents	178
Frances bay	160
—— cay	113
—— —— anchorage	113, 115
—— point	94
—— port	94
Francis bay	241
François	299
—— anchorage	301
Frederik knoll	243
Frederichsted	252
—— coal	252
—— consular agent	253
—— directions	252
—— hospitals	252
—— population	252
—— port charges	253
—— provisions	252
—— telegraph	253
Free point	149
Fregate anchorage	301
—— cove	301
—— de Haut island	285
Fregatte island	266
French cay	53
Frenchman's bay	140
—— cap	212

	Page.
Frenchman's cay	238
French wells	49
Friar's cap	142
Friendship bay	209
Frigate channel	314
—— islet	312, 314
Frios cays	218
Fry's bay	276
Fungy Bowl	256

G.

	Page.
Galafre river	93
Galatea rock	131
Galera pass	99, 101
Galeras port	203
Galion	299
—— bay	300
—— pilots	300
Gallardo bank	224
Galliot cut	43
Galveston	10
Garanacha bay	98
Garden key light	11
Gaspar point	26
Gatas cays	219
Gauche river	180
George island	38, 235
Georgia river	144
Geronimo point	98
Gibb's hill	18
Gibara	119
—— bay	119
—— coast pilots	119
—— consular agent	119
—— river	119
——, Saddle of	118, 119
Gibraltar wharf	119
Ginger island	236
Gingerbread ground	27
Glass window	39
Glover island	319
Goat cay	25, 29
—— Head	275
—— —— channel	275
—— island	138, 139, 266
—— point	318
Golding cay	31
Gomere bank	161, 162
Gonaïves	195
—— bay	194
Gonave bank	191
—— channel	190
—— island	190, 191
Goodwill plantation	292

	Page.
Gorda cay	26
—— channel	91
—— point	103, 161, 162
Government hill	52
Governor harbor	40
Goyave bay	316
Gozier island	282, 284
Grampus shoals	255
Gran Boucand point	200
Granchora	166
—— anchorage	166
Grand Anse bay	317, 318
—— —— du Diamant bay	295, 298
—— —— —— anchorage	298
—— Bacolet	316
—— bay	294, 310–313
—— Anse d'Arlet bay	298
—— Caicos island	51
—— Caiman island	81, 156
—— —— anchorage	156, 157
—— —— caution	156
—— Case bay	264
—— cay	24
—— Cul-de-sac Marin	246
—— —— —— —— anchorage	305
—— —— —— —— bay	305
—— —— —— —— river	305
—— Goave bay	190
—— Gosiers bay	179
—— islet	200
—— Mal bay	316
—— Mouton shoal	202
—— Savanna	293
—— —— anchorage	293
—— —— supplies	293
—— Pauvre bay	316
—— point	198
—— port	257
—— reef	189
—— Turk island	53
—— —— anchorage	54
—— —— pilots	54
—— —— trade	54
Grande Anse	288
—— bay	263, 283
—— Coulée channel	286
—— Estero Colorado	207
—— pass	282, 287
—— Passe	282, 328
—— Pierre bay	194
—— point	187
—— Terre	280
—— Vigie point	287
Grange point	203
Granja shoals	204

	Page.
Grass cay	240
Grassy bay	16, 18
—— anchorage	17
Gravois point	185
Gray's Inn wharf	149
Great Abaco island	23
—— —— anchorage	23
—— Bahama bank	13, 27, 66
—— Bird island	278
—— Camanoe island	235
—— Carenero cay	162
—— Cay a l'Eau	184
—— —— channel	290
—— Cayemites island	189
—— Cruz bay	240
—— Egg island	33, 38
—— Exuma	41–43
—— Grouper island	265
—— —— reef	265
—— harbor	23, 236, 245, 253, 255
—— —— cay	29
—— Inagua island	50, 57, 60
—— Isaacs light-house	13
—— —— rock	26, 27
—— islet	215
—— Krum bay	214
—— Lameshur bay	240
—— Marigot bay	198
—— North Side bay	244
—— Piñero island	214
—— Piton point	306
—— Ragged island	61, 62
—— —— beacon	61
—— reef	183, 184
—— river	144
—— —— directions	144
—— St. James island	245, 247
—— Stirrup cay	28
—— Thatch island	238, 239
—— —— tides	239
—— Tobago island	246
Green bay	135
—— cay	31, 46, 245, 249
—— —— anchorage	36
—— island	273, 278, 320
—— —— harbor	143
—— Turtle cay	24
Gregerie channel	243
Grenada island	309, 315
—— coasts	319
—— currents	7, 315
—— government	315
—— winds	316
Grenadines, the	309
—— currents	315

INDEX.

	Page.
Grenadines, tides	315
Grenville	319
—— bay	316, 319, 320
—— caution	319
Gris Gris point	246
Gros-Cap point	303
—— island	303, 305
—— —— bay	303, 304
Grosse cay	181, 182
—— pointe	207
Grotte rock	301
Grouper shoal	255
Gua cays	74, 79
—— point	78
Guadeloupe island	279–287
—— —— climate	281
—— —— earthquakes	7, 282
—— —— mails	280
—— —— north coast	280
—— —— population	279
—— —— telegraph	282
—— —— west coast	285
—— —— —— currents	286
—— —— —— winds	286
—— —— winds	281, 282
—— reef	222
Guadiana bay	98
—— point	98
—— river	98
Guajaba river	116
—— island	117
Guajabana, mount	113
Guajaibon river	104
Guana bay	279
—— island	279
Guanabo river	107, 164
Guane	98
Guane Guamas river	98
Guanaja	117
—— river	117
Guanajivo point	222, 223
Guanayara river	89
Guanica	220
—— directions	220
Guanico point	121
Guanima river	92
Guaniquilla point	224
—— shoal	224
Guano islet	235
Guanos point	72, 107
Guantanamo	73
—— river	73
Guarabo river	88, 89
—— —— anchorage	89
Guaraguao	167

	Page.
Guarda-Rays point	71
—— de Yacabo cove	71
Guardawaya river	216
Guanrabo point	86
—— river	86
Guayaibon river	104
Guayacanes	166
—— anchorage	170
Guayama	217
—— reef	216
Guayanilla bay	220
—— point	220
—— river	220
Guayos cay	88
Guijano	221
Guillermo cay	115
Guinchos cay	64, 65, 67
Gulf stream	3, 7, 9, 11–14, 66, 106
Gun cay	132–134
—— light	26, 27
Gustaf	266
—— harbor	266
—— port charges	266
—— trade	266
Gustavia	266

H.

	Page.
Hache island	255
Haines cay	29
Haiti, currents	6, 7
Half-moon bay	136
—— —— cay	137
—— —— (southern)	139
Halifax	316
—— steamer	14, 54
Halle point	194
Hamilton	13
—— harbor	16, 18
—— island	14
Hammock rock	118
Ham's bluff	249
Hans-Lollik	246
Harbor island	21, 38, 39
—— point	41, 240, 255
Hardy bay	318
Harrison point	321
Hat island	264
Haut du Cap	201
—— fonds	204
Hanlover point	51
Havana	7, 8, 10, 11, 12, 68, 103, 327
—— docks	105
—— fevers	104
—— hospitals	105

INDEX.

	Page.
Havana, imports and exports	105
—— pilotage	105
—— population	104
—— provisions	105
Hawk's Nest	55
—— —— sand-spit	45
Hayti	158
—— minerals	158
—— mountains	158
—— port charges	159, 160
—— ports of entry	159
—— rivers	158
—— weather	159
Healthshire hammock	136
Hen and Chickens islets	26
Henne bay	195
—— point	195
Henry bank	27
Hermanos passage	212
—— rocks	212
Hermitano, Le	205
Herradura cays	113
Herrero river	227
Hetzel shoal	8
Hidden harbor	73
High cay	30
Highborn cay	43
—— cut	43
Highbreaker rock	256
Hillaby mount	320, 321
Hillsboro inlet	12
Hillsborough bay	313
—— village	313
Hobson breaker	61, 63
Hodgo point	278
Hog cay	62
—— fish cut	16
—— island	31, 33, 34, 318, 319
Hogsnest point	240
Hogsty reef	60
Hole-in-the-wall	13, 23, 35
Hole town	322
Holguin	119, 120
Hominaji point	171
Hondo river	89
Hook sand	36
Hope bay	150
Horseshoe channel	273
—— reef	167, 311
Hospital bay	188, 195
Hotte, mountain, La	178, 187
Hueros cays	79
Humacno port	216
—— port charges	216
—— river	216

	Page.
Hunt bay	141
Hurricane hill	270
—— hole	31, 329
Hurricanes	2
—— frequency of	2
—— indications of	2

I.

Ibard point	187, 188
Icacos bay	216
—— cay	216
—— point	109, 110, 216
—— rocks	212
Icague bay	199
—— point	198
Iguanojo point	86
—— river	86
Ilet, river, Le	184
Inis anchorage	71
—— beach	71
—— river	71
Inagua custom-house	21
Indian cays	25, 91, 94, 95
—— creek	273
—— group	91
—— river	8, 94, 294
—— rocks	237
Indio passage	221
Industry tree	43
Inez de Soto cay	100
Ingles point	77
Ingleses point	99
Inner Barracks reefs	141
—— Brass island	247
—— las Manchas	222
Invisible rocks	235
Ireland island	14, 16, 18
—— —— dock-yard	14
Irois	187
—— point	187
Iron mountains	104, 106
Irvin's bay	320
Isaac shoal	11
Isabelle bay	205
—— cape	203, 204
—— de Torres	205
Isle of Pines	91, 93, 94, 95
Isleta cay	169
Islets, the	178

J.

Jaba point	72
Jacagua port	218
Jack-a-Dan isle	313
Jackson port	207
Jack Taylor reef	93

	Page.
Jacmel	180
—— bay	180
—— —— anchorage	180
—— coal	180
—— consular agent	181
—— pilots	180
—— population	180
—— port charges	181
—— steamers	180
—— trade	180
Jagney point	100
Jaimanita river	164
Jaina river	173
Jaitecoco hill	124
Jamaica	50, 53, 74, 127, 152
—— bay	48
—— climate	129
—— currents	6
—— description	129
—— earthquakes	129
—— hurricanes	129
—— N. coast currents	152
—— N. coast winds	144
—— NE. end	151
—— population	129
—— towns	129
—— trade	129
—— winds	1
James cistern	40
—— fort	277
—— hill	59
—— point	39
Jaragua	123
—— point	123
Jardine cays	93
Jardinillos bank	91, 92
Jarro point	119
Jaruco river	107
Jarry mill	234
Jatibonico river	82, 84, 85, 92
Janco ravine	69
—— river	69, 70
Jaula cay	117
Jayan river	164
Jeremie bay	188
—— consular agent	189
—— point	188
—— population	189
—— steamers	189
Jibacoa river	107
Jicaco islet	164
—— point	164
Jicaquito bay	204, 205
Jiguero point	222, 323, 324
Joa bay	73

	Page.
Jobabo	87
—— bay	88
—— point	84
Jobos port	217
Johnson reef	240
Jojo bay	70, 71
—— point	70, 71
—— river	70
Jost Van Dyke island	231, 240, 245
Joulter cays	31
Juan d'Olio	170
—— Louis cays	91, 92
—— Rabel bay	197
—— Saez hill	116
Judge bay	278
Juif bay	186
Julia cape	209
Jumintos	62
Juniper hole	51
Jupiter inlet	8, 12
Jururu, Puerto de	119
Jutias cay	99, 100
—— pass	100

K.

	Page.
Kahouanne islet	246
Kansas reef	181
Kelly house	130, 131
Kendal point	323
Kettle Bottom shoals	278
Key Biscayne	10
—— West	12, 13
—— —— entrance channel	10
—— —— harbor	10
—— —— northwest passage	10
King rock	246
Kingston (Jamaica)	54, 133, 134
—— coal	133
—— consulate	134
—— directions	136
—— east channel	134
—— harbor	133
—— —— tides	136
—— pilots	134
—— population	133
—— port charges	134
—— quarantine	133
—— repairs	134
—— south channel	135
—— steamers	134
—— supplies	133
—— telegraph	134
—— turning marks	134
—— (Tortola)	238
—— anchorage	238

	Page.
Kingston, directions	238
Kingstown	307
—— anchorage	307
—— authorities	308
—— bay	307
—— coal	308
—— hospital	308
—— population	308
—— port charges	308
—— salutes	308
—— steamers	308
—— supplies	308
—— telegraph	308
Kitridge point	321, 323
Knoll point	243
Knox wharf	147
Kurca reef	167

L.

	Page.
Ladder landing	267
—— point	266
Lagoon hill	59
Lamentin point	192, 193
Landrail point	49
—— anchorage	49
—— rock	38
Lang bank	251
Lanzanillo anchorage	112
—— cays	112
Larague reef	189
Large islet	314
Largo banks	213, 214
—— cay	93
Lark bank	238
—— channel	31
—— point	41
Latanier's point	183
Lateriana river	208
Lavandera islets	213, 214
—— point	100
Lavanderas ledge	65
—— reef	64
Layon river	293
—— anchorage	293
—— valley	292
L'Ecu, port-à	197
Lee Stocking island	43
Legare anchorage	10
Leinster bay	241
Lena cay	97
Leogone	191
—— point	190
Leonard's hill	275
Levantado cay	161
Levantados reef	162

	Page.
Levera bay	320
—— island	316, 320
Leviza cay	101
—— pass	101
Lignum Vitæ cay	29
Ligro point	195
Ligna port	124
Liguanea mount	136
Lima bank	215
—— point	215
Limbé channel	199
—— island	199
—— anchorage	199
—— point	199
Lime cay	132, 134
Limlair bay	313
Limon port	208
Limonade bay	203
Limones cay	78
—— point	79
—— river	78
—— shoal	79
Lirio point	161
Little Ambergris cay	53
—— Bahama banks	13, 23, 24
—— —— current	22
—— —— tides	25, 26
—— Caicos island	51
—— Camanoe island	235
—— Cayemetes island	189
—— Cayman	157
—— Cruz bay	240
—— —— anchorage	240
—— —— direction	240
—— Egg island	38
—— Exuma	41, 43
—— Grouper islets	265
—— Guano cay	23
—— Hans-Lollik	246
—— harbor	236, 245
—— —— cay	23
—— Inagua island	60
—— Jost Van Dyke	245
—— Martinique	314
—— —— anchorage	314
—— —— caution	314
—— Marigot bay	198
—— Mushroom	315
—— Pedro point	140
—— Piñero island	214
—— Piton	306
—— Port Français	200
—— Ragged island	61, 64
—— —— anchorage	61
—— St. James island	247

INDEX.

	Page.
Little St. Vincent	314
—— Thatch island	238
—— Tobago	314
—— island	346
—— Wickham cay	239
Liverpool shoals	203
Livisa, port	121
Lizard rock	243
Llana cay	52
—— point	70
Lobos cay	65, 67
Locos cape	106
Loggerhead key	11
Loiza river	227
Loma de Banao mountains	85, 86, 87
London Bridge rocks	316
Long Acre point	141
—— banks	30
—— bay	143, 151
—— cay	32, 48, 52, 63
—— —— anchorage	53
—— —— custom-house	21
—— island	138, 278
—— —— custom-house	21, 41
—— point	252, 318
—— —— anchorage	318
—— —— shoal	318
Long's wharf	138
Lorton rock	38
Louisa Augusta, fort	249
Loup de Ste. Marie	302
—— Ministre	302
Lovango cay	246
Low cay	155
—— —— anchorage	156
—— —— shoals	155
Lower White Horses	195
Luana point	141
Lucea point	144
Luquillo	227
—— mountains	211

M.

Macaguanigua river	125
Macao point	105
Machos de Fuera cay	83, 86
Mackie bank buoy	29
Macoris, consular agent	170
—— point	207
—— port	169
—— river	169
—— —— caution	170
Macouba point	302
Madame river	207
Magdelina point	170
Magua river	164

	Page.
Maguina landing	104
Mahault bay	286, 288
Maho point	184, 185
Maiden cay	132
—— island	276
—— rock	132, 135
Majagua point	220
Majana bay	92, 93
Mala Pass anchorage	177
—— Pascua cape	216, 217
Malagueta	118
Malanilla shoal	25
Malano point	23
Malcolm bay	141
—— point	141
—— road	52
Maldonado point	227
Maleo island	241
Mamelles, the	280
Mammee bay	143
Mamora bay	273
Man island	39
Man-of-War anchorage	54
—— bay	54
—— cay	24, 42, 63, 257
—— channel	63, 64
—— point	273
Managua papa	104
Manati, mesa de	118
—— point	85, 118, 164
Mancha de Tierra	222
Manchioneal harbor	151, 152
—— —— anchorage	152
—— —— caution	152
—— —— supplies	152
Manel	67
Mangle Prieto point	82
—— point	120
Mangles cay	97, 109
—— group	91, 95
—— point	91, 93, 102, 104
Mangrove harbor	255
Mauroux island	244
Mantua	98, 99
Manueco, El	118
Manuel Goumez cays	82
Manzanillo	78
—— bay	79, 203
—— cays	78, 79
—— point	203
Maravi port	124
—— —— supplies	124
Marca de Limones	78
Marchas de Fuera cay	85, 87
Marechaux cape	180

	Page.		Page.
Maria Aguila point	78, 89	Matanzas port	108
—— port	148, 149	—— provisions	108
—— —— anchorage	149	—— railroad	107
—— —— directions	148	—— water	108
—— —— pilots	149	Mate cays	81
—— —— quarantine	149	—— channel	81
—— —— supplies	149	Maternillos light-house	67
Marias point	149	—— point	110, 117
Marie Galante	288	Mathew Town road	58
Mariel port	103, 104	Maya point	107, 109
—— table	103	Mayabeque river	92
—— table-land	102	Mayaguez	223
Marigot	264	—— bay	222, 223
—— bay	264	—— hospitals	223
—— harbor	305	—— officials	223
—— point	199	—— population	223
Marin point	299	—— port charges	223
—— village	299	—— provisions	223
Marina cay	235	—— river	222
Marinavo bay	118	—— steamer	223
Mariguana island	50	—— trade	223
Market fish cay	29	Mayero island	310, 311
Mavors bill	41	—— —— anchorage	311
Marquesas keys	10	Maymon river	165
Martin Garcia point	176	Maysi cape	126
Martinique	292	—— reef	126
—— caution	299	—— —— caution	126
—— currents	291	Mead point	260
—— island	295	Medano	111
—— —— authorities	297	Medanos de Manati cays	83
—— —— climate	295	Media Luna cays	80, 115, 223
—— —— government	295	—— —— reef	216
—— —— hospital	297	Medina islet	111
—— —— port charges	297	Meeren cay	240
—— —— salutes	297	Mella bank	182
—— —— steamers	297	Melones point	221
—— —— telegraph	297	Memory rock	25
—— —— U. S. consulate	297	Mercurias rock	246
—— —— water	297	Meseta point	220
Mary cays	52	Mesto bay	182
—— point	241	Michelle point	292
Music harbor	86	Middle cay	153, 154
—— port	88	—— —— anchorage	154
Mata port	125, 126	—— ground	30, 37, 40, 44
—— —— supplies	126	—— passage	221
Matainsa port	220	—— point	58, 319
Matanzas	8, 68	—— reef	275
—— boat landing	108	Miel, Playa de	125
—— coal	108	—— river	125
—— currents	6	—— —— water	125
—— exports	108	Milk river	139
—— hospitals	108	—— —— consular agent	139
—— imports	108	Mills breaker	15
—— pilots	108	—— —— channel	16
—— population	108	Mingo cay	246

		Page.
Minos		168
—— point		168
Miragoane		190
—— anchorage		190
—— bay		190
—— consular agent		190
Mira-Por-Vos islets		49
Mississippi river		7
Mitan cay		200, 301
—— channel		299, 300
Mizpa bank		90
—— point		90
Moa, Cayos de		122, 123
—— creek		122
—— Ensenada de		122
—— river		121, 122
—— Sierra de		122
Moco point		141
Molasses reef		59
—— road		58, 59
Mona channel, currents		6, 7
—— island		209
—— passage		56, 209, 210
—— currents		210
Moncrieff hill signal-post		321, 324
Mongon cape		177
Monito island		210
Monk hill		274
Monkey shoals		270
Monte Chico islet		204
—— Christi		158, 327, 328
—— —— bay		203
—— —— islet		204
—— —— shoal		202, 204
Montego		145
—— bay		144, 145
—— —— directions		145
—— consular agent		145
—— population		145
—— supplies		145
Montezuma shoal		310
Montron point		193
Mont Serrat church		107
Montserrat island		270, 271
—— —— anchorage		271
—— —— government		270
—— —— population		270
—— —— products		271
—— —— tides		271
Moors point		239
Morant bay		131
—— cays		127, 128
—— —— anchorage		128
—— —— current		128
—— —— water		128

		Page.
Morant point		130, 151, 152
—— —— caution		130
—— —— reef		130
—— —— winds		132
—— port		130, 131
—— —— buoys		130
—— —— consular agent		131
—— —— water		131
Mordazo cays		80
Moretes port		208
Morgan's bluff		31
Morillos islets		216
Morne á Vigie		193
—— au Diable		294
—— de Gaespes		193
—— Fous cliff		294
—— Fortune		304, 305
—— Rouge point		181, 182
Morris bay		275
—— shoal		137, 139
Morro castle		74, 104, 107
—— island		225, 226
—— point		104
Moselle shoal		26
Mosquito bay		244, 255, 257
—— cay		182
—— cove		144
—— hill		275
—— island		235
—— point		244
—— river		104
—— shoal		258
Mouchoir bank		57
Moulacique point		306, 307
Mount Bruce		292, 293
—— Daniel		293
—— Hardman bay		318
—— José		94
—— Ojo del Toro		77
—— Pelée		295
—— Soufrière		307
—— Turquino		76
—— Tartane		300
Moustique bay		197
—— point		197
Mouton de Haut		247
—— rock		288
Mucaras reef		64
Muertos beach		70
—— cays		66
—— island		217, 218
—— water		218
Muhlenfels point		243
Mula point		258
—— port		258

348 INDEX.

	Page.
Mula point anchorage	258
—— —— directions	258
—— —— shoals	258
Mulas point	120
Mulatas channel	58
—— reefs	58
Murray anchorage	17
—— bay	16
Mushroom rock	44, 314, 315
Mustique island	310

N.

	Page.
Naguabo	215, 216
—— consular agent	216
—— customs regulations	216
—— port charges	216
—— river	215
Naguarage bay	123
Najallo river	173
Napoleon, Fort	289
Naranjal anchorage	177
Naranjo port	120
Narrows, The	269
—— anchorage	269
Nassau	32, 33
—— anchorage	34
—— custom-house	21, 30
—— harbor	31, 32, 33
—— —— bar signals	34
—— —— east channel	34
—— island	51
—— steamers	33
Navas, port	123
Navassa island	127
Navidad bank	57
Navy island	150
Nayba passage	165
Necker island	235
Needham point	324
Negra point	69
Negril harbor	113
Negro Point light	208
Negro rock	223
Neiva bay	174, 177
—— river	158, 172, 176
Nettle point	151
Nevis island	269, 270
New bank	143
—— bore	155
—— Fall cliff	323
New Providence island	31, 35, 36, 44
Nicholas channel	65, 67, 110
Nicolao reef	111
Nigüero point	29
Nina shoal	217

	Page.
Nigua river	173
—— —— caution	173
Nipe, Port	120
Nisaito anchorage	177
—— river	177
Nisao point	172, 173
—— river	173
—— roadstead	173
—— water	173
Nisibou river	165
Nombre de Dios bay	100
Nonsuch bay	279
Norman Island	236, 237
—— pass	237
—— Pond bay	43
North Bemini island	26
—— Caicos island	51, 52
—— Cat island	27
—— cay	32
Northeast cay	128, 153, 253
—— —— directions	153
—— bank	39
—— breaker	49
—— Providence channel	39
North Negril point	143
—— rock	15, 44
—— —— channel	16
—— sound	156, 278
—— Wager rock	262
—— —— anchorage	269
—— West channel	24, 30
—— —— Providence channel	22, 28
—— —— point	58, 59
Nueva Gerona	94
Nuevitas	116, 118
—— anchorage	118
—— consular agent	118
—— entrance	117
—— harbor	118
—— population	118
—— steamers	118
—— supplies	118
—— telegraph	118
—— tides	118
—— trade	118
Nuevos Grandes	118
Nurse bank	63
—— channel	63, 64
—— —— beacon	64
—— —— cay	62

O.

	Page.
Obispo islet	212, 213
Ocampo river	71
Occidental point	209

INDEX.   349

		Page.
Ocho Rios		148
—— bay		148
—— supplies		148
Ocoa bay		174, 176
—— gulf		174
—— point		175
—— road		175
Ohio shoal		8
Ojo del Toro mount		77
Ola Grande reef		216
Old Bahama bay		307
—— —— channel		64, 65, 67
—— —— winds		67
—— Fort point		144, 145
—— harbor		138
—— road		269
—— anchorage		269
Oistin bay		323
Olbian reef		298
Ora Cabeza		148, 149
Orange bay		143, 150
—— cays		13, 27, 30
—— islet		143
—— point		143
—— town		267
Orient bay		264
Orneu rock		244
Outer Brass island		247
—— Reef bar		62
Oyster pond		264
Ozama river		158, 171
—— —— tides		171
—— —— winds		171

P.

Packet rock	242
Padre point	91, 119
Padrepino port	206
Pagee point	149
Paix, fort	197
—— consular agent	198
—— —— directions	198
—— —— steamer	197
—— —— trade	197
Pajaros point	123, 234, 235
Palada cays	253, 254
Palanca cay	92
Palancos shoal	122
Palenque, port	173
—— point	174
Palisades	132, 134
Palm point	130
Palmas point	120
Palmetto bay	149

Palmetto point	59, 272
Palmillas point	167, 168
Palomas Cay anchorage	84
—— —— group	84
Palominos islet	213
Pan de Azucar	72, 87, 100
—— —— Sama	120
Pan of Matanzas	13, 67, 106
Panton cove	28
Parattee point	140, 141
Paredon del Medion	115
—— Grande cay	115, 116
—— point	110
Parham	278
—— harbor	278
—— sound	278
Park bay	191
Parker bay	142
—— —— leading marks	142
Pasa Caballos point	89
Pasabanao point	83, 85
Pascal cay	161
—— point	182
Paso Real	98
Passage islands	253
Passages from the Bermuda islands	19, 20
Passe à Caret	286
Pastillo, port	218
Patillas bay	216
—— port	216
Patit cay	29
Pava, port	174
Peake bay	138
Pear cut	64
—— tree bottom	147
Pearl point	234
—— rock	296
Pearns hill	275
Pechems point	208
Pedernales bay	179
—— point	179
Pedro bank	152, 153, 155
—— —— current	155
—— —— soundings	152
—— bay	140
—— bluff	143
—— cays	153, 154
Pelegrino reef	224
Pelican bank	138, 139
—— cays	23, 137, 138, 139, 192
—— channel	138
—— harbor	23
—— island	237, 321, 322, 324
—— point	263
—— rocks	263

	Page.
Pelican shoals	322
Pena Ahujercada point	215
Penas Altas ridge	107
—— Blancas	224, 225
Peniston	234
Penniston cay	55
Penoncillo point	219
Peñuelas river	220
Pères river	206
Pérez point	197
Perla cays	78, 79
Pero point	131
Perseverance bay	244
Pesta	191
Petatillos sand-banks	95
Peter island	236
Petit Bourg	245
—— Cannouan	310
—— Cul de sac Marin	282
—— Goave bay	190
—— —— consular agent	190
—— —— steamer	190
—— Martinique islet	301
—— Nevis	310
—— Rivière bay	194
—— Trou anchorage	177
—— —— tides	177
—— —— de Nippes	190
Petite Anse	201
—— d'Arlet	304
—— Gonave	191
—— Rivière	190
—— —— village	189, 190
—— Terre islands and islets	284, 285
Philips reef	51, 54
Philipsburg	263
—— consul	263
—— population	263
—— trade	263
Picket rock	27
Pickle bank	157
—— beacon	10
Pico del Potrerillo	86
—— Tenerife	321
Picolet fort	202
—— point	180, 201
Piedra point	115
Piedras bank	215
—— cay reef	91
—— Gordas point	71
—— point	91
Piéges bay	179
—— point	179
Pierre head	194, 195
—— Joseph bay	188

	Page.
Pig point	62
Pigeon cay	31, 62
—— island	137, 138, 139, 303, 304, 310
Pilon islets	81
—— cay	81
—— de Azucar	208
Pilot rock	256
—— channel	256
Pilote river anchorage	298
Piment port	186
Pimlico islands	37
Pinalillo point	98
Pinar del Rio	98
Pinels Island reef	264
Piñero islands	213, 314
—— point	214
Pinipinicho cays	80, 81
Pinsonelle cay	209
—— channel	209
Pintado bank	69
—— point	69
Piragua islets	213, 214
Pirata mount	257
Pirogues rocks	190
Pitajaya port	221
—— channel	40
Pitman caves	40
Piton Crève-Cœur hill	299
Pitons du Carbet peaks	286, 295
—— peak	303
Pître cay	179
Place Bertin	296
Placeres Blancas	106
Plaisance mill	282
Plana anchorage	47
—— cays	47
Plantain Garden bay	151, 152
—— —— anchorage	152
—— —— river	152
Plata port	205, 206
—— population	206
—— port charges	206
—— steamers	206
—— trade	206
—— winds	206
Plateau du Carbet	296
Platform point	179, 195
Playa Blanca	69, 70
—— de Andres	170
—— Caleta	69
—— Vieja	175
Playita	106
Plum point	133, 134
—— light-house	137
Plumajes point	97, 98

INDEX. 351

	Page.
Plymouth	271
—— consular agent	271
—— supplies	271
Point à Pitre bay	282
—— —— —— coal	283
—— —— —— consul	284
—— —— —— directions	284
—— —— —— hospital	283
—— —— —— pilot	284
—— —— —— population	283
—— —— —— port charges	284
—— —— —— provisions	283
—— —— —— salute	283
—— —— —— steamers	284
—— —— —— telegraph	284
—— —— —— trade	284
—— Agabama	87
—— Arbalatos	102
—— Caleta	69
—— Casilda	87, 88
—— des Fous	295
—— Frances	91
—— Hicacel	74
—— Jaquet	294
—— La Mare	296
—— Maria Aguila	87
—— Maternillos	68
—— Michelle	292
—— Nigra	69
—— Purgatorio	101
—— Vigie	304
Polink point	137
Poloma cay	161, 262
Ponce bay	218
—— port	218-220
—— —— consular agent	220
—— —— harbor rules	220
—— —— population	219
—— —— port charges	219
—— —— trade	219
Pond point	254
Porpoise rocks	244
Portail point	288
Port Antonio	150, 151, 327
—— —— consular agent	151
—— —— directions	151
—— —— eastern harbor	150
—— —— port charges	327
—— —— supplies	151
—— —— western harbor	150
—— —— —— —— beacons	150
Port au Prince	191, 194
—— —— climate	191
—— —— coal	191
—— —— consular agent, vice	192

	Page.
Port au Prince hospitals	192
—— —— —— inner harbor	191
—— —— —— pilots	192
—— —— —— population	191
—— —— —— port charges	192
—— —— —— rock	191
—— —— —— salutes	192
—— —— —— steamers	192
—— —— —— supplies	191
—— —— —— trade	192
Port Agunento	124
—— Baitiqueri	72
—— Banes	120
—— Baria	119
—— Bay	124
—— Boma	125
—— Cabonico	121
—— Cannova	121
—— Castries	304, 305
—— Cayo Moa anchorage	121
—— Cebollas	121
—— Colorado	164
—— Cueva	124
—— Egmont bay	318, 319
—— Francais bay	200
—— Guantánamo	73
—— Henderson	134
—— Howe	45
—— Jicaco	164
—— —— pilot	164
—— Livisa	121
—— Ligua	121
—— Louis	286
—— —— anchorage	286
—— —— population	286
—— —— provisions	286
—— Macao	164, 165
—— Macoris	169
—— Maravi	125
—— Maria	148
—— Masio	87
—— Mata	125
—— Moule	287
—— —— anchorage	287
—— —— mail	287
—— —— pilot	287
—— —— signals	287
—— Naranjo	120
—— Navas	123
—— Nelson	46
—— Nipe	120
—— Nonnettes	185
—— —— bay	185
—— Palenque	173
—— Royal	131, 132

INDEX.

	Page.
Port Royal bay	273
—— —— currents	132
—— —— point	132
—— —— spit	133
—— —— winds	131
—— Salut	185
—— Sama	120
—— Taco	123
—— Tanamo	121
—— Tanas	85
—— Viejo	173
—— Vita	119
—— Yuma	165
Portillo	77
—— harbor	76
Portland bight	137
—— —— directions	137
—— cay	137
—— barbor	49
—— point	137
—— reef	137
—— ridge	139
—— —— caution	139
—— rock	152, 153, 155
—— —— anchorage	153
Portsmouth	294
Portugal point	198
Portuguese shoals	135, 136
Potter cay	36
Poules rock	190
Powell point	40, 45
Practicos point	82
Predicator point	179
Prickly bay	318
—— Pear island	235
—— —— anchorage	235
—— —— mark	235
—— —— tides	235
—— point	318
Priestman river bay	151
Prince Rupert bay	291, 294
—— —— bluff	292
Princes bay	308
—— peak	193
Principe port	117
Privateer bay	237
Protestant cay	250
Providence channel	13, 35
Providenciales beacon	52
—— island	51, 52
Prune island	312
Puerca point	214
Puercos river	101
Puerta point	70
Puerto Baracoa	69

	Page.
Puerto Cabanas	103
—— de Jururu	119
—— de Manati	118
—— del Mariel	103
—— —— Rio Moa	121
—— Escondido	73
—— Gorda	121
—— Juanita	327
—— Martel	166
—— Masio	88
—— Rico coast, general directions	228
	229, 230
—— —— currents	6
—— —— island	211
—— —— —— custom regulations	211
—— —— —— population	211
—— —— —— port charges	211, 212
—— —— —— products	211
—— —— winds	1
—— —— river	107
Puga cay	87
Punta Cana	165
—— de Afuera cay	97
—— —— la Cruz	161
—— —— las Heches	161
Punta de la Sabanilla	89
—— Largo shoal	228
—— Yagrumage	121
Puntanal	166
Puntilla	222
—— sand-spit	226, 228

Q.

	Page.
Quatre isle	309, 310
Quebrado de Moa	121
Queen's channel	31
Quemada point	69
Quiabon river	167, 168
Quicksands	10
Quintus beacons	37

R.

	Page.
Rabbit islet	310
Rabbit rock	27
Rabihorcado cay	82
Raccroc Cochon bay	179
Raccoon cay	62
—— cut	62
Rackum cay	132, 133
Rafael cape	164
Ragged island	62–64
—— channel	63
—— custom house	21
—— harbor	62

INDEX.

	Page.
Ragged point	324
Rama point	125
Ramos islet	213
Ramée bay	286
Ram head	239
Ramier cay	182
Ramville islet	301
Rancho del Cuba anchorage	176
Ranchos point	174
Ranchitos bay	165
Rapado cay	99, 101
—— Chicos cay	99
—— Grande cay	99
Raquette islet	183
Rat cay	182, 200, 277
Ratones island	219, 220
Ravient reef	141
Raye bay, La	306
Real port	221
—— river	164
Rebecca shoal	10
Rebellines cay	97
—— —— anchorage	97
Red bay	31
—— Head point	280
—— islet	312
—— point	244
—— —— shoal	244
—— rock	258
Redonda island	270
Redonde islands	289
Redondo mount	164
Redman channel	101
Reed point	270
Reef bay	240
—— beacons	9
Regalle cay	182
Rendezvous bay	240, 260
Renon, port	183
Rhode bank	213
Riding anchorage	55
—— rocks	27
Rincon bay	224
—— port	208
Ringdove rock	237
Riocito anchorage	177
Rio Bueno	146, 147
—— —— anchorage	146
—— —— water	146
—— Casa	94
—— Grande	150
—— Juero	110
—— Seco	70
—— Tacre	70
River fort	272

	Page.
River point	150
Road bay	260
—— harbor	237
—— town	237
Robert harbor	301
—— —— anchorage	301
—— town	301
Robertson shoal	139
Roca cape	207
Roche à Bateau bay	186
—— —— anchorage	186
Rochelois bank	190
Roche l'auvre	199
Rock point	26
—— sound	40
Rocky point	130, 139
Rodriguez bank	222
Rojo cape	178, 221
Rolleton	42
Romano cay	116, 117
—— —— harbor	117
—— river	168
—— —— anchorage	168
—— —— directions	168
—— —— water	168
Roncadora pass	99
Ronde islot anchorage	315
Rosario	92
—— cay	93
—— channel	91, 93
Roseau bay	306
—— river	292
—— roadstead	292
—— telegraph	292
—— town	292, 293
—— valley	291
Rose island	35, 314
—— bay	286
Rouge rock	258
Round bay	239
—— hill	138, 264, 275
—— —— bluff	144
—— —— rock	234, 235
—— —— passage	236
Roussolle bay	178, 179
Rousselin point	188
Rover point	150
Roxo cape	179
Royal island	38
Rucia point	205
Rum cay	46
—— —— custom-house	21
Runaway bay	147
Rupert rock	243
Russell island	38

1018—No. 85——23

INDEX.

S.

	Page.
Saba bank	267, 291
—— island	266
—— —— anchorage	267
—— —— description	266
—— —— landing	266
—— —— provisions	267
Sabana bay	174
Sabanilla	107
Sabinal cay	117
Saddle hill	269
—— mount	275
Sage mount	237
Sagua la Grande exports	112
—— —— —— harbor	111, 112
—— —— —— imports	112
—— —— —— pilotage	112
—— —— —— population	112
—— —— —— reef	111
—— —— —— river	111, 113
—— —— —— supplies	112
Sail rock	248, 310
Saint Ann	147, 148
—— —— bay	147, 148
—— —— anchorage	148
—— —— consular agent	148
—— —— land wind	148
—— —— peak	148
—— Aubin isle	302
—— Augustine shoal	226
—— Bartholomew	265
—— —— description	265
—— —— products	265
—— Catherine point	16, 17
—— Christopher island	268
—— Croix	248, 253
—— —— north coast	249
—— David bay	294
—— —— island	14
—— David's harbor	319
—— —— head	16, 17
—— —— point	319
—— Domingo cay	61, 64
—— Elair cay	309
—— —— point	309
—— Eustatius island	267
—— —— coast	268
—— —— population	267
—— —— products	267
—— —— winds	268
—— —— islet	290, 291
Saint François	282
—— George	16, 316, 317, 318
—— —— anchorage	17, 46
—— —— authorities	318

	Page.
Saint George bay	46
—— —— cape	182
—— —— channel	16
—— —— coal	317
—— —— fort	196
—— —— harbor	16, 316
—— —— island	14, 17
—— —— islet	290
—— ——, liberty	317
—— —— supplies	317
—— —— telegraph	317
—— Helena shoal	226, 227
—— Honoré, port	200
—— James bay	245
—— —— channel	247
—— John island	239, 241
—— Johns	276, 277
—— —— coal	277
—— —— channel	277
—— —— consul	277
—— —— harbor	276
—— —— hospital	277
—— —— island	290
—— —— pilot	277
—— —— point	143
—— —— port charges	277
—— —— provisions	277
—— —— trade	277
—— Joseph, fort	202
—— Kitts island	268
—— —— government	268
—— —— population	268
—— Louis bay	182, 289
—— —— winds	182
—— Luce cay	298
—— Lucea	143
—— —— harbor	143
—— —— directions	143
—— —— supplies	144
—— —— water	144
—— Lucia	299, 321
—— —— island	303, 304
—— —— current	307
—— —— government	303
—— Lucie inlet	8
—— Margaret bay	150
—— Marie	299
—— —— anchorage	302
—— —— islet	302
—— Mark bay	193
—— —— point	193
—— —— river	206
—— Marks bay	316
—— Marthe point	296
—— Martin island	263

	Page.		Page.
Saint Martin island, caution	264	Salt river point	249
—— Nicolas mole	196	—— Water Money rock	248
—— —— population	196	Salto de Joho point	70
—— —— salutes	196	—— la Punta Negra	69
—— —— supplies	196	Salut, Port	185
—— Paul's anchorage	290	Sama port	120
—— —— island	290	Samana	162
—— Peter island	289	—— bay	160
—— Pierre bay	296	—— cape	160
—— —— city	301	—— cay	47
—— —— roadstead	296	—— directions	162
—— —— —— anchorage	296	—— gulf	163
—— —— —— currents	296	Samphire cay	37, 40
—— Thomas harbor	241, 243	San Autin river	110
—— —— island	241	—— Carlos de Aguadilla	224
—— —— earthquakes	7	—— —— port	224
—— —— islet	290, 291	—— —— anchorage	224
—— —— —— north coast	244	—— —— consular agent	225
—— —— steamers	14	—— —— population	224
—— Vincent	317, 321	—— —— steamers	224
—— —— islands	307, 309, 312	San Cayetano bay	100
—— —— rocks	61	—— Felipe	108
Sainte Anne	292, 328	—— —— cay	91, 115
—— —— anchorage	282	—— —— cays	95
—— —— hills	240	—— —— group	91
—— Marie	285	—— Fernando de Nuevitas	118
—— Rose mount	240	—— Juan	208, 225, 227
Saintes, Les	289	—— —— cape	211
—— islands	224	—— —— coal	225
Salo-Trou	179	—— de los Remedios	113
—— anchorage	179	—— —— directions	227
—— river	180	—— —— harbor	227
Salée bay	186	—— —— caution	228
—— river	283	—— —— directions	227
—— —— bay	197	—— —— inner	228
Salina point	48, 197	—— —— hospitals	226
Salinas bay	221	—— —— Morro	228
—— de Coamó	217	—— —— peak	91
—— —— directions	217	—— —— pilots	226
—— point	173	—— —— population	225
Saline channel	314	—— —— steamers	226
—— point	59, 299, 318	—— —— supplies	226
—— rock	314	—— —— telegraph	226
Salomon, Point	194	—— —— trade	226
Salt cay	53, 55, 56, 65, 66, 248	—— —— wharf	169
—— anchorage	35	—— Lorenzo bay	164
—— bank	65	—— Pedro	169
Salt island	236	—— —— bay	86
—— islands	138	—— —— rock	169
—— key	10	—— Salvador	45
—— Pond canal	58	Sancti Spiritu	85
—— —— hill	57, 59	Sand cay	55, 56
—— river	138, 249	—— Hill point	140
—— —— bay	199	—— —— range	140
—— —— mound	251	—— key	66

	Page.
Sandy cay	25, 245, 311
—— island	260, 276
—— isle	313
—— isles	320
—— point	47, 145, 254
Sans nom	285
—— Souci anchorage	301
—— —— cove	301
Santa Barbara bay	160, 161
Santa Barbara de Samana	162
—— —— —— consular agent, vice	163
—— —— —— population	162
—— —— —— port charges	163
—— —— —— steamers	163
—— —— —— supplies	163
—— —— —— tides	162
—— —— —— winds	162
—— Clara bay	110
—— Cruz	80, 84, 248, 253
—— —— del Ceibo	169
—— —— —— river	169
—— —— north coast	249
—— —— river	107
—— —— tides	253
Santa Isabel	99
—— Isabella bay	209, 210
—— Lucia river	98
—— Maria	99
—— —— cay	115
—— Monica rock	237
Santaren channel	65, 66
Santo Domingo	1, 50, 53, 158
—— —— island	158
—— —— —— minerals	158
—— —— —— mountains	158
—— —— —— port charges	159, 160
—— —— —— ports of entry	159
—— —— —— river	158
—— —— —— weather	159
—— —— port	170
—— —— —— coal	172
—— —— —— consul	173
—— —— —— directions	171
—— —— —— population	172
—— —— —— port charges	173
—— —— —— port regulations	172
—— —— —— steamers	172
—— —— —— supplies	172
—— —— —— trade	172
—— —— southeast coast, tides	166
—— —— winds	1, 159
Santiago islet	216
—— port	216
—— de Cuba	68, 72, 74

	Page.
Santiago de Cuba coal	75
—— —— —— exports	75
—— —— —— imports	75
—— —— —— piers	75
—— —— —— pilots	75
—— —— —— provisions	75
—— —— —— railroads	75
—— —— —— steam tugs	74
—— —— —— steamers	75
—— —— —— telegraph cables	75
—— —— —— water	75
Saona island	167, 168, 211
—— —— bank	167
—— —— caution	167
Sardinero anchorage	210
—— —— tides	210
—— river	74
Savan islet	310
—— rock	310
Savana island	248
—— passage	248
—— —— tides	248
—— la Mar point	72
Savanna sound	40
—— la Mar	142, 164
—— —— anchorage	142
—— —— consular agent	142
—— —— directions	142
—— —— supplies	142
Savannah point	149, 150
Schoolmaster shoal	149
Scorpion point	256
—— rock	243
Scotch bank	238, 254
Scotland	320
Scott head	292, 293
Scrub cay	254
—— island	234, 235, 261
Sea Cow bay	238
Sea Venture shoals	17
Seal reef	262
Seal's cove	141
Seasons, dry and rainy	1
—— hurricane, general directions for	5
—— sickly	1
Sebalto point	163
Seco river	70
Seine bay	256
Seringapatam shoal	318
Seringue bank	188
—— point	188
Serpent island	253
Settlement bay	257
—— point	25

	Page.
Seven Brothers	204, 205
—— islands	203
Severino castle	107
Shaddick point	260
Shannon beacon	37
—— —— cay	37
—— shoal	153
—— —— caution	153
Shark islet	247
—— rock	253
Sheerness bay	149
Ship channel	41, 43, 44
—— —— cay	44
—— head	150
—— rock	150
Shirley heights	273
—— point	238
Shoe Hole road	37
Shrimp shoal	255
Sierras de Sancti Spiritu	86
—— Morenas	111
Signal hill	241, 252
Siguanea bay	94
Siguapa anchorage	109
—— town	110
Silencio point	126
Silla de Caballo	211
—— —— Romano hill	116
Silver bank	57
—— —— currents	57
—— cay	32
Simon	299
—— anchorage	301
—— cove	301
Simpson bay	263
Sin Fondo bay	178, 179
Singe bank	299
Sir Francis Drake channel	234, 237
Sister islets	256, 257
—— rocks	313
Six Shilling cay	37
Slaney point	238
Slaughter harbor	28
Small point	135, 136
Smith cay	74, 75
—— cays	43
—— channel rocks	36
Snug bay	256
Soboruco cliffs	69
—— rocks	91
Soco river	169
—— —— anchorage	169
Soldier cay	257
—— key	10
—— mount	258

	Page.
Soldier point	213, 214, 255
Sombrero island	7, 233, 259
—— key	66
—— rock	71
Somerset island	14, 18
Sopers hole	238
Sosua, port	206
Soufriére bay	292, 306
—— —— anchorage	292, 293
—— hill	271
—— mount	280, 292
—— peak	303
—— port	207
—— town	306
—— —— caution	306
—— —— directions	306
Sound	245, 253
—— bay	257
——, Lee channel	254
——, Leeward passage	245, 247
——, Middle channel	245, 247
——, —— ground	254
——, South channel	245
——, Weather channel	254
——, Windward channel	245, 256
Sounding, bank of	233
—— Bemini islands	26
—— Booby point	151
—— Caicos island	51
South cay	48, 153, 154
—— —— shoals	154
—— channel	135
—— Dog rock	44
Southeast cay	128
—— —— channel	24
—— knolls	135, 136
—— Negril point	143
—— point	41
—— —— light	324
—— —— reef	323
—— Riding rock	27
—— rock	44, 63
—— Side Landing	206
Southwest bank	55
—— —— bay	33, 35, 312
—— —— cay	128, 153, 154, 255, 256
—— —— —— anchorage	154
—— —— —— point	156
—— —— —— rock	155
—— —— channel	290
—— —— reef	31
—— —— road	244
Sow islet	290
Soye point, La	204
Spaniard rock	264

Spanish point	271	Terre-Basse point	263
Spar beacon	27	—— d'en Bas	288, 289
Speights town	322	—— Haut	288–290
Squalls in the West Indies	6	Tetas de Managua	104
Start point	50	—— Bella	110
Starve Gut bay	140	—— la Vinda	113
Statia island	267	Thatch island	238
—— coasts	268	—— cut	238
—— population	267	Thiery island	300
—— products	267	Thomas bay	178, 179
—— winds	268	—— mount	275
Statira shoal	59	Thorn hill	143, 144
Steamer lines	75, 90, 93, 108, 110	Three-fathom banks	135
Stevenson rock	41	—— Rivers bay	186
Stocking island	42	Thunder channel	31
Storms in the West Indies, law of	5	Tibiz point	169
Stracham cay	41	Tiburon bay	187
Stragglers	245	—— cape	127, 182, 187
Straits of Florida	8	—— port	187
Stream point	255	—— supplies	187
Sugar-loaf channel	290	Tichfield	150
—— mount	265	—— peninsula	150
—— passage	290	Tides, Antigua	279
—— point	289, 290, 302	—— remarks on	1
Sugar-loaves	303	—— Windward islands	262
Swimmer rock	53, 56	Tierra Baja road	198
Syndare islets	266	—— cays	86
		Tinosa cay	182
T.		Tintamarro island	264
Tabara river	176	Tintorero point	70
Tablazo shoal	226	Toar beach	124
Table hill	276	Tobago cays	310, 312, 321
Table rocks	178	—— anchorage	311
—— de Mariel	103	Tobasco point	99
Taco port	123	Toc Vers islet	266
Tacre river	70	Toleto point	98
Tallabacoa river	86	Toney rocks beacon	55
Tamiso cay	161, 162	Tongue of the Ocean	30, 64
Tampa	10	Tony beacon	33
Tanamo, port	121	—— rock	33
Tantes rocks, Les	315	Torbec	183, 184
Tapiou bluff	180	Tororu islet	204
—— de Cahonane	186	Torrecilla point	170, 171
—— du Petit Goave	190	Torrens point	267
—— rock	305	Tortola channel	193
Tupoon creek	257	—— island	237
Tarpum bay	40	Tortuga island	197, 198
Tarquino mountain	74	—— channel	198
Tartane	301	—— currents	193
Tavora river	176	—— keys	11
Telegraph cable	104, 107	Tortugas islands	106
Tennessee reef	10	Tortuguero	176, 225
Tercero cay	205	Tortuguilla	117
Terremoto cay	221	Toulan point	182
—— passage	221	Tour d'Estaing	202

INDEX. 359

	Page.
Tourmaline reef	222
Tow rock	234
Trabuco cay	93
Treasure point	237
Triangles	242
Tributarios de Nimeros	115
—— de Cuba	78
Trinidad island	317
—— —— currents	7
—— port	84, 86, 87, 89
Trinité, port	301
Triumph reef	10
Trois Islets anchorage	297
—— Pitons	293
—— Rivières point	197
Trompeuse rocks	201
Trou de Forban	182
—— Jacob bay	179
—— —— cliff	179
True Blue bay	318
Truyes bay	178
Tunas	85
Turkey key	242
Turk islands	53, 54, 57
Turk's island	51
—— —— passage	56
Turners bay	240
—— point	239
Turquino mountain	74, 145
Turtle Dove cay	244
—— harbor	10
—— head	36
—— heads	135
Twelve Apostles' bluff	188
Twin islets	256
—— pass	256
Two Brothers cay	240
—— —— rock	245
Tyrrel bay	308, 313
—— anchorage	313

U.

Ucarls village	215
Union island	311, 312
United States	8, 10, 12, 50, 53, 57
Upper White Horses	133, 196
Usine d'Arbousier	284
Uvas cays	100
Uvero bay	209
—— cays	80

V.

Vaca point	160, 257
Vacho island	182, 183
Vacia Telegas point	227

	Page.
Vaez point	124
Vaisseaux bank	288
Varadero bay	109
Vases bay	178
Vauclin anchorage	301
—— cove	301
—— mark	299
—— mountain	295, 299
—— pass	299
—— point	299
Vavas point	221
Vega Real, La	158
Vela cay, La	112, 113
Verde cay	61, 64, 111, 115, 116
—— —— tides	116
—— —— water	116
Verreur point	194
Via river	175
Viejo de Azua, Puerto	176
—— —— —— directions	176
—— Frances cape	207
Viejo, port	173
Viento point	216
Vieques island	214, 257
Vieux bay	307
—— Bourg	183, 185
—— fort	289
—— —— anchorage	289
—— —— islet	289
Vigie point	197, 305
Vinagera reef	99
Virgin Gorda island	234
—— —— anchorage	234
—— —— sound	235
—— islands	231
—— —— currents	6
—— —— description	231
—— —— earthquakes	7
—— —— tides	232
—— —— winds	1
—— peak	234
Virginia key	8, 12
Vita port	119

W.

Wag Water river	160
Walker cay	24
Washer island	256
—— passage	256
Washes cay	212
Water cay	62, 65, 255, 257
—— island	244
—— —— anchorage	244
Watering bay	313

INDEX.

	Page.
Watling's island	50
Watson rock	246
Wax cut	43
Welk rock	247
West bay	33, 35
—— Cabria hill	293
—— Caicos island	51–53
—— Dog islet	235
—— harbor	138
—— —— directions	138
—— India islands	1, 50, 56
—— Indian hurricane	2
—— Indies earthquakes	7
—— —— squalls in the	6
—— middle rock	135
—— —— beacon	136
—— —— shoal	135
—— mountain	241
West point	143
West reef	52
Westerhall point	319
Whale cay	24
—— channel	24
—— rock	253
Whistling cay	240, 241
White bank	44
—— Horse rock	249
—— Horses	140
—— House point	141
—— —— anchorage	141
—— point	263
—— rock	314, 315
—— shoal	138
—— Wall cliff	267
Wickham cay	233
Willoughby bay	273
—— anchorage	273
Winds, Cape Maysi to Baracoa	126
—— general remarks on	1
Windy hill	270
Windward channel	127
—— —— currents	6, 127
—— islands	2, 303, 304
—— —— currents	6
—— —— earthquakes	7
—— —— winds	1
Woodbridge bay	292
—— —— anchorage	293
—— —— water	293

	Page.
World's End reef	311
Wotten Waven estate	291
Wreck hill	16
—— reef	135, 136

X.

Xagua	89
Xagua bank	91
Xaymaca	130

Y.

Yabucoa bay	216
—— port	216
Yagua shoal	82
Yaguaneque harbor	121
Yaguasey creek	122
—— point	122
—— shoal	122
Yagrumage, Ensenada de	121
—— punta	121
Yallahs bay	131
—— hill	129, 130
—— point	131
Yamaniguey anchorage	123
—— river	123
Yaque river	203
Yara river	78
Yasica river	207
Yeacos point	109
Yeague point	200
Yeguada river	163
Yellow bank	44
Yoguanabo river	89
Young islet	308
Yufri shoal	228
Yuma bay anchorage	166
—— —— water	166
—— river	163
Yumuri anchorage	123
—— river	108, 126
—— valley	107
Yunque, el	211

Z.

Zacheo island	210
Zancudo islet	213
Zarza de Fuera cay	83, 85, 87
—— point	85
—— river	85

www.ingramcontent.com/pod-product-compliance
Lightning Source LLC
Chambersburg PA
CBHW020307240426
43673CB00039B/730